Arthur Cridland

I'll Take It

A Down-to-earth Guide
to Running Fine Retail Stores

How to make money
by doing it right
in retail

First U.S. edition. Adapted from Arthur Cridland's StOReS System of Retail Selling.
Printed in Canada

Analytic Business Services Inc.

255-1027 Davie Street, Vancouver BC V6E 4L2 Canada
Voice: 604/876-9017 Fax: 978/246-5696 E-mail: analytic@telus.net

Canadian Cataloguing in Publication Data

Cridland, Arthur,
  I'll take it

  Includes index.
  ISBN 1-55212-254-9

  1. Retail trade--Management. 2. Customer services. I. Title.
HF5429.C74 1999   658.8'7   C99-910641-4

This book is published *on-demand* in cooperation with Trafford Publishing.
On-demand publishing is a unique process and service of making a book available for retail
sale to the public taking advantage of on-demand manufacturing and Internet marketing.
On-demand publishing includes promotions, retail sales, manufacturing, order fulfilment,
accounting and collecting royalties on behalf of the author.

Suite 6E-2333 Government St., Victoria, B.C. V8T 4P4, CANADA
Phone   250-383-6864   Toll-free   1-888-232-4444 (Canada & US)
Fax   250-383-6804   E-mail   sales@trafford.com
Web site   www.trafford.com   TRAFFORD PUBLISHING IS A DIVISION OF TRAFFORD HOLDINGS LTD.
Trafford Catalogue #99-0023   www.trafford.com/robots/99-0023.html

 10   9   8   7   6   5   4

ISBN 155212254-9
9 781552 122549

PREFACE

I'll Take It summarizes the essentials of running a fine retail store. It's based upon the author's *StOReS System*. The *StOReS System* is a broad generic manual which retailers tailor to the needs of particular stores. *StOReS* is an acronym of *Structured Operation of Retail Stores*. The *StOReS System* provides the structure necessary for successful operation of fine retail stores. Its subtext is *How to Make Money by Doing It Right in Retail* and its mode of presentation is as *A Down-to-earth Guide to Running Fine Retail Stores*. The *StOReS System* is a major treatment of the hands-on side of retailing.

I'll Take It meets the special needs of those requiring a version of the outlook on retail selling found in the *StOReS System* in the format of a traditional book. Some retailers will find *I'll Take It* adequate for their purposes, while others will use it as an introduction to the *StOReS System* before introducing it into their stores. *I'll Take It* reformats, and in places condenses, the material found in the *StOReS System*.

There is also a difference between the two publications in the amount of practical support. *I'll Take It* explains the retail system set out in the *StOReS System* but leaves it up to the individual retailer to put the system into practice. On the other hand, the *StOReS System* gives practical help and support in setting up the system in a particular store.

I'll Take It has a different approach from that taken in the *StOReS System*. The *StOReS System* has a *Seller's Volume* aimed directly at sellers and a separate *Manager's Volume*. Most sellers make use only of the material directed at sellers. Managers keep some of the material directed at managers to themselves. Managers will choose to share other material needed for managing the store with chosen sellers as they set up *Special Jobs* for them. Sound management calls for passing on as many jobs as possible to sellers. Training for these *Special Jobs* stands apart from the general training of all sellers. In contrast, *I'll Take It* aims solely at managers but also provides them with helpful material for use with their sellers. While it contains material covered in the *Seller's Volume* of the *StOReS System*, it's the job of the manager who chooses not to work with the *StOReS System* to direct this material to the sellers.

I'll Take It is notable for its positive attitude to retailing. Its title of three small words reflects this attitude, for while small, they are the most desirable words a retailer can ever hear. *I'll Take It* guides managers in showing their sellers how to get customers to utter these three little words. It shows managers how to work positively with sellers in a store where it's a pleasure to shop

Contents

INTRODUCTION

Making money by selling at retail is a simple idea. Buy items at a price, then sell them at a higher price to cover costs and take a profit. With enough capital it's easy to rent a store and stock it. It's easy to make some sales. Then the problems begin. What at first looks so simple turns out to be full of traps.

Without a system for running the store, problems are endless. You thought you'd run the store, but the store runs you. You thought the sellers would work for you, but you work for the sellers. Your sellers make few sales and the store is always a mess. You're always telling them what to do, but their questions are endless. They still get it wrong even when you tell them what to do. They quit without any reason just when you get used to them, and it's rarely for a better job. Finding qualified sellers to replace them is next to impossible.

The store of your dreams becomes an endless round of toil and pressure. A weekend off is a luxury and there's little point thinking about a holiday. Take a week off and the store may fall apart. The profits you dreamt of remain dreams. They seem lost in a distant fog. You need help and you have no time to get it.

I'll Take It presents a down-to-earth program for running retail stores. It's an entire system and its aim is to create a store that works for anyone who runs it or who sells in it. It's a system for a store that works reliably, smoothly and profitably from day-to-day. It plans to get sellers who begin with a low level of skill to produce outstanding sales. It sets up an orderly store customers know they can trust. *I'll Take It* gives practical advice to present and soon-to-be owners and managers of fine retail stores. Target users of *I'll Take It* run stores that people in retail describe as destination stores, specialty stores or quality stores. These are stores that people go out of their way to visit, often traveling across town or from out of town to shop in them. Other stores can make use of parts of the system. Ideally the store will have a working manager for up to five to eight sellers. This store can stand alone, be part of a chain, or be a department of a larger store.

I'll Take It talks mainly of sellers, rather than staff or employees.[1] Put the stress on seeing that everyone who works for you sells for you, even if they only do so part of the time. This includes the manager. The only exceptions are outside specialists like bookkeepers and accountants who come to do a specific job under contract.

Above all else, sellers in retail stores need to know how to make sales. In most retail stores the training of sellers is wrong. Again and again sellers say the wrong things to customers. Again and again sellers behave in the wrong way to

---

[1]A side benefit of the word "seller" is that it's sexless without being awkward like "salesperson."

customers. Without knowing it, they make sure they sell as little as possible. Often the person who trains them has little idea of what really makes customers buy. Often there's no training of sellers or so little training that it amounts to no training. *I'll Take It* has as its central axis a series of *Steps for Selling*. They let sellers make high sales without giving the sellers a bad name for forcing customers to buy. They get sellers to make sales without putting customers on the defense.

Lead into the *Steps for Selling* by getting sellers to keep away from the greatest mistake of retail—asking customers, "May I help you?" Then teach the roles of *Open* and *Closed Questions* in selling. Then on to the *Steps for Selling*.

Stress the importance of knowing the store, greeting customers and talking to customers. Have sellers get around the defense of customers who say they're "Just looking" when they're in the store to buy. Find out what it is that customers want to buy before showing them anything. Teach sellers how to show items to customers and how to get around the roadblocks customers put in the way of sales. At the right time, have sellers ask customers to buy without asking customers to buy. That way, if need be, it's easy to go on selling with no loss of face.

See that sellers ask all customers to buy before they leave the store. Give them the skills to sidestep the knockout blows customers deliver to say they're not buying. Have sellers keep customers who buy busy while they write up the sale. Have sellers follow the steps needed at the cash drawer to complete the sale.

Survey all customers so you know where they came from. Register customers and sales. Praise customers for buying, a most important step, and invite them to return. Say good-bye to customers. Then shape up the displays and storage and do the after-sale paperwork. Write *Thank-you Notes* to customers.

I'll Take It gets sellers and managers to live and breathe the *Steps for Selling*. For the crazy truth of retail stores is that day-to-day jobs push selling aside. Selling slips into the background as background jobs take over and consume the store's productivity.

I'll Take It gives you the tools needed to set sales goals. It gives you the tools to measure each seller's sales. Setting sales goals results in sellers who know they must answer for their actions. Living up to a standard is a fair exchange for the support you give them and for the rewards they gain. Sellers develop responsibility when they know they must answer for what they do. Sellers become skilled professionals when they take responsibility.

Turning sellers loose armed with the *Steps for Selling* and with sales goals is only the beginning. To sell well, sellers need to feel the ease that comes from knowing how the store works. To become free agents in selling, sellers need to feel the support of the store's routines behind them. Sellers need to get the support systems right before they sell. Getting it right with the store comes before selling. That's the only way to be free for selling. Making sales is the *Front End* of running a store. The *Back End* is the support structure that frees sellers to make sales. Put the *Back End* in place quickly. Then work on the *Front End* with every seller every day.

I'll Take It deals with the *Back End* of selling by setting out a support structure for sellers. Show sellers how to cut large difficult jobs into small easy jobs. Let them know how and why to keep the store clean and neat. Give them the skills to handle phone calls and reps who visit the store. Show them how to protect the store from thieves. Go over the details of shifts and schedules. Make sure they can do the daily figuring every retail store needs, both by hand and with a calculator or with a computer.

Be sure sellers can record sales so the store has data about its activities. Show them how to use cash registers (or a point of sale system,) calculators and charge card machines. Make sure they know how to open a shift, run a shift and close one down. Be sure they can do the paperwork and know how to fit *Background Jobs* into the gaps between customers. Show them how to keep track of sales and items sold during the shift. Be sure they know how to do the jobs the store needs each day. These include making price changes and pricing items for sale, receiving and handling deliveries, taking stock and placing orders.

Sellers sell well when their rewards relate to their sales. Sellers who receive rewards for making sales like to make sales. They want to make more sales. *I'll Take It* gives help with the ideas behind paying commissions and the details of setting them up. Commission payments are the real key to profits in retail sales. They push sellers into better selling while they lower the percentage of sales you pay your sellers. Managers who think they don't pay commissions live in a dream world. They pay a percentage of their sales to sellers as wages. That's the commission they pay. Paying commissions drives up sales, makes you pay more cash to sellers, but that ends up as a lower percentage of sales. Fear is one reason some retailers don't pay commissions. They know too little about them to trust themselves to pay them. Greed is another reason. Some try to keep the extra profit for themselves, but without the commissions there's no extra profit. To make money see that the people who work for you make money too.

Relating rewards to sales can lead to cutthroat competition among sellers for customers. Commissions alone are a mistake because they can soon turn your sellers into a hungry wolf pack that drives customers away. *I'll Take It* therefore balances a system of commission payments against *The Wheel* that controls the order in which sellers sell. The role of *The Wheel* is to share customers among sellers. This stops sellers skimming the easy sales. Sellers learn to sell when it's their turn and they learn to make their turn pay.

A good commission system raises sales, but sellers get jaded. *I'll Take It* gets managers to watch for falling sales and inject new interest to boost sales back up again. Sellers push to make sales when they can win prizes by selling well. *I'll Take It* gives a model for games to get your store's sales rising. Then it's easy to bring in your own games and draw on ideas from your sellers for games. Prizes can be small or large, depending on the sales the games bring to you.

Training sellers begins when managers interview and choose them. It's important to get off on the right foot at interviews. Make sure you hire sellers with the right attitude. Let them know what you expect of them. This is the time to be up front with all your special needs. Set the framework you need right from the beginning. That works better than letting sellers take things for granted and having to correct them later. From the first contact, managers constantly train sellers. *I'll Take It* stresses that training and coaching sellers are the main functions of managers. Often in retail selling, training is a one-shot deal or a series of one-shot deals. Sometimes there's no training. *I'll Take It* stresses the need for managers to train sellers daily.

I'll Take It's stress on training and coaching allows stores to face the real world of sellers. This is simply that sellers come and sellers go. Often they go when it's a bad time for managers to have them go. For weak retail managers it's always a bad time when a seller leaves. The reaction of weak retail managers to normal turnover of sellers is to whine about how hard it is to find qualified sellers and how ungrateful sellers are. Then they advertise for experienced sellers, hoping to put the job of running their stores on someone else's shoulders. Neither do they give any thought to the strength of those shoulders, nor to the values of their owner. Those who think they can escape the staffing problems of retail stores live in some other world, not this one. The only qualified sellers you need are those you qualify in your store for your store. Do everything you can to keep them. Above all, make your store an interesting place to work. Take care when you find sellers qualified for someone else's store. You may have to work hard to qualify them for your store. They may work out in your store, but it's often easier to train bright and eager beginners. Managers who ask for qualified sellers have given up on their stores. They've turned the control of their stores over to someone else. They usually have trouble finding the level of skill they need and settle for something less. Instead of this, the trick is to get ordinary people to give more than ordinary service.

I'll Take It measures how well sellers sell through a number of *Scores* which sellers track. A store needs measurements of how well sellers sell to raise its chance of success. Sellers' *Scores* quickly show managers which skills they need to improve. Managers zero in on these skills and help sellers improve them. Managers give the training and coaching needed to get sellers to improve their

Scores. This is a system of constant action and feedback. Managers use sellers' *Scores* to bring sellers to the *Third Level of Selling*.[2]

Where do managers get the time to give sellers so much training and coaching? Most managers who skip training and coaching sellers claim they're too busy. They can scarcely do what they already have to do without training and coaching sellers every day as well. These managers are doing the wrong things. *I'll Take It* teaches them a different way of managing. The stress is on developing management skills and setting up all routine jobs so sellers do them instead of managers. The stress is upon making the circle of routine jobs larger and larger, week by week.

Look around usual retail stores and you'll see sellers have a lot of down time between customers. To beat their boredom they chat with other sellers, read books, listen to the radio, and so on. *I'll Take It* channels this down time into useful activity. It does this through the use of two tools, *Daily* and the *News System*.

Daily is a checklist of sellers' jobs that managers build up gradually. Without *Daily*, sellers will limp along. They'll not do the jobs that need doing, or they'll always be asking the manager what to do. The store will work poorly. Stores without a list of jobs limp from one crisis to the next. Sellers who don't know what to do or when to do it run managers ragged. These stores are out of control. Their managers work for the sellers, rather than the sellers working for the managers. Their managers are "too busy" to train sellers in the *Steps for Selling*.

With the *Daily* checklist, sellers know what to do next between sales. Their days are full and interesting. Make sure sellers always have something useful to do between sales. All sellers work on a variety of *Background Jobs* necessary to keep the store going. This way sellers feel more useful and less bored than when they hang around with nothing to do. Sellers do several types of *Background Jobs*. There are the *Usual Jobs*, done by the next available seller, and the *Special Jobs*. *Special Jobs* need special training for chosen sellers to do them. It's by adding *Usual Jobs* and *Special Jobs* that managers free their time for training and coaching. The aim is to get many sellers involved in *Special Jobs*, so managers are truly managing instead of doing. An important part of management is getting things done through the actions of others.

The *News System* makes sure all sellers keep up-to-date on changes in the store. In an active store there's a constant posting of *News Sheets* and exchange of messages. These make sure everyone knows what's going on. Word of mouth from one seller to another will help the spread of news. Word of mouth helps the spread of news and makes news stronger, but you need something more certain for

---

[2]First Level: Sell something to everyone. Second Level: Sell higher priced items. Third Level: Sell more items.

the main system of spreading news. Nor can managers rely on telling sellers one by one. Another advantage of *News Sheets* and messages is that managers get feedback from them. Of course, managers must stay in personal contact with sellers too. They must be there for sellers' questions. Good managers encourage questions but at the same time cut out the need for them. They do this by good training and by making it clear to sellers that they're responsible to act for the store.

Use the *News System* to give sellers jobs beyond those listed in *Daily*. Some of these jobs are one-shot deals. Others make their way into *Daily* later.

Sellers' Meetings play an important role in the *News System* of a fine store. They bring all sellers together for important developments. They're good places for brainstorming, for pumping up sellers and for praising good sellers. They're good places to make bonds between managers and sellers.

A store using *I'll Take It* captures everything it does in *Guide Sheets*. The *Guide Sheets* record what the store does and doesn't do and the reasons for these decisions. The *Guide Sheets* record all actions that take place in the store. They set out the complete needs of the store clearly and fairly. *Guide Sheets* pay attention to all the details and let managers keep sellers on track. They include the little things easy to overlook that soon add up to the difference between a fine store and a run-of-the-mill store. With *Guide Sheets* sellers quickly learn a system that sells items to customers. *Guide Sheets* let you pass on a system to all sellers rather than limiting you to serving all customers personally. Managers use the *Guide Sheets* in training. Then *Daily* points sellers to *Guide Sheets* so they can do the *Background Jobs*.

Guide Sheets make training easy. Each one covers a single topic which sellers and managers can easily understand. Each is short enough so sellers and managers take them in their stride easily. *Guide Sheets* are the concrete record of what needs doing, why it needs doing and how to do it. People need a sense of purpose in their lives and *Guide Sheets* make purposes clear to sellers. People are born with a desire to work and to please others. They hunger for order in a crazy mixed up world. Make demands on people and you give a form to their lives that makes them feel good. People want to do the best job they can. People love to work when they do it well. But before they can begin a job they must know what to do.

It's common to find sellers on the job for months, limping through jobs nobody told them how to do properly. Sellers need more than general statements about what they should do. Sellers must know the actions that lead to sales and support selling. Sellers become frustrated when they only hear, "Sell more." They need to know the actions to take to sell more. Often sellers who seem to be lazy are sellers who don't know what to do. *Guide Sheets* address the needs of sellers and managers.

Each *Guide Sheet* has a series of numbered topics. These numbered topics give the base of a control system used for tracking sellers' training and coaching. Each seller has a *Training Log* listing all actions needed in the store. It needs more than writing down the actions in *Guide Sheets* and expecting sellers to take them. Nor is it enough to tell sellers what to do and expect them to do it. A few will do the job well, but most will do their idea of the job. Many will forget some of the actions. Then they'll feel uneasy and become frustrated. Anger builds in frustrated sellers. They take it out on people around them. They sell poorly. Sellers need a training and coaching program. The marks of this training and coaching are "showing how" and "telling how," with frequent *Personal Daily Attention*. Notes in each seller's *Training Log* give a way of knowing how well training and coaching are going for each seller.

It needs more than training sellers once and expecting them to do the job well. With basic training they'll do better than without it. They'll do a good job. Some will do a good job for a long time, but most will taper off. None will do the great job that a fine retail store demands daily. To get that, give your sellers more support. That demands daily coaching. The mark of daily coaching is prompt and frequent feedback. People love work when they do it well and someone recognizes them for it. Your sellers will reward you with successful selling for this type of support. Sellers who make sales like to make sales. They want to make more sales.

Training and coaching work well when there's a fair way of seeing how well sellers are selling. *I'll Take It* sets out a system of *Scores* that measure how well sellers sell. The *Scores* single out areas sellers need to improve. This system works well because it's fair. It works because sellers know what they must do. Pep talks and pushing sellers are out of place in it. These give only short-term gains, if any. It's hard to talk people into changing. People have to know what to do to be successful. People do feel good when they know what they're doing. They do follow good plans. They do answer well to the support of daily training and coaching. They do learn to answer for their actions. They do develop responsibility. They do like honest measurements of selling when they get high rewards for high sales. Take note of sellers' *Scores* and get ready for some surprises. Get ready to keep and look after some sellers you don't like. Get ready to retrain some sellers who are coasting in your store. You'll have to let go any who refuse to answer to retraining.

I'll Take It also uses the *Training Logs* to review sellers quarterly. Even though managers give daily feedback and coaching, frequent formal reviews keep sellers on track.

There are two approaches to using the *Guide Sheets*. During training the approach to *Guide Sheets* is through a series of *Outlines*. The *Outlines* come before the *Guide Sheets* and act as an index to them. For day-to-day operation of the store the approach to the *Guide Sheets* is through *Daily*, the checklist of the store's actions. Key all actions in *Daily* to *Guide Sheets*. That makes training stronger. Sellers know they can look things up when they forget them.

I'll Take It is partly a base for your store and partly a model for your store. No two stores are alike, even if the stores are similar. All stores have a common pattern of needs, but each store is unique. Stores differ in their layouts. They differ in the equipment they have. They differ in the aims and values of management. One store needs sellers to dress casually but in fashion. Another needs sellers in conservative suits. Another needs sellers to dress like punks. Whatever the style, each store needs to let its sellers know how to dress. It's simple to prepare *Outlines* and *Guide Sheets* to fit the situation. Each store will also need to put together its own version of *Daily*.

To see how *I'll Take It* hangs together think of it as an automobile. The *Steps for Selling* are the wheels that keep turning to move the vehicle. The *Scores* and *Games* are the engine that drives the wheels. *Daily*, the *News System* and *Training* take care of navigation and steering. *Background Jobs* are the maintenance and gas which keep the vehicle moving.

Most *Guide Sheets* will cover a job that sellers or managers need to do to keep the store running. They will tell what to do and why to do it. They will tell it in simple direct English without jargon. A few *Guide Sheets* will cover topics sellers and managers need to know as background material. *Guide Sheet* titles are direct commands to act, like: "Greet customers." Each *Guide Sheet* breaks the job into a series of steps or topics. Like the *Guide Sheet* titles, the topics are mainly direct commands to act, like: "Greet without asking questions." Each topic stands out as a numbered heading with an explanation following it.

The *Outlines* manage the *Guide Sheets*. They point to lower level *Outlines* or to *Guide Sheets*. Like the *Guide Sheets*, the titles of *Outlines* are mainly direct commands to act, like: "Clean the store."

Some *Guide Sheets* will have *Forms* to use with them. *Forms* need to have the number of a related *Guide Sheet*, so *Guide Sheet* 15-17 explains the use of *Form* 15-17. For ease of use and tracking the supply of forms, keep them in a separate *Forms* binder.

Managers need to learn management skills. They need to get the right sellers and to schedule them. They need to maintain *Daily* and keep the *News System* going. Above all else, they train sellers, particularly in the *Steps for Selling*. They review sellers quarterly. They use sellers' *Scores* to drive the store and they set up games to keep the sellers selling. They see that sellers keep the store's records and they put together the store level summaries of selling. They see that the store's selling records get to the bookkeeper on time and in good shape. They pay the sellers and pay the store's bills regularly. They keep the store supplied with items to sell. Once the store's *Scores* are high enough, they advertise and promote the store. Managers begin by doing many of these jobs themselves. Their skills as managers show themselves by how well they organize sellers to do many of these jobs under their guidance.

Advertising comes last for managers. A common myth of weak managers is that advertising will make up for the sales their messed up stores are killing. Chances are advertising is the last thing a store needs if it has enough foot traffic for it to survive. A store best makes use of advertising only when its *Scores* show that the customers it already has are buying as much as they should. Unless you're off the beaten track, don't pay a single penny to advertise until you have the right *Scores*. *This advice alone will more than pay you for the price of I'll Take It in a single week.* Move cautiously when your store's *Scores* show it's time to try advertising. *I'll Take It* shows you how to go about advertising and how to measure the results of ads. Placing ads without measuring results is like burning money. Some advertising pays, but most advertising is a waste of money.

I'll Take It is a hands-on approach to running retail stores. It deals only with the practical matters of making stores work. It's about making your store come alive. It makes no attempt to cover matters retailers must or may need to know, but don't relate to day-to-day activities. Thus there's no advice on choosing bankers, accountants and lawyers. Nor is there advice on the roles of proprietorships, partnerships and corporations. Nor is there advice on financing or buying stores. Nor is there advice on renting or building stores. Nor is there advice on insuring stores. *I'll Take It* supposes your store is already in play or that you're about to put it into play. Somehow, for better or for worse, you have your store together and now find you need help on day-to-day matters. Or, you have your plan for a store together and want to hit the floor running. *I'll Take It* takes off from the point where you've put your store together. It addresses the problems of how to run the store.

I'll Take It is also deliberately silent on an important topic, the layout and decor of your store. Successful fine stores look, sound and smell good. They have a special feel about them. The options for layout and decor are endless and they're personal. This is where you give of yourself to create a unique store that excites customers. Your store is truly your store. Only you can make it like no other store.

While *I'll Take It* has much to say about preparing records for bookkeeping, it's silent on the details of bookkeeping. All retailers have to be able to read financial statements. Some may have to do their own bookkeeping until they make enough cash to pay a bookkeeper to do it for them. Master the elements of bookkeeping you need to know from a standard bookkeeping text. Bookkeeping is bookkeeping is bookkeeping. *I'll Take It* offers nothing on the topic.

Finally, some words about computers. You may come across people who say you can't run a modern store without a computer. These people often have something to sell you. Usually, they want to sell you a computer and some software. To sell to you they may need to convert you to their beliefs. The reverse is true. You can't run a store with a computer if you can't run a store without a computer.

A computer will help some retailers to run a store better than without it. These are retailers who already have good computer skills. They'll use a word processor as a matter of routine. As they use *I'll Take It* they'll see the places where spreadsheets and databases will help them. They may have the skills needed to integrate a *Point Of Sale System* into their store operations. There's a large gap between what computers can do and what a given person can make them do. There may be repeated problems in keeping your computer running. It may be fun to a computer junkie to spend three days tinkering with a tape backup system to make it work properly, but can your store afford that kind of down time? There's a real danger of a computer becoming a tool that takes energy away from running your store. Everything is fine as long as the computer works for the store. Once the store starts working for the computer, it's headed for trouble.

Some retailers can't tell a byte from a bite. For them a hard drive is getting stuck in a traffic jam. They can put aside computers for a while. First make your store work. You'll put in long hours to keep your store's records in shape by hand, but it'll pay off. You'll know how your store works. Think about computers when your store is making money and your management structures are in place. You may want to get involved yourself or you may use other people, but you'll know what you want for your store. The computer systems that work well are those based on systems that work by hand. Once you have a paper system that works for you, speed it up with a computer system when you can afford one. A side benefit is that when your computer system breaks down, you'll be able to run your store by hand. Make no mistake, your computer system will break down.

As sure as night follows day, whatever someone tells you your computer system will cost, it'll cost a whole lot more. It'll cost you twice, three times, ten times or even more times than you'll think it will. It'll eat up lots of your time. It may do exactly what you want, but it may frustrate and disappoint you. There are people who'll make light of these realities, but they are realities. Prepare for them when you take this plunge. It's a plunge you should take when your store prospers.

The most important thing for a manager to do in a store is to train and coach sellers in the use of the *Steps for Selling*. Everything else is subordinate to this training and coaching. That's not to say that everything else is unimportant. Everything else is important, but it fits around training and coaching sellers in the use of the *Steps for Selling*. Because of the crucial role of the *Steps for Selling*, managers will find it useful to review them before reading the rest of the book. First review *Tune Up for the Steps for Selling*. Then review the *Steps for Selling*. Then read the rest of the book with the *Steps for Selling* hovering in the background. Continually ask yourself, "How will I fit this into managing the *Steps for Selling*?" Resist any temptation to start using the *Steps for Selling* before, or instead of, using the rest of the information in the book. The *Steps for Selling* are a powerful tool, but they are dangerous to use alone. They fit into a context, and without this context they could harm your store rather than improve it

CHAPTER 1

MANAGEMENT SKILLS

Managers of retail stores need management skills. The way to make money in retail is through the efforts of other people. The golden rule is, "never do anything yourself if someone else can do it for you." It's easy to fail by trying to do everything for yourself. New store owners may well find themselves tracking inventory by hand because they can't afford to pay someone to do it for them. They may not be able to afford equipment to help with the job. It's a serious mistake if they track inventory by hand to "save money" when money is at hand to pay for help or equipment. The manager's job is to see that other people work efficiently and effectively. Likewise, there's a duty is to see that equipment is right for the job and is a sound investment.

Working through other people can have pleasant surprises. Often we find others can do things better than we can. Train them well and let them run with their jobs. Sometimes managers will have to settle for people doing jobs less well than they can do them themselves. That's perfectly OK, as long as the job gets done well.

Managers will find it repays them always to be open to new management ideas through readings, discussions and the courses they take. The topics of this chapter have great value to the management of retail stores but by no means cover all needs.

Seek Other People's Input

Managers can't do their job alone. There's a lot of free advice and there's a lot of cheap advice. There's expensive advice too. Whatever its source, seek it and weigh it up before following it. Mine the free advice first and then mine the cheap advice. Move deliberately when seeking expensive advice.

Listen carefully to customers who shop in your store. Make sure sellers let you know what customers say about the store. Be eager to learn what's good, what's bad, and what's neither good nor bad about your store.

Brainstorm — Brainstorm with your sellers. Your sellers will give more when they know you value their input. They'll have more interest in ideas they're part of than ideas that come from above. Brainstorm with other merchants. Ask friends and relatives for input on your store.

Run phone surveys — Ask customers how you're doing. Ask what you could do better. Listen politely and thank customers for their input. Give special thanks to customers who tell you bad things about your store. Many customers lack the courage to do this. Ask those who have the courage to tell you more. A few customers like this can help you get your store ahead.

Run Focus Groups — Invite groups of customers to lunch or dinner. Wine and dine them well. They pay back with views on your store. The groups are *Focus Groups* because they focus on problems. General input is fine. Take all you can get, but focus on problems.

Call *Focus Groups* when you have problems or have big decisions to make. Talk about new ideas for items and for advertising. Talk about ideas on new directions for the store. Explain what you're trying to do and why you want to do it. How do customers react? Ask everyone to tell you a good and a bad point about your store.

Mix with positive people — Some people run down and tear apart other people and their ideas. Honest talk about faults is one thing but steer clear of people who are going nowhere with their lives. They can only help you go nowhere too. Suffer them politely once and strike them off your list. Hang out with people who are going somewhere with their lives.

Make your own decisions — Hear all opinions you can, then make your own decisions. It's your business and nobody can make decisions for you. All the experts and all the well-wishers in the world can't run your business for you. Fall into the trap of believing they can and your business will slide downhill.

Set and Reach Goals

Set goals for yourself and your sellers. Without goals you drift. Set goals and you know where you're going, and you can see how well you're doing. Setting goals comes before making plans to get to the goals. Set short-term goals and long-term goals. Beware of only going after short-term goals. Do at least a little work on your long-term goals each day.

Set clear-cut goals — Goals are clear-cut or they're not goals. Goals like "to increase profits" or "to increase sales" aren't clear-cut. They aren't goals, they're dreams. Here are some clear-cut goals:

- Cut returns to suppliers by 50% by July.

- Joe to develop six new Openers by next Friday.

- Raise next year's sales of cut glass by 20%.

- Raise March sales by 15%.

Set goals you can measure — The goals in the above list are goals you can measure. You can see how close you are to goals you can measure. Then you can step in to keep things on track for the goals. Sellers will push to reach goals they can measure. Sellers will push for the 15% goal when they see March sales running at 13% increase. They won't push "to increase sales."

Set goals with deadlines — Goals are only goals when they have deadlines.

Set goals sellers can reach — Sellers will give up on impossible goals. There's little point asking for 100% increase in sales when 10% is more likely. There's little point expecting Joe to change from your worst seller to your best seller in a week. There must be a reason for you to think sellers can reach the goals you set. Perhaps your store is getting better known each year and it's reasonable to expect 10% yearly increases in sales. Only go higher than this when you provide support for doing so. Perhaps you train sellers in a new way to sell items. Perhaps you bring in a new line of items that customers seek eagerly—you may have cornered the market on Cabbage Patch dolls at just the right time. Perhaps you run a series of ads on TV.

Set goals that challenge sellers — Set goals too low and sellers ignore them. Sellers need to struggle and then feel the glow of success. There's little point asking for 2% increase in sales. That won't make sellers glow. Set sales goals at 10% increase or more. Set no sales goals rather than set sales goals below 10% increase.

Write goals down and read them daily — Goals aren't goals until you write them down. Keep a list of your own goals. Post the store's sales goals in *Daily*. Give sellers their own sales goals each week. Let sellers keep their own goal sheets. Review past and coming goals with sellers each week. Goals aren't goals unless you read them over daily to keep them in mind. Goals become clearer when you read them aloud. Reading them aloud fixes them in your mind.

Keep goals in order — It's easy to have too many goals. Some are more important than others. List them in order of importance. Give the most important goals the most attention. Draw a line through your list of goals to separate active and inactive goals. Remove goals from your list if they remain inactive for a long time. Work on the top two or three goals.

List actions needed to reach the top goals — List as many actions as possible for the top goals. Here's a list of actions to help the sales of cut glass:

- Prepare a window display of cut glass by next Friday.

- Prepare a highlighted in-store display of cut glass on Tuesday morning.

- Skim through four library books on cut glass for interesting facts on Saturday.

- Read articles on cut glass and pressed glass in *Encyclopaedia Britannica* on Saturday.

- Browse articles in back issues of *New Glass Review* on Saturday.

- Phone a list of cut glass manufacturers from the *Thomas Register* for hints on selling cut glass by the end of May.

- Write three scripts to turn customers from ordinary glass to cut glass during the next *Sellers' Meeting*.

Be sure the actions you list are actions, not thoughts. "Need facts on cut glass" isn't an action. "Ask librarian for help in locating facts on cut glass" is an action.

Work Through Others

Train others to do your work. Turn jobs into lists of steps needed to get them done. Write them up as *Guide Sheets* and train sellers to do the jobs for you. Do nothing yourself that you can get someone else to do. Doing a job because you've always done it is a trap. Trust others to do it, even if they don't do it as well as you. Doing a job because you like doing it is a trap. Let one of your sellers do it if it's that nice. Free yourself to deal with challenges that only you can handle.

Be the training person instead of the answer person — Train your sellers, or they'll sweep away your time with endless questions. They'll lean on you. You'll work for them, rather than they'll work for you. You'll always be under pressure. You may snap at your sellers and put them under stress too.

Playback all instructions with "Tell me," or "Show me" — Most managers fail to get feedback when they give instructions. Most managers give instructions to others and act as if they'll do the job well. People often only hear some of the words. They daydream. They're lost in thoughts about their own problems. They give their attention to other things happening around them. They get bored.

People often don't understand some of the instructions, but they rarely say so. People look at things from their point of view rather than yours. Many prefer to do things they like doing rather than what you want them to do. People often haven't answered for their actions before. It's a new idea for them. People often invent shortcuts that do less than you want.

Many managers who give instructions ask the listener, "Do you understand?" and believe the answer when it's, "Yes." Most people who don't understand something say, "Yes" in answer to, "Do you understand?" Some say nothing. Some just nod their heads. It's rare to get, "No" for an answer. People rarely admit they didn't catch on. They bob their heads and say, "Yes." It's rare for managers to check answers. Find out how much sellers understand by checking the playback.

Show John the steps for handling a return on an item bought with an American Express Card. Now say, "Do you understand?" When John says, "Yes," say, "OK here's my receipt for the sale. It's your turn now." Watch to see that John can do it properly. Repeat this until John gets it right.

Take a gentle approach with new sellers. "OK, let's run through it again. This time you tell me what you're going to do" is gentler than "Tell me." "It's your turn now" is gentler than "Show me." Only use "Tell me" and "Show me" by themselves when you're sure sellers know you mean them no harm.

Checking the *Playback* gets easier after a while. People learn that every time they answer, "Yes" to, "Do you understand?" you'll meet them with, "Tell me" or "Show me." So they listen with care and ask questions as they go.

Get commitments on jobs you give to others — Begin by letting others know what you expect them to do. Let them know the result you want. Let them know how you want it done if you want them to do the job your way. Let them know which tools to use if you want them to use special tools. Let them know how to use the tools if there's a special way to use them. Run a *Playback* to check they know what you want. Get them to agree to do the job. Ask, "Can you do this job for me?"

Agree on a price if it's an outside job. Agree on a deadline. Suggest a deadline that works for you: "Can you finish this job by Thursday?" Ask, "How soon can you finish this job?" when someone can't finish the job by your deadline.

Drive home the deadline. Ask, "Are you sure you can finish the job by Thursday?" For someone who works for you: Ask, "Can you finish it by Thursday and still do your other jobs?" Get a commitment. Say, "OK, I'm relying on you. I'll expect it Thursday. How about 2 o'clock?" "I'm relying on you," makes it clear the deal is one-on-one. It shows that you trust the other person. "I'll expect it Thursday," stresses the agreement you've made. "How about 2 o'clock?" drives the hook home. It prevents Thursday sliding into Friday and Friday into Monday.

Head off foot dragging — Sometimes you want action by a date but others want to drag their feet. People are good at finding reasons they can't do things. Go over your needs again and ask for the date you want. Then say, "Surely that's reasonable, isn't it?" This gives people a chance to go along with you. It's easier to say, "Yes" than to say, "No" when you put it like this. It also gives people a chance to tell you why it's not reasonable. Then make a new offer.

Honor the commitments people make to you — Enter appointments on your calendar to pick up jobs. Respect them as you respect other appointments. Be there on time to pick up jobs. You'll make problems for yourself if you check Thursday's job on Wednesday of the following week. People will learn that "2 o'clock Thursday" means "about a week from Thursday." Some of your jobs will vanish into thin air if you miss checking your jobs.

Thank people and give praise for jobs well done. "Thanks for finishing the new price list, Marcia. You've done a really good job. Now everyone in the store will find life easier." Follow this pattern:

Thanks   Thanks
Job   for completing the new price list,
Name   Marcia.
Praise   You've done a really good job.
Benefit   Now, everyone in the store will find life easier.

Check how jobs are going — Check how it's going when a job will take a long time. Make several entries on your calendar to ask "How's the job going?" Asking how it's going keeps your job in mind. It'll renew the commitment. You'll hear about any unexpected problems. You'll have time to change your plans if there's a delay.

Deal with broken commitments — Let people know you're upset when they don't finish jobs at the agreed time. "I'm upset that you haven't finished this job as you agreed." Let them know why you're upset. "This means we won't be able to sell the new items over Thanksgiving weekend."

Sometimes there's a good reason for a delay. Say you expected a warning. "Yes, I can see how that would delay you. But I'm upset that you didn't warn me so I could change my plans. I was relying on you." Keep this warning on a delay hidden when you get the commitment on the job. It weakens the commitment if you ask people to warn you if the job won't be ready on time. They know you'll accept a delay and they won't push themselves. It's different with people who can only give a half a commitment. "I'm not sure I can do it by Thursday. I'll try, but it's going to be tough." Then say, "OK, but let me know how it's going on Wednesday."

Find someone you can rely on when someone breaks commitments twice.

Keep after jobs until people finish them — Keep jobs on your calendar until people finish them. Get a new commitment and make a new calendar entry when someone's late with a job. It's easy to forget to make the new entry and have a job die on you.

Get the names of people you phone — Ask the name of the person who answers the phone. Start with, "Hello, this is John Smith of Flowers Unlimited. Who's there, please?" Try "Hi, my name's John Smith. What's yours, please?" if you get a job title instead of a name. Say, "Pleased to meet you, Michael. Can you please help me with..." Knowing names makes your dealings more personal. You also know the person to get back to if a problem develops.

Get Sellers to Come Along

Bring sellers into plans and decisions. Sellers buy into plans and decisions when they're partly theirs. Your plans and decisions become their plans and decisions. Sometimes you can bring in sellers from the beginning. That's always good. Sometimes you've decided on a plan of action. Then bring in sellers on the details. Brainstorming with sellers is a good way to begin. Follow brainstorming by giving sellers *Odd Jobs* and *Special Jobs*. Bring in as many sellers as possible.

Let sellers know what's happening — Use the *News System* and *Sellers' Meetings* to let sellers know things are going to happen, before they happen. Let them know why things are happening. Let them know their roles in what's happening. Let them know you're depending on them to do things in new ways.

Beat "can't-do" sellers with a trial period — Many sellers like the challenge of new ideas but some fear change. Some are comfortable as they are. Some see change as a threat to their security. They're full of reasons why new ways of doing things won't work. Answer "can't-do" sellers like this: "I certainly understand the problems you've raised. Still, the fact remains we have to do something to improve profits. We have to start now, not at some time in the future. The plan we're looking at now is the best we've been able to come up with. So here's what we'll do. We'll give this plan a sixty day trial and then see if it's doing what we want. Those of you who feel uneasy, please put those feelings aside for sixty days. Give it your best and we'll see what it looks like then."

Set the trial period. Set long trial periods for big changes and shorter trial periods for small changes. Be there during the trial period to see what goes on. Be there during the trial period to build up the changes you're looking for.

Tie up the loose ends — You have some loose ends to tie up when you use a trial period. Fail to tie them up and you'll have problems. Talk one-on-one with sellers who are against the new ideas: "Frank, I know that you feel uneasy and I'm grateful to you for letting me know. This is a hard job and I need all the support I can get. I'm looking to you for leadership in getting the others to give this thing a fair trial. Can I rely on you to put your personal feelings aside for the next sixty days? Can I rely on you to become a booster for this project?"

You have a real problem if a seller won't go along. You'll have to show you control the store: "I'm sorry Frank, but I can't run a divided store. I'm satisfied that it's worth trying this thing for the next sixty days. I'm telling you it's part of your job to support it."

It's time to say good-bye to Frank if Frank doesn't change after this. Frank may say he'll go along with the sixty day trial but not do so. He may plan to go along but his bad-mouthing gets the better of him. "Frank, you told me you'd put your personal views aside and support this thing for sixty days. Yet I keep hearing you bad-mouthing it. I can't run this store with you working against me. Is this something you can correct, Frank?"

It's likely that Frank will come into line, at least for a while. You'll have to keep your eye on him. Be sure to thank him for his support when Frank changes.

Know Your Sellers

Be friendly to all sellers. Strike a balance. Be friendly but avoid pushing into private lives. You can be friendly without being friends.

Aim to know what makes your sellers tick — Philip is an opera buff. Jane plays tennis. Ann is a serious long distance runner. Mary goes bowling on Tuesday nights. Odette is planning to become a lawyer. Jim dotes on his granddaughter, Michelle. Keep yourself posted on your sellers' interests.

Learn about sellers by being around sellers — A direct approach sometimes works poorly. Much of what you learn comes out in working side by side. Pitch in with sellers on some of the store's *Background Jobs*. Take small groups of sellers to lunch. Throw a picnic now and then. Go bowling, play pool or whatever with sellers from time to time. Make sure sellers truly enjoy these events. It works against you if sellers have to put up with your events.

Play no favorites and make no judgments — There's no reason you have to like your sellers or their values. It's easier for you if you do, but that can be a luxury you can't afford. Your interest in sellers is in how well they sell. Sellers will lose morale when you're friendly to some but not to others.

Set an example to your sellers — Get things done and do them well. That helps develop a desire in sellers to do things well themselves. Much of the success of a store comes from the manager's attitude. Sellers catch the flavor of the manager's attitude.

Get a Head Start

Plan your day. Set aside time at the start of the day to plan what you're going to do today. Another way is to plan the next day at the end of each day. Plan without other people around to break in on your thoughts. Some people get up before the people they live with and plan today. Others find somewhere to hide in the evening and plan the next day. Include in your day plan:

• Actions from your list of goals.

- Actions from your daily calendar.

- Appointments and other commitments.

Stop your day plan from becoming a wish list — Aim to finish today's plan today. Include only one or two extra items. Long lists defeat the purpose of a day plan. They force you to spend time managing lists of items you don't get done. They make you feel you're not getting anywhere.

Use prime time well — Most people have a time or times of day when they work best. Do your most important work during this prime time. People who don't get much done usually kill their prime time. They do many short easy jobs during prime time. They make a lot of phone calls they could make later. Then they put off the important jobs because they've worn themselves out. They do more short easy jobs instead. They blow away most of their days like this. It's better to jump into an important job in prime time.

Get more prime time by starting prime time early. There may be some people whose biological clocks set their prime time late in the day. Many people who believe this have taught themselves to put things off. Early prime time pays off. Push in a few less important jobs in breaks from prime time. Then get back on prime time and do less important jobs when prime time peters out.

Use push time well — Push to get jobs done. You've done two jobs and you're wondering if you have time to do a third. It would be easier to do the filing that's stacked up instead. Push the third job. You're in push time. There's a reason you're wondering if you have the time to do the job. You know you do have the time to do the job but you'd like to put it off. It's a bad habit you've fallen into. You know when there's no time to do the job. You don't have to wonder about it.

Fix Problems Quickly

Act on problems quickly. Problems stay around if you ignore them. Hoping problems will go away doesn't work often. Do something about them. The longer you wait, the harder it is to do something about a problem. Maybe you learn to live with it. Maybe you push it aside till it crashes down on you. Maybe you bottle it up till it explodes from you in anger.

Fix problems quickly when you know how to fix them. Look for ways to fix problems when you don't know how to fix them. Work out what you're going to do before you start to do it. This isn't the time to fly by the seat of your pants. Nor is it the time to delay action. Get the facts, then act.

Be positive — Act as if sellers want to do a good job but don't know how to do it. Show a real interest in finding the cause of the problem and fixing it.

Fix problems, not people — Keep your attention on the problems. It won't help to knock the people or make them feel small. Let them know how you see it. Ask if it's so. Let them know what you expect them to do. Ask, "Can you do it?"

Focus on the problem — Come directly to the point. Be matter-of-fact. Many trainers lead into problems with an apology. They beat around the bush trying to be kind. That's no way to go about it. Problems are normal. Solving them is normal. "Joan, let's work on some *Openers* to help you sell more."

Make it clear there's a problem. Deal with the problem only. Some trainers want to play the good guy. They want to soften the blow. So they sandwich problems with praise. "John, you've made good sales this morning but you're still not racking the shoes you don't sell. Other than that, you're our best seller." A mixed message like that won't do the trick. It buries the problem in the praise where it gets no attention. John comes through as a lovable rascal. He'll only hear the praise. John deserves lots of praise, but not now. He needs to get the message that he must rack the shoes he doesn't sell. He needs to know he has something to fix. He needs a simple direct message. "John, let's talk about the need to keep the rack in good shape."

Be more direct if he doesn't improve. "John, let's talk about the problem your mess makes for everyone else in the store."

Move towards the solution — Focus energy on where you want to go. This is **do** energy. **Do** this, then **do** that, then **do** the next thing. Energy focused on what you want to get away from will bog you down. This is *don't do* energy. *Don't do* this, *don't do* that, *don't do* the other. A little *"don't do"* may be useful, but most of it spins wheels. Avoid it if you can. *"Don't do"* sends a mixed message. Why talk about what you're not going to do? Just do what you're going to do.

There are always some people who do what you ask them not to do. Sometimes they mishear you. Sometimes "don't" makes a thing more attractive. Why draw attention to it?

The briefcases are selling poorly because Mary stacked them in a dark corner without price tags. Try a "do" approach. "Mary, let's see what we can do to get these briefcases sold. How about a pyramid of them under that spotlight? How about the top one open to show the pockets for pens and papers? How about a couple of them expanded to show they take a lot of papers? How about using those bright new colored price tags to price them?"

Compare this with a *"don't"* approach and it's easy to see which way will get Mary to make a good display for you. "Mary, I *don't* see how you'll ever sell those briefcases. *Don't* pile items in the corner like that. *Don't* make a dull display like that again. *Don't* display items without prices."

Fix problems with "we" — Even when you know how to fix problems, sellers do the fixing. Forcing sellers to do it your way works poorly. Things work better when sellers agree with you. Sometimes sellers have ideas that help fix problems. It's easy to make fixing these problems a "we" effort.

Follow a Plan for Big Problems

Recognize big problems. A big problem is one you decide to pay special attention to. It might be big because it hurts your sales. It might be big because of the sellers involved—perhaps two sellers don't get along. It might be big because you tried to fix it before and it's still a problem. It might be big because there's a lot of detail to cover. Whatever the reason, it's going to take more time to fix than most problems.

It's a big mistake to treat a big problem as a small problem. It's tempting to save time this way, but you'll pay for it later. It's a big mistake to treat a small problem as a big problem. That'll waste time and you'll lose the respect of your sellers.

Call problems situations — Call problems situations to make them easier to handle. "John, let's talk about the situation with the window displays." That gets better results than "the problem with the window displays."

Put problems into numbers when you can — You're ahead when you can say what the numbers are. Then you can describe problems clearly and set clear goals. John's *Hit Value* is $20 and you want John to raise it to $25 in March and $30 in April. The numbers let you measure progress as you support John in reaching the goal.

State problems clearly — Highlight problems so there's no avoiding them. Joan is in the office in answer to the invitation "Let's talk about the situation with special orders." Let Joan know the facts: "Joan, I've been going over the figures on special orders. It turns out there were 45 for the whole store in June and you placed 29 of them."

Underline problems — Underline that there are problems: "We have to do something about these figures, Joan. A special order makes us lose twice. We miss the profit on the sale of an item we have. Then the costs of special handling make us lose money on every special order. We lose even more when customers don't pick up their special orders and we have to sell them as markdowns."

Seek input and listen to it — Find out how the sellers see the situation. "How do you see this situation, Joan?"

Listen while sellers answer. "I didn't know we lose money on special orders. I thought we prided ourselves on meeting customer needs. I thought by writing special orders I was building the store's image. It's a pain to write them and now I find that for putting in the extra effort I get blamed. We never seem to have what customers want."

In this case Joan's words show she lacks some facts she needs to know. Review her *Training Log* later. Review the training program if necessary. Joan is willing to work to build the store, but she's headed in the wrong direction. She's angry and she's upset because the store doesn't carry enough items.

Support sellers — Support what you can from the sellers' input. "I appreciate you wanting to satisfy customers and build the store's image. Those are things I like to hear from sellers."

Beware of going outside the sellers' input to support sellers. That's using praise to water down correction. Support sellers for giving input if there's nothing to support in the input. "Thanks for letting me know how you feel, John."

Develop a plan together — It's important that sellers help make plans. Plans work better when sellers pitch in. Let them feel they pitched in even when they don't pitch in. Be sure all the seller's miffs and mistaken views come out. Talk about all of them. Talk about all your points of view. Hold nothing back.

Explain, ask, talk over and agree — Go topic by topic. Begin with a topic that's easy for the seller to accept. State your point of view on the topic. "We lose money on special orders, so we pay no commissions on them. You'd put money in your pocket if you sold something we have instead of writing a special order. You'd not have the pain of writing the special order either. And you'd feel that we appreciate you better."

Ask, "Does that seem reasonable to you?" Let sellers answer. "I'd like the extra cash. I'd like not writing the orders. But I don't want to sell customers items they don't want."

Agree with the answers if you can. "That's perfect. Never sell customers items they don't want. They'll not buy again."

Suggest a way to go and get some agreement. "Joan, if we can work out a plan where you sell customers only what they want and you write no special orders, could you go along with it?"

"Well, I'd like to, but I don't see how to do it."

"OK, we'll work out how to do it. Can you go along with it when we've done that?"

"Yes, if I don't have to sell customers items they don't want."

"Fine. We agree on that."

Go through the rest of the topics in the same way. "The stock we carry shows the kind of store we are. We've chosen an area of sales and we aim to be the best in that area. We find out what most of our customers want and we keep it in stock. We add new items and get rid of old items as times change. We can't carry every brand and model. There's not enough money, space or time to do that. Nor is that a service to customers. We act as a filter for customers. Customers shop here because they know they can rely on us. We stock our store well. We usually have the items customers want. The hard part is finding out from customers what they want. Does that seem reasonable to you?"

"Well it's a good store. Most customers find what they want, but many ask for items we don't have."

"There are a few customers who know exactly what they want and won't settle for anything else. Most customers have a need or a want they partly understand. Sometimes they say what they want by asking for something they know about. So, they may ask for a brand or model. Or they may describe something they hope exists. The seller's job is to find out the want or need that lies under what customers ask. Then the seller sells an item that fills the need or want. Does that seem reasonable to you?"

"Selling what customers need or want is reasonable. I'm uneasy with not believing what customers say."

"I agree. It's not a matter of belief. It's a matter of knowing what customers are like. Suppose I ask to buy Brand 1 because I know it does A, B and C. You stock Brand 2 because it's better quality at the same price. It does A, B, C and D. D is something I hadn't known about and I'd like. Wouldn't you serve me better by selling me Brand 2?"

"Yes that's true."

"The *Steps for Selling* show you how to find out customers' needs and wants. There are several steps between *Schmooze* and *Ask All Customers to Buy* that help. *Find Out Why Customers Want to Buy* and *Show-&-tell the Chosen Item* are the ones to start with. Some sellers find it hard to use these steps. Suppose we go over these steps and do some role playing based on them. I'll play the role of a customer buying a stereo. Does that seem reasonable to you?"

"Yes."

"Let's see how it works with you writing no special orders for a while. Instead of writing special orders, ask questions and make sales. Pass customers along to other sellers if you get stuck. Afterwards find out how the other sellers handled them. Does that seem reasonable to you?"

"OK. I can try that."

Sum up the plan — State the plan clearly. "The plan calls for you to review the *Steps for Selling*, beginning with *Find Out Why Customers Want to Buy* and *Show-&-tell the Chosen Item.* I'll support you in this by playing the role of a customer. To support yourself in this effort, write no more special orders for a while. Pass customers along if you find you can't make a sale from items on hand. Then find out how other sellers dealt with them."

Sum up the benefits of following the plan — List the benefits sellers can expect. "By following this plan:

- You'll only sell customers what they need or want.

- Your sales will improve and you'll earn more commissions.

- You'll have less paperwork.

- You'll feel we value your efforts better than you feel we do now."

Get a commitment — Ask, "Do you agree to this plan?" Most sellers agree if you've fully involved them in the plan.

Try for a trial period when sellers aren't fully willing to agree with a plan. Ask, "Can you accept this plan for a trial period?" Find out why sellers won't go along with trial plans.

Begin again if you haven't really involved sellers in the plans. You may both need to take a break to think things over before you begin again.

Now and then you'll find sellers who won't involve themselves in any plan. They may test how far they can go with you. Say good-bye to them.

Enter your commitments in your calendar — Decide on dates and times for follow-throughs. Write them in your calendar.

Follow Through on Changes

Follow through to see that things change. Always follow through when you train sellers. Ask for change, expect to see change, and check that change takes place. That's your commitment to the process. Asking for change and following through is training. Asking for change and not following through is nagging. It's easy to nag instead of training. Then sellers don't take you seriously. Write your times for follow-through on your calendar.

Act as if sellers will change — It's easy on you when you ask for change and you get change. Act as if change is normal. That sets the tone for change to take place.

Step in when you don't see the change you want — Make it clear you're not seeing the change you want to see. Draw up a new plan for change with a deadline. Follow the plans for fixing problems. Let sellers go when resistance to change is firm.

Punishments like doing the store's nasty jobs only build bad feelings. Not only do the punished sellers feel angry about the punishment, but sellers who normally do these jobs begin to feel they're being punished and bad feelings also grow in them.

Keep on Top of Harassment

To harass is to annoy, badger, bother, pester, plague, pressure, provoke, subject to stress, tease, torment, vex, worry. Make it clear to your sellers that you won't put up with any form of harassment. That includes not only sexual harassment but also harassment based on race, national origin, religion, sexual orientation, mental or physical state, or age. That includes teasing.

Make sure sellers know they'll be open to discipline if they harass anyone who works with them or for them. They may lose their job. The law requires you to take prompt and proper action on harassment. The law requires you to act whether or not the victim wants you to act. Make sure sellers know it's OK to make a good faith report of harassment. There's no penalty even if they're wrong.

Give sellers guidance on harassment — Give your sellers examples of actions that are OK and those that aren't. Encourage them to use simple tests. Does what you say, write or do relate to work? Would your sister or mother like someone to say, write or do it to her? Has someone told you they're upset by something you wrote, said or did?

Give sellers guidance on dealing with harassment — The first line for an harassed seller is to politely ask the harasser to stop. The second line is to involve the manager. When the manager fails, the third line is to go above the manager, to the mall manager or to head office. Other lines are through a local support group or a state or federal human rights commission or council. Underline your commitment to fighting harassment.

Talk openly against harassment of all kinds — Let your sellers hear you talk against harassment often. Build an atmosphere that makes it clear you won't put up with harassment. Talk out against harassment instead of against any harassers you deal with. Keep everything you know about any case of harassment private. Talk about cases of harassment only with the people involved.

Bring the people together — Someone being harassed should talk to the harasser about it. Only some people being harassed will be able to do that. Others will tell you about it instead. Some will talk but get nowhere and then tell you about it. Bring the people together and get the talk going. Get the problem out on the table.

Get the harasser to see the harassment — A lot of harassment boils down to being insensitive to other people. Often harassers admit what they've done but claim it's harmless. Be firm with the harasser. "Pat, you may see this as harmless, but it isn't. You may not mean to harm, but you're causing harm. Is this something you can change?"

Get the harasser to apologize — See that anyone who agrees to change apologizes for the harassment. "Pat that's fine. Now if you'll apologize to Chris, we can all put this behind us." The matter ends when the harasser apologizes.

Be firm when the harasser won't apologize — Go over the facts. "Pat, let's review this so we're all clear. Chris says you said so & so and you admit it. Acting like that is out of place in this store. To put it all behind us, all you have to do is apologize to Chris, but you refuse to do it."

Tell what will happen. "Pat, this is a most serious matter. I'm giving you until the end of tomorrow to think it over. I'll ask Chris to make a written complaint if you haven't apologized by then. Then I'll deal with that formally."

Get the written complaint at the end of the next day. Then begin the process of firing the harasser.

Hear out word against word — Sometimes one person says it happened while the other says it didn't. Without witnesses you're stuck. You can't make a judgment and you shouldn't. Harassment may have taken place, but perhaps the accuser is lying.

Bring the people together and talk about the issue. Make it clear you take it seriously. Make no threats. Make it clear you'll review any recommendation on the job if the alleged harassment involved a threat to job security. Write a note to each seller's file. "Date, X alleged that Y said …, Y denied it. No action taken.

CHAPTER 2

MANAGEMENT DECISIONS

There are a number of basic management decisions to make about the nature of a retail store. Sound management calls for reviewing these decisions from time to time, but only changing them after careful thought. Having a firm framework stops the store from drifting into difficult situations which lead to unneeded expenses and a drain on profits.

General control of a store comes from writing a *Mission Statement*, which defines the store's role and sets its limits. Other control comes from being clear how you will deal with customers who ask for special orders, for mail orders or for layaways. Stores recording sales with electronic cash registers or computers may have decide whether to control inventory by entering items as PLUs or SKUs.

Mission Statement

The *Mission Statement* tells sellers what business the store is in. Stores that try to be everything to everyone end up limping along with no clear purpose. It's important to make decisions about what you want the store to be. The *Mission Statement* includes the kind of items the store sells and sets out its values. It's a guide to steer the store day-to-day. It keeps the store on track when it's under pressure and when others push the store to be something else. It stops the store wasting energy by spreading itself too thin. Sellers are at ease with customers when they know what the store stands for. Stores with *Mission Statements* are like ships with rudders—they get where they're going. The *Mission Statement* brings everyone's mind into focus. But it doesn't have these benefits by magic. Everyone needs to read it deliberately every day in a way that makes it a fresh document to them.

Only you can write your store's *Mission Statement*. You'll go through several versions before you get it right. Your *Mission Statement* will repay you by keeping your store on track. Some sample *Mission Statements* follow.

The Model Train Center

Sales of the major brands of high quality model trains in gauges N to O including a full range of accessories, model kits and magazines.

Notes:

The major brands of model trains are: Athearn, Bachman, Bowser, Fleischmann, Hornby, Kato, LGB (Lehmann-Gross-Bahn,) Lionel, Mantua, Marklin, Polks Aristo, Rivarossi.

The gauges of model trains are:

Scale	Gauge	Decimal inches	Approx. inches	True mm	Approx. mm
1/220 of 56.5 inches	Z	0.257	1/4	6.52	6.5
1/160 of 56.5 inches	N	0.353	11/32	8.97	9
1/120 of 56.5 inches	TT	0.471	15/32	12.00	12
1/87 of 56.5 inches	HO	0.649	5/8	16.50	16.5
1/64 of 56.5 inches	S	0.883	7/8	22.42	22
U.S. 1/4 inch = 1 foot	O	1.250	1 1/4	31.88	30
1/48 of 56.5 inches	O	1.177	1 1/4	29.90	30
1/32 of 56.5 inches	#1	1.766	1 3/4	44.80	45
1/22.5 of 56.5 inches	G	2.511	2 1/2	63.80	64

Most gauges are based on the Standard Gauge of 56.5 inches. Note that Gauge O has a different base in the U.S.

We carry only the gauges on the shaded lines.

The Sound of Stereo

Retail sale of mid to high quality stereo equipment at premium prices. Our sales depend on customers noticing the knowledge and reliability of our sellers.

Grandpa's Toy Store

Retail sales of toys that are safe, old-fashioned and educational or just plain fun, for children from birth to the age of ten.

Notes:

A safe toy is one that passes required and voluntary safety standards. See the standards filed in *Daily*.[3]

---

[3]Required standards: Code of Federal Regulations, Commercial Practices 16, Part 1000 to End. U.S. Consumer Product Safety Commission, Division of Regulatory Management, Office of Compliance and Enforcement, Washington D.C. 20207 (301) 504-0400.

To be old-fashioned, the design must be one that a child born before 1850 could have played with. This is well before the invention of dry cell batteries. The material of the toy doesn't matter. Plastic stacking blocks are OK. The historical fit of the toy matters. Batman is out.

The Garage—Code of Ethics

To have a sense of personal obligation to each individual customer.

To perform high quality repair service at a fair price.

To hire the most skilled mechanics obtainable.

To continually upgrade the technical training of our staff.

To only use proven replacement parts of high quality distributed by reputable firms.

To itemize all parts and labour on the service invoice.

To retain all parts replaced for customer inspection.

To guarantee all new parts for 90 days or 4,000 miles.

To uphold the high standards in our profession.

To guarantee our work performed.

Ron Tremblay

Ron has this posted for all his customers to see in Vancouver, British Columbia. He also prints it on his invoices. Notice how he adds his name to his code. It shows his pride in what he does.

The Daffodil Clothing Company

The Daffodil Clothing Company is a small "off-price" retail chain. Prices on current fashions and our own labels are 30% to 70% lower than the regular retail price.

Special Orders

Decide how you're going to act when customers ask you to place special orders for them. Placing special orders brings a new layer of actions and expenses into your store, so be sure special orders really pay off for you. This payoff can be in producing profit or in developing loyal customers.

Voluntary Standards: F963-92 Standard Consumer Safety Specification on Toy Safety. 1992 Annual Book of ASTM Standards, vol. 15.07. End Use Products. American Society for Testing and Materials, 1916 Race Street, Philadelphia PA 19103-9965 (215) 299-5585.

One way is to limit orders to usual items — Only "special order" items you are going to order anyway because you've temporarily run short. Stick to your store's mission and choose your stock well. Then you cut down on special orders. Should you be out of an item you usually carry when a customer wants it, order it. You were going to order it anyway.

Use requests for special orders to examine what you carry — Sometimes customers ask for an item within your mission that you've overlooked. Now's the time for a trial order.

Are your sellers on track? — Sometimes customers ask for special orders because your sellers are bad at suggesting other choices. They may even suggest needs to customers. Give extra training to sellers who come up with unneeded special orders.

Go for special orders when they pay — Special orders are an important source of profit in some stores. There are so many book titles that no store could carry them all, even for a single subject. Special orders are a routine part of the business.

Keep track of costs — Special costs go with special orders. Estimate the costs before you begin. Then track the costs to be sure of them. There's the cost of sellers' time for taking orders and for making orders. Often you have to buy a minimum number of items. You'll get the costs of pricing and displaying the extras. Then you may have to sell them at a loss.

You may decide to take a loss on special orders as a cost of building regular customers. Be sure to track how much regular trade you get from customers who make special orders.

You can fall into a trap. A discount store sells cheaper than you and provides no service. Its customers come to you for special orders. You end up providing a service for the other store.

Collect prepayments for marginal special orders — Sometimes a special order program limps along with minor profit because too many customers don't pick up their orders. Try collecting prepayments before abandoning the program.

Mail Orders

Usually setting up for mail order while setting up for retail is a recipe for disaster. Mail order isn't something to do "on the side." Obviously, a strong established retail store can also operate a successful mail order business. It needs to find out how to run a mail order business, which is quite different from running a retail store. Then it sets up mail order as a separate business or as a department of the retail store.

The reverse is a little easier. Most mail order businesses have at least a small amount of casual walk-up business. There are always some local people who like to check out who they're buying from. Let the walk-in trade tick over until the mail order is strong. Then consider whether it's enough to justify opening a proper retail store.

Retail stores that pay percentage rent to a landlord will need a separate business for mail order. They'll need legal advice on how to protect themselves from claims on their mail order profits by their retail landlord.

Avoid drifting into mail order. It's tempting to send something by mail as a special favor to a customer. Although the store doesn't handle mail orders, a seller decides to mail something anyway. These special favor mail orders cost a lot and they are strictly amateur bumbling. There's the time and expense of buying packing materials at retail. There's time spent packing and shipping the items. Shipping may cost more than allowed for. There may even be brokerage charges across a border. Steer clear of falling into this pit.

Layaways

Layaway: A customer holds an item by making a down payment. The store keeps the item until the customer has paid for it. The customer visits the store to make payments to pay off the debt. Then the customer takes the item.

Customers usually want the things they buy right now, so the use of credit cards has largely replaced layaways. Despite this, layaways are still alive in a surprising number of stores. These are the main users of layaways:

- Customers who've used up their normal sources of credit.

- Customers who buy items for future special events, like a birthday or a marriage. They use layaways to force themselves to put money aside for the event.

- Customers using part of the food allowance to buy something special.

- People who feel uneasy with credit.

- People of a cultural origin that frowns on credit.

Ignore layaways unless you have a number of customers asking for them. Layaways will only increase your trade when your situation is right. These are the problems you face with layaways:

- Increased record keeping.

- Special supplies to keep track of layaways.

- Need for storage space.

- Cash tied up while the items are in storage. The markup on the items must allow for the cost of cash tied up while items are in storage for the items themselves and the storage.

- Customers who back out of the layaway agreement. Some stores make charges when customers can't finish the payments rather than refunding all cash paid. This may be suitable for an auto parts store, but it's not suitable for a fine retail store. Such charges are reasonable but that won't stop customers from disliking them. You'll lose customers and they'll bad-mouth your store to others. Customers you treat well will be loyal to your store.

- Getting stuck with out-of-season items by customers who back out. Include this cost in the cost of backouts.

Watch how often backouts happen and work out the cost including the cost of out-of-season items. End your layaway program if backouts eat up the profit from the program.

PLUs or SKUs?

PLUs are *Price Look Up Reference Numbers*. SKUs are *Stock Keeping Units*. PLUs give firm control of the items you sell, but to use PLUs you must first store them in the memory of the electronic sales recording equipment. For each item you record a unique number, a brief description, and its price, before you begin selling it. Do this in an orderly fashion and it repays you with much information about your inventory.

Instead of entering a PLU for each item before selling, it's possible to enter SKUs while selling. Typically, the seller will face a prompt like "ENTER PRICE/DEPT." The seller then enters a price and presses a key or chooses an abbreviation for the department. The seller might press key [M] for Maternity Wear, or select an abbreviation from a displayed list.

Stores that use SKUs have no need to enter numbers, descriptions and prices before selling items. They have no need to number the items they sell. While these look like time-saving advantages, at the end of the day the store only knows how many items were sold in each department and their selling prices. There is no way of relating a specific price to a specific item. It's hard to know when sellers charged wrong prices, whether by accident or design. The number of departments in use is likely to be small. Such a system can only work well where there is a limited number of departments, each with a limited number of items, and with the items having recognizable prices.

The approach taken here is that it is well worth the extra effort to work with PLUs. They give better control of inventory and of sellers. To allow for missing PLUs and labeling errors set up a single department for problems. This will allow sellers to make the sale at the correct price when they know it, or at what seems a reasonable price. Then it's important to correct errors in labeling and programming right away. It's also important to "refund" the problem and "resell" it as the correct item. Clear these error up no later than the day they occur and take steps to avoid similar errors in the future.

CHAPTER 3

GET SELLERS

Your sellers are your store. They will make it or break it. Whether they make it or break will depend on their way of thinking and how well you train and coach them. Their way of thinking is basic. Although they will come to you with a developed way of thinking, how they behave in your store will depend on how you handle them as you interview them and train and coach them. Your task will be simpler if you choose well in the beginning.

Look for These People

You won't always get ideal people, but you'll get the best available people if you have a clear picture of the people you want.

Look for people with a good attitude — An attitude is a firmly held point of view or way of looking at things. Note that it's not just a point of view or a way of looking at things. It's firmly held. You can rely on it.

A good attitude is the most important point to look for in people you hire. You can change anything else that's wrong when the attitude is good. People with a good attitude can learn anything you need them to do in your store. You'll keep your customers when your sellers have a good attitude. The bad attitude of sellers is a leading cause for losing retail customers. These are some things that show a good attitude in people:

Accept responsibility for their lives. They look to change themselves when things go wrong. They don't blame others.

Commitment to self-improvement. They are people who want to grow. They're not content to flow with the stream. They want to do something with their lives. They'll take guidance.

Energy for the job. These are people who'll put everything they have into the job. They know that no matter where they work, they really work for themselves. They want to do a good job. They'll accept that what other stores call excellence is your normal standard.

Keen to sell. These are people who like selling. They're proud of selling and want to learn to sell better. They stand opposite people who think selling is something decent people don't do. They stand opposite people who sell because they can't get a "better" job.

Like what you sell. They're excited about the items you sell. They can support the prices you charge.

Look for people who relate well to other people — Get people who like people. Get people who like talking to people and do it well. They make good eye contact but don't stare. They hold their bodies well. They smile as they talk. They're warm and they use people's names. They have good voices and project them well. They're up-to-date with what's happening in the world.

Look for people who are honest and open — Get honest people. You'll trust them with your property and your cash. There's no staying power without honesty. It builds trust, respect and loyalty. There's no place in your store for dishonest people.

Get people who are open with other people. You need to know about things that go wrong right away. You need to know about things that go wrong from the people who handled them. You need sellers who talk about it when they get upset with one another. You can't run a store when people bottle things up.

Let your people know if they're dishonest or closed, you'll say good-bye to them. Let your people know if they're honest and open they can survive mistakes. Let them know you'll support them to change.

Look for people with goals in life — Get good sales from sellers with goals in life. Many sellers with goals will move on from your store. It's better to use them as they pass through than not use them at all.

Forget retail experience — Get bright people and train and coach them to do the job you want done. You can use people who've worked in other retail stores. There's no need to hold it against them. You'll have to train out some bad habits as well as training them. Forget the fantasy that you'll get some people with retail experience and your store will run itself. The best you can hope for that way is a run-of-the-mill store. Nobody is qualified for your store when your store is unique.

Find the Sellers You Need

Hiring is strictly a matter of business and it's up to you to make sure you don't stick yourself with sellers you don't want or can't fire. Build these points into your search strategy:

Hire only sellers you're willing to let go — It's hard for some managers to let sellers go. It's even harder to let relatives and friends go. It's as hard to let your investor's relatives and friends go. Some people can do it. At 3 pm the boss lets a seller go who happens to be her son. At 6 pm as a parent she gives him sympathy for losing his job. You need something solid between the two of you to do that sort of thing. Ask yourself if your husband will still be your husband if you let him go. Ask yourself if it's a risk you want to take. Ask yourself if you want to risk your friendships before you hire friends.

Make hiring sellers strictly a business deal. Keep yourself free to let sellers go who don't work out. Your business will suffer if you hire sellers you can't let go for emotional or political reasons. You're on solid ground when you're sure you're willing to let anyone go who doesn't work out.

Sellers who want to get on will leave you when they know you favor sellers close to you. You'll end up with those who feel you owe them something and those too dull to move on.

You serve your relatives and friends badly when you let them prosper as a favor. You take away their chance to succeed for themselves.

Keep your irons in the fire — Watch you don't force yourself to take anyone who comes along. That's what happens if you wait till someone leaves and then start looking for a new seller. Write a simple ad and usually have it running somewhere.

Alert Person to Sell Eyeglasses
```
Up to $x/hour after training. No experience necessary.
Part time. Call 123-1234.
```

An ad like this is all you need. Cycle your ad through local newspapers and employment agencies. Look for the places that have free listings. High schools, women's centers and retired people's groups are a beginning.

Take applications from everyone who turns up asking for work even when you haven't a position available. Give at least a brief interview. Keep the facts on file if you can't employ now. Then you'll have some people to call in times of need. Keep a list in order of your interest in the people. Note offers and refusals on the list. Write nothing on the applications. You may have to show them if someone charges you with job discrimination.

Headhunt as you shop — Carry business cards when you shop. Look for good sellers who might make less than you pay. Give them your card and say, "I like your selling style. Please call me to talk about improving your position." Headhunting in your own mall will make you some enemies you may not wish to have. Think hard before you do it there.

Pay your sellers a headhunting bounty — Pay a reward to your sellers for anyone they bring in. Say, $50 or $100 when you employ someone they find. Pay the same amount again if the person is with you after three months.

Choose managers from within — Choose them from the sellers you know. You signal your sellers that you don't respect them when good positions go to outsiders. They learn they have no chance to better themselves with you. Good sellers leave you. Only use outsiders with special skills, like bookkeepers and accountants. Hire them as consultants for a few hours at a time.

Keep an extra seller — Employ one seller too many rather than one seller too few. That way you have a bridge when someone leaves. It sounds like a waste but it's not. You pay a commission on sales rather than a flat wage. Employ as many sellers as you like, as long as they're making their commissions. The number of sellers you need usually turns out to be a range rather than a number. You'll know you need 6-8 sellers rather than needing 7 sellers. Keep to the high end of the range.

Get two for one — You need a new seller, so get two part-time sellers instead. Then see how they work out. Let one go and get another part-timer or let one go and put the other on full-time.

Replace your worst seller with a hot new prospect — Poor sellers keep slots warm for good sellers. Joe is ticking along. He pays for himself, but that's it. You've trained him and supported him, but he can't move his sales up. Joe is keeping the slot warm until someone better shows up.

Take Applications

Begin all employment with a written application.

Employment Application and Agreement

Last Name _____ First _____ Middle _____ Phone _____

SSN _____|____|_____ Driver's License _____

Address _____
         Apt. No - Street No & Street   City   State   Zip

Employed?   Y/N   Date Available _____   Referred by _____

Available	Mon	Tue	Wed	Thu	Fri	Sat	Sun
From							
To							

Employment: List Present or Last Position First

	Yr & Mon	Name & Address	Phone	Supervisor	Job	Pay/hr	Reason Left
From							
To							
From							
To							
From							
To							

Education or training useful for job _____

Exclusions: List all present or former employers, educators, coworkers, supervisors, personal references and others you wouldn't want us to contact for information about you.

On the back of this form tell us in your own handwriting why you want to work for our store.

I certify that my answers are true, correct and complete to the best of my knowledge. I authorize investigation of my personal and employment history. This investigation includes, but isn't limited to, all statements contained in this Application and Agreement or made in interview(s). I authorize all persons not listed by me above under Exclusions to provide information on my employment, education, character and qualifications. I understand that false or misleading information given in my Application and Agreement or interview(s) is just cause for rejection of my application or dismissal in the event of employment. In the event of employment I understand that my employment is terminable at will at any time for any reason. I agree that I'll always follow all rules and regulations as set by management. I understand that the management won't tolerate discrimination or harassment of any kind by or of its employees.

Signature _____   Date _____

Make sure applicants fill the form in fully

Get references from earlier jobs. What people have done in the past and how they've done it give the best clues to what you can expect from them. Get character references for people new to the work force. Ask for school or personal references. You trust your sellers with a lot in your store. Check them out before you hire them.

Exclusions are people applicants don't want you to talk to about earlier jobs. Most people won't fill in any exclusions. That's fine. You can network when there are no exclusions. You have John Smith as a reference, but John Smith says the applicant worked mainly with Marion Ownby. You're free to contact Marion Ownby.

Make sure you get the sample of handwriting. Your sellers will write the records your business depends on. You need to know you can read them. Asking why they want to work for your store gives them something to write about that's of interest to you and samples their handwriting.

Make sure applicants sign and date the application — Without a signature and date you have no application.

Check the legal part of the application form — The legal part at the bottom is mainly standard. Only your lawyer can tell you how well it will hold up in your location. Say clearly that the employment is terminable "At will." That means if either you or someone working for you thinks the job isn't working out, either of you can say good-bye to the other. It's important that all employment in your store is "At will."

Weed out don't-wants — Some people who apply will be wrong for your store. People successful in other areas rarely work out. You don't want a welder who's sitting out a temporary downturn in welding. You want someone who's aiming for retail sales.

Check All References

Check all references of people you interview. People put their best foot forward when they want a job. They often tell half-truths and lies. Many employers gloss over checking references. They don't do it at all or they check only the easy ones. Check them all, including those needing long distance calls. You trust your sellers with the items you sell and your cash. Know who they are. You trust the success of your business to your sellers. Know how well they work. What someone did in the past gives warning of what they'll likely do in the future. Some people learn from their mistakes but most people go on making the same mistakes. Give people a chance, but keep your eyes open for your business. Look for real evidence of change. The promise to change isn't enough.

Use a *Reference Check Sheet* to force yourself to stick to a pattern of checking.

Reference Check Sheet

Applicant _____
Checked by _____ Date _____
Reference _____ Phone _____
Company _____ Position _____

Did your company employ the applicant?   Y ☐ N ☐

From? _____ To? _____ Job Title? _____

Kind of work? _____

Any promotions? _____

Are earnings of $ _____ per hour correct?

Did applicant lose time because of poor health?   Y ☐ N ☐

Was applicant late often?   Y ☐ N ☐

Did applicant follow instructions well?   Y ☐ N ☐

Did applicant take responsibility?   Y ☐ N ☐

What was the applicant's attitude? _____

What are the applicant's strengths and weaknesses? _____
_____
_____

Any work related conflicts? _____

Why did applicant leave? _____

Would you rehire?   Y ☐ N ☐ Why not? _____
_____

Would you recommend me to hire the applicant?   Y ☐ N ☐

Is there anyone else I should speak with about the applicant?   Y ☐ N ☐

Take control of the call — Be polite and act as though it's normal to get facts on applicants. You get more facts when you're sure of yourself. Say you're calling, "to check on some facts for a job application." That's less threatening than calling, "to ask for a reference." Asking for "facts" gets more than asking for "information" on someone. "Facts" suggests common knowledge. "Information" suggests private knowledge.

Begin with simple facts of record, like job title and kind of work. Keep evaluations and sensitive topics till later. Sometimes the references won't tell you much. They may fear lawsuits. They may give only name, title and length of employment.

Sometimes what you get from references depends on how you talk to them. Sometimes it depends on whom you talk to. Some people are natural talkers and tell a lot without you saying much. Point out that you have the applicant's permission to talk with the reference when you hit a wall. Point out that you need facts to look at the applicant fairly. Say that unless you get the facts you can't give the applicant the job.

Respect other people's trust in you — Make it clear to the reference that your call is between the two of you. Never carry back facts to an applicant. The applicant says she left her last job to go on a trip to Europe. Her boss says she fired her for being late too often. It's not your place to tell her what her boss said. That's between you and her boss. Do ask her how often she's late. Do make your expectations for sellers being on time clear to her. Do ask her if she can live up to them. Check that she comes in on time if you hire her. Be ready to let her go quickly if she hasn't learned from her last firing.

Check references before you interview — Sometimes what a reference tells you makes it clear you don't want an applicant. What you learn from a reference may point out questions you'll need to ask in an interview. You risk not checking references if you plan to check them after the interview. Your desire to hire may become so strong that you put the references aside. You may run short of time and get swept into hiring.

Allow for biases — People who give references may have biases. They may have only good things to say about someone they like. They may have only bad things to say about someone they don't like.

Talk to the earlier references — It's a mistake to talk only to the last reference. Imagine a retailer has a seller who's at the low end of the sales scale. Imagine also that he suspects the seller is dipping into the till but can't prove it. The retailer would like to get rid of the seller, but doesn't have the guts. Now you phone and ask for a reference. You get a glowing reference because it solves the retailer's problem to pass the seller on to you. Two years later someone else calls for a reference and he's eager to give the true story. Time also gives a maturity to people's views. They may see things more clearly and with less passion.

Sort out differences after you interview — In rare cases something the applicant says makes it worth your while to crosscheck with a reference.

Interview Applicants

Prepare to spend time on the interview. Schedule at least two hours for the job but prepare to spend less time with applicants who prove to be unsuitable.

Make no promises of job security — Say nothing during an interview that suggests any kind of job security. Make no direct promises. Say nothing applicants can take as indirect promises.

Work from Interview Sheets — With an *Interview Sheet* you'll have a standard pattern to what you find out about applicants. Build up a stock of past interviews. Then you can compare new interviews with those of sellers who already work for you. You force yourself to be fair with people you hire when you work from an *Interview Sheet*. Change your *Interview Sheet* as you get experience with interviews. It'll change over time, but there'll be enough there to compare with old interviews.

Interview Sheet

Name _____
          Last, First, Middle

Interview by _____

Date _____

Application

	Writes neatly	Y ☐	N ☐
	Showed interest in the store	Y ☐	N ☐

Interview

●	Good attitude	Y ☐	N ☐
	Positive person	Y ☐	N ☐
	Bright person	Y ☐	N ☐
	Nice person	Y ☐	N ☐
	Sure of self	Y ☐	N ☐
	Polite	Y ☐	N ☐
	Takes feedback well	Y ☐	N ☐
	On time for interview	Y ☐	N ☐
	Makes eye contact	Y ☐	N ☐
	Smiles	Y ☐	N ☐
	Well dressed	Y ☐	N ☐
	Dressed for the job	Y ☐	N ☐
	Well groomed	Y ☐	N ☐
	Speaks clearly	Y ☐	N ☐
	Easy to listen to	Y ☐	N ☐
	Throws voice	Y ☐	N ☐
	Speaks well	Y ☐	N ☐
1	Has goals	Y ☐	N ☐
2	Is growing	Y ☐	N ☐
3	Gives to the job	Y ☐	N ☐
4	Likes the store	Y ☐	N ☐
5	Has ideas on store	Y ☐	N ☐
6	Positive on attendance	Y ☐	N ☐
7	Relates to people	Y ☐	N ☐
8	Knows self	Y ☐	N ☐
9	Other questions	Y ☐	N ☐
10	Questions from references	Y ☐	N ☐
11	Special skills	Y ☐	N ☐
12	Asks about job	Y ☐	N ☐
A	Agreements	Y ☐	N ☐
B	Displays well	Y ☐	N ☐
C	Math	Y ☐	N ☐

Keep attitude first in mind — Keep your main interest in the attitude of applicants. With *Interview Sheets* you can bog down in details. Treat them as your way of taking a picture rather than using them as a score sheet. Correct failings when the attitude is right. At interviews applicants may dress poorly for the job. They may make poor eye contact. They may not smile. Feed their failings back to the applicants directly and evenly. Give applicants a chance to change. That's better than keeping quiet and writing them off.

Say, "John, our sellers have to smile at customers easily. Is that something you can do?" and wait for an answer and a smile. Say, "Mary, the way you're dressed now isn't right for this job. The way we

Questions

1 Tell me something about your interests in life
1 How do you see yourself five years from now?
2 How have you changed in the last three years?
2 What kinds of criticism have you had from other managers you've worked for?
2 How do you think you could improve yourself?
3 Why are you interested in this job?
3 What is there about you that makes you a good worker?
4 What do you think about this store?
5 What would you do to improve this store?
6 What do you feel is a good reason for missing work?
6 What do you feel is a good reason for being late?
7 How do you enjoy working with people?
7 What types of people upset you?
7 How do you deal with them?
7 In what ways are you easy to work with?
8 In what ways are you hard to work with?
8 How do you deal with stress?
9 Other questions.
9 Why are you changing jobs/did you leave your last job?
9 Tell me about a typical day in your present/last job.
9 What has been the most interesting job/project in your life?
10 Questions from checking references.
11 Anything else bearing on the job you'd like to tell me about yourself?
12 Anything you'd like to ask me about the job?

A Agreements

Take Pride in Selling

Look at Selling As a Helpful and Friendly Job
Look at Selling As a Skilled Job
Feel Good about the Items, the Store and Selling
Sell Fully to All Customers

Know What the Store Expects from You

Be Honest and Open
Dress and Groom Yourself Well
Work Free of the Effects of Alcohol and Drugs
Work Unusual Hours
Be on Time
Leave the Good Parking for Customers
Smoke and Chew Far from the Store

dress is informal but neat and in fashion. Are you able to dress like that? Are you willing to listen to ideas from me and some of the other sellers on dress?" How do they respond? Do they seem to be people who'll grow?

Bring applicants up to get good service. How far down in the barrel you go depends on your needs. You can be picky when you have more applicants than you need. Chances are you'll have to bring some applicants up to your level. Make sure they're willing to come up to your level, then bring them up. They'll be glad you did it. There are too few employers ready to bring out the possible in people. Sellers you bring up will know they have an unusual boss. They'll give you good service.

Step around outlawed questions
— Ask only questions directly related to doing the job. Put every question you ask to this test and you'll protect yourself from problems. Keep away from all questions, speech or actions that could lead to a charge of discrimination or harassment. Keep them out of all advertising, all interviews and all job applications. Never ask applicants to send photos of themselves.

Remember this is a job interview, not a social event. Questions you ask to put someone at ease may make it look as if you plan to discriminate. You might find a person's name interesting and ask about it. It looks as if you asked about national origin. You might ask a woman

Use the Phone for Business
Keep the Store's Secrets
Control Your Visitors
Keep to a High Standard of Personal Conduct
Give First Class Customer Service
Keep Up with World, National and Local News
Give and Take Praise

B Displays well

Display has good impact	Y ☐	N ☐
Sign has good content	Y ☐	N ☐
Sign shows good art skills	Y ☐	N ☐
Sign has good impact	Y ☐	N ☐

C Math

Work with Numbers

Round Decimals
Work Out Percentages
Use a Hand Calculator
Use a Simple Business Calculator

about her family because you have an interest in the people you meet. It looks as if you try not to employ women with small children.

Consult your lawyer before you ask any question on these topics:

- AIDS.

- Age or date of birth.

- Arrests or conviction of crimes.

- Citizenship, nationality, national or social origin, family tree.

- Dependence on alcohol or drugs.

- Education not specifically needed for the job.

- Languages not used on the job.

- Marital or family status.

- Mental or physical handicaps that don't affect ability to do the job.

- Other sources of income.

- Political beliefs.

- Pregnancy, childbirth or children.

- Race, color, ethnic origin.

- Religion or non-religious beliefs.

- Sex or sexual orientation.

Avoid asking outlawed questions indirectly. "When did you graduate from high school?" is a way of asking age. "Where did you grow up?" is a way of asking if someone was born in this country.

Sum up the interview on one sheet — Use page one of the *Interview Sheet* to sum up the interview. Score interview points "Yes" or "No." You'll fool yourself if you play games with sliding scales. Applicants are either OK or not OK for each point. Points like being on time for the interview and being well dressed you'll see right away. Points like "Makes eye contact" and "Speaks well" will come out as you talk. Some points will come out only as you ask questions.

Follow a plan for questions. The points where you need to ask questions have a number beside them. These numbers key to the list of questions on the *Interview Sheet*. Add questions of your own as you get experience with interviews.

Question fairly — Steer clear of leading questions. Leading questions make clear the answer you want to hear. "You'll always be on time, won't you?"

Avoid coaching answers. You coach answers if you give hints when applicants get bogged down. It's another way of getting answers you want to hear. You might as well not bother to ask questions if you coach answers. Try asking a question a different way or move on to a different question.

Follow the 20/80 rule. Aim to talk 20% of the time and let applicants talk the other 80%.

Bounce from applicants' answers to ask more questions. You dominate the interview when you use answers as a jump off point to talk about your views. You find out little about applicants when you spend time talking about yourself.

Give applicants a fair hearing. Listen fully to what applicants have to say. Avoid pushing them into pigeon holes. Learn who they really are.

Build up trust before asking sensitive questions. Let applicants feel at ease with you before you ask sensitive questions. Sometimes you deal with applicants who lost their last job. That's sensitive, but you'll want to know why applicants lost jobs.

Make sensitive questions sound normal. "There are many reasons for people leaving their jobs. Please tell me what happened in your case."

Accept the answers to sensitive questions. "I see. Thank you for telling me." Avoid any judgments or negative comments.

Get the facts you need to know — What's the attitude like? In the interview, attitude is top of your list. It's the most important thing about people. That's why it has a big star beside it on the *Interview Sheet*.

Can you live with the handwriting? You know the handwriting from the application. Is it neat enough for your store's records? Is it neat enough for everyday messages?

Do applicants show an interest in the store? Thoughtful applicants will look the store over and want to know what they're getting into. Some will let you know the store excites them.[4] You're dealing with a good prospect when the reaction is honest and they have other strengths.

Watch for bubble heads. They're excited by the store. They're keen. They look right for the part. They have little to back up their bubbles.

Watch for applicants who like the store but say nothing. Ask them what they think about the store. Give them feedback on being open with you. Push them in the right direction. See how they react to feedback.

Check off other general points at the end of the interview. Is this a positive, can-do person? Is this a bright person? Is this a polite person? Can applicants handle feedback?

Make sure applicants are at ease with you before you give them feedback. Give feedback when you're asking questions or bounce it from anything you see. "John, we've found we need to show we're paying attention to customers to sell well. One thing we do is make good eye contact. I notice nobody has taught you how to do that yet. As we talk, look at my face. Look at a point above my nose when you feel you want to look away. Look about half an inch higher than my eyebrows. Move you eyes about on my face, so you don't stare. Keep looking at me and meet my eyes from time to time. Is that something you can do?"

Ask questions by numbers. Plan your questions, but follow ideas that come to you as you listen to applicants. The numbers key to sample questions on the *Interview Sheet*.

Find out about goals. You're better off with sellers who have goals even if they'll outgrow your store and leave you. Make exceptions for applicants with spirit. A retired person with no great goals can be good. So can someone returning to the work force who's grateful to survive. Steer clear of applicants who are just putting in time with their lives. Find people who accept change in their lives. Steer clear of rigid people.

Find out how your job will fill people's needs. Find out what they'll bring into the job. At least they should be grateful for the job and show they're willing to please.

Get applicants to tell you what they think about the store. This is almost a leading question because applicants looking for a job will rarely run the store down. Ask it to get applicants to commit themselves. Thoughts become truths when people put them into words. You want your sellers to tell you they love your store. Set the pattern at the interview. Then keep at it.

---

[4]You've probably got a dull store and need to do something about it if this happens only rarely. Applicants have a fresh view of your store. They see it as fresh customers see it.

Ask applicants how they'd improve your store. Most applicants won't have any ideas. They scarcely know your store yet. Someone may say, "I'd try brighter lighting in the windows." You know you have someone who'll add to your store. You signal you expect people to pitch in when you ask them for advice at the interview.

Ask about being on time. Applicants aren't going to tell you they miss work and come late. So ask them about good reasons for doing so and see what comes out. People often talk more freely when the question suggests there are good reasons for doing bad things.

Look for people who set high standards for themselves. "I miss work only when I'm so ill I have to go to a doctor. It's been three years since my last time. I usually get to work ten minutes ahead of time. I suppose it would be OK to be late if the bus crashed. That's not something that ever happened to me."

Some people have given themselves permission to miss and to come late. "You have to miss work when you're ill. Sometimes you're late if you miss the bus or the bus is late." These facts are true but they don't show a high standard. You'll have to ask questions to get more details. Nobody can quarrel with missing work when ill. Ask, "How often are you ill each year?" Ask, "How often are you late each month?" Perhaps this is a person who rarely misses and is rarely late. The answer may reflect a way of speaking rather than a bad attitude. To clear doubt, make clear what you expect. "People who aren't late get up early enough to get to the bus stop in time. They plan to arrive ten minutes ahead of time and have a coffee before work. That way they only miss their coffee if the bus is late. Does that describe you? Are you willing to change if it doesn't describe you?" For some people taking days off and being late are habits. People who take days off when the weather is fine or when there is powder snow won't work out. People who are late because they oversleep or have a hangover won't work out.

Find out how applicants relate to other people. Find out what applicants know about themselves. Ask questions on any other topics important to your store.

Ask questions that came up when you checked the applicant's references. Remember to keep the references' trust in you.

Let applicants tell you anything about themselves they think bears on the job. Answer any questions applicants want to ask you.

Begin training now — Begin training at the interview. Make it clear you have standards for your store right up front. At least in a general way, cover material from the sections *Pride in Selling* and *What the Store Expects from Sellers* in Chapter 8 *Make Expectations Clear* as listed on the *Interview Sheet*. This material covers important basic ideas related to attitude. Let applicants know what you expect and ask them questions. This way you'll learn more about the applicants and start them in the right direction.

Have applicants set up a display — Let applicants know all sellers in your store set up displays. Choose applicants who rise to the challenge. A good sense of style is a help here, but you don't need an artist. Now is the time to set the standard and weed out applicants who back off.

Have applicants set up a display and make a *Highlight Sign* as if for a new item.[5] The heading "Displays well" in the *Interview Sheet* points you to a check list for scoring the display. Have on hand sample items for the display and materials to write a sign. Tell applicants, "This is a new item in the store. We're going to sell it at $19.95. Your job is to set up a display and write a sign to interest customers in buying the item." Then leave them in peace while they do it.

Test arithmetic and calculators — Have applicants show what they know about arithmetic and calculators.

At least in a general way, cover the material from the section *Work with Numbers* in Chapter 11 *List Sales* to see where the applicant stands. The "Math" section of the *Interview Sheet* lists this material. The sections you use and the level you accept is up to you. Know what you're getting and how much training you'll have to give. Put most stress on simple arithmetic. Make sure applicants understand this is a survey, not a make or break test.

Make a decision — Review the Application Form and the results of an interview. You have three choices:

1. No interest in the applicant.

2. Put the applicant on hold. You think you can work with the applicant at some time in the future.

3. Interview the applicant again. Ask applicants who look good to come for a second interview. Offer jobs to those who still look good at the close of the second interview.

Let applicants know your decision — Keep to a standard for dealing with applicants. Let everyone know where they stand with you. Leave no applicants dangling. It's tough to tell applicants they haven't got the job, but tell them anyway. It's easy to skip this. It's a sign your people skills are low if you don't deal openly with applicants you turn down. Tell applicants on hold you've decided

---

[5]Be sure any tests you use for hiring or promoting relate directly to the job. Avoid things like handwriting analysis and casting of horoscopes. You'll find them hard to defend. For math scores collect some comparison scores. Compare with scores of sellers who do the job well. Make sure you keep all test scores to yourself.

not to expand at this time. Let them know they impressed you. Let them know you'd like them to work for you some time in the future.

Interview Applicants Again

A second interview is a powerful tool. It gives you the chance to drive home the active nature of your store and to tie up any loose ends. Put the accent on the training parts of the interview.

Go over feelings — How do you feel about offering the job? How do applicants feel about wanting the job?

Ask any left over questions — Now's the chance for you to ask more questions. Does the applicant have more questions to ask you?

Go over some things before the final decision — Summarize the main facts of the interview. Tell applicants, "The plan is to go over some things before either of us makes a final decision. We'll repeat some of the exercises from the interview. Then we'll do some more exercises so you get a better feel of the store." Ask, "Is that OK by you?" Go over the materials covered in the interview.

Offer the job if it feels right — In the end it comes down to a feeling. Structured interviews gives you a good basis for developing your feelings about applicants.

Set up a work schedule for applicants who accept. Introduce the new seller to any other sellers who are working. Put out a *News Sheet* on the new seller. Let sellers know there will be a new seller in the store.

Hire drivers subject to a good driving record — Say to applicants who will drive for you, "I can hire you on condition you can show me a good driving record." In most states drivers can get an abstract of their driving record from the state's department that licenses drivers. Lay in a stock of request forms. Check off the records you wish to see. Fill in your name and address as the person to receive the abstract. Have the store mail the request and pay for the abstract. Before mailing the request ask the applicant, "Will there be any problems with this, Joan?" Start the applicant working in the store, but hold off on driving until you see the abstract.

Hire and Pay Sellers Legally

Although hiring and paying sellers has red tape around it, it's an area where playing by the rules pays off. The fuss needed to do things right is nothing compared to the fuss you'll get if you stray outside the law.

Follow INS[6] rules set out in the *Handbook for Employers* (M-274.) The handbook shows how to fill in *Form I-9 Employment Eligibility Verification*. Get the handbook and several I-9 forms from your local INS office. Get bulk copies of *Form I-9* from the Superintendent of Documents.[7] You can photocopy extra I-9 forms. To stay legal, copy both sides of the form onto one sheet of paper.

Ask to see proof of identity and right to work — The back of *Form I-9* lists the many items that job seekers may show you. One choice is to see one item that proves both identity and right to work. Another choice is to see one item that proves identity and another item that proves right to work. Part 8 of the handbook has pictures of many of these items.

Take any listed documents as proof of identity or right to work. Take the documents offered and check that they're on the list as suitable for proof of identity or right to work. Try to choose which items you'll accept and you may find yourself answering a charge of discrimination.

Take documents that will run out soon. You can't turn down job seekers because their papers will run out soon. They may be able to renew them. Turn them down and you may find yourself answering a charge of discrimination.

Show no preference to U.S. citizens — Equally qualified aliens with the right to work in the U.S. have as much right to a job as a U.S. citizen.

Have sellers sign in. Have all sellers fill in and sign their part of *Form I-9* (Section 1) when they begin work. Check that sellers fill in every item. Each item sellers miss or report wrongly can cost you a fine.

Fill in all items on your part of *Form I-9* (Section 2.) Each item you miss or report wrongly on each form can cost you a fine.

Later you may have to fill in Section 3. This is to update the facts that change or to use when you re-hire a person. Leave Section 3 blank at the time of original employment.

Hang on to completed I-9 forms — It's easiest to keep completed I-9 forms for three (3) years after sellers stop working for you.[8] Keep the forms in a separate file

---

[6]Immigration & Naturalization Service, Washington, DC 20536 (800) 755-0777. Look in the phone book under Government Listings in the White Pages for the local office or connect to http://www.ins.usdoj.gov on the Internet.

[7]Superintendent of Documents, U.S. Government Printing Office, Washington, DC 20402 (202) 783-3238 or connect to http://www.access.gpo.gov/su_docs on the Internet.

[8]The rules call for keeping the forms until the later of: a) three years after the start of work; b) one year after the end of work.

rather than spread out through sellers' files. Then it's easy to take them for audit.[9] You may only get three days notice to present the forms for audit.

Cheating will backfire on you — Cheaters may suffer legal penalties. Managers who cheat lose their reputation for honesty. They send a signal to their sellers that they cut corners. Soon their sellers cut corners on them. Managers who cheat put the fate of their business in other people's hands. It's easy for sellers who fall out with their managers to turn them in. Managers who cheat always live with extra stress. They never know the twists. A young lady is in the country illegally working at a store. She has a falling out with her boyfriend who turns her in. The store owner gets the visit from the federal agents.

Check sellers' names and Social Security Numbers — Follow IRS[10] rules set out in the Employer's Tax Guide (Circular E.)

Ask to see *Social Security Cards*. Copy names and *Social Security Numbers* from *Social Security Cards*. That makes sure you get them right. It's not enough to ask sellers for their names and *Social Security Numbers*. Seeing the card makes sure you're dealing with people who have *Social Security Cards*.

Check for cards that have "Not for Employment" on them. *Social Security Cards* carried by students and temporary residents with no right to work have these words on them. Check cards for alterations.

Sellers without a *Social Security Card* should apply for one. Sellers using a name different from that on the *Social Security Card* should apply for a new card. Follow through on sellers who apply for new cards. Make sure you see the new cards. Let the SSA[11] know when a seller stalls you on showing you the new card.

You risk a fine for every W2 income tax form you turn in without a *Social Security Number*.

Have sellers fill in Form W-4 — Each new seller must fill in an Income Tax Withholding Form (W-4.) Get copies of Form W-4 from the IRS.[5]

Put everyone on the payroll — Your bookkeeper can set you up to handle the payroll details the right way. Be sure you can do it right if you're your own

---

[9]The INS may ask to see these forms. So may the Department of Labor (DOL.) So may the Office of Special Counsel for Immigration Related Unfair Employment Practices (OSC.)
[10]Internal Revenue Service, Department of the Treasury, Washington, DC 20224. Look in the phone book under Government Listings in the White Pages for the local office, or begin exploring from the bottom of http://www.irs.ustreas.gov/prod/cover.html on the Internet.
[11]Social Security Administration, 6401 Security Boulevard, Baltimore MD 21235. Look in the phone book under Government Listings in the White Pages for the local office, or connect to http://www.ssa.gov on the Internet.

bookkeeper and paymaster. Be sure you can meet the deadlines and follow the rules set out in the IRS's *Employer's Tax Guide* (Circular E.)[5]

Take the required deductions from paychecks. Required deductions from paychecks include federal, state and local income tax withholding, contribution to Social Security, state disability deductions, authorized deductions for health or life insurance, and tax deferrals. Make sure you include commissions, spiffs and prizes as pay as well as wages. Make sure you pay required overtime.

Set aside seller benefits — Keep a set aside account for seller benefits. These include sick pay and vacation pay. Provide benefits for all sellers after the legal time period. Usually, when someone has worked for more than six (6) months you must pay benefits. Check your local laws for the time limit. A few weeks before this limit is a good time to review whether you want to keep sellers.

Employ managers as exempt workers Some workers are exempt from overtime provisions. *Federal Fair Labor Standards Act* (FLSA) and some state laws exempt certain jobs from overtime pay provisions. Usual exempt workers are company officers and directors, owners, executives, managers, outside sales representatives, professional staff, supervisors and technical staff.

Steer clear of the independent contractor dodge — The dodge looks OK. Instead of employing people, pay them as freelance agents. First get sellers to fill in a form that you think protects you. Now pay cash against signature for hours worked. That frees you of the bother of putting people on the payroll and making deductions, or so you think.

Sellers like it because they get more cash. You don't take out the deductions. Sellers should do that, but they don't. It's too much bother for them, just as it's too much bother for you. They think it's smart to cheat on their taxes. That's not your problem. That's the sellers' problem, or so you think.

There's a fly in this ointment. Probably the IRS will apply tests like these to see if the sellers are independent contractors:

- Have the sellers incorporated or registered a business?

- Can the sellers show they work for several clients, or are you their only client?

- Are the sellers free agents working without direction from you? That's to say do they work for you like a plumber or an electrician works for you.

Your sellers will fail these tests. You'll owe the tax they didn't pay, plus fines and penalties.

Set Up Files on Sellers

Begin with a simple file of facts on your sellers.

Seller's Fact Sheet

Legal Name: Last _____   First _____   Middle _____

SSN ____|__|____   Driver's License _____   Phone _____

Date of Hiring _____|__|__
                    Month Day Year

Home Address _____

Number of exemptions claimed on your W-4 tax form _____

Military or draft status _____

People to call in case of emergency:

Name _____   Phone _____
Name _____   Phone _____
Name _____   Phone _____
Name _____   Phone _____

Anything else you wish to add:

Set up a separate file for each new seller — Start a new file when you employ someone. First crosscheck you've seen proof of identity and are sure the person can work legally in the U.S.

Begin by having the seller complete a *Seller's Fact Sheet*. Collect facts (age, marital status, dependents) you couldn't collect on the job application if you feel you need them. Be sure you don't use them to discriminate when you decide whether to keep or promote sellers. The seller's file is the place to keep all facts about a seller. It's the place for copies of notes you write to the seller. It's the place for copies of notes you make about the seller.

Act as if sellers can review their files — Most states allow sellers to review what's in their files. Sometimes there are limits to what sellers can see. The simplest plan is to act as if sellers can review everything. Put nothing in sellers' files that you want to keep from them. Then you can be open with your sellers about their files.

Keep the sellers' files in a locked cabinet — Sellers shouldn't be able to look through each other's files. Make sure only those who need to use sellers' files to do their jobs may use them. You may only need to lock part of a filing cabinet to protect the sellers' files. Drill holes for metal screws and put a padlock and hasp on the top drawer of a file cabinet. Padlock the top drawer. Otherwise someone can take out the drawer above the files and reach down to them.

Support Sellers Fully

Give everything you can to the sellers you hire. Make hiring a serious commitment to support. Put yourself on the line for the success of new sellers. It's your failure if sellers fail. Give sellers that kind of commitment when you hire them. Sort the losers out at the interview and don't hire them. Hire only sellers you can and will work with.

Play no favorites — Support everyone you hire. Leave none to swim alone. Put no limits on training and coaching for all sellers. Have no reservations on the support you give to all sellers. Give more support when you find yourself not liking someone. Your aim is selling, not liking. Make sure you don't put a death wish on a seller.

Turn problem sellers into model sellers — Sellers sometimes upset you. Take your feelings out in supporting them for selling. Get them to please you by how well they sell. It's too easy to push sellers aside when they upset you. That's not the way to go. Getting rid of someone's the easy way out. You hire Fred to help with the flower arrangements. Instead of doing them in order of need, Fred does them in order of interest to him. He takes all the fancy ones and ignores the run-of-the-mill arrangements. Suddenly, you have nothing to sell and there's Fred enjoying his artistic creations. You get steamed and let Fred go. That's failure. Not Fred's failure, but your failure to get Fred on track. The aim of discipline is to improve what sellers do, not to get rid of them. Work with sellers instead of nailing them.

Push beginners over the hump — Get new sellers up to speed fast. Set a goal for training and a goal for reaching a commission level. Then push the new sellers there. Train them and support them and keep training them and supporting them. Train, train and train again and again and again. People need to repeat an action six to eight times before it becomes a habit. In our busy world we look for instant solutions. We're usually too busy to do the job properly. Get out of that habit.

A few sellers can't or won't learn to sell. They don't meet their goals when others do. Give them strong support. Give them extra training and coaching. Make sure they have customers to sell to. It's time to say good-bye when you're sure the problem lies with them and not with you. Make your decision on sellers by the end of the 6th week of employment. Watch out, it's your reputation on the line. You're going to have to let new sellers go if they don't reach their goals. That's failure— your failure, not theirs. You selected them as sellers you could support to reach their goals. You didn't make it. You didn't make it because you didn't give them enough support. There's no other reason. Put the blame on yourself, not on somebody else.

Let Sellers Go Fairly and Firmly

Letting sellers go is a sensitive area full of traps for the unwary and full of tension for the faint-at-heart. It pays to be clear on where you stand with this issue from the beginning. Be clear on definitions:

Let someone go: Lay someone off or fire someone.

Lay someone off: Dismiss someone without fault because of events beyond your control, usually lack of business.

Fire someone: Dismiss someone who's unable or unwilling to do the job.

Know where you stand — In theory you may dismiss sellers with or without cause at any time. Likewise, sellers may stop working for you with or without cause at any time. These are important rules for free enterprise and personal freedom to exist.

A number of laws limit your freedom to dismiss sellers. Among them are equal opportunity laws and laws on harassment. There are also laws that protect whistle blowers who report improper business practices. Some of these laws are obvious. Others are less obvious and may sneak up on you. As long as you break no laws, you're free to dismiss sellers with or without cause at any time.

Contracts and agreements limit your freedom to dismiss sellers. Your right to dismiss sellers will change if you enter into contracts or agreements with them. Such agreements may also limit when and how sellers may leave you. The agreements may be directly between you and sellers or between you and a union. You may have agreed to hire a seller for a stated period. You may have agreed only to dismiss sellers for failure to meet the terms of a contract.

Be careful what you put in handbooks. One view is that handbooks aren't contracts since they don't completely define the terms and conditions of work. On the other hand, some employers have found themselves bound by their handbooks. In handbooks, claim they aren't contracts. On the other hand, write them as if you'll have to stand by them.

Develop a way of firing sellers — Avoid blind firing. Some lawyers recommend firing sellers with no warning and refusing to discuss the firing. Before you do this, make sure your lawyer backs you up. Such action is rarely in your best interest. It's easy to open yourself to a charge of breaking the law. That's specially so when you fire a minority person, a woman or an old person like this. Many sellers you fire like this will look for a way to get back at you. It's not good for morale in the store. Sales may suffer. Other sellers may leave. They may decide your store isn't a good place to work. It'll give your other sellers a poor impression of your common sense and humanity. Be sure there's good reason for it when you fire a seller like this. You'll pay a price for it.

Stick with "At will" employment but act as if you can only fire with cause. Fire only for a reason. Make this your moral code. Make sure the sellers you fire can't do the work or won't do the work. Let sellers you fire know why it's happening. Sellers expect you to tell them why you fire them.

Follow a graded response to problems with sellers. Go through a series of steps. Being fired shouldn't surprise the seller who's being fired. Abandon a graded response only in cases of gross misconduct like theft[12] or challenging supervision.

Forget what sellers do on their own time. Sellers' off duty conduct is no concern of yours unless you can show it harms your business interests. One exception that may concern you is a seller working also for a rival store.

Sellers you lay off are a special group. There's not much else you can do when you don't have enough business to support all your sellers.

Prepare to state why you let someone go. State laws may require you to sign a statement saying why you let a seller go if the seller asks you to do so. Check the wording with your attorney before you sign a statement. The easiest statements to sign are those that place no blame on the seller. This includes statements such as, "Discharged owing to a seasonal drop in business." Sometimes you'll have to place blame on the seller as in, "Discharged for repeated lateness." Tell the truth. In some states you'll pay more unemployment insurance for discharging sellers without cause than for discharging them with cause. Check how much it will cost you to chicken out or cover up for a seller. The requirement to say why you discharged a seller doesn't limit your "At will" relationship. You can say you discharged a seller without cause. Make a statement like this rarely. Reserve it for times when you want to change a situation without going into the whys and wherefores.

Lay sellers off firmly and kindly — Let some sellers go during business downturns. Select your weakest sellers and lay them off. Lay off the most recent hires when sellers are equal. Call sellers in and say something like, "Frank, as you know, business conditions are hurting our sales. There's no way we can carry all the sellers we have. I have to let some sellers go and I've chosen you as one of them. I wish things were different, Frank, but they aren't. Frank, you can rely on me to give you full support in finding another job."

Only explain how you chose to let sellers go when sellers push the issue. Then explain how you made your choice. That means when you select your weakest

---

[12]While dishonesty and theft are good grounds for dismissing sellers on the spot, they may be hard to prove. As in a court, the accused has the right to confront witnesses.

sellers, have the facts at hand. That means when you choose the most recent hires, look their hiring dates up in their files. Be able to defend your choices if you have to.

Tie up the loose ends. "Please let me have your key to the store and your key to the cash drawer. Then I'll give you the final payment we owe you and we can go our separate ways. I'm really sorry about this, Frank."

Review your support before you fire a seller — Every time you fire a seller you chalk another failure on your record. Sometimes you can't escape the failure. That's OK. Chalk up your failure and move on. You certainly can't run your store with sellers who don't work out.

Sometimes you can escape the failure but you tell yourself you can't. It's easy to seek the causes of failure in other people. There's comfort in placing the blame on someone else, even though there's stress in it too. You soon have a high turnover of sellers. Your store becomes marked by stress and becomes a hard place to work.

Each seller is a valuable resource. You put a lot into getting, training and coaching sellers. Protect and develop your investment. Review your support before you fire sellers. Have you trained and coached them without holding back? Did you get busy elsewhere and let the training and coaching slide? Did you give them 100% and more, or did you write them off at some time? Did you put them in mental pigeon holes that made it easy to look down on them?

Give support now if your support was lacking. Say to sellers, "Look, things haven't gone as they should. Let's start again." Have the courage to face your bad habits and break them. You have to begin again anyway when you fire sellers and replace them.

Firing a seller is an extreme action. It's cruel to fire a seller when there's no need to. Avoid firing a seller to get even or as a punishment. Avoid firing a seller just for the hell of it. Firing a seller is your last weapon. Use your last weapon last, not first. Use it as little as possible. Fire a seller only when you're free of ego. Fire without name calling. This is no time for fixing blame. Firing a seller when you're hot and in a rage is a big mistake. Make a snap decision in anger and you may be the one who feels the heat. There are plenty of lawyers looking for clients fired without good cause. Make sure you're without pride when you fire someone and make sure you don't gloat when you've fired someone. Fire after thought and while free of the desire to fire. Make your decision to fire a seller a sound business decision. Give it thought and take the steps to make sure it's a fair decision.

Review your interviews when support doesn't work — Do your homework when you fire someone. Your support didn't work because you were training the wrong horse. You chose the horse. Review how you choose sellers. Are you clear who you're looking for? Are you finding the sellers you need? Are you taking and reviewing applications well? Are you checking all references? Are you interviewing properly? Do you need more or better interview questions? Are you interviewing applicants again properly? Somewhere in that list something is wrong. Find out where and correct the mistakes.

Fire sellers who resist support — Some sellers won't let you support them. They may go through the motions with you, but then go their own way. They may know better than you. Perhaps they do, but not for your store.

First try to fix the problem. You have no choice but to fire the seller if you can't fix the problem. Now you have some homework to do. For new sellers, again you're training the wrong horse. Review what's wrong as you would when support doesn't work. For sellers who used to accept support, find out how you lost contact. Something changed in the seller or in how you give support. Find out what that is. Try to backtrack with the seller you have and get things right if the fault is with you. Build protection against repeating this failure into how you deal with sellers.

Fire sellers who won't change their faults — Some sellers do things badly and won't change. Some sellers come in late and no matter how much you're on their case they still come in late. Some sellers take too many days off without notice. You tell them they're out of bounds several times. They still take time off without notice. The examples are endless. These are sellers who destroy themselves. Keep them and they'll destroy you too. You have to let them go.

Move quickly on bad choices — Make a clear choice on whether you want to keep new sellers. Set a time for serious review of new sellers. Set this time for yourself without telling new sellers about it. Sellers may think they've become permanent sellers if you tell them about this review and they pass it. Set the time for review by how much training and coaching you've given and by the selling results you see. Make your decision and act as soon as the time is up. Mark your calendar so you're sure to do this review. Otherwise, you'll have poor sellers slide in with you.

Record graded responses to sellers with problems — Try to solve every problem. Be able to show you tried to solve the problem and failed in case you have to fire a seller.

1. Talk about the problem. That's the normal way to deal with a problem. Write nothing down.

2. Talk again and write a dated note to the seller's file. Note that you talked first informally and now you've talked again. This is strictly a note to remind yourself of the steps you're taking. The seller doesn't get a copy.

3. Write a dated note to the seller. State the problem and state why it's important to solve the problem. State that you've talked about the problem twice. State the improvement you expect to see. Also state when you expect to see the improvement. At the bottom of the note include a receipt for the seller to sign. Call the seller in to pick up a copy and sign the receipt on your copy. File your copy in the seller's file. Write another dated note to the seller. Say what happens if you don't see the improvement. Say the seller's employment will end if the problem isn't solved by a date.[13] At the bottom of the note include a receipt for the seller to sign. Call the seller in to pick up a copy and sign the receipt.

4. Give a final written warning to the seller before the firing deadline. Write down everything you've done. Include copies of all earlier notes. Say this is now the final chance. Say that failure means the end of employment by a date. At the bottom of the note include a receipt for the seller to sign. Call the seller in to pick up a copy and sign the receipt.

5. Fire the seller after checking that you're clear to fire. Check that the seller still isn't meeting standards. Check that you told the seller about the faults. Check that you counseled the seller on improvements needed. Check that you warned the seller of firing for not improving. Check that you've reached the firing deadline. Fire the seller.

The seller may refuse to sign a receipt for a note. Have a witness present and call in the seller again. Ask for the signature in front of the witness. Fire the seller on the spot for refusing to obey a work order if the seller refuses to sign the receipt. Have the witness write and sign a note outlining the refusal. Keep this note in the seller's file.

Remove sellers from being on final warning when they improve. Write a note removing them on the understanding they stay at the improved level. Give a copy to the seller and put a copy in the seller's file.

Fire sellers politely and firmly — Stay firm in your decision. This is no time to waver and bargain. You've already gone over the other choices if you've made the decision properly. You've now made a decision, so make it clear you've made a decision. Make no apology for firing a seller. Base firing only on sound business reasons. Tell the facts simply and clearly. Let sellers know you're firing them because they're not working out. Be honest and direct. Be calm. Be friendly and strong. Fire with the least harm to the person as possible.

"Michael, we've talked about you being late several times. I've given you two written notices telling you it's not acceptable. Today you were late again, so I've

---

[13]Try graded discipline. Try suspension or no promotion. Keep firing as your last option.

decided it's time for you to move on. Please let me have your key to the store and your key to the cash drawer. Then I'll give you the final payment we owe you and we can go our separate ways."

"Jane, we've talked about your failure to meet our standards for shaping up the displays and storage. I've given you three written notes and made it clear that you must be up to standard by today. You've had fair warning that if you're not up to standard it's the end of you working with us. You're still not up to the standard we require, Jane, so it's time for you to move on. Please let me have your key to the store and your key to the cash drawer. Then I'll give you the final payment we owe you and we can go our separate ways."

Make the final cash payment. The final cash payment due will vary according to your agreements and the laws that apply to your store. Pay any unused sick leave and any unused vacation pay. Most states require these payments.

Two week's severance pay is typical after working for a year, but most states don't require you to pay it. You'll have to go on paying it if you begin paying it. You can't pay it to some and not to others. That's discrimination. Check your local laws on whether to describe it as "severance pay" or "pay in place of notice." It may affect your sellers right to unemployment payments.

Make a payment for the period of the notice if you have to give notice when you let sellers go. Have the seller leave right away. It won't help your store to have an upset seller working for a week or two.

Keep firing between you and the seller — Firing a seller is a private business matter. It's not something to gossip about with other sellers.

CHAPTER 4

GET NEWS TO SELLERS

A formal *News System* using *News Sheets* and *Messages* makes sure all sellers get news about the store. In a busy store there's lots of news. Stick to a plan that everyone follows. This plan will involve the sellers providing feedback that they received and acted upon the news item.

Talking to sellers is good for training and coaching them. With news, it's hard to reach everyone. Talking to a few sellers and hoping they spread the news works poorly. Talking to each seller about simple news items is a poor use of your time. It works poorly when you have many sellers on several shifts.

Tack notices on a bulletin board and they sink into the background. Many sellers ignore them. You get no feedback and control. Sellers pin the notices over one another and your store looks messy. Even if the mess is out of sight by customers, your sellers learn it's OK to be messy. Tack notices on the cash register and you're on the way to being just another sloppy store. The place for *News Sheets* is in the *News Sheet* section of *Daily*. The place for *Messages* to sellers is in the *Message Pocket* of *Daily*. The place for replies to *Messages* from the manager is in the *Message Pocket* of the *To Manager* binder.

Make sure you don't get news and training mixed up. Training has too many parts to handle completely as news. Some training can begin with a *News Sheet* directing attention to *Guide Sheets*. Finish the training in person.

Sellers' Meetings play an important role spreading news, but they never replace the *News System*. News items that you bring up at *Sellers' Meetings* also go into the *News System*. Although *Sellers' Meetings* play other important roles, they form a separate section of this chapter.

News Sheets

News Sheets have news that everyone needs to know. *News Sheets* get facts to sellers fast. Look at the sample *News Sheet* to see how simple *News Sheets* are:

News Sheet 5 November 1994/1

First	Last	Initials	Date	Time
A. J.	Dennison			
Catherine	Bloor			
Christine	Johansenn			
France	Netepan			
Mahasti	Mogoshi			
Megan	Russell			
Tina	Hildebrand			

Leave Cash Register Turned on at Night

At night take out the cash register key from the REG position, *not* from the OFF position.
This will leave the display on.
This will let the batteries inside the cash register re-charge overnight.

Most *News Sheets* are short and easy to understand. Some warn you about topics for the next *Sellers' Meeting*. Others spell out topics from the last *Sellers' Meeting*. Keep *News Sheets* as short as you can. It's usually time to write a *Guide Sheet* when you find yourself writing a long *News Sheet*.

News Sheets have a shorter life span than *Guide Sheets*. Many *News Sheets* have news of passing interest. Although you'll change the contents of many *Guide Sheets* from time to time, most soon become stable.

Messages

Messages have news for one person. Think of the *Messages* as *News Sheets* for one seller. Put *Messages* in envelopes. Recycled envelopes are OK for most *Messages*.

Sellers' Meetings

Run *Sellers' Meetings* to stay in contact with your sellers. Meetings add to your personal contacts and your contacts through the *News System*. When time is available use parts of *Sellers' Meetings* for training. Short topics, preliminary training, and important topics work best. Follow through in the *News System* and with *Training Sessions* as usual.

Get value — Make *Sellers' Meetings* pay off. Work out a *Meeting List* of useful topics for each meeting. Make sure you spend the time well. Weed out simple topics you can deal with through *News Sheets*. Aim to meet for 45 minutes to an hour. Run a tight schedule and don't let latecomers change it.

Meet often or now and again, as long as the meetings pay off. It's easy to fall into a pattern of meetings for their own sake. You decide to meet each Wednesday and you do. The meetings take on a life of their own. Special meetings stand out as important. With special meetings you run the risk of putting off calling them.

Go all the way — Hold meetings your sellers are eager to go to. You can hold meetings at your store, but hold as many as you can afford at a good hotel or restaurant. Include a meal. Put as much cash as you can afford into making your sellers feel special. A good pattern is a morning meeting at the best hotel in town. First you eat, then you meet. A good plan is to begin breakfast at 7 am. Then have all plates, coffee and so on cleared away by 8 am. Then meet till 9 am.

Make sure all sellers go to all Sellers' Meetings — All sellers go to all *Sellers' Meetings*. Sellers go to *Sellers' Meetings* even if they're not working a shift on the day of the meeting. Pay call-in pay to sellers who have to come in specially for them. Sellers can only miss a meeting if they're on holiday or ill. Expect usual *Sellers' Meetings* to last from 45 minutes to an hour. Expect *Sellers' Meetings* with a meal to last from an hour and 45 minutes to two hours. Unless you plan carefully you may have to pay some sellers overtime pay.

Only sellers for the day go to early morning pump-up meetings.

Announce times of *Sellers' Meetings* in a *News Sheet*. Include a *Meeting List* so sellers know what you'll talk about.

In your training make sure sellers know that *Sellers' Meetings* aren't the place for gripes and bitches. Settle gripes and bitches one-to-one. It's wrong to bring them up at *Sellers' Meetings* and drag everyone else into them.

Choose two recorders — You need sellers to write for you—you'll be too busy running the meeting.

Choose a seller to write down the main events of the meeting. Choose a seller who writes neatly. Keep a record of what took place and you'll be in a good position to follow through on decisions. Keep the records in the *Meetings* binder.

Choose a seller to write with felt markers on an easel pad. An easel pad that's about 27″ x 34″ is a good size. Choose a seller who writes quickly and neatly.

Talk about new stuff — Normal training at *Sellers' Meetings* will bore your sellers. Get everyone to grow at meetings. What's new? Where are we going? How can we get there?

Brainstorm solutions to problems — Your sellers are full of ideas to solve your problems. Put the seller who writes quickly and neatly beside the easel pad. Then throw problems out to the sellers. Let everyone feel they're part of the solution. Write down all the ideas your sellers come up with. Act as if they're all good ideas, even the dogs. Never rank the ideas at the meeting. Rank and test the ideas later in private. Sometimes everyone senses a good idea when it comes. They jump in to praise it or make it better and you're clear you have a winner.

Show-&-tell new items — You've ordered new items or you're thinking about ordering them. Show them to your sellers. Get their reactions on the items and how to sell them. Write them on the easel pad.

Head off fixed minds — Some sellers see changes as threats. Explain their benefits to the store and to sellers at meetings. Let the fears come out. Calm sellers down.

Pump up sales — Get the sellers worked up for sales. You may have new items to sell or new ways to sell old items. You may have new prizes to give to good sellers. The best way is to let the sellers know after breakfast on a big selling day.

Begin on time — Reward sellers for being on time by starting on time. You punish sellers who are on time if you wait for sellers who are late. Talk to sellers who are late more than once privately. Ignore sellers who are late once. There are many good and bad reasons for being late.

Keep to the Meeting List — Kill new topics that come from the floor. Say, "That's an important topic. Let's list it to talk about it at a future meeting. For now, let's keep with the current *Meeting List*." Keep "Other Business" off the *Meeting List*. It defeats the purpose of having a *Meeting List*. It sets you up for time-wasters and ramblers.

Never take new items from the floor. Meetings like that go all over the place. Sellers let the manager know if they have items for *Sellers' Meetings*. Put them on the *Meeting List* for the next meeting if they're of general interest. Most of them aren't of general interest. Settle them one-on-one.

Kill asides — Take control quickly when talk strays from the topic. "That's an interesting story, Mike. Perhaps you can finish it next time we lunch together. For now, let's go on with the business at hand." End private talks. Ask the sellers who start private talks to share what they're talking about if it's to the point. Ask them to stick to the point if their private talks aren't to the point.

Head off motor mouths — Sellers who can't stop talking will destroy your meetings if you let them. Let sellers state their views but stop them rambling. Be polite but firm. Stop them with: "Frank, we have limited time on this issue. Please make your point so we can move on." Talk with motor mouths privately. Make it clear you expect them to improve their style. Take the view that they have a lot to offer. Help them to offer it better than they're doing now.

Invite the views of quiet sellers — Invite quiet sellers to talk. Many of them have good ideas.

Protect speakers from butt-ins — Protect each speaker's right to a fair hearing. It's OK for others to comment or ask questions. It's not OK for others to butt in and upset the speaker. Many sellers have good ideas but express them poorly, so make sure to hear them out.

Protect speakers from sellers who butt in because they don't listen. Some sellers don't listen because they're not the one on stage. Some don't listen because they're bored. Stop them with: "Mary, please let's listen to Jane now."

Protect speakers from sellers who butt in because they can't wait. Stop them with: "Calm down Frank, you'll get your chance soon. Just now, let's listen to what Mary has to say." Make sure to give Frank his chance later.

Protect speakers from sellers who butt in to pay back criticism. Stop them with: "OK Jane, we see you don't like what Mary is saying about you. At least she's saying it openly. Please let her finish. Then you can have time for your view." Make sure Jane gets her chance to talk.

Protect speakers from sellers who use a joke to shoot down an issue. Sometimes a serious issue gets pushed aside because someone treats it as a joke. Stop this with: "OK, nice joke, but let's get back to the issue." Take the seller aside later and make it clear that jokes are OK as long as they don't undercut issues.

End each item by stating its results — State clearly what you decided for each item. Include commitments for named sellers and deadlines for getting jobs done. Make it clear that actions will flow from decisions.

End on time or early — Never go over the time stated for a meeting. Close the meeting when you finish early.

Schedule your follow up on commitments — Schedule check points on your calendar for each commitment. Check on progress until sellers finish the jobs. Check on progress until you finish your jobs.

CHAPTER 5

TRAIN SELLERS

Most people who work as sellers in your store want to do a good job. To do a good job they need to know what to do. They need to know what you expect of them. Training sellers is letting them know what to do and what you expect of them.

In many retail stores sellers get little training. The managers are too busy running the store for them to have time for training their sellers. Sometimes they give token training and rely on their sellers "catching-on." Often they fool themselves. They believe they have little need for training if they only hire "experienced" or "qualified" sellers. They fail to ask themselves why well-trained sellers would beat a path to their door. They fail to realize that if their stores are one of a kind no-one else can qualify sellers for it. The best they can hope for is for sellers who "caught-on" in some other store.

Nothing can replace training your sellers. The training you give has to cover everything that happens in your store. Sellers will reward you for that kind of support with high sales. Customers will find it a pleasure to shop in your store.

Turnover of sellers gives less pain when you train your own sellers. Once you develop a training system, training new sellers becomes routine. It takes time to train new sellers, but turnover is part of the retail world. It's better to deal with it than become a run-of-the-mill store. You're not at the mercy of your sellers when you train them. Many managers live in fear their sellers will quit. With a good training program, you know you can replace your sellers.

Cut down turnover of sellers by training them. Some sellers leave for better paying jobs. Some sellers leave because of changes in their personal lives. Most sellers leave because they're bored and frustrated. They make few sales. They wait around between sales. They lack a sense of purpose. They've little chance to become successful. They're not satisfied with what they're doing. Train your sellers and you reduce their boredom and frustration.

Some turnover of sellers is good for your store. As you use your training system, you'll gradually improve it. Replace sellers with better trained sellers. Replace jaded sellers with fresh eager sellers.

Train While Interviewing

The smart manager uses interviews to begin training. This training is brief and it needs repeating after hiring. Its importance lies in:

- Sending a message to sellers that their attitude needs to be in line with the store's values and expectations.

- Gaining sellers' commitment to the store's values and expectations.

- Making it clear to sellers that the store's management is action-oriented.

The main topics are on the sample *Interview Sheet* in Chapter 3 *Get Sellers*. Go over them in summary form with sellers. Take every opportunity to get sellers to commit themselves to the store's needs. Certainly, no job-seeker is likely to report having a low standard of personal conduct. Yet committing to having a high standard is a strong factor in having one.

Flying Start

The *Flying Start* is the training you give to all new sellers before turning them loose on the selling floor. Turning sellers loose and hoping for them to sell leads to disaster. So does letting them sell until you get ready to train them. It slips too easily into no training. There are two parts to the *Flying Start*:

1. Back-end training.

2. Front-end training.

Back-end Training

The *Back End* of retail includes all non-selling jobs that support selling. It includes things like operating the cash register, setting up displays, cleaning the restrooms. The back-end training for the *Flying Start* includes only basic back-end jobs. Thus it includes operating the cash register, but not setting it up for the day, nor producing the daily selling reports. It includes tidying displays, but not setting up new displays. It includes using the price list, but not learning the prices of all the items on sale. It does not include jobs that old hands may think of as unpleasant and wish to push onto new hires. Heavy duty cleaning of the restrooms comes in later training.

Front-end Training

The *Front End* of retail includes all selling jobs that bring sellers into direct contact with customers. Complete the *Flying Start* back-end training before giving the *Flying Start* front-end training. Complete the *Flying Start* front-end training before sending sellers onto the selling floor. Back-end training solidly in place frees sellers to concentrate on front-end training. It frees them to make sales. It cuts down on sellers getting all in a dither. When sellers fumble at the cash register, there's a risk of losing sales. There's an even greater risk of losing customers who see your store as one that flies by the seat of its pants.

Training Sessions

The major part of training takes place in sessions for individuals or small groups. These sessions call for a flexible approach. While training a group takes less of your time than training individuals, it also takes more of your sellers away from selling. Training individuals, or two or three people at a time, gives your sellers more personal attention than they would get in a larger group. Only you will know the situation in your store and probably you'll handle it differently at different times. Make sure you keep the store selling and handle the training without slighting one for the other.

Write the Training Manual

When your training program is only in your head you have no training program. You'll train differently each time, overlook things, possibly even ramble. Write it down. When you write it down you have to decide what you want your sellers to do. That's not to say your program is cast in stone. Far from it. You'll change and improve it often. For computer jockeys a word-processing program can be a great help. But don't worry about that. True cut-and-paste, with scissors and glue, serves quite well. Better to put your effort into the training program rather than into learning how to use a word processor.

Writing down your training program is not to say that you have to give a wooden delivery. As you gain confidence in presenting your program your presentation style will mature. The important point is to be clear. A clear written training program presented woodenly still puts you ahead of the pack.

Write down your training plan even if you can train sellers perfectly well without notes. Otherwise you've trapped yourself. You'll always have to be there for training. With a written plan you can train others to train for you. Your store has more value with a written training plan. It helps you when you want to sell your store.

You're in a trap if you use a key person to train your sellers with no written plan. Your training plan leaves too when that person leaves.

You'll follow a pattern each time you train if you write down your plan. You'll have a system that includes everything your sellers need to know. You'll have something to improve if you write down your training plan. You can make changes. You can fit the pieces together so they work better.

It's nice if you can write well, but simple writing is enough. Make clear points, use simple words, use short sentences and let the grammar worry about itself. Can your sellers understand it? If so, OK. If not, let them tell you and then change it. The rest of this section deals with the writing style and the format of your training manual.

Style of Writing

Bear these words in mind as you write: — short, small, direct.

Short — Write topics as short as possible, but not too short to understand. It's the same with each title, each sentence, each paragraph. Write sentences short on commas. One or none is ideal but now and then it's OK to use more. Avoid semi-colons. Avoid explanations in brackets.

Word-processing programs usually have style checkers which flag long sentences and paragraphs. Although they check style and not grammar, software writers usually call them grammar checkers. You can get on without one perfectly well. Develop the habit of chopping up long sentences, particularly those with many commas in them. Aim for sentences no longer than 12 words. Aim for paragraphs with no more than three sentences.

Although few words are usually better than many words, watch for the cases where this isn't so. "Support each point by proof material" surely reads more clearly as, "Support each point with material that proves it."

Small — Use small words in place of long words. "It's appropriate to request customers to purchase…" becomes, "It's OK to ask customers to buy…" The short word need not have exactly the same meaning as the long word. Some long words, like "application" in "job application" have no short words that clearly replace them. Use them without guilt.

Direct — Make simple direct statements. Avoid the passive voice, which is indirect and lacking in warmth and ownership. Compare the passive "John is loved" with the active "Anna loves John."

People who say, "Please talk to me about last month's sales figures when you're not too busy" but mean, "Let's talk about last month's sales figures right now" are polite but unclear. People who state directly what they mean are easier to deal with.

Issue calls to action: "Find out the reason for buying", "Listen to customers", "Take control of the items," and so on. This is not to show who's boss. It's to show clear ideas and direction. Sellers will like this support.

Format of the Training Manual

Training materials are easy to use when you set them up as simple *Guide Sheets*. Each *Guide Sheet* deals with a single topic. Number the *Guide Sheets* and group similar *Guide Sheets* together. For example: *Guide Sheet* 6-1, *Guide Sheet* 6-2, *Guide Sheet* 6-3, *Guide Sheet* 7-1, *Guide Sheet* 7-2, *Guide Sheet* 7-3. This makes it easy to add or delete *Guide Sheets* as the need arises. Simply give a new *Guide Sheet* a letter after the number, like *Guide Sheet* 6-2A.

Here is the first page of *Guide Sheet* 23-5 from the *StOReS System*.

Guide Sheet 23-5

Notice Buying Signals

Buying Signals: Words or actions customers use to say "I'm close to buying" in a roundabout way.

1. **Watch for shorthand for "I'll take it"**
   - Some customers buy by asking how they can pay.
     "Do you take personal checks?"
     It's safe to act as if these customers have asked to buy.
   - Customers are close to buying when they think of taking the item home.
     "Do you deliver?"
   - Customers are close to buying when they think of living with the item.
     "How long is the warranty?"

2. **Watch for the moments when your silence sells the item**
   - Customers have asked to buy when they ask the price.
     Tell the price, shut up and let customers finish the sale.[1] You're past "Just looking" when a sale doesn't follow a customer asking the price. Go on with schmoozing or finding out why customers want to buy.[2]
   - Customers want to buy when they ask a partner.
     "What do you think, John?"
     The ball is now in the partner's court. Let the partner speak next—you'll kill the sale if you step in. Either you make a sale or the partner puts up Roadblocks to the sale. After the partner speaks, sell to the partner. You know the customer who asked the partner the question wants to buy. Go around the Roadblocks the partner puts up.
   - It's time for you to shut up when customers show signs of deep thought.
     They're working at selling the item to themselves for you. They look as if they're stewing things over. They may pace the floor. They may stroke their chin. They may fold and unfold their arms, and so on.

3. **Watch for signs of great interest in buying**
   - Customers want an item if they pick it up while you're selling to them.
   - Customers want an item if they stop listening to look at the item when you're talking to them.
   - Customers want an item if they knock it's price.
     This is a strong buying signal. They're asking for your help. Sell them on the value of the item.

4. **Trust your feelings**
   - Sense when customers want to buy.

---
[1]Guide Sheet 22-10 *Ask All Customers to Buy.*
[2]Outline 27 *Use the Steps for Selling.*

Backtrack to Outline 29   – 1 –   © 1995 Arthur A. Cridland

The *Guide Sheet* has a direct command for a clear short title: *Notice Buying Signals*. In this case there's a definition of "Buying Signals." A series of numbered topics follow, each a brief and clear command. Within each topic there are simple bulleted points. Where needed there are brief explanations of the bulleted points.

Outlines placed before the *Guide Sheets* allow managers and sellers to find the *Guide Sheets* they need. *Guide Sheet* 23-5 has a footer under the footnotes pointing back to *Outline* 29, *Make the Steps for Selling Stronger*.

Outline 29

Make the Steps for Selling Stronger

Know What You Sell
Guide Sheet 23-1

Know Prices
Guide Sheet 23-2

Contract Customers to Stay
Guide Sheet 23-3

Focus on Customers
Guide Sheet 23-4

Notice Buying Signals
Guide Sheet 23-5

Develop Personal Customers
Guide Sheet 23-6

Outsmart Hagglers
Guide Sheet 23-7

Sell More to Sold Customers
Guide Sheet 23-8

Switch Customers to Items We Carry
Guide Sheet 23-9

Know the Promises That Make Customers Act
Guide Sheet 23-10

Let Customers Think They're Bothering You
Guide Sheet 23-11

Burn Your Business Cards
Guide Sheet 23-12

Know Birth Signs
Guide Sheet 23-13

Listen Deeply
Guide Sheet 23-14

Outline 29 has a footer pointing back to *Outline* 1, *Seller's Topics*, which is the starting point for sellers.

Outline 1

Seller's Topics

Take Pride in Selling
Outline 2

Know What to Expect
Outline 3

Keep Up with Things
Outline 7

Learn How We Do Things
Outline 8

Tune Up for the Steps for Selling
Outline 26

Use the Steps for Selling
Outline 27

Make the Steps for Selling Stronger
Outline 29

Boost Scores to Boost Sales and Profit
Outline 30

Play Games to Push Sales Up
Outline 31

Outline 1 is the natural start for sellers, who can drill down to deeper *Outlines* and to the *Guide Sheets*.

Some *Guide Sheets* will show sellers how to fill in forms. Give the form the same number as the *Guide Sheet*. Thus, *Form* 15-4 *Seller's Customer Flow Summary,* goes with *Guide Sheet* 15-4 *Fill in the Seller's Customer Flow Summary*. Give the form a title similar to the title of the *Guide Sheet* whenever possible. Keep copies of the forms the sellers will use in a *Forms* binder or file and keep the form masters in a special *Master Forms* binder or file. Protect the master forms carefully to make sure sellers don't fill them in and leave you having to prepare new forms.

Follow a Training Plan

It's not enough to write *Outlines*, *Guide Sheets* and *Forms*. Follow a plan for training.

Set up Training Jobs for formal training — Formal training is training supported by *Guide Sheets*. Set up the *Guide Sheets* and other support needed as *Training Jobs*. *Training Jobs* usually begin by letting sellers know about the job and its *Guide Sheets*. After sellers study the *Guide Sheets*, managers train sellers until sellers get the *Training Job* right.

Kick off important Training Jobs at Sellers' Meetings — Some *Training Jobs* are important enough to deal with them at *Sellers' Meetings*. Some *Training Jobs* may need more than one *Sellers' Meeting*. Cover *Training Jobs* at regular *Sellers' Meetings* or call special meetings to kick off *Training Jobs*. Calling special meetings makes *Training Jobs* really stand out. Drive home important ideas in the *Training Jobs* at *Sellers' Meetings*. Get sellers behind the *Training Jobs* at *Sellers' Meetings*. Then follow through with further training.

Use the News System to set Guide Sheets — Set *Guide Sheets* for all sellers or for groups of sellers by *News Sheets*. Set *Guide Sheets* for one seller by a message in the *Message Pocket*.

Write follow-throughs on your calendar — Follow through on each seller quickly. Suppose you set *Guide Sheet* 5-1 *Keep on Top of News Sheets, Messages and Guide Sheets* by a *News Sheet* you posted on the evening of Monday, March 28th. The work schedule shows Mary Jones will open the store at 9 am on Tuesday, March 29th. Mark your calendar to talk to Mary as soon as possible after noon on Tuesday, March 29th:

Tuesday, March 29th 1994
3:30 pm Mary Jones Guide Sheet 5-1 (28 March.)

The work schedule shows Jane Smith will next work at 10 am on Wednesday, March 30th. Mark your calendar for Jane as soon as possible after noon on Wednesday:

Wednesday, March 30 1994
4:00 pm Jane Smith Guide Sheet 5-1 (28 March.)

At the times of the calendar entries check to see if the sellers have initialed the *News Sheet* and the *Guide Sheet*. Unless there's good reason for delay, talk to sellers about items they've not initialed. Let sellers know they can't skip. Look for replies to *Guide Sheets* set by messages in the *To Manager* binder.

Track Training Jobs in Training Logs — Make note of all training in each seller's *Training Log*. Setting up and reviewing *Training Logs* is basic to an effective training program. A separate section of this chapter covers *Training Logs*.

Make entries in the *Training Log* each time you train sellers. Review each seller's *Training Log* at a fixed time each week. You're only partly training if you train without checking that sellers know what to do. Expect little improvement. Some sellers ignore jobs set for them. Some sellers ignore jobs unless you push them.

Check playback and follow through for informal training — Informal training is one-on-one without *Guide Sheets* to support it. You show someone how to do something. Check the playback of informal training.

Follow through on this training. See the seller using the training or see the results of the training. Add a note to the *Help List* to watch for the seller using the training. Mark your calendar to see the results by a certain time.

Use Training Logs

Training sellers without keeping a record of their training is like throwing money into the wind. Keeping a record of training closes the loopholes in training. It is the foundation for coaching.

Know what your sellers know — Train sellers little by little. There's no way to show sellers everything at once. Keep track of what each seller knows. Know what they know when you ask sellers to do things. Know what to train next when you train sellers again.

Close out "Nobody told me" — Tell sellers what they need to know to do the job. John worked in a run-of-the-mill store for six months. Yet he refunded $500 cash for a return on an item paid with a bad check. Asked why he didn't follow the rules on taking checks, he answered, "Nobody told me about them." Asked why he didn't follow the rules on refunds, he answered "Nobody told me about them." Close out "Nobody told me" in your store.

Get rid of "Should know" — In run-of-the-mill stores managers think their sellers should know things. You hear "Should know" when things go wrong. "Should know" often comes from an angry, bitter or annoyed manager. Mary should know how to write up VISA charges. John should know how to work the cash register. The sellers standing around talking should know how to sell to the customers they're ignoring. "Should know" managers generally have one or more of these faults:

- They don't train their sellers.

- They don't check that sellers understand their training.

- They don't coach their sellers after they've shown them what to do.

- They don't review their sellers' training routinely.

- They don't keep track of any training they do.

- They rely on the experience sellers gained in some other store.

- They fool themselves by pretending things are true.

- They haven't accepted they must answer to themselves for their sellers and their store.

"Should know" is a warning flag. Hear yourself use it and know it's time to change your ways.

Measure training simply — Track training by what sellers can do. Either Mary knows how to make a MasterCard charge or she doesn't. Either John knows how to dust the window displays or he doesn't. For each action there's a level that's OK. See that everyone reaches it. It's that simple. Sliding scales don't work. Thoughts and feelings enter the picture when you rate sellers 1-10, 1-5 or Excellent-Good-Fair-Poor-Unacceptable. Sliding scales fool you. They give a gray and fuzzy picture. Go for a sharp "let's get this simple job done" picture.

Keep Training Logs on sellers — Keep *Training Logs* to track the training of sellers. Make a copy for each seller. Store it in a *Duo-Tang* or similar binder. Keep it in the seller's file in a locked file cabinet. Use *Training Logs* to support sellers in their work. Avoid calling them evaluation sheets. They record what sellers can do. They give credit to sellers. The only way they're evaluation sheets is they evaluate how well managers support sellers.

Start Training Logs with the Trainer List — Note each training event by number, date and trainer's name.

Training Log

Seller   <u>Quentin Jones</u>

! Attention Next, D Date Set, C Check-off OK, P Playback OK, S Seen OK, Q Quarterly Review OK

1 <u>27</u> <u>Ma</u> <u>94</u> <u>Barbara Bateman</u>
2 <u>28</u> <u>Ma</u> <u>94</u> <u>Barbara Bateman</u>
3 ___ ___ ___ _____
4 ___ ___ ___ _____

The *Trainer List* has the *Event Codes* used on the rest of the *Training Log*:

!	Attention Next	Used when planning future training
D	Date Set	Allow enough time between D and C
C	Check-off OK	Seller initialed and dated Guide Sheet as read
P	Playback OK	Seller showed or told skill to trainer
S	Seen in Action	Trainer has seen seller using the skill
Q	Quarterly Review OK	Trainer accepts this skill for the Quarterly Review

Training is in the order!, D, C, P, S, Q. Check! before D, D before C, C before P, P before S, and S before Q.

The rest of the *Training Log* looks like this:

22-13 0 Ask "How Did You Hear about Our Store?" 17!18D19C21S
22-13 1 If You Haven't Asked This Question Yet, Do So Now 20P
22-13 2 It's Important Information for Planning Advertising 20P
22-14 0 Register the Customer or the Sale 17!
22-14 1 Say "Please Let Me Put You on Our Customer List"
22-14 2 Answer Customers Who Ask Why You Register Them
22-14 3 Try for Birthday by Asking for Birth Sign
22-14 4 Use Phone Number as a Reference Number
22-14 5 Enter Non-Registering Customers in the Drawing
22-14 6 Try to Remember the Registered Customers by Name
22-14 7 Register the Purchases of Registered Customers

Use the training event number in the rest of the *Training Log*. The date lets you know how long ago the training took place. The trainer's name lets you cross check with the trainer. Get off on the right foot. Note your name even if you own one store and manage it yourself. Act as if you'll prosper and have others train for you in the future.

Line 22-13 0 is the title of a *Guide Sheet*. Line 22-13 1 is its first numbered topic, 22-13 2 is its second numbered topic, and so on. To make a *Training Log*, make a list of titles and numbered topics for every *Guide Sheet*. This way you use the same topics through all stages of training and coaching.

Handwritten entries record the training of the seller. The entry 17!18D19C21S is a record of training. The numbers 17, 18, 19, 21 are entries on the *Trainer List*. Look at the *Trainer List* to get the name of the trainer and the date of the training for each number:

- The 17th trainer on the *Trainer List* entered ! (Attention Next.)

- The 18th trainer on the *Trainer List* entered D (Date Set.)

- The 19th trainer on the *Trainer List* entered C (Check-off OK.)

- The 21st trainer on the *Trainer List* entered S (Seen in Action.)

Make follow-through entries on your desk calendar — Follow through on each seller quickly. Suppose you set *Guide Sheet* 5-1by a *News Sheet* you posted on the evening of Monday, March 29th. The work schedule shows Mary Jones will open the store at 9 am on Tuesday, March 30th. Mark your calendar for Mary as soon as possible after 10 am on Tuesday, March 30th:

Tuesday, March 30th 1993
10:30 am Mary Jones Guide Sheet 5-1 29 March

Check the seller's check-off — Talk about it right away if the seller hasn't done the check-off on time. "Any problems with the *Guide Sheet,* Mary?" Then straighten out any mistaken views. Be clear that you expect sellers to check off *Guide Sheets*.

Move into the Playback as soon as you can — Talk with the seller. Try to get the playback without putting sellers on the spot. The best way to get the playback is by giving *Personal Daily Attention*. The playback comes out as you chat. Sometimes you can skip the playback because you see the seller using the skill. You can then check off "Playback OK" and "Seen in Action" at the same time.

Sometimes things don't work that well and you have to ask for the playback. "You've checked the *Guide Sheet* off nicely, Mary, so let's chat about the *News System*. Let's role-play and you train me on how we run the *News System*." Suppose Mary tells you about everything but messages. Prompt her with, "How about messages, Mary?" The playback is OK if she tells you about messages.

Otherwise, talk with her about messages. Then enter, "Chat with Mary about messages" on the *Help List*. Check the playback again after that until Mary gets it right and you can check off the playback.

Let the seller know you're pleased. "That's fine, Mary. You're really on top of the *News System*."

Move to Seen in Action — Work with the *Help List* to watch for items *Seen in Action*. Write Mary 5-1 News on the *Help List*. This is your daily reminder to help Mary until you clear this item from your *Help List*.

Sometimes you'll see things in action without doing anything about them. For *Guide Sheet* 5-1: You look in *Daily* and see Mary initialed and dated *News Sheet* 1. You look in the *Guide Sheets* binder and see Mary initialed and dated *Guide Sheet* 5-1. In the *Message Pocket* you see a message in her handwriting to another seller.

Sometimes you'll have to step in and help. For *Guide Sheet* 5-1: Mary was the last seller to initial and date *News Sheet* 1. You saw this in *Daily*. Mary didn't move the sheet to the *News* binder. Mary replied to the message from you. She put her reply in the *Message Pocket*, not in the *To Manager* binder. Mary needs help.

Update the *Training Log* and the *Help List*. Her entry in the *Help List* becomes Mary 5-1 3 News Sheets to News binder.

Talk about items needing help right away. Deal with these items now if the seller is in the store. Otherwise, deal with them the next time the seller comes in. Talk, don't write. Go one-on-one to help sellers. Help them with what troubles them and with their mistaken views right away. Let sellers know when they're doing right. Writing won't get you one-on-one. Writing is too stiff. It's too easy to give the wrong idea. Writing is too official. Talk matter-of-factly and pleasantly. Get sellers doing things your way without making them feel guilty. Help them to catch on:

"Mary, when you're the last one to initial a News Sheet, please put it in the *News* binder. *Daily* gets cluttered if we leave old News Sheets there. Then fresh News Sheets get lost in the old ones. Then sellers overlook the fresh News Sheets."

"Mary, please put replies to messages I send you in the *To Manager* binder. This is the one place I look for everything that sellers want me to know. I don't like to work against sellers while they're using Daily."

Help with outstanding items until they're complete. Work from your *Help List* each day. Get sellers up to standard. Then scratch their entries from the *Help List*.

Check that you're training sellers — Check all sellers' *Training Logs* monthly. Are there at least three entries a week on each *Training Log*? New sellers need many more entries.

Review Sellers Quarterly

Schedule *Quarterly Reviews* for every seller. Review sellers even though you're in touch with them daily. With the stress on day-to-day training it's easy to skip regular *Quarterly Reviews*, but you still need them. A formal review is an event. People pay attention to and react to events in their lives. Formal reviews put sellers in touch with themselves in a way that nothing else equals.

Let sellers know exactly how they're doing. Let sellers hear praise for a job well done. Let sellers learn where and how they must improve. Let sellers pause and consider themselves. Let sellers commit themselves to their goals. Sellers need to know how they're doing.

Sellers guess how they're doing when you don't tell them how they're doing. They sometimes guess wrongly. Sometimes you have sellers who do a good job but think they're below standard. They become unsure of themselves, get low in spirits and their sales fall off. Some of them slink off to another job. You lose sellers when they think they're doing a good job but think you don't prize them. Let them know you prize them if they're doing a good job. Let sellers know if they're below standard. Then they know they have to change. Sellers below standard can only change after you let them know they need to change.

Base reviews on Training Logs — Reviews are simple. They are really summary training sessions. Start from the seller's *Training Log*. Use normal management skills. Use training skills in summary form. Reviews are a big deal for sellers. That's because for them they're events.

Get agreements to improve — Come to agreements with sellers on what they need to improve. One seller may need to raise the *Item Count* for the month to 1.3 by the end of May. Another seller may need to raise the *Hit Value* for May to $45. Get sellers to say they can and will make the goals. Make some agreements as goals. For good sellers work out a plan together to get better. Here it's a matter of focusing sellers. Make some agreements binding. For sellers who are too low give 30, 60 or 90 days to improve. To bring new sellers up to low level selling, give two weeks to improve. Tell these sellers they improve or they say good-bye.

Learn to live with Quarterly Reviews — Keep to the review schedule. It's easy to put reviews off or give them less often than quarterly. It's OK if you review every four months. Space them longer than that and you're on slippery ground. Reviews every six months are too far apart.

CHAPTER 6

COACH SELLERS

Training sellers is not enough for your store to be a winner. Training is the lead up to coaching and it is coaching that makes your store great. Training sellers is letting them know what to do and what you expect of them. Coaching sellers is making sure they know what to do. It is also making sure they are doing things well in the way that you expect them to do it. Coaching is "Training with Wings." Coaching is a never-ending job, so you have to keep track of it. Enter everything you do, plan or agree to in the sellers' *Training Logs*.

Coaching makes your training fly. Coaching is all about support. Are things really clear? Have your sellers really understood? Are sellers really doing what you want them to do? Have they begun to cut corners? Are they doing what they want to do rather than what you want them to do? Have they started to forget the training? Do they need that little extra support to go over the hump?

Check that sellers know what to do — After training it's time to check that sellers know what to do. Expect little improvement when you train without checking. Some sellers ignore jobs set for them. Some sellers ignore jobs unless you push them. Sellers who do jobs well still need the support that coaching gives. Learning is more than a one-shot deal.

Check that sellers are doing what you want them to do — After training sellers know what you want them to do. Then check that they're putting what they know into action.

Keep at it — Train, then coach, coach and coach again, and again and again. People need to repeat an action six to eight times before it becomes a habit. In our busy world we look for instant solutions. We're usually too busy to do the job properly. Get out of that habit.

Judge your success in training and coaching sellers — Score your store on the absence test. How long can you leave your store knowing it will run as well without you as it will with you there? That's a good measure of how well your training and coaching program works. In the beginning it's only an hour or two. Aim to increase this time gradually to days, weeks or months.

Follow a Coaching Plan

Map out how you're going to coach. Then coach daily, all through the day. Training and coaching are the most important things a manager does in a store.

Give all sellers Personal Daily Attention — Keep in touch with all sellers daily. Take an interest in all sellers. Ask lots of questions in a cheerful way. "How'd it go with that last customer, Marcie?" "Finding it any easier to duck 'Just looking,' John?" "How'd you come up with that great idea for the handbag display, Mary?"

Let new sellers know they never get in trouble for being honest. Make sure new sellers know they can tell you their problems openly. Ask questions to help, not to put sellers on the spot.

Work the Help List daily — The *Help List* is a list you use to help the sellers. "Watch Mary greeting customers and praise her," is a typical entry on the *Help List*. Work the *Help List* each day. Strike off items and add new items as needed.

Use the Four Ways of Coaching — Use *Straight Flip*, *Shoulder Tap*, *Question*, and *Feedback Session*.

Straight Flip: See something that needs training while you're in verbal or visual contact with the seller. Make a suggestion to flip the seller in the right direction. "John, try counting the cash like this …" No need for a long speech. It's like oiling a squeaky door. Say a few words and move on. Check for progress later.

Shoulder Tap: See something that needs training while you're out of verbal or visual contact with the seller. Tap the seller's shoulder to get attention. Make a suggestion to flip the seller in the right direction. Check for progress later.

Question: Ask a question about an action the seller is working on. "How's your *Hit Rate* coming along, Mary?" Shut up and listen. Make a comment when there's progress. "Fine. Keep at it, Mary." Talk about it when there's a problem.

Feedback Session: Set up time for a full blown feedback session. Talk about something that needs changing and work out a plan together. Aim for two feedback sessions with each full-time seller each week.

Praise sellers — Praise the things sellers do right. Look for things sellers do right and praise them. "The store looks wonderful, Mary." "Excellent sales for a Monday, John." "Thanks for staying late yesterday. You really brought us up-to-date, Catherine." "The new window display is a real knockout, Joan." Make sure good sellers know they're good.

Make praise a habit. Praise without thinking about it. Praise without fail. Praise on impulse. Make praise your thing. You can't give too much praise. Keep on praising. You can't praise something once and get it over. Praise doesn't work like that. Praise the same thing often.

Praise far more than you correct. Give a mountain of praise for every molehill of correction. Sellers will bear you ill-will if they feel you're always correcting them. Go out of your way to improve your score of praises. Keep a daily score of praises and corrections if praising sellers isn't natural to you. Aim for many praises for few corrections.

Praise now, not later. Praise right away when you see something done right. Delayed praise is less praise. Delayed praise adds one more item to your *To-do List*. Delayed praise easily turns into no praise.

Praise in words, not in writing. Writing delays praise. It breaks the rule "Praise now, not later." Writing is more work than telling someone right away. Praising sellers in words right away puts you close to sellers. Writing is stiff and far from your sellers.

Train and Coach the Steps for Selling

Make sure you spend time every day training and coaching the *Steps for Selling*. It's the most important work you do in the store.

Put the Back End in place first — All the everyday jobs in a store make up the *Back End*. Knowing how to use the cash register and how to write credit card drafts. Knowing how to do the day's paperwork and how to answer the questions customers usually ask. These and all the other jobs like them make up the *Back End*.

Selling is the *Front End*. Make sure sellers have the *Back End* in place before they sell. That takes pressure off learning and improving the *Steps for Selling*. Sellers who make sales and find they can't do the back-end jobs get upset. Upset sellers sell poorly. Good back-end skills set sellers free to sell.

Build sellers up to the Third Level of Selling — First get sellers to sell something to everyone. At this stage it doesn't matter how much they sell. Nor does the value of their sales matter. Get them selling something to everyone. This is the *First Level of Selling*.

Second get sellers to sell higher priced items. Give them the courage to sell higher priced items. That's where your profit lies. This is the *Second Level of Selling*.

Third get sellers to sell more items to each customer. Get sellers to sell a number of high priced items to everyone. That's how you raise your profit level. This is the *Third Level of Selling*.

Build sellers up as you build a house. First build the basement. Then frame it. Then put on the roof. Start building the roof first and you'll get nowhere.

Roof	*Third Level of Selling*	Sell more items
Framing	*Second Level of Selling*	Sell higher priced items
Basement	*First Level of Selling*	Sell something to everyone

Focus on starting to sell and asking customers to buy — Starting the sale is the problem. It takes guts to start to sell. It's easy to shy away from customers. Put your first efforts with sellers on the early *Steps for Selling*. Get them to start selling to everyone. Sellers must start a sale to have a chance of making a sale. Asking customers to buy makes sellers uncomfortable at first. Let sellers slide on asking customers to buy and sales will be poor.

Stress self-ending Show-&-tells — Self-ending *Show-&-tells* take the pressure off sellers. Sellers who only need to ask a few customers to buy are more willing to ask them. Keep stressing the importance of asking all customers to buy. Otherwise sellers get out of the habit of asking customers to buy.

Base coaching only on facts — Base coaching on things you see or hear, or on *Scores* you measure. Keep hunches, guesses and snap judgments out of coaching. React only to what you see, hear or measure.

Coach to improve one action at a time — Single out one action to improve. Improve that action, then move on to the next action. Trying to improve several actions at once leads to disaster. It confuses sellers. It gives them an out because they have no focus. Aim to improve a single *Score* when you're improving the *Scores*.

Coach or praise — Coach when you see things sellers need to change. Coach without blaming. Be matter-of-fact. Share in the job by using "Us" or "We." "Let's try it this way, Joan." "Frank, let's work on greeting customers." "Let's see if we can put together some new *Openers*, Mary."

Praise when you see things that sellers are doing right. "You brought that customer through those *Roadblocks* nicely, Mary." Praise all sellers much more than you coach them.

Never mix coaching and praising. Sellers will filter out part of the message. There's a time for coaching and a time for praising and they're different times. Most sellers will take the praise and block the coaching. Why would they take the coaching seriously when they can roll in the praise? The coaching is just an aside if they're so good. Some sellers won't hear the praise. After a while they'll feel they get a lot of coaching but get no results.

Give rapid and regular feedback — Aim to coach or praise after all sales. Sure, you won't see every sale. You'll be busy with other things at times. Then you'll see a sale. Move right in and coach or praise.

Speak right away. That's the best kind of feedback. Speaking now beats speaking later. Spoken feedback beats written feedback. Written feedback is late and it's far from the event. Forget seller of the month awards.

Use the Four Ways of Coaching — Use *Straight Flip*, *Shoulder Tap*, *Question*, and *Feedback Session*.

Keep in mind how hard it is to learn — Coach, coach and coach again, again and again. People need to repeat an action six to eight times before it becomes a habit. In our busy world we look for instant solutions. We're usually too busy to do the job properly. Get out of that habit. See that sellers get it right. Instead of giving up on sellers, take them through training once again and then start coaching them again.

Be able to do it yourself — Be able to show the skills that you coach others to develop. All managers spend part of their time selling. Mangers must sell at least the lowest expected of other sellers. Expect good sellers to sell more than managers. Good managers aim to coach sellers to sell better than themselves.

CHAPTER 7

CONTROL THE STORE WITH DAILY

The most reliable way of controlling a store is to use a checklist of everything that takes place in the store. Since all sellers use this checklist every day we can call it *Daily*. Because there's a clear list of jobs, sellers know what to do. Each day sellers step their way through *Daily*. There's little need for you to tell them what to do. Sellers who use *Daily* get the jobs done that support selling. This gives a strong background which frees the sellers to sell. Sellers step from their jobs and sell when customers come in the store. As long as there are customers in the store, sellers keep selling. Sellers step back into the jobs listed in *Daily* between customers.

Start *Daily* as a simple list with only a few entries, then make it grow. Smart managers know that the more they put into *Daily*, the fewer routine jobs they find themselves doing. This frees them for the important tasks of training and coaching sellers and of developing the store.

Daily lists only things that sellers do. Managers also run *Manager's Daily* to keep themselves on track. Naturally, any jobs that managers can move from *Manager's Daily* to *Daily* frees that much time for other work. It's easy to overlook jobs. They do it all the time in sloppy stores. *Daily* helps us avoid the signs of a store that's limping along:

- It's 3 pm on November 6th. The date on the charge card imprinter is November 3rd.

- It's 11.10 am on a slow Wednesday. So far there are no sales but the floor still needs mopping.

- It's 3 pm, the store's busy and the next shift begins at 4 pm. John skipped pre-counting his cash in the slow time between 2 and 3 pm. Now he'll be in a rush at close out.

- Joan knows she should phone the bank for the rate on the Canadian dollar. She means to do it. It keeps slipping her mind and suddenly she's busy with other things. Anyway, "It's the same as yesterday, so it's no big deal." Fred felt the same way yesterday. So did Mary the day before. So did Nancy the day before that. Turns out we're giving customers 90 cents on the dollar and the bank's giving us 80. Today we took in 600 Canadian dollars. Good-bye $60.

- The printing tape on the cash register wore out two weeks ago. Since then, we've been giving out receipts that customers can't read. With each receipt the store sends a message that it doesn't care about its customers.

Work from *Daily*

This section covers general topics in preparation for working with *Daily*.

Work from Daily all day, every day — Sellers never outgrow the need to use *Daily*. That includes managers and owners. That includes sellers hired yesterday and sellers hired years ago. After a while some sellers may think, "I know all that. I do it all without looking at *Daily*." That's not possible. There are too many jobs to do. The jobs sellers do change too often.

Do the jobs in the order listed — The order in which sellers do the jobs changes. Add new jobs and stop doing some jobs. It's too hard to do the right jobs in the right order without help. Sellers go through *Daily* job by job, from beginning to end. They slide a 6-inch ruler down the page.

Do the jobs every day unless noted otherwise — Some jobs in *Daily* have a note on how often to do them. Examples are: Mondays, Third Wednesday in the Month, Monday and Friday. Sellers do the jobs without a note every day.

Finish jobs on time — Some jobs in *Daily* have a note telling when to finish them. These times are guides. Sellers may run behind time when sales are good. Some jobs have a time span allowed for them. These times guide sellers in their work and keep the manager under control. Sellers let the manager know when these times are wrong.

Drop any job to make a sale — Jobs fill the time when sellers aren't making sales. Sellers drop them and sell when customers are in the store.

Know the major job groups — *Selling Jobs* and *Background Jobs* are the two major job groups. *Selling Jobs* are the jobs that directly bear on making a sale. They include talking to customers, writing sales slips and collecting cash. *Background Jobs* are the jobs you need to do to let you sell. They include pricing items, setting up displays and keeping the store neat.

Know the kinds of Background Jobs — *Opening Jobs* are *Background Jobs* that get the store ready for opening. These are jobs it's best to do without customers under foot. They include setting up paperwork and setting up the cash tray. Sellers finish *Opening Jobs* before they open the doors for customers.

Early Jobs are *Background Jobs* that get the store ready for the day. They're like *Opening Jobs* but sellers can do them while customers are around. *Early Jobs* are easy to drop when customers come in. They include sweeping the floor and tidying the displays.

Usual Jobs are *Background Jobs* that sellers do most days. They do them between serving customers and drop them to sell. They include pricing items, receiving deliveries and dusting.

Odd Jobs are *Background Jobs* that need doing from time to time. There's no pattern to them. Many of them are one-shot deals. Suppose a supplier sends some items in ugly plastic bags. You decide to take them out of the bags and sell them loose from a basket. Taking the items out of the bags and setting up the basket is an *Odd Job*. Sellers do *Odd Jobs* between customers and drop them to sell.

Special Jobs are *Background Jobs* that need special skills. The manager picks sellers and trains them to do *Special Jobs*. It's a way of spreading the workload. After a while most sellers have one or more *Special Jobs*. *Special Jobs* are like *Usual Jobs* but only sellers trained for *Special Jobs* do them. With other *Background Jobs* it's first come, first served. Sometimes the manager will arrange it so others sell while a seller does a *Special Job*. An example of a *Special Job* is preparing the stack of credit card drafts for deposit in the bank.

Closing Jobs are *Background Jobs* sellers do at the end of their shift. Sometimes that's after they close the store. Sometimes that's after another seller has taken over. Like *Opening Jobs*, these are jobs it's best to do without customers under foot. They include counting cash and finishing paperwork.

Change-over Jobs are *Background Jobs* sellers do at the change of a shift. For the seller coming in some of the jobs are the same as *Opening Jobs*. For the seller going out some of the jobs are the same as *Closing Jobs*. Some jobs sellers only do at change over. They include switching cash trays and switching cash drawer keys.

Training Jobs are jobs sellers do as part of their training program.

Set Up *Daily*

Build Daily gradually — Begin *Daily* with a few jobs only. Add a few more jobs to *Daily* later. Give the sellers time to get used to them. Then add a few more jobs. Go on like this until after a while you'll make few changes. Bring *Daily* into your store step by step when you start. Get your sellers involved in putting *Daily* together. It's a mistake to dump a whole new *Daily* on your sellers. After a while *Daily* will list all the jobs you need your sellers to do. Then your store will grow and change. You'll decide to do some things differently. You'll do some new things. You'll stop doing some of the things you do now. Change *Daily* to keep your sellers on top of the new ways you want things done. Warn sellers about changes in *Daily* by *News Sheets*. Direct the sellers' attention even to small changes. For big changes train sellers as well.

Use only one side of the paper — You will cut and paste, add sheets and remove sheets. So, life will be easier if you use only one side of the paper.

Key jobs in Daily to Guide Sheets — The ideal is that each job in *Daily* refers to a *Guide Sheet*. For example: "Clean the Store (*Guide Sheet* 6-9.)" Keying jobs to *Guide Sheets* backs up your training. Trained sellers know where to look for a refresher. Mark *Daily* so new sellers know which jobs you expect them to do. In an emergency, even an untrained bright seller can find out how to do things in the store from *Daily*.

Key jobs in Daily to Guide Sheets gradually — You'll have more jobs than *Guide Sheets* when you start *Daily*. Put the jobs in without keying them to *Guide Sheets*. For example: "Clean the store." This lets your sellers know you expect them to clean the store. Letting sellers do the cleaning that occurs to them is better than them not cleaning. Write the *Guide Sheet* later. It'll let sellers know how and when to clean the store. Then train sellers using the *Guide Sheet*.

Key new *Guide Sheets* to jobs in order of importance. Perhaps for your store a *Guide Sheet* on cleaning the store is a low priority. The sellers may be cleaning the store well enough without one. The store may not be as clean as you'd like, but you may have more urgent problems. Perhaps you have a problem with shortages in the cash drawer. It's urgent that you prepare the *Guide Sheet* "Cash Drawer Report" and train sellers to use it. It comes ahead of a *Guide Sheet* for "Clean the store."

Include clock times and job times in Daily — Put clock time markers in *Daily* to make it strong. People do jobs at their own pace unless they work to a standard. List jobs like this:
Job 1... (*Guide Sheet* 6-8)
Job 2... (*Guide Sheet* 16-5)
Job 3... (*Guide Sheet* 6-12)
Job 4... (*Guide Sheet* 9-2)
10:00 am
Job 5 Open doors to customers
Job 6... (*Guide Sheet* 12-2)
Job 7... (*Guide Sheet* 12-6)
11:15 am
...
Job 15... (*Guide Sheet* 10-3)
3:00 pm

Put job times in *Daily* to make it stronger. This gives sellers a sense of how well they're doing. List jobs like this:
Job 1... (*Guide Sheet* 6-8) [2 min]
Job 2... (*Guide Sheet* 16-5) [5 min]
Job 3... (*Guide Sheet* 6-12) [10 min]
Job 4... (*Guide Sheet* 9-2) [10 min]
10:00 am
Job 5 Open doors to customers
Job 6... (*Guide Sheet* 12-2) [10 min]
Job 7... (*Guide Sheet* 12-6) [5 min]
11:15 am
...
Job 15... (*Guide Sheet* 10-3) [4 min]
3:00 pm

Be fair with times. It's better to allow 15 minutes for a 10 minute job than 10 minutes for a 15 minute job. Let your good sellers guide you on times. Ask for and accept the feedback they give you. Timing jobs well prevents you from overloading sellers.

Leave time for selling. It's too much to ask sellers to do jobs that take an hour between 10 am and 11 am. There might be customers in the store even if it's the worst hour of the week. One way to deal with slow times is to plan large blocks of clock time. For example: 2½ hours of jobs between 10 am and 2 pm on Mondays. Be sure your sellers know that selling time beats other time. Be sure they know you'll support them in this. Look in the cash register before you complain when your store's dirty and messy. Your sellers were right to sell instead of cleaning the floor if sales were better than usual. Your sellers were right to sell instead of redoing the displays that customers knocked over. Thank them for it. Skip complaints about the mess or you'll spoil their triumph. They'll learn that you prefer a tidy store to high sales if you complain about the mess. They can stay late to clear up the mess. Other sellers can clear up the mess tomorrow. Do you need to schedule more sellers at this time?

Include support for the jobs in Daily — Look at each job in *Daily* to see if it needs support. Suppose you price most items with a label gun. Dolls are different. Here you use blue string tags for boy dolls and pink string tags for girl dolls. You buy the string tags from an out-of-town supplier. Remember the blue and pink string tags for the dolls when you add the job "Price new items" to *Daily*. You must have them on hand to price the dolls. Somewhere in *Daily* you need another job that makes sure you have enough on hand. Perhaps you'll enter a line item in "Check usual supplies."

Slice up the jobs in Daily — Cut up big jobs into bite-sized chunks. For example: Between yearly inventory checks, spot check stock quantities a few items a day. That'll keep you on top of mistakes without being a big burden.

Cut slices off jobs done under pressure. For example: Sellers can't count the cash and charge card deposit until the end of the day. They can pre-count cash and sales drafts more than once during the day. At the end of the day counting will be fast.

CHAPTER 8

MAKE EXPECTATIONS CLEAR

The *Back End* of retail covers all those non-selling jobs that support the *Front End* of retail—face-to-face selling to customers. When sellers have the *Back End* in place it frees them for selling. They can use the selling skills they have to the maximum and they can work on improving them. When managers push sellers to sell without their back-end skills in place, the sellers stumble and fumble. They lose heart and they lose customers for your store.

Work out a graded plan for training and coaching the back-end skills. When Mary is a new seller she must know how to operate the cash register before she makes sales. She can learn about daily cleaning of the restrooms later because one of the old hands can cover that. The graded plan in a store will reflect the store's special needs and the staffing levels for shifts.

Pay attention to the back-end training that you can handle during the interview. A good start here sets the tone for the training to come. The rest of this chapter deals with important areas for back-end training.

Pride in Selling

Make sure your sellers take pride in selling. Give them the point of view that supports that pride.

Look at Selling As a Helpful and Friendly Job

Many people knock selling, but the reality is that sellers help customers solve their problems and live contented lives. As they sell, sellers grow personally.

Sellers help customers by selling to them — Customers have problems on their minds when they're in a store. Sometimes the problems and the answers to them are clear. Sometimes the problems are clear but the answers aren't. Sometimes even the problems aren't clear. Customers have ideas that nag at them. They may believe they're "Just looking," but the items you sell are on their minds. They're "Just looking" in your store, not some other store.

Sellers give customers facts, help and advice. They help customers to feel sure of themselves when they make decisions about the items they buy. They find out what problems customers have. Sellers satisfy customers by solving their problems. They help someone when they make a sale.

Sellers develop social skills by selling — As sellers sell, they learn skills for relating to customers. Selling brings them in contact with many different and interesting people they wouldn't normally meet. They also meet some difficult people. Now and then they meet someone they don't like at all. They learn to deal pleasantly with all of them. They learn to be friendly. The skills they use in selling are valuable in their everyday life.

Sellers grow by selling — Sellers throw away old ways as they learn new skills. Selling forces them to face their habits. It forces them to know what they can do and see what they have to do to get things done. As they learn new skills, they change. They learn the skills to make sales, but there's a spill-over into daily life.

Look at Selling As a Skilled Job

The reason that people knock selling is that most sellers they meet lack selling skills. If the law allowed untrained brain surgeons to operate, brain surgeons would have a worse reputation than sellers.

Lack of service turns customers off — See no service at its "best" in the starkly lit barns of the discount houses. Customers roam from aisle to aisle searching for their needs. Now and then they find someone who points them in the right direction. Perhaps what's there meets their needs. Supposed lowest prices reward shopping like this. Sometimes the prices are low but sometimes they're as high or higher than prices in other stores. Getting tired or upset is an almost certain result.

No service has become the rule in most department stores. Department stores have cut themselves down to go up against discount stores. Their sellers leave customers alone too often when they need help. Many specialty stores model themselves on department stores. Department stores were once good models. Once they gave service but now it's rare. Modern specialty stores need a better model.

Untrained sellers turn customers off — Sales training in many stores amounts to pushing sellers onto the sales floor and hoping for the best. Stores are full of sellers who have little idea of how to sell. Many go from customer to customer with little success, repeating, "May I help you?" like a trained parrot. Stores are full of sellers who know little about items or where the items are in the store. Stores are full of sellers who don't know what's in stock and don't know prices. These untrained sellers deserve better treatment. They'd gladly give good service if someone would show them how to do it.

Wrongly trained sellers turn customers off — One end of the scale is wrong training that comes from lack of knowledge. The trainer teaches ways of selling that don't work. Some of these trainers use the ways of selling that sellers use on them when they're shopping. There are so many untrained sellers in stores that they see mainly bad ways of selling.

The other end of the scale is wrong training that comes from a wrong attitude. Trainers teach sellers to use "hard sell" ways of selling. They breed pushy sellers. Pushy sellers make sales, but they have few repeat customers.

Retail selling is a professional skill — Only when sellers approach selling as a professional skill do they have a satisfying career. Professional skills change retail selling from a low paying dead-end job into a good living. They change retail selling from a boring job to a challenging and exciting job.

The system of selling presented in *I'll Take It* gets sellers to say and do the right things. It uses proven ways of selling which fit into a general plan for running retail stores. These ways of selling make sales happen now and turn customers into regular customers. These ways of selling result from trials by skilled sellers who've carefully looked into how well they work. These ways of selling are easy to understand, but sellers need discipline to use them correctly. Sellers must practice and measure how well they sell. These ways of selling need sellers who commit themselves to improvement. They need sellers who know there are no short cuts to being top.

Feel Good about the Items, the Store and Selling

Make sure sellers are wild about what they sell and where they sell. It's the only honest form of selling. Anything less cheats customers.

Choose sellers with real passion for the items you sell — Strong good feelings about the items on sale helps sellers to sell them. Customers feel the sellers' love for the items when sellers sell items that interest them. Customers will notice if they fake an interest. Faking it will kill sales.

Make sure your sellers are selling only items they'd like family and friends to buy. They sell best if they always speak well of the items they sell. They sell well when they use the items they sell. It comes through to customers when sellers put their money where their mouth is. Perhaps your sellers can't afford to use the items you sell. In that case, they have to want to use them. What sellers know from personal use can help them sell, but they may need to keep their views in check. They give customers only the few facts they need to know to help them buy.

Choose sellers comfortable with your prices — Sellers sell well when they feel the prices are right for the items in the store. The right price isn't the same as the lowest price. Perhaps some items are cheaper elsewhere. Suggest these possibilities for the other store:

- It may show too little profit on sales.

- Whether the owner knows it or not, the other store may be on its way out of business.

- It may be the wrong place to sell the items. They're close-outs at low price.

- It may choose to lose money on some items to create the image of a store with bargains.

- It may price items one way today, another way tomorrow.

- It may use a poor way for setting prices.

- It may use a way to set prices with a mistake in it.

- It may be less pleasant to work or shop in than your store.

- Its prices may be too low to pay its sellers well.

- It may have no hidden benefits and no training programs.

Sellers who aren't at ease with prices can't sell well. They support the items weakly and customers notice it. Encourage sellers to talk about prices with you if they feel prices are wrong. Sellers hurt sales when they act as if prices are too high in front of customers. A store will have problems if its prices aren't right. Customers will notice and will shop elsewhere.

Choose sellers comfortable with selling luxuries — Good prices for luxuries are high prices. Customers who want and can afford luxuries expect to pay high prices. Paying high prices for high quality items sets the buyers apart from other people. Sellers won't sell many fine watches if they can't see the value in a $3,000 watch. Nor will they sell many if they think it's wrong to spend $3,000 on a watch. Better for them to work in a drug store and sell cheap watches.

Customers feel good when they buy luxuries. There's a special glow people get when they buy something they've dreamed about. Remember how excited you felt when you bought your first new automobile? Remember the pleasure you got from the stereo you'd always wanted? Think back to the pleasure of your first new bicycle. Sellers have the good luck to share in the excitement as they help customers to buy.

Make sure sellers go along with the needs and wants of customers. Some sellers feel customers are just like them. They feel they can decide customers' needs for them. Good sellers are much more sensitive to human nature than that. They sell customers only what customers need or want to buy.

Choose sellers who support the store fully — Make sure sellers are always positive about your store. Make sure they're positive to customers even if there are things wrong in your store. Managers are human, so they're sometimes wrong about things. All businesses need to better themselves. Everything won't be perfect in a store. Sellers whining to everyone about the store's bad points won't change anything. Encourage sellers to discuss problems with you and make wise changes where they can. Let sellers who don't support your best efforts find themselves a different job.

Sell Fully to All Customers

Make sure your sellers sell customers everything they want and need. Yes, that will help your bottom line, but that's not the reason for doing so. It shows a shameful lack of respect to sell customers anything less than they want and need.

Sell fully or you fail customers — Always sell as much as customers need or want to buy. Selling fully makes life easy for customers, respects their time and gives them pleasure. Find out customers' needs or wants and sell them their needs or wants. Then sell the items that naturally go with what they need or want. That way customers use their shopping time fully. Their lives are easy and they're happy. Sellers who fail to sell fully fail customers.

- Mary bought the green shoes in Honolulu. She remembered the seller with regret when she tried to buy green shoe laces in Omaha.

- Alonzo bought the hammer but forgot the nails. The same guy sold him the glass but not the putty.

- Clarissa bought a new ribbon for her typewriter. At home she found that she also needed paper.

- Frank was dressing for an important date. Suddenly he found that he had no belt to go with his new trousers.

Respect customers' values — Make sure your sellers stay open to customers' values. Respect the choices customers make. Sellers' personal values are theirs alone. Sometimes they can use them to help a sale, but see that they steer clear of using them to stop customers from buying. Certainly the tight pink pants and bright green blouse match poorly. Why spoil the clear pleasure the customer gets from them? The seller may see them as ugly but the customer doesn't. Shirt A sells like hotcakes, but you're stuck with shirt B because most customers find it ugly. Sell shirt B to customers who choose it and like it. Sensitive sellers keep what they think about shirt B to themselves.

Never save for customers — Some customers want to buy as little as possible as cheaply as possible. It's a flaw in their nature that sellers respect. Trouble lies ahead if people who want to buy little and cheaply become sellers. They think other people shop like them. They suggest savings and shortcuts to customers. They force customers to go along with them. They think they're the good guy but they're using strong arm tactics. Sellers who save for customers turn customers off.

Customers want to feel they can afford the best even when they can't. Sellers who treat them as though they can't afford the best turn them off. They'll spoil the pleasure customers are enjoying. Then customers may leave rather than buying something they can afford instead. It's not a seller's job to shatter customers' dreams. Let customers work through their dreams to what they can afford. Sellers go along with their dreams. After customers work through their dreams for themselves, they'll willingly buy what they can afford.

Sellers who save for customers fail to let the needs, wants and dreams of customers guide them. They make customers suffer.

- Mary wanted to stay in a fine hotel during the two day meeting. The travel agent suggested something cheaper. The room was in a less pleasant hotel. There was no view of the ocean. Mary wasn't part of the group at the main hotel and she had less fun than others at the meeting.

- John usually replaces the fan belt on his car every year. Now he's stuck on a lonely road. The mechanic decided to save him a few dollars and replace the belt next year.

Sellers who save for customers undercut the store. Saving for customers lowers short-term sales. Sales are missing the extra cash for the fancy room and the fan belt. Saving for customers also lowers long-term sales. Next time, Mary uses a different travel agent. Next time, John uses a different service station. They never go back to the places that made them suffer.

It's fine when you try to sell to customers fully and they save for themselves. It's fine when saving for a customer's the only way to make a sale. Sellers fail customers when they take it on themselves to suggest savings without feedback that customers want savings.

Customers want quality items and easy shopping — Most customers want to buy items that truly suit their needs. They prefer the highest quality they can afford. It's poor service to sell them less than they can afford. Most customers like to buy where it's pleasant and easy to shop.

What the Store Expects from Sellers

It's important to be clear what you expect from sellers right from the beginning. The more you tell them up front when they're new with you, the better for you in the long run. Make sure you include all the nasty stuff. Then it won't jump out and surprise someone.

Insist on Honesty and Openness

Insist on honesty with people. Being honest is the only way we let people know they can rely on us. People can lose everything they have in this world. They can suffer lots of bad luck. People still respect them if they cling to their honesty. A high standard of honesty is a person's most important quality. Honesty builds the trust, respect and loyalty of other people. Without honesty people have no staying power.

Insist on honesty with the store — Find sellers who respect the trust the store places in them. Sellers handle the store's items, supplies, materials, and money. You ask them for facts about their selling and the jobs they do for the store. There's a temptation to bend the facts to look better. Sellers who made 2 sales to 10 customers may think they look better by reporting 2 sales to 4 customers. Once or twice it may work. It shows when someone does this sort of thing often. Then you know you have someone you can't work with. Make up your mind that only honesty will do for your sellers—there's nothing else you'll accept. Dismiss dishonest people.

Insist on honesty with co-workers and managers — Make sure your sellers let people know about it right away when they mess up. People who admit their mistakes right away gain the respect of other people. It's better to learn about a mistake from the person who made it rather than from someone else. It's better to know someone made a mistake than to suspect someone. The only way to survive a huge mess-up is to own up to it right away. It's silly to lie about it. Make it clear that liars don't survive in your store.

Insist on honesty with customers — Making false claims about the items or the store will backfire. Make sure it's aluminum when sellers claim it. Make sure it's guaranteed for life when sellers claim it. Make sure it's solid oak when sellers say it is. Let customers know if the parts out of sight are fiberboard. Sellers will turn customers off forever if they find them making false claims. They'll never shop in your store again. Make sure your sellers find out the facts if they don't know them.

Insist on openness with co-workers and managers — Make sure your sellers let their co-workers and managers know how they feel about things that upset them. Stress that politeness is the aim. But it's better to risk making waves rather than bottling up feelings and boiling with them until they explode. Get your sellers to tell the person who needs to know. Griping about things behind people's backs won't fix anything. Talking things over openly leads to solutions.

Encourage sellers to let people know how they feel about the things that please them. Get them to speak up when they see something they like or when someone does something that pleases them. Giving praise makes others feel good and makes the praiser feel good too.

Dress and Groom Yourself Well

Neat and proper clothes for selling show your customers your sellers care. Get the clothes right for your kind of store and customers will trust your sellers.

What the sellers wear will be different in different stores. Some stores call for business suits. Others call for informal clothes. Still others call for shocking fashions or fancy dress. Some call for neat coveralls.

Let your customers guide you. Customers are most at ease with sellers who dress as they do or who dress how they'd like to dress. In some cases customers expect sellers to wear uniforms.

In stores that sell fashions, see that sellers wear only the fashions currently in stock. Make this a condition of employment. Naturally you sell the fashions that sellers wear to them at cost. Your sellers become walking models in your store.

Whatever you choose for your store, let your sellers know what to expect. Avoid a lot of detail. Be sure your dress code doesn't discriminate against any groups. Give feedback so sellers know where they stand. Give a lot of positive feedback. All of us like it when someone tells us we look good.

Good grooming always helps sales, even in a tire store. Insist on it. Here's some guidance for sellers in an upscale store:

Dress casually but fashionably — Choose fashions our customers will like and understand. Customers know our store for its fine appearance—dress to support the store.

Leave jeans and running shoes at home — Jeans and running shoes are below the image we want. They may be smart and fashionable to the in-group, but they're still jeans and running shoes.

Wear a watch — Wear a watch with large clear numbers. Sellers need to keep track of time.

Wear no signs that turn off some customers — Customers have strong feelings on some of life's problems. Abortion is a good example. Many customers support it fiercely. Others oppose it fiercely. Wear a button or T-shirt supporting one side of the issue and you'll turn off some customers. What you support on the issue is your affair. It's no part of selling. Leave your signs at home.

Groom yourself well — To groom yourself is to keep yourself clean, neat and tidy. A poorly groomed seller kills sales.

Get it right — We'll let you know how you're doing on dress and grooming. We'll suggest changes for the future when you're trying but missing the mark. Turn up poorly dressed or groomed and it's back home to get it right. There's no pay for the time it takes you. Two send-homes in 90 days are as much as we'll put up with. After that, it's time to say good-bye.

Work Free of the Effects of Alcohol and Drugs

Expect sellers to come to work ready to work. Spaced out sellers do their jobs poorly. It's up to them to keep themselves free of the effects of alcohol and drugs. It's not your job to keep track of how sellers live. Judge sellers strictly on results. React to:

- Damage to equipment.

- Damage to our public image.

- Low morale.

- Low quality.

- Poor decisions.

- Poor performance.

- Problems of behavior.

- Repeated absences.

- Repeated lateness.

- Safety problems.

- Waste.

Counsel sellers to improve. Say good-bye to sellers who don't improve. Sellers stack the cards in their favor by staying free of the effects of alcohol and drugs.

Work Unusual Hours

Retailers work unusual hours. Some of the best times for retail sales are when other people play or get ready to play. Professional retail sellers expect and look forward to working at these times.

Work when others play

- *Easter*—We're open from Good Friday through Easter Monday.

- *The week before Labor Day and Labor Day weekend*—That's when others are getting a last fling of summer vacation or are getting ready for school.

- *The day after Thanksgiving*—That's our busiest day of the year.

- *The week before Christmas*—During the week before Christmas we're open as long as there are shoppers.

- *Christmas Eve*—On Christmas Eve we're open as long as there are shoppers. After that, we prepare for the sale that begins the day after Christmas.

- *The day after Christmas*—That's when we have a sale.

- *The first two weeks of January*—That's a school vacation period.

- *All other public holidays.*

Some sellers may be off at these times but most will work. Make it a condition of employment for sellers to be open to work at unusual times.

Work late night shifts — Some late night shifts end after public transport has closed. Schedule these shifts only from the pool of sellers who agree to work late night shifts. For some sellers, make this a condition of employment.

Take inventory — Count everything in the store twice a year. Count outside normal store hours. Schedule most sellers to count to get the job done quickly. Sellers get overtime pay or call-in pay if they qualify. Make it a condition of employment for sellers to be open to take inventory.

Go to Sellers' Meetings — *Sellers' Meetings* are part of the work schedule. Sellers get overtime pay or call-in pay if they qualify. Make it a condition of employment for sellers to be open for *Sellers' Meetings*.

Fill in for other sellers — Sometimes things go wrong and normally scheduled sellers can't make it. Sellers have to be willing to drop things to help the store through these times. Sellers get overtime pay or call-in pay if they qualify. Make it a condition of employment for sellers to be open to fill in for other sellers.

Take running breaks when needed — Running breaks are breaks taken in pieces. Sometimes a seller is alone in the store, or the store's busy, when it's lunch or coffee break. Take the break time in the store split up between serving customers. Sellers get the same break time as they usually get, but it comes in pieces. Sellers get an extra hour of base pay when they take a running lunch break. Make it a condition of employment for sellers to be open to take running breaks.

"At will" employment — No statement above in any way changes the nature of a seller's "At will" employment.

Be on Time

You can't run your store with sellers who aren't on time. This is especially so for sellers who open the store in the morning.

Let sellers know what to expect for being late — Expect sellers to start on time. Question the reasons for being late for sellers late two (2) times in a ninety (90) day period. Make being late three (3) times in a ninety (90) day period beyond the normal limit. Unless there are good reasons for being late, subject sellers to discipline. This may include dismissal. Keep a record of the times sellers are late in their files.

Let sellers know what to expect for leaving early — Leaving early is the same as being late. Being late once and leaving early once is the same as being late twice.

Require a warning for planned absences — All sellers need to take some personal time off. Make sure sellers let you know about it ahead of time so you can arrange a cover for them.

Call in for unexpected emergencies and illnesses — Have sellers call as soon as they can when it's clear they can't make it. Expect them to have someone call for them if they're unable to call. Take calls at home if you need to. Require sellers to keep the store's number and the manager's home number in their pocket diary. Require all sellers to carry a pocket diary.

Give only one warning to sellers who skip calling in — Not calling in is a mistake sellers make only once. The second time a seller is a no-show without a call-in it's time to say good-bye. The store's in a tough spot when sellers don't show up, but if they call in, roll with it. The store's in an impossible spot when sellers don't show up and don't call in. Act as if a seller has quit when absent two (2) scheduled days without calling in.

Be clear on too many absences — Four (4) absences in a 90-day period is too many. The reasons for more absences will come under question. Require sellers to present a written record from their doctor at their expense when it seems necessary. Too many absences will lead to discipline, which may include dismissal. Keep a record of absences in sellers' files.

Leave the Good Parking for Customers

Reserve the parking space near your store for customers. There's no reason for sellers to use this prime space.

Make space for customers — The more parking spaces there are near the store, the better for sales. Some customers need to be near the store to carry out the items they buy. Some customers are lazy. They won't walk across a parking lot and won't park on a nearby street.

Use public transport — Even the largest parking lots fill up on busy days. Seller's who use public transport support the store's sales. Seller's who use public transport help reduce traffic jams and pollution.

Park and walk if you must drive — Park in a nearby area away from stores and walk in. Make believe you live only ten minutes from the store. Park there and walk in. Take this chance to get some daily exercise. Park only where shoppers don't park. Although sellers have as much legal right as shoppers to park on a public street, professional sellers choose to give up that right.

Park safely — Make sure sellers park only where they feel their car's safe and they feel safe walking in. Use public transport if there's nowhere like that ten minutes from the store.

Smoke and Chew Far from the Store

Make sure sellers who smoke or chew keep these habits out of the store.

Follow the store's no smoking rule — This store is a no smoking area. Most cities have a bye-law against smoking in stores. Even if your city doesn't, make it a rule in your store. There are good health reasons for not smoking.

Keep the store and items clean and pleasant — Smoke makes dirt and leaves odors. Dirt and odors get in the air and make it unhealthy and unpleasant. They get in the items you sell and lower their value.

Smoke on breaks well away from the store — See that sellers move well away from the store to smoke. Smokers hanging around the doorway are no part of a fine retail store. The store looks cheap if sellers hang around smoking outside the door. Men look like barkers outside a blue night spot. Women look like hookers waiting for johns. Timid customers shy away from the store. Some customers feel uncomfortable making their way through the smokers.

Chew far from the store — Chewing has no place in a store. It looks crude and it's rude to customers. Sellers need an empty mouth to talk to customers. Move well away from the store to chew.

Use the Phone for Business

Abuse of the phone will cost you three ways:

1. Extra phone costs.

2. Lost time while your sellers are on the phone.

3. Sellers who lack focus—it's unlikely the lack is only with the phone.

Keep the phone free for business calls — The store's phone is for business use. The store's out of business when sellers block the phone with personal calls. See that sellers make few personal calls and keep them short. Here's an example of a personal call it's OK to make: "Hi there, Jack. I get off at 7:30. Can you pick me up? Good. Thanks. I'll be at the usual place by 7:35. See you then. Bye!"

Cut off problem friends — Friends who call sellers at work for a chat are a problem. Train sellers to deal with them firmly from the beginning: "Jane, I'd like to talk to you, but I'm at work. Give me your number and I'll call you tonight at about 7:30." Then they'll learn you mean business.

If Jane continues to talk: "Jane, give me your number and I'll call you at 7:30." If Jane goes on talking: "I'm sorry Jane, I have to hang up." Hang up. If Jane calls back, ask the manager to talk to her.

Make personal calls from a pay phone on a break — Train sellers to make personal calls outside the store.

Use the Quick Phone List — The *Quick Phone List* beside the phone lists:

*   Emergency phone numbers.

*   Everyone who works for the store.

*   Numbers the store calls often.

Keep the Store's Secrets

The facts in your store belong in your store. They're neither for sharing with outsiders nor are they for casual gossip.

Sellers keep facts about the store to themselves — Sellers see and use facts the store keeps to itself. Examples are how to set prices, sources of items, sales figures. Sellers keep these and other sensitive facts within the store. Limit access to sellers who need to use these facts to do their jobs. Seller aren't free to talk about them with customers or other outsiders. For example, it's easy for customers who don't know retail expenses to think normal markups are high.

Sellers keep facts about customers to themselves — Sellers see and use the names, addresses and phone numbers of customers. Keep these facts within the store. Talk about them only with sellers who need to use them to do their jobs. It's important that the store's customers know they can trust it.

Keep facts about sellers to yourself — Keep facts in sellers' files locked up. Only a few people need to use them to do their work. They're not free to tell or show anything in these files to outsiders or to other sellers.

Train sellers to stonewall outsiders who ask for secrets — Sellers say to outsiders: "I don't know. You'll have to ask the manager about that."

Keep the store's secrets in the store — No one may remove or make copies of any documents, records, reports, data, or computer software without the manager's approval. Telling or showing the store's secrets to outsiders can lead to sellers losing their job. Loss of secrets could have serious effects on the store's business.

Sellers agree to keep the store's secrets after quitting — Require sellers to agree not to share the store's secrets with any other individual or company after they quit working for your store. Make this a condition of employment.

Control Visitors

Drop-ins are friends of sellers who drop by to chat. You don't want them in your store. Watch out for the "managers" of poorly run nearby stores who stop by to shoot the breeze with your manager and sellers.

Make sure sellers friends and relatives aren't drop-ins — It's fine for sellers to show their friends and relatives through the store. That's different from them dropping in to visit. It's fine if sellers' friends and relatives are customers. That's different from them dropping in to visit. Visitors always change the mood in the store. They never help sales. Visitors take a seller's attention from customers. Customers feel they're butting in on the seller's personal life and they leave without buying. Several visitors at once turn the store into a clubhouse. Customers are even less likely to buy when there's more than one visitor. Have sellers meet their visitors outside the store during breaks. It's up to sellers to train their visitors to respect the times that they work.

Make sure people who pick up sellers aren't drop-ins — Pick-you-ups who come early and hang around in the store kill sales. They send a signal to customers that says, "Hurry up. We're about to close. Shop some other time." They hover and fidget around the store. Pick-you-ups in the store when sellers are closing put pressure on the sellers. They make the sellers make mistakes. They delay closing. Have sellers' pick-you-ups meet them away from the store. Be sure they stay away from the doorway and the store window.

Keep to a High Standard of Personal Conduct

Make sure sellers take their personal conduct seriously. Most stores act as if their sellers follow good rules of personal conduct without spelling the rules out. The following lists contain the most obvious actions a store can't put up with from sellers or others working for the store at any of its locations. They also apply while representing the store elsewhere. These lists don't include everything unacceptable. Despite these lists, all employees remain employed "At will."

Severe actions — These actions are so serious that they'll cost sellers their job:

- Acts of sabotage.

- Acts or threats of violence.

- Any action taken on purpose that undercuts our efforts to make a profit.

- Being drunk or under the influence of drugs or controlled substances.

- Being in the store or other work place out of scheduled work hours without he manager's or supervisor's OK.

- Breaking any of the store's rules on purpose.

- Breaking security or safety rules.

- Careless actions that put the life or safety of another person in danger.

- Changing the store's records or other documents.

- Creating conflict or lack of harmony on purpose.

- Criminal acts.

- Destroying or damaging the property of others on purpose.

- Destroying or damaging the store's property on purpose.

- Dishonesty.

- Fighting or stirring up a fight.

- Gambling.

- Giving a false reason for a leave of absence.

- Giving away or selling the store's secrets to other people or businesses. This includes employees who have no need to know them.

- Giving false data to the store.

- Handing in an untrue time slip or other record of time worked.

- Immoral or indecent conduct.

- Intimidating or coercing fellow employees on or off the premises.

- Limiting work output on purpose or encouraging others to do the same.

- Lying about sick or other leave.

- Making false statements on an application for employment or other work records.

- Using poor security or safety practices on purpose.

- Personal use of the store's equipment or property without the manager's or supervisor's OK.

- Personal use the store's equipment for profit.

- Possession of firearms, weapons or explosives.

- Possession or removal of any of the store's property without first getting an OK from the manager or supervisor. This includes written, printed and electronic documents, as well as other property.

- Refusing changes in your work schedule.

- Refusing to help out on *Special Jobs*.

- Refusing to obey lawful work orders.

- Refusing to work as scheduled.

- Refusing to work overtime.

- Running a lottery or other system of gambling.

- Spreading facts from sellers' files.

- Theft of other people's property.

- Theft of the store's property.

- Use, possession or sale of any quantity of a drug or controlled substance— except for medications prescribed by a physician which let you work well.

- Working for a business we're up against while employed by our store.

Less severe actions — These actions will result in discipline, including possible dismissal:

- Any act of harassment.

- Being absent or late too many times.

- Being below our standards of dress.

- Being indifferent or rude.

- Being untidy and/or dirty.

- Blocking the work of another employee.

- Breaking the store's rules.

- Buying the store's items for resale.

- Careless damage of property.

- Chewing in or near the store.

- Disorderly or hostile conduct.

- Eating and drinking outside the allowed eating and drinking areas.

- Failure to meet production or quality standards as explained to you by the manager or supervisor.

- Horseplay.

- Leaving work before the end of a workday without the OK of the manager or supervisor.

- Leaving your work station during your work hours without the OK of the manager or supervisor, except to use the restroom.

- Loitering or loafing during working hours.

- Making, adding to, or failing to correct, unsanitary conditions.

- Mistakes due to carelessness or failure to get instructions.

- Not being ready to work at the start of a workday without the OK of the manager or supervisor.

- Not filling in your time slip daily.

- Not following our policies.

- Not reporting an absence or late arrival.

- Not reporting damage or an accident right away.

- Posting, removing or altering notices without permission of the manager or supervisor.

- Selling items or collecting money for charities or others without the manager's or supervisor's OK.

- Sleeping on the job.

- Smoking in or near the store.

- Soliciting.

- Speeding or careless driving in any vehicle.

- Spreading rumors or nasty gossip.

- Stopping work before the scheduled time.

- Unsatisfactory or careless work.

- Using obscene or abusive language.

- Using the store's phone for long personal calls.

- Using the store's phone for too many personal calls.

- Wearing unsafe clothing.

- Writing or ringing up your own order.

Give First Class Customer Service

Customers will know your store for customer service only if it gives customer service. Giving customer service takes more than claiming to give it. You can get your sellers to wear buttons saying "I'm a Customer Service Specialist." You can put up posters saying "Customer Service is Our First Job." You can advertise that you're "Widely Known for Excellent Service." These are idle boasts unless you do give first class service. The risk with boasts like these is that those who make them rarely follow through with training. They put their efforts into the boast and then feel they've done something about service. They may tell their sellers to give service, but not tell them how to do it. They give lip service instead of service. It's better to train your sellers to give service and not boast that you give service.

You'll pay a cost for customer service, but it's your best form of advertising. Now and then a customer will abuse you. That's part of your cost of service.

Be careful what you consider customer abuse and be careful how you try to cut down on abuse. A customer may buy a dress or a suit and try it on at home before returning it. After 2 or 3 returns the customer is satisfied. It causes you work but that's OK. You're seeing one end of how customers deal with things. Customers at the other end keep items they don't like.

Customers who make returns are good for your store. They're satisfied assertive customers and they tell their friends they're satisfied. You can be sure they'll boost your store, especially if they get hassles in other stores. Their friends know that if you'll satisfy these unreasonable oddballs, you'll certainly satisfy them. Their friends begin to shop with you. Most of them keep what they buy. Those who make returns are busy out there advertising your store for you.

It's abuse when a customer wears an item to a party, soils it, then asks for a cash refund. People will hear about it if you refuse the refund. Only they won't hear the customer soiled the item. They'll only hear you're a tough store to deal with. Make the refund cheerfully, but let the customer know you're sending the item to charity. Also contract that customer on returns pleasantly. "I'm sorry the item wasn't suitable. I'm sure my favorite charity will be glad to get it. Usually, we don't make returns on items we can't resell, but there's no problem on this return."

For abuse that's an oddity of a good customer, you'll keep the customer and get good advertising from the return. Follow the terms of the contract you made on returns with a "customer" where abuse gets out of hand. You said "Usually, we don't make returns on items we can't resell," so you can now refuse the return.

Sometimes you can abuse yourself. Learn from the case of the butcher who opened ten large expensive cans of ham for a neurotic shopper. She turned down each one, saying, "That's too fatty. Please open another one." After the first one, you or I would say, "I've seen a lot of these hams, Ma'am. They're all like this one. They all have some fat. Would you like me to cut the fat off this one for you or would you prefer a packaged ham?"

Sellers are the store — Sellers are the store when they deal with customers. Customers form opinions of the store by how sellers treat them. These opinions soon become facts in their minds. See that sellers accept that they're responsible for the success of the store.

See that sellers smile and speak with a friendly tone of voice. Sellers are the face of the store. The first ten to fifteen seconds with a customer usually decide how things will go. That's something sellers can control. Let customers see and hear they're glad customers are in the store. See that sellers thank customers for stopping by. See that they make customers their friends.

Act for the long-term interest of the store — The short-term interest of the store is to make sales. The long-term interest is to develop regular customers. The short-term interest always takes back seat to the long-term interest. Get sellers thinking not only of how to make this sale, but of how to make sure this customer comes back again and again. Let sellers pretend they're customers when they don't know how to handle problems. Then they give customers the service they'd hope to get.

Think of today's sale as the long-term value of sales. Customers who spend $100 today may do so five times a year. That's $500 from each of them. Customers who spend $500 this year may spend $5,000 over ten years. Today's sale of $100 sets the pattern for $5,000 of sales. That's what's riding on every sale a seller makes.

Treat customers like guests in your home — Get sellers to act as they do when they have guests in their homes. Not just any guests, but guests they'd really like to be their new friends. Have the same warm feelings to customers as you do to friends. Make your customers your friends. Treat them with courtesy and respect.

Smile when you talk to customers — You look good when you smile. Smiling gets you off on the right foot—it takes control of how you feel. Smiling is catching—it puts customers in a good mood. Smiling cuts through anger. It's hard to be angry with someone who greets you with a smile.

Speak with a friendly tone of voice — How you say something counts a lot more than what you say.

Program yourself for selling when you wake up — Attack the day positively. Tell yourself it's going to be a good selling day and it will be. Our days follow our first thoughts in the morning. We can make our days flow smoothly or we can place roadblocks in the way.

Snap out of negative thoughts. Snap the opposite into its place when a negative thought comes. "What a lousy day." Snap! "What a beautiful soft gentle rain."

Steer clear of people who live their lives in a black cloud. Drop them from your life if they won't change. They'll only pull you down.

Snap out of negative words. Get rid of words like, "can't," "don't know," "impossible," "should have." Snap into the opposite.

Snap out of insult words. Get rid of words like, "dummy," "fool," "idiot," "jerk," "mooch," "nerd," "pigeon," "stupid," "turkey," and worse.

Be true to your word — Do what you say you'll do. Do it when you say you'll do it. Learning to do things right the first time helps you keep true to your word.

Under-promising and over-delivering helps you keep true to your word. Promise for Thursday when you think you can get it ready by Wednesday. That's better than promising for Wednesday and not getting it ready till Thursday.

Sell as if there are other stores in town — Customers may come to us, but we're breaking into their time to sell. They're not breaking into our time. You'll lose customers when you sell as if we're the only store in town. Always give customers a cheerful greeting and good-bye.

Satisfy customers — There's a cost to getting customers. It costs about five times as much to get a new customer as it does to keep a customer we already have. Bad attitudes and lack of interest by sellers cost us customers.

Customers who get upset make snap decisions to shop elsewhere. They don't reason it out. They don't say it's just this seller. They don't say this seller's having a bad day today. They act on their feelings. It's a big loss when a seller kills today's sale and drives a customer away. There goes today's $100, this year's $500 and a long-term $5,000.

Make sure customers get what they want. Sometimes customers are wrong, but make them feel right. Work things out so they're OK to you and to customers. Upset customers spread bad tales about the store.

Satisfy yourself — Pride yourself on your customer service. Feel the satisfaction of a job well done. Without that commitment to customer service, a seller's job lacks a focus. Without a focus in your job, you've no game to play. People without a game to play amount to nothing. Satisfy customers and you satisfy yourself.

Let other sellers sell — Respect the need of other sellers to focus on customers to sell. It breaks the natural flow of selling if you butt in on other sellers while they're selling. Then their sales suffer. A seller may be the only person who can tell you something to get you out of a tight spot. That's tough—customers come first. Plan ahead and keep yourself out of tight spots.

Treat other sellers well — Treat the sellers who work with you with the same as you treat customers. Customers will see it if you treat other sellers badly and they'll be uncomfortable. It'll rub off when you deal with customers. You can't change gears that easily.

Keep Up with World, National and Local News

For your store's *Awareness Program* select examples of newspapers and magazines. Try to give choices. Ask your sellers for their ideas. Get help from your local library.

It's important for sellers to read a magazine based on the items you sell. A sports magazine for a sports store, a photography magazine for a photography store, and so on. You may wish to name a specific magazine here, or you may wish sellers to read more than one. Sometimes there's no one-to-one match for your store's items. So look for something close that will help your sellers. Sellers in a toy store might read a magazine on early childhood. It might be more valuable for selling than a magazine on toys.

Many cities have a city magazine. Its title often features the name of the city. Birmingham Magazine, Los Angeles Magazine, San Diego Magazine and Phoenix

Magazine are examples. A number of states have state magazines. Alabama Magazine, Alaska Outdoors and Arizona Highways are examples. There are also regional magazines like Pacific Northwest. The Gale Directory of Publications and Broadcast Media is a good place to start looking for publications like these. Most cities have several free weekly newspapers covering different districts of the city.

See that your sellers follow the *Awareness Program*. Chat with your sellers. Now and then set a pop quiz on recent events. Give it to all sellers by the *Message Pocket* in Daily.

Have something to talk about with customers — Have something to talk about if you want to talk to customers. Find out what's going on in the world. Read, look at and listen to the local, national and international news. Stress positive news that interests many people. Steer clear of news topics that stir up people.

Follow the store's Awareness Program — To work in your store sellers must commit to developing awareness of the world around them on their own time. Explore and know the city and its surroundings. Keep up an interest in standard tourist places. Know about new places and events that interest tourists. Read one daily newspaper that covers world and city events. Listen to or watch one daily news broadcast on radio or TV. Read one weekly news magazine like *Time* or *Newsweek*. Read one weekly newspaper that covers the store's district of the city. Read one monthly magazine based on the store's state or city. Read one monthly magazine that bears on the items the store carries.

Give and Take Praise

People who think well of themselves give praise generously. They also accept praise from other people politely and without embarrassment.

Praise other stores to make customers think well of ours — You'll sound like a whiner if you knock the stores we're up against. Once you start to knock others you'll do it again and again. You'll become a whiner and you'll turn customers off. You'll sound not sure of yourself. You'll make it worse if you also boast about our store. Customers like to shop in stores with a nice guy image.

Customers know you're sure of yourself if you give praise warmly. Say, "Yes, that's a fine store. We learn a lot from them." Or, "Yes, that's a store that keeps us on our toes." You can say, "Yes, we keep up with what they're doing" about any store, even a lousy store. Say nothing at all if you can't say something nice.

Praise other items to make customers feel sure of ours — Some customers know about items we don't carry. Always praise items that customers know about. Then customers who think Brand X is good know you have good judgment. They'll be more likely to listen to your views on our brand. Say, "Brand X refrigerators are excellent. In this store we're committed to Brand Y because …" Stick to the benefits you know our brand offers, even if you know there are problems with Brand X.

Thank customers who praise you or the store — From time to time a customer will praise you or the store. All you need to do is say, "Thank you." You can add, "It's kind of you to mention it," if you wish.

What Sellers Can Expect from the Store

It's important to be clear what sellers can expect from the store right from the beginning. The more you tell them up front when they're new with you, the better for you in the long run. Make sure you include anything that may disappoint them. Then it won't jump out and surprise them. Be aware that as you tell sellers what they can expect, you can also tell them what they can't expect.

The More You Sell, the More You Get

The fruits of retail truly ripen for owners when their sellers earn commissions on sales. For management's details on commissions and other payments to boost sales, see *Pay a Commission on Sales* in Chapter 17 *Boost Sales and Profits*. This section deals with commissions and other payments from the point of view of the seller.

Begin with base pay — Pay only base pay only while sellers learn the back-end skills. Tell sellers you'll pay them so much an hour and that's it. There are no extras. Sellers want more than base pay, so help them learn the back-end skills as quickly as possible. Then they can start earning more.

Earn more by selling more — Pay sellers by the amount they sell when they have the back-end skills. Look at sellers' sales figures and pay them a percentage of sales. We call paying a percentage of sales, "paying a commission on sales." A commission is the seller's rake-off. It gives sellers a piece of the action every time they make a sale. Pay a commission on sales to get sellers to earn more by selling more.

Sellers always get base pay — It's natural for sellers to worry that they'll work hard and get paid less than a wage. It's possible that nobody comes into the store when sellers are working. Sellers may sell only a small amount while they learn to sell. Sometimes sellers sell a lot and other times they sell very little. It's hard for sellers to plan their lives without knowing if they'll earn much. Protect sellers by paying base pay. Pay a wage against commission. Each pay period pay sellers the base pay for the hours they work so they can rely on a fixed base amount. At the end of the month work out what they've earned on commissions. Take away the base pay they've already received from the commissions and write a check for the extra. Sellers keep the base pay if the commission is less than base pay. They get no extra check but they give nothing back. Base pay compares well with pay in stores where there's no chance to earn a commission. Sellers can only win on this deal.

Beat goals to get more — Set sellers a sales goal each week. For the hours a seller works each week, work out sales for a like period last year and adjust the sales for inflation. Based on that, set a sales goal.

For sales the same as last year's adjusted sales, sellers get 6% commission. For reaching the goal, sellers get 8% commission. For the goal plus 10% of the goal, sellers get 9% commission. For the goal plus 20% or more of the goal, sellers get 10% commission.

Sell no-commission items to snag real sales — A commission is a share in the profit on an item There's nothing to share when a sale makes no profit..

We sell sale items for no profit. Sometimes we sell sale items at a loss. We use them to draw customers into the store. Our hope is these customers will also buy other items. Sellers get no commissions on sale items. Sellers make their commissions on the other items they sell along with the sale items.

We sell markdowns for little or no profit. Some items we buy to sell at a profit sell poorly. We mark them down and sell them for what we can get. Sell them like sale items. They make fine bait on the hook to get customers to buy other items. Sellers get no commissions on markdowns. Sellers make their commissions on the other items they sell along with markdowns.

Price changes aren't markdowns. Sometimes we get items we think we can sell at a better profit than usual. Then it turns out we can only sell them at the usual profit. We have to lower their prices, but as they're making a profit sellers still earn commissions on these items.

There are no commissions on special orders. There are too many expenses that go with special orders to rely on making a profit on them.

There are no commissions on seller's discount sales. Likewise, there are no commissions on mall discount sales. There are no commissions on other discounts. Sometimes we sell defective items "as is." Sometimes there are other reasons for a discount on an item. The rule is that discounts carry no commissions. Like markdowns, they make fine bait on the hook to get customers to buy other items.

There are no commissions on top of spiffs. Spiffs give you more cash than a commission. Sellers can't take a commission when they take a spiff.

Pay commissions to help expand the customer base — One of the *Steps for Selling* has sellers ask new customers, "How did you hear about our store?" It's part of the deal that sellers ask this question of all new customers. Sellers get no commission for the sale if they miss asking the question and reporting the answer.

Sellers send *Thank-you Notes* to get commissions. One of the *Steps for Selling* has sellers send a *Thank-you Note* for sales above a certain price. It's part of the deal that sellers send a *Thank-you Note* to get a commission. Sellers get no commission for the sale if they skip sending the *Thank-you Note*.

Feature spiffs — A spiff is a special cash payment sellers get as soon as they sell an item. A spiff is a special bonus that takes the place of a commission. It's more cash than the usual commission. Sellers get no commission on the item if they also get a spiff.

Most spiffs work like this: Suppose the store buys an item at $50 to sell at $100. At 10% commission the seller gets $10 and the store gets $40 to pay its expenses and make a profit. It turns out the item sells poorly and the store lots of them. One solution is to mark the item down. The store gets $30 to pay its expenses when the item sells for $80. Perhaps there's a slight profit at this price but there may be a loss. Since it's a markdown, the seller gets nothing. Instead, focus the sellers on selling this item instead of marking it down. Keep the price at $100 and offer a $16 spiff. Every time sellers sell one of these items sellers get the spiff right then and there. They get the money in hand, so they see the connection between the sale and the cash. They get $16 instead of $10. That makes them happy and makes them push to sell the item. The store now gets $34. While it's less than the $50 it wanted, it's better than $30.

Spiffs end when they turn into markdowns. Sometimes the spiff makes little change in the sales of an item. Mark the item down and the spiff ends. Selling the item at $80 brings the store close to break-even. Selling it lower still means the store's losing money.

Make it clear to sellers that spiffs are between them and the store. Never talk about spiffs where customers can overhear you.

Here's another way to use spiffs: Place a large order at a discount on an item that sells well at a good profit. Now focus sellers on moving the item with a spiff. Do this only when your sellers are tuned in to spiffs and hunger for them. Sometimes it takes sellers a while to realize how much extra they can earn from spiffs.

Work on having spiffs in your store once sellers hunger for them. A spiff is a special event and it always helps your store to have special events to perk sellers up. This is especially so when the events lead to more cash for sellers. A store with spiffs is a store that's got things going on.

Sellers earn their way into the good times — Some time slots are better than others. We swap sellers when we think a seller can do better than someone who's in a good slot. Keep up your selling to stay in a good slot.

This is how we're paying now —There's no guarantee that we'll always pay like this. We're looking for a way for us all to make extra cash. We think paying commissions will do that but we'll make changes if we need to do so.

A Safe Workplace

The safety poster is available from the Occupational Safety and Health Administration (OSHA,) U.S. Department of Labor.[14] Contact the local office at the address in your phone book. OSHA may refer you to an agency operating an approved State Safety Plan. This is often the State Department of Labor or its like.

Complete Occupational Safety and Health Administration Form 200 each year if you have more than 11 people working for you. This is a summary of injuries and illnesses.

Prepare an emergency exit plan for your store. Write your plan down and put it in a safety *Guide Sheet*.

Locate at least two exits far from each other for use in a fire emergency. Always keep these exits unblocked. Always keep exit routes unblocked too. Mark emergency exit routes with signs.

Train everyone in the use of the plan. Include a way of accounting for everyone outside the store after an emergency exit. Include a plan for helping physically impaired people if you employ any.

Provide the store with fire extinguishers. Maintain them properly. Show the sellers where they are. Show them how to use the extinguishers.

Review your emergency exit plan and your fire extinguisher needs with your local fire department.

Include these points in your safety *Guide Sheet*:

Put safety ahead of all other matters

- Always work safely. This store follows all safety rules and regulations.

- Study the safety poster in the storeroom.

- Know where we keep the first aid kit.

- Report any unsafe practice you see.

---

[14]200 Constitution Avenue N.W., Washington D.C. 20210

- Report any safety hazard you see.

- Report anything that needs repair. We'll do something about it.

- Report all injuries to the manager right away. Report even slight injuries.

- Report it to the manager if you or another worker become ill.

- Follow common sense safety rules

Practice fire safety

- Know where the fire extinguishers are.

- Know how to use the fire extinguishers.

- Keep all fire doors closed. Never wedge them open.

- Know the emergency exit plan for the store.

- Many liquids can catch fire. This is true of some cleaning fluids. As far as possible, use them outside the store. Use them carefully inside the store. Know which fire extinguisher you'll use before using liquids that can catch fire.

- Smoke only in smoking areas.

- Empty ash trays into the toilet.

- Put used matches into the toilet or run water over them in the sink.

- Pour cold water on burns.

Practice electrical safety

- Plug electrical machines directly into wall sockets.

- Avoid the use of 3-way plugs and extension cords with extra outlets.

- Make sure 3-prong electrical plugs still have the third prong on them.

- Check the condition of any extension cords you use.

Take care on stairs

- Walk, never run.

- Take stairs one at a time.

- Store nothing on stairs. Stairs are not shelves. Stairs are for walking only.

Take care when lifting or pulling loads

- Get help when lifting loads that weigh more than twenty pounds.

- Get help when moving furniture.

- Bend at the knees and keep a straight back when lifting loads.

- Keep loads close to your body.

- Avoid twisting your body when lifting loads.

- Lift loads smoothly without jerking them.

- Move heavy loads on a dolly or a chair with wheels.

- Keep your back straight when pulling loads. You can hurt your back pulling loads as easily as lifting loads.

Use chairs and steps safely

- Sit firmly and squarely in chairs. Place your rear firmly at the rear of the chair.

- Make sure all four legs stay on the floor. Rocking a chair on its two back legs is dangerous.

- Stand on a step stool rather than standing on a chair.

- Make sure any chair you stand on is solid. Keep off chairs that fold, roll or tilt.

- Keep off the top two steps of the step ladder. They're to hold the step ladder together. It's too easy to overbalance if you stand on them.

Keep the store and your work area neat and clean

- Put rubbish in proper containers right away.

- Keep the aisles clear.

- Keep exits clear.

- Wipe up all spilled liquids so nobody slips on them.

Push dollies and pushcarts with care around people

- Watch for people who step backwards into pushcarts.

Get the facts on supplies and equipment

- Read all labels before using products new to you.

- Run machines only after someone shows you how to run them safely.

- Operate vehicles only when you have a valid license for the vehicle.

Take care around office and store

- Walk, never run. It's too easy to run into people and things.

- No horseplay or practical jokes.

- Close cabinet doors and desk drawers after use.

- Open doors slowly. Look through the vision panel to be sure nobody's behind a door.

- Stack items only to safe heights.

- Know the emergency exit plan.

Freedom from Harassment

It's important to make your sellers aware of the seriousness of harassment. Also make it clear that sellers carry the burden of their own harassments. The store will not answer for a seller's harassment of another person. People who harass answer personally for their actions and their effects. The store will provide no legal, financial or other help to anyone accused of harassment in a legal action.

Avoid upsetting words or actions not related to work. Say, write or do nothing that upsets people, unless it relates to work. These are some of the obvious forms of harassment:

- "Accidentally" brushing against someone's body.

- Acts of intimidation and violence.

- Asking for sexual services.

- Giving an unwelcome kiss.

- Giving unwanted gifts.

- Grabbing someone.

- Improper touching.

- Leering or ogling.

- Making ethnic slurs.

- Making racial jokes.

- Making suggestive jokes or lustful comments.

- Put downs.

- Putting up sexual pictures.

- Refusing to accept no for an answer.

- Teasing.

- Writing suggestive, racial or ethnic comments.

- Forced sexual relations are the extreme form of sexual harassment.

Stay above the line

You ask someone who's your equal at work to the local coffee shop.
You ask someone who depends on you for promotion for a date.

You accept "No" from someone who doesn't ask you to ask again.
You keep after someone for a date.

You make eye contact while speaking to someone.
You let your eyes roam all over a person's body.

You give someone a friendly pat on the shoulder.
You pat someone on the behind.

You say someone looks nice today.
You say someone's got great legs.

Avoid turning a false step into harassment — It's a false step when you upset someone without meaning to do so. Sometimes it's a real surprise to find something you normally do upsets someone. It's a good plan to say you're sorry and never do it again when that happens. We can all make false steps without meaning harm. It's harassment when you go on upsetting someone who's asked you to stop.

You avoid the issue if you try to prove it doesn't matter. You avoid the issue when you claim what you did was harmless. It's the same when you accuse the other person of being a bad sport or of being too serious. Accept that you upset someone. You see it one way but another person sees it differently. You may see your words or actions as harmless, but they harmed someone.

Always tell the manager about a power harassment — A power harassment is harassment by a person who can affect your career. It's harassment by a person with the power to hire or fire you. It's by a person who's able to change your rate of advance. It's by a person who's able to help or block your career. Typically, the harasser offers job security in exchange for sexual favors. Sometimes the harasser makes the offer openly. Sometimes the offer is disguised so the harasser can deny it took place. Sometimes it takes the form of a joke.

You can never be sure you've cut off a power harassment. It need only occur once. You've said no. The harasser appears to accept your answer. You can never be sure when the payment for saying no will fall due. You've no choice but to tell a person higher than the harasser about a power harassment.

Equal Opportunity

Employment with us is without regard to age, sex, national origin, race, color, creed, political belief, sexual orientation, marital status, status as a disabled veteran, status as a veteran of the Vietnam era, the presence of any physical, mental or sensory disability that doesn't stop someone carrying out needed job functions. We base employment on ability to do the job.

Equal opportunity applies to, but isn't limited to, recruitment, selection and placement, rate of pay, promotion and transfer, discipline, demotion, layoffs and terminations, working conditions, testing and training, awards, compensations and benefits.

Sellers' Discounts

Follow the rules for sellers' discounts yourself. Sellers will notice if you walk out of the store with items without paying and without a receipt. They may be your items, but you flash two signals to your sellers:

1. Inventory control is sloppy in your store. Who's to be sure whether we have 10 watches or 11 watches? What's to keep sellers from helping themselves?

2. You're willing to cheat the business. The sellers will pick up on that. Sellers feel they can cheat too when they see that the boss cheats.

This is a business you're running. Buy from it like the rest of the sellers.

Work out the discount — Make it clear that your sellers can only take discounts on items priced to make a profit. Allow no discounts on give-away prices.

Normally priced items — Sellers who buy normally priced items for their personal use may deduct 40% from the listed price. That means sellers can buy an item you sell at $10 for $6.

Markdowns — Sellers who buy markdowns for their personal use may deduct 40% from the original listed price, not from the marked down price. You price an item at $10 and it sells poorly, so you mark it down to $7. Sellers may buy it at $6. Sometimes the marked down price is lower than the sellers' discount. A $10 item marked down to $5 goes for $6 at the sellers' discount. It's better to buy it as a customer.

Sale items — You sell sale items at cost or at a loss. There are no sellers' discounts on them.

Discounted items — You sell discounted items at cost or at a loss. There are no sellers' discounts on them.

Buy for personal use — Discounts apply to items for sellers' own use. Sellers' own use includes the members of their immediate family and gifts that they give to others. Sellers may not take discounts on items:

- As a favor for a special customer.

- For friends or for relatives outside the immediate family.

- To sell them for profit themselves.

Should anyone press sellers for a discount they shouldn't give, they should explain that they could lose their job over it.

Buy from another seller — Always have another seller ring up discount items. That way it's a clear and open sale. Get a receipt from the other seller so there's no misunderstanding on taking items from the store.

There are no commissions on sellers' discount sales. Selling to another seller is a professional courtesy.

Keep the receipt with the items — All items leaving the store have a receipt with them. There are no exceptions. We reserve the right to inspect all packages and parcels entering or leaving our premises.

Mall Discounts

Managers of other stores set their own mall discounts. Mall discounts in other stores are up to the other stores. All you can do is let other stores know what you do in your store for people who work in the mall. You can ask other managers to follow the same or a similar system.

Let your mall discount apply to all staff who work in the mall: the staff of all other stores and the staff of the mall, from janitors and security staff to managers. Follow a plan based on *Sellers' Discounts*.

Normally priced items — Mall staff who buy for their personal use may take 15% from the list price. That means they can buy an item we sell at $10 for $8.50.

Markdowns — Mall staff who buy markdowns for their personal use may deduct 15% from the original listed price, not from the marked down price. A $10 item sells poorly, so you mark it down to $9. Mall staff may buy it at $8.50. Often the marked down price is lower than the mall discount. A $10 item marked down to $7 goes for $8.50 at the mall discount. It's better to buy it as a customer.

Sale items — No mall discounts on them.

Discounted items — No mall discounts on them.

No commissions on mall discount sales — Mall discounts are a professional courtesy to the people your sellers work with.

Holidays and Vacations

These are the usual paid legal holidays recognized by many states:

New Year's Day	January 1st.
Martin Luther King's Birthday	Third Monday of January.
Presidents' Day[1]	Third Monday of February.
Memorial Day	Last Monday of May.
Independence Day	July 4th.
Labor Day	First Monday in September.
Veterans Day	November 11th.
Thanksgiving Day	Fourth Thursday in November.
The day after Thanksgiving Day	
Christmas Day	December 25th.

[1]Honors the births of George Washington (February 22nd) and Abraham Lincoln (February 12th.)

The Monday after is a holiday when holidays fall on a Sunday. The Friday before is a holiday when holidays fall on a Saturday.

Some states have no recognized paid legal holidays. Give some paid holiday days even if you don't have to give them. You want people to know you as a fair employer.

Some states or businesses add or swap one or more of these holidays:

- Easter Sunday (Between March 21st and April 25th.)

- Good Friday (Friday before Easter Sunday.)

- Day Before New Year's Day (December 31st.)

- Abraham Lincoln's Birthday (February 12th.)

- George Washington's Birthday (February 22nd.)

- Columbus Day (Second Monday in October.)

- Christmas Eve (December 24th, ½ day.)

- Seller's Birthday

- Seller's Marriage Anniversary (Give a like holiday to unmarried sellers.)

- Seller's Child's Birthday (Give a like holiday to sellers without children.)

- Jewish or Other Religious Holidays.

Pay base bay for vacation pay if that this is legal in your state. Besides costing less, paying base pay encourages sellers on commission to take vacation time when sales are low. You may have to pay some other hourly rate. It may be the average hourly rate earned for a given period. You may want to pay more than base pay so sellers know your store as a good place to work.

Take holidays and vacations to refresh — Holidays and vacations give sellers time to rest and relax. Holidays and vacations are times for sellers to enjoy themselves doing special things. They need time off or they'll burn out. Everyone must take some holiday and vacation time. Provide the best holidays and vacations you can because it helps you keep good sellers.

Serve time to take paid holidays and vacations — All holidays and vacations are unpaid until sellers have worked full-time for at least six (6) months.

Work full-time to take paid holidays — List the paid holidays in your store. List any days the store closes, usually New Year's Day, Thanksgiving Day and Christmas day. They're paid holidays for those who've worked full-time for 6 months. Let sellers know you're open all other days. For legal holidays you are open, those who've worked full-time for 6 months get like time off. The manager will set like time off after talking with sellers and reviewing the needs of the store. Some sellers may take the holiday off on the legal holiday day but nobody can rely on it. It depends on how many sellers you need that day. Let sellers ask to be off on one of these days if it's important to them. Try to fit them in, but make no promises. Keep a *Holidays List* of those who've worked on each holiday day in the past. The fewer times a seller worked on a holiday before, the more likely the seller is to work this time. Try to be fair, but make no promise to be fair. The needs of the store come first.

To qualify for holidays with pay sellers must work the scheduled workdays before and after the holiday.

Take religious holidays — Let sellers take time off for their religious holidays. They may use sick leave if they have any available. Otherwise the time off is without pay. Tell sellers to let you know their plans at least two (2) weeks in advance.

Build annual leave — Full-time sellers and half-time sellers qualify for paid vacation time. They begin to build vacation pay after they complete six (6) months of work for the store. Some sellers finish six months of work by the 1st through the 15th of the month. They build vacation pay for the full month. Some sellers finish six months of work by the 16th through the end of the month. They build vacation pay from the first day of the next month.

The hours of vacation sellers build depend on how long they've worked. This is a possible plan. All vacation hours earned are base pay. Full-time sellers work 40 hours a week. Half-time sellers work 20 hours or more, but less than 40 hours a week. Part-time sellers who work less than 20 hours a week don't build annual leave.

Full-time Sellers		
Years Worked	**Vacation Hours Earned Each Month**	**Total Vacation Days Earned Each Year**
Less than five (5)	6.66	10
Five (5) but less than ten (10)	10.00	15
More than ten (10)	13.33	20

Half-time Sellers		
Years Worked	**Vacation Hours Earned Each Month**	**Total Vacation Days Earned Each Year**
Less than five (5)	3.33	5
Five (5) but less than ten (10)	5.00	7.5
More than ten (10)	6.66	10

No other sellers build paid vacation time. Sellers build no vacation pay when they're on leave. Sellers can carry vacation time over to the next year until the end of April. The idea is to get sellers to take their vacations early in the year. After April 30th, sellers lose any vacation time that's owing from last year.

The manager works out the time periods sellers take for vacation bearing in mind the needs of the store. Get sellers to make their needs known as far in advance as possible. Try to honor them, but it may not be possible. The manager spreads out the sellers' vacation periods. It may not be possible for all sellers to take their vacation as a single period. Someone with three weeks of vacation may have to take two weeks and one week, or three separate weeks. Have sellers let you know if it's important to keep their weeks together. Try to do so, but it may not be possible. Since vacation pay is base pay, it's smart for sellers to take their vacation at times when things are slow in the store.

Sometimes a paid holiday falls during a seller's vacation period. Sellers choose whether to take an extra day of vacation or of holiday pay.

The purpose of vacations is for sellers to rest and relax. Avoid paying sellers instead of them taking vacations.

Pay any unused vacation pay when sellers stop working for the store.

Sick Leave and Medical Emergency Leave

Sick leave is for personal short-term illness. Medical emergency leave is paid short-term leave to care for others. Sellers may take medical emergency leave to care for a sick spouse or domestic partner, a child, a sick parent, or a brother or sister who lives in their home.

Lump sick leave and medical emergency leave together. For ease of use shorten "sick leave and medical emergency leave" to "sick leave."

Workers' Compensation has first call. This sick leave plan doesn't apply for illness or injury covered by Workers' Compensation. In this case we give way to state law.

Full-time and part-time sellers who've worked for at least six (6) months may take sick leave.

Sellers on sick leave receive base pay for up to two times the average weekly hours worked on scheduled work days. Suppose sellers work eight hours a day, Monday through Friday. After they've worked for six months they may take eighty hours sick leave a year. Suppose sellers work four hours each Sunday. After six months they may take eight hours sick leave a year.

Any time off during a working day counts first against sick leave. Keep the score in hours, so sellers don't lose a whole day or half day when they see a doctor. After sellers have used their sick leave, any time they take off counts against their earned vacation time. After they've used their vacation pay, time off is without pay. Make sure sellers let you know ahead of time when they know they'll be taking sick leave.

At the end of the calendar year pay any unused sick leave. Pay any unused sick leave when sellers stop working for you. Time taken off before sellers have worked for six months is without pay.

Disability Leave (Including Maternity and Child Care Leave)

Lump disability, pregnancy and child care together. Disability leave includes: leave for disability or illness; leave for pregnancy and maternity;[15] leave to care

---

[15]Pregnancy is the condition of being with child, while maternity is the state of being a mother. To some people maternity includes pregnancy.

for a newly adopted child. It's odd to bundle pregnancy with disability, but that's done under the Federal Pregnancy Act. Include care for a newly adopted child as an alternative to pregnancy. This lets you treat men and women the same.

Sellers who've worked for a year or more may take disability leave. Disability leave is unpaid leave. It lasts for up to ninety (90) days. Sellers may ask for extra thirty (30) day periods if necessary. The maximum time for disability leave is one (1) year. Lay off sellers who are away from work for more than the allowed period of disability leave. They're welcome to apply to work with you again, subject to your usual hiring plans.

Tell sellers to give as much notice as possible of their need for disability leave. Ask for a report on a seller's need for disability leave from an appropriate professional person for each period of disability. These reports are at the seller's expense.

Pay any sick leave due to sellers when disability leave begins. Pay any vacation time owing to sellers if they ask you to.

Sellers earn no sick leave or vacation pay during a leave of more than thirty (30) calendar days.

Ask sellers to give as much notice as possible of their return from disability leave.

For illnesses or physical conditions needing medical treatment, ask for a doctor's report before sellers return. This must say that continued employment in the present position won't risk the seller's health or the health or safety of others. This report is at the seller's expense.

Attendance or job performance may suffer before or after disability leave. Allow for this to the extent required by law. You need not change the work load or give fewer than usual work hours.

Funeral Leave

Full-time and part-time sellers may take funeral leave.

Death of an immediate family member — Sellers will receive base pay for scheduled work hours on up to three days in a row for a death of an immediate family member that occurs locally. Sellers will receive base pay for scheduled work hours on up to five days in a row for a death that occurs out of town.

Other deaths — Sellers will receive base pay for scheduled work hours for one day.

Extra time — Sellers may take additional unpaid funeral leave.

Leave for Jury Duty and Other Time in Court

State and federal laws require you to give sellers time off for jury duty. Never say or hint that you'll help someone get out of jury duty.

State and federal laws may not require you to pay anything to your sellers on jury duty. Pay something unless your back is really against the wall. A store is part of a just society. It pays to play your part. One plan is to pay the difference between jury pay and normal pay. Another is to pay normally and let the sellers keep the jury pay as extra.

Avoid having sellers turn the jury checks over to the store in return for normal wages. It causes extra bookkeeping and possible tax problems. Set limits on how many days and hours of jury duty you'll pay for. Set a qualifying period of employment before you pay for jury duty.

Serve on a jury — The law requires us to allow sellers time off when called for jury duty. We're proud to cooperate on this important civic duty. Let us know within forty-eight (48) hours of receiving a jury summons.

Payment for jury service — Any money the government pays you for jury service is yours to keep. We'll help you avoid losing money because of jury service if you've worked for us at least six (6) months. We limit our help to scheduled work hours during a maximum of ten (10) business days. We'll pay the difference between your jury pay and your regular pay. We base this on your average hours and pay for the past six (6) weeks. To receive jury duty pay, give us a statement of jury service and pay. The court will let you have this document. You must return to work on any day or half-day you're free from jury service.

Testify for the store — All sellers who testify for the store are at work. We pay for all hours in court. We base your hourly pay on your average pay for hours worked during the past six (6) weeks. All sellers summoned to court in any action related to the store must first talk with the store's attorney.

Go to court for other reasons — Sellers may take other time off to appear in court. This time is without pay.

Leave for Military Duty

Full-time staff may take leave for military duty. This leave is for people called to active or reserve military duty or full-time duty with the National Guard. It lasts up to six (6) months. Leave for military duty is unpaid. Sellers may apply any unused vacation pay and sick leave to their military leave if they choose. To take leave for military duty:

• Show your orders to the manager as soon as you receive them.

- Enter military service directly from working in the store.

Apply for re-employment within ninety (90) days of your discharge. Show your discharge papers.

Leave to Vote

It's important for citizens to vote in local, state and national elections. The polls are open long hours so sellers can usually vote before or after work. Sellers can take up to two (2) hours leave to vote if they need to vote during working hours. Leave to vote is unpaid leave. Sellers can use any unused sick leave or vacation leave for leave to vote if they wish. Have sellers let the you know they'll be taking leave to vote at least two weeks ahead of time.

Worker's Compensation

State law requires you to pay part of sellers' earnings into an Industrial Insurance Plan. Many people call the Industrial Insurance Plan "Workers' Compensation." The law requires you to take and send in sellers' payments from each paycheck they receive. The law also requires the store to pay part of each seller's coverage.

The Industrial Insurance Plan covers sellers for work related injuries and occupational illnesses. It covers sellers for all approved medical, hospital and related services needed for their treatment and recovery. It also gives wage replacements should sellers be unable to work for a while.

Unemployment Insurance

The store pays all costs of sellers' coverage by the Federal/State system of unemployment insurance.

Only workers unemployed through no fault of their own qualify for unemployment insurance payments. They must be physically able to work and must take any suitable worked offered to them right away. They must actively seek work by making personal contacts with possible employers during each week they claim benefits. Workers who quit work without good cause get no benefits. Neither do discharged workers nor suspended workers and persons who refuse suitable work offered to them.

To receive benefits, workers must have worked 680 hours in a base year, or in the last four completed calendar quarters.

Social Security

The law requires sellers to pay part of their earnings to a fund for Social Security Insurance. You must take and send in their payments from each paycheck they receive. For every dollar sellers pay into the fund you also pay in a dollar.

"At Will" Employment

Guard the "At will" employment status jealously—do nothing that clouds it. Write nothing in a *Guide Sheet*, *News Sheet*, *Message* or other written document that undercuts the "At will" status. Say nothing in interviews, *Sellers' Meetings* or face-to-face that goes against the "At will" status.

Avoid the terms "permanent employment," "permanent employee," "regular employment," "regular employee" and the like. Avoid the words "temporary employment," "temporary employee" and the like. Where you have temporary workers, it follows you also have permanent workers. Avoid the terms "trial period" or "probationary status" and the like. Where there is a period of trial or probation the period after the trial or probation is permanent.

Trying to have your cake and eat it may lead you into trouble. Telling sellers it's a condition of employment to stay through the Christmas rush can haunt you when you let them go in May. So can asking for two weeks notice when sellers quit. You may have to give two weeks notice, or two weeks pay, when you let them go.

Understand "At will" employment — All employment with your store is "At will." This means that either a seller or the store can end the employment with or without cause, with or without notice, at any time, except as otherwise provided by law.

"At will" employment applies to all employees without regard to the length of employment. "At will" employment applies to all employees without regard to any benefits or awards given to employees.

"At will" status is a condition of your employment by our store. Our store neither expresses nor implies any contract of employment other than "At will." No events arising from your employment will alter your "At will" status unless specifically set out in writing and signed by you and the owner of the store.

Payday

Follow standards on payday. Most states require you to have a regular payday. Paydays usually can't be more than a month apart. Payday once a week or once every two weeks is usual in retail.

Pay once every two weeks. You halve bookkeeping and paperwork when you pay every two weeks instead of weekly. Only pay once a week when you see a business need to do so. Perhaps other retailers in your area pay once a week and you must do likewise to get sellers.

Some retailers claim your sellers are less likely to steal from your till if you pay them weekly. They claim that sellers who are poor cash managers get desperate during the second week.

Pick up your paycheck every second Thursday — We pay you by work periods. Each work period is two (2) weeks long and ends at midnight on a Sunday. We get the checks ready to pay you by the afternoon of the following Thursday. Suppose a work period runs from Monday, April 11th to Sunday, April 24th. We have the checks ready on Thursday, April 28th. The manager gives you your paycheck on Thursday afternoon.

Pick your check up the next time you come to work if you're off work on Thursday afternoon. It's on you own time and expense if you're off work Thursday afternoon but come in to pick up your check. Call ahead to make sure the check's ready. The manager will mail your check to your home address or your bank if you prefer.

Let us know ahead of time if you plan on cashing your check at the cash register. We can only cash payroll checks if we have enough cash on hand.

Expect deductions from your paycheck — The law requires us to make deductions from your paycheck. These may include federal, state and local income tax withholding, state disability deductions and other authorized deductions. We list all deductions on your pay stub.

Complete a W-4 form — The income tax deducted depends on your earnings and on the number of exemptions you claim on your W-4 form. At the end of the year we give you a W-2 form telling you the total income tax deducted for the year.

Head Hunting Payments

Sellers may know people they think would work well in your store. Have sellers let the manager know about them. Then have them apply, mentioning the seller's name. For each person you hire, pay the seller a hundred (100) dollars when you hire. After six (6) months of satisfactory service, pay another hundred (100) dollars. These payments don't apply to staff whose job it is to hire people.

What Customers Can Expect from Sellers

It's important to be clear what customers can expect from sellers right from the beginning. The more you tell your sellers up front when they're new with you, the better for you in the long run.

Know the Store's Mission

The *Mission Statement* tells us what business this store is in. Stores that try to be everything to everyone only limp along, so we've made some decisions about what we want to be. The *Mission Statement* includes the kind of items we sell and sets out our values. It's a good guide to steer us day-to-day. It keeps us on track when we get mixed up or when others push us to be something else. It stops us wasting energy by spreading ourselves too thin. Sellers are at ease with customers when they know what the store stands for. Their mind has a focus to it.

Read the Mission Statement every day — Make sure all sellers read the *Mission Statement* before they begin selling on a shift. File it in *Daily* so they see it every day.

Help Customers Meet Their Personal Needs

Customers have needs that may not relate directly to selling to them. Go out of your way to service these needs promptly and politely.

Direct customers to the washrooms — Many customers ask where the washrooms are. Have sellers give clear directions to the nearest washrooms and to other washrooms. In some shopping centers the washrooms get crowded at certain times. You score points with customers when you direct them to less crowded washrooms off the beaten track.

Direct customers to the pay phones — See that your sellers can give directions to the pay phones. Many customers will ask where they are. Telling them cuts down on customers asking to use the store's phone. There's no gain by offering to let them use the store's phone.

Let customers who ask use the store's phone — Some customers will ask to use the store's phone. You'll let them use it if customer service is the prime thing on your mind. Seeing the phone can act as a trigger to customers asking to use it. Fewer customers will ask to use it if you keep the store's phone out of sight. Have a long cord on any phone customers may use. Then you can control where customers use it. Put in phones with the dial on the base instead of on the handset. Dial for customers. The problem with a cordless phone is you risk losing control. Customers can stroll to one side and dial an overseas number.

You may need another phone if the store's phone is too busy to let customers use it. You need it for the business you're missing. Try a phone that only reaches local numbers when you go to more than one phone. That's the one to let customers use.

Suppose you're swamped by customers using the store's phone. Then you'll have to tell customers the phone is "tied up for a while." Direct them to the pay phones. Give them the coins to use the pay phone if you have to.

Some reps also ask to use the phone. Quick calls to make contacts are OK. Longer calls to get business done for our store are OK. Watch for reps who try to use our store as their office. Let them know you want to keep the store's phone clear for business use. Be polite, but you can be plainer with reps than with customers.

Direct customers to banks and bank machines — Some customers ask for a bank or a bank machine. See that sellers know the nearest ones. Keep a list of the nearest branch of all major banks, with directions on how to get there.

Call taxis for customers — Keep a list of taxis in the *Quick Phone List* by the phone.

Know the Tourist Places

Always have something for tourists. You can start with a brochure on your town from the tourist office. Customers like it when you think about them like this. Develop a *Tourist Sheet* with the help of your sellers. List the "must-see" places. Have the sellers add personal comments like "Spend at least 2 hours at the Science Museum, it's super fun—Cindy Jones." Include a restaurant list. Put personal comments for each restaurant. "This is my favorite restaurant. Try the crab fettuccine—Tom Jones." First put the restaurant list together from the sellers' ideas. Then send sellers to restaurants as a reward for good selling. Have them bring back a report and add it to the list.

Put together an Awareness Program — Keep a library of tourist books and maps for use in the store. Have sellers read parts of the books and use the maps from time to time. It's OK to share them with tourists, but keep them in the store. Keep a supply of city maps from the Tourist Bureau to give to tourists. Also have a ferry schedule on hand.

Use the Tourist Sheet — Tourists often ask about your town. Make a list—*Our Favorite Places*. Include restaurants. Tourists go for this personal touch. Give copies to customers who show an interest or who look like tourists. See that all sellers know about all places on the list. See that they know how to get to all places on the list. Ask sellers for ideas on updating the list. *Our Favorite Places* can help to get sellers schmoozing with customers.

Know How Customers Can Buy

Spell out what your store takes in addition to U.S. cash

Credit and debit cards — List all cards the store takes.

U.S. and Canadian checks — List your check policy. Unless there's good reason not to, take personal checks or travelers checks from anywhere in the U.S. or Canada.

List the Canadian cash you take — Take Canadian bank notes, travelers checks and personal checks. Take no Canadian coins, not even the $1 and $2 coins Canadians call loonies and toonies, unless your bank will take them from you.

Know the rate of exchange on Canadian cash — The seller in charge of the day posts the rate on the Canadian dollar as *Today's Rate*. Have all sellers check the rate as soon as they come on shift. Check that sellers can tell the rate without looking at *Today's Rate*.

Put items on layaway — See that sellers know about layaways if you take them.

Take All Returns

Take all returns without question. Commit to customer satisfaction. It's in your interest as well as in the interest of customers. Every upset customer tells ten others while every satisfied customer tells five others. By taking returns you replace ten bad reports with five good reports.

Take returns politely — Say nothing to make customers who make returns feel foolish. Be cheerful and smiling. Some customers do feel foolish about making returns. They may apologize for making trouble. Let them know it's OK to make returns. Some customers are tense when making a return. They expect it to be difficult. To defend the return they need to make you or the store wrong. They can be sharp and hostile. They can be angry and loud. Help them through this difficult time. Keep calm. Being sharp and hostile yourself won't help to set things right. Let customers vent their feelings fully. They'll feel better once they get them out. Accept their point of view. Apologize: "I'm sorry you had to go through this, Mr. Jones." Let them know it's OK to make a return.

Ask to see the receipt — The easiest returns are those where the customer has the receipt. That way we know the customer bought the items from us. The price and how the customer paid are clear.

Use judgment on the return if the customer has no receipt. In most cases, trust the customer. That's easy if you made the sale yourself or if you know the customer. That's easy if the customer's a registered customer. Otherwise, go by your feeling about the customer.

Ask for an ID card if you suspect a shoplifter is turning stolen items into cash. Say nothing about shoplifting. Some customers may ask why you need an ID card. Say, "That's our policy on returns without a receipt." Give no other explanation. Repeat this explanation as many times as necessary. Some customers may protest about you not trusting them. Smile and say, "I'm sorry, Sir—but that's our policy on returns without a receipt." Usually don't refuse to do something because of a policy. This case is an exception.

Asking for an ID card won't upset most customers. Shoplifters won't like to show you their ID card. Say to customers who can't produce a receipt or an ID card, "I'm sorry for the trouble this causes, Sir. I'll be happy to take the return when you come back with your receipt or ID card." Prepare a *News Sheet* when a suspicious customer tries to make a return without a receipt or an ID card. Let the other sellers know what happened. Shoplifters trying to turn items into cash often try again on a different day with a different seller.

Ask customers what they need to make them happy — Say, "I'm sorry that you've had this trouble, Mrs. Jones. What do you need to put this right?" Sometimes customers want to replace a flawed item with a good one. Sometimes they want a discount on an item. Sometimes they want to put the price towards a different item. Sometimes they want their money back. These solutions are all fine. Sometimes customers have other ideas. These solutions are fine too if you think they're reasonable and you can handle them. Now and then customers will make outrageous demands. Perhaps a customer demands you fire the seller who made the sale. Perhaps a customer asks for a free trip to Hawaii to make up for frustration and lost time. Smile, as if the customer made a joke. Say, "A trip to Hawaii would certainly be nice, but that's beyond me. I can certainly give you your money back."

Suggest other items when it's right to do so — Often customers return items because they don't meet their needs. It's clear the sellers who made the sales didn't find out the needs fully. Perhaps you can do that now and sell something else instead of giving money back. Put no pressure here. Only sell something else if the customer goes along with it easily.

Customers don't have to tell you why they want to return items. Never press them if they don't want to tell. Most customers do tell you why they're making a return. Let the manager know the reason when they tell it to you.

Take back destroyed items — Sometimes customers destroy items and then return them. Take the items back. The items didn't work out as the customer expected. Stand by what you sell. The cost to the store is a form of advertising. Customers will speak about the store with respect. Refusing to accept the destroyed items will spread bad publicity. Customers will only say you refused to take a return. They won't say they destroyed the items.

Keep returns out of normal selling steps — There are only two cases where sellers mention returns while selling:

1. The customer brings up returns. "Can I get my money back if I buy this and don't like it?" "Certainly. You can get your money back with no problems."

2. The seller uses the *Buyer Protection Plan* to make a sale.

Sellers who suggest, "You can return it if you don't like it," get too many returns. They plant the idea of returns in customers' minds. They plant the idea that the items are low quality. These seeds grow and invite returns. Even the mildest customer returns items for the smallest reasons.

Keep Cool with Angry Customers

Even if you run your store perfectly your sellers will have to deal with angry customers from time to time. Give them the tools to turn angry customers into loyal repeat customers.

Keep cool even when customers are rude — Sometimes customers get angry. It never helps to get angry too. It never helps to judge the customer. Control any angry self-talk that goes on in your mind. Instead tell yourself customers are going through a tough time. Tell yourself you need to help them.

Let customers let off steam — Let everything that's making customers angry come out. Wait till customers go flat before you say anything. Angry customers are wonderful. Get them to spill the beans. Make your attitude one of, "Tell me more." Angry customers want to buy. They want a fair deal they can understand. Their anger comes from a frustrated desire to buy.

Agree with complaints — Agree with complaints and tell customers the problem in your words. "I see—it's impossible to follow the instructions for putting the chest of drawers together."

Say you're sorry — Share in customers' feelings by saying you're sorry. Say, "I'm sorry you've had to go through this." Say, "I'm sorry I've caused you so much pain" when the anger's aimed at you.

Avoid anger words when talking to angry customers. Avoid the words "anger," "angry" and "upset." Getting angry or upset are things people do to themselves. You'll never calm customers down by suggesting they're angry or upset. "Suffering pain" or "going through something" comes from things other people do. That's the picture to paint for angry customers.

Suggest a solution or ask for advice — Try one or more what-ifs. "What if we put it together for you?" "What if I show you how we put them together?"

Find out the needs. Sometimes you can't try a what-if because you're not sure what the customer wants. The fireplace you sold smoked up the house. Is the customer looking for a way to stop it smoking? Does the customer want you to clean the whole house and replace all its furnishings? Ask, "How do you see us making this problem go away?" Accept the answer when it seems reasonable and you can handle it, or try some more what-ifs.

Thank customers for letting you know about problems — As they leave, thank customers for bringing problems to you. By that time some of them feel they've made too much fuss. Let them know the meeting pleased you. Avoid any backbiting, even in your own mind. Keep your thoughts about customers positive and make sales.

Suggest a Taxi for Delivery

For most stores, delivery services are a thing of the past. So unless yours is the unusual store that's found how to make deliveries pay, fall back on suggesting a taxi for delivery.

Say, "No" politely when customers ask for deliveries — Say, "I'm sorry but we don't make deliveries ourselves."

Act as if most customers take a taxi for deliveries — Continue with, "Most customers who need a delivery take their items in a taxi. I can easily call one for you. Would you like that?" Suggest a station wagon taxi if the items are very large. Suggest a taxi that takes a credit card if spare cash is a problem. Call a taxi from the *Quick Phone List*.

Offer to put the items on hold for be-backs — Some customers want the taxi later. Some customers want to call friends or family for a ride. Offer the use of the store's phone. Some customers want to go home and return with a vehicle. Sell the items now and you're sure you've made the sale. Some customers say they'll come back to buy later but usually that's the last you see of them. Say to these be-backs, "That's fine—let's make the sale now and I'll hold the items for you. That way you can be sure of the items and there'll be no delay when you're ready to go." Suggest buying now to be sure of the items even when the store is overstocked on an item. Who knows what'll happen next? Perhaps a tour bus will come in and everyone will buy the same item.

Special Orders

Always take "orders" for items you carry but are out of stock. If you've decided against other orders, let your sellers know this. Let them know:

- Special orders are more expensive than normal stock.

- Special orders need special attention.

- Customers often don't pick up special orders.

- You stock a wide choice of items that customers need.

- You usually have enough items for customers to choose from.

Let customers know when items come back in stock — Sometimes customers see something and decide to buy later. They ask about it later when it's out of stock. Offer to let customers know when it's back in stock if it's an item we usually carry. Get each customer's name and phone number. Add it to the *Customer Call List* in the *Receive and Handle Deliveries* section of *Daily*. Call the customer when the item comes back in stock. You get the chance to make the customer your *Personal Customer*. Get the customer to come at a time you're working and ask for you by name

If you've decided special orders pay off for you, spell out the steps for taking them.

Hold Items for Customers to Help Sales

Although holding items for customers has its own problems, sometimes holding an item turns "no sale" into a sale.

Hold items when customers ask — Sometimes customers ask if you'll hold items for them. Often it's something heavy or awkward. They may want their hands free while they do other shopping. They may need to call or go for an automobile. Sometimes they don't have enough cash with them. They ask to pay a deposit and return with the rest of the cash.

Suggest holding the items when customers waver — Where some customers ask if you'll hold the items, others waver—they sway to-and-fro, they feel or show doubt. You know they want the items. They make all the right noises. Suddenly, they realize the items are awkward or find they haven't enough cash. Then they make the wrong noises. You're going to lose these sales unless you do something about them. That's the time to offer to hold the items. Suggest a hold only when you must do it to make a sale. There's little space to store holds.

Ring up the payment or part payment — Get a payment to hold the items. A payment makes the customer return. The more you get the more likely the customer will return. Most customers expect to pay when they ask you to hold. Act as though you expect full payment unless you're holding it because of lack of cash. Tell customers they'll only need to show the receipt to pick up the items quickly.

Choose when to hold with no payment — You can choose to hold items with no payment. Sometimes customers phone first and head for the store to pick up the last of an item. Perhaps you know the customer. You can make a good impression on customers who came out with no cash by holding items for them.

Write a Hold Slip — Write on a blank sheet from a note pad and follow this pattern:

HOLD FOR	*Maria Gonzales*
PHONE	*123-1234*
UNTIL	*4 pm Wed, March 23rd 1994*
TOTAL	*39.95*
PAID	*20.00*
TO PAY	*19.95*
RECEIPT	*12345*

Jean Jones 11.30 am Wed, March 23rd 1994

Make a contract on the pick up time. Ask customers when they'll pick up, then say, "I have this down for pick up by 4 pm today. OK?" Wait for an answer. Ask again if you need to. That fixes the need to make the pick up in the customer's mind. It cuts down complaints from customers who come for items late and find we've sold them.

Be clear about payments. Write the total for the items on the *Hold Slip*. Take away the amount the customer has paid. Write the amount left to pay. Include the receipt number. Write down the three amounts so we're clear on payments. Include the receipt number as a cross-check. One seller may have to deal with another's *Hold Slip*. A seller may have to deal with a customer who's lost the receipt.

Fix Hold Slips on bags, not items — Tape or staple *Hold Slips* on bags not on items. Keep the items in good shape. Sometimes customers don't come back for holds. We need to be able to sell them to someone else without marking them down.

Store the items in the Hold Area — Look in the *Supplies and Materials List* for the *Hold Area*.

Check receipts when customers pick up holds — Ask to see the customer's receipt if another seller made the hold. "Please let me see your receipt so I can find the right items." It's your decision on releasing items without a receipt. Usually, there's no point making a fuss. We've had no problems with false claims so far. Write down the customer's ID card if the items are expensive or you feel uneasy.

Finish sales — All cash paid at the time of the hold was a prepayment. Suppose the total was $39.95 including tax and the customer paid $39.95. Change the prepayment of $39.95 to a payment when the customer picks up the items. Suppose the total was $39.95 including tax and the customer put down a part payment of $20. Change the prepayment of $20 to a payment when the customer pays the other $19.95.

Phone overdue holds and set a new pick up time — *Daily* has someone check the *Hold Area* for overdue holds regularly. Phone and make contact once. You may need to leave a message for someone on a different shift to try at a different time of day. Set a new time for pick up when you make contact. Write the new time on the *Hold Slip*.

Flush overdue holds — Keep holds moving. Some customers don't pick up their holds. Sometimes sellers can't make contact with the customer by phone. Sometimes the customer sets another pick up time but still doesn't pick up the items. Return the items to the active stock. Put the *Hold Slip* in the *Flushed Holds Pocket* in *Daily*.

Refund on flushed holds that are out of stock — Try to keep the sale alive when customers come late for holds. Check the *Hold Area*. The hold may still be there. Check the *Flushed Holds Pocket* to make sure someone flushed the hold. Finish the sale if the items are still in stock. Make a refund when the items are out of stock. Be pleasant but clear to the customer.

"I'm sorry, Mrs. Gonzales. We called several times but got no answer. So we returned the items to stock. All I can do is give you a refund. Is there something else you'd like instead?"

"I'm sorry, Mr. Jones. We returned the items to stock when they weren't picked up as arranged. All I can do is give you a refund. Is there something else you'd like instead?"

Refuse Requests for Mail Orders Politely

It's only now and then that a customer asks about mail orders. Mail order is a separate way of doing business. To take mail orders we'd need to set our store up to handle them. At present it's not a direction we plan to go.

Say, "No" when customers ask for mail orders — Be polite—say, "I'm sorry but we don't handle mail orders."

Avoid special favor mail orders — We'll either do mail orders properly or not at all. At present our decision is not to do them.

Refuse Requests for Personal Charges Politely

A personal charge is a charge made against a customer's signature or on the store's own credit card—we have neither system. Personal charge systems cost a lot to set up and run properly. Systems set up by dabblers always lose money for the store. Be polite—say, "I'm sorry but we only charge against major credit cards."

Layaways

Make sure sellers know what layaways are in case customers ask for them.

If you don't take them, sellers say, "I'm sorry but we don't handle layaways. Would you like to place it on a credit card?"

If you take them, spell out the steps for handling them. Always begin by keeping the layaway open but trying to avoid its paperwork and storage. Say, "Yes, a layaway's fine, or would you prefer to use a credit card?"

CHAPTER 9

KEEP ON TOP OF THE STORE

The material in this chapter aims at keeping basic order and tidiness in the store. While Chapter 12 *Run Shifts*, covers background jobs that sellers do before, during and after selling, the topics here are a more basic background to running the store.

Schedule Sellers

Follow local employment standards covering meal breaks, rest breaks, overtime pay, and so on. Keep these rules in mind as you set schedules. Check your state's employment standards. Check with the Department of Labor and Industries or its equivalent. Ask if there are any city standards. The models used here may vary from those in your state and city.

Be flexible — Lean backwards to give sellers the schedules they want. Get sellers to let you know their needs. Perhaps some sellers go bowling on Tuesday nights. There's no point asking them to work then if others can do so. Remember there are limits to what you can do. You have a commitment to keep the store open for customers. Many of them shop at times normal people take off. Times like Friday nights, Christmas Eve, and so on. Sellers aren't normal—they're in retail, so they work when most people play. They're good times to make money. Sellers may be working with you because they can fill certain time slots. There'll be times when sellers' personal needs and the store's needs clash. The store's needs always come first. Be tough when you have to, but don't let that be your usual way.

Avoid scheduling sellers too often — You'll solve your short-term problem, but lose when burnout comes. Be careful to give sellers enough rest between shifts. It's unwise to follow a late night Friday with a Saturday morning shift.

Fit good sellers into good slots — Put your good sellers on weekends. Let slower sellers mind the store on Mondays and Tuesdays.

Schedule unusual hours — Include any extra unusual hours as part of the sellers' normal schedules. You may have to pay overtime or call-back pay. Keep costs as low as possible, without giving up the unusual extra hours.

Check that call-back is OK under the employment standards you live by. Schedule *Background Jobs* if call-back is out of the question.

Watch the costs of overtime pay — As you schedule, bear in mind the costs of overtime pay. Most local standards require you to pay time and a half for any hours a seller works over 40 hours a week. Some require overtime pay for any hours over 8 hours a day. Find out if you can let sellers work 10 hours a day, four days a week, without paying overtime. Here's how overtime pay works supposing base pay is $5 an hour and you only pay base pay:

40 hours	@	5.00	=	200
10 hours	@	7.50	=	75
50 hours				275

Suppose you pay commissions and commissions on sales for 50 hours amount to $370. $370 for 50 hours work is $7.40 an hour. Ten of those hours were overtime at time and a half. That's $11.10 an hour. You still have to pay 10 x $3.70 ($37) to come up to legal standard.

Know the extra cost when you put your hotshot sellers on overtime. Their overtime pay relates to base pay when base pay is more than they earn on commissions. Otherwise it relates to what they earn.

Employ sellers less than full-time to avoid paying overtime. That way you have some room to work with when there's a push and you need sellers to work extra time.

Pay a shift premium when you have to — All stores have dead shifts. You're open Monday mornings, but you rarely see a customer. You need someone to keep the store open and do *Background Job*s. Normal pay is minimum wage paid against commissions but there are few commissions on a dead shift and base pay rarely attracts anyone. You may have to pay extra to get sellers to work these shifts.

Check your local standards to make sure you can pay different rates for shifts at different times. Keep the shift premium separate from base pay. It's special extra pay for working a special shift. It ends when you move the seller to a normal shift.

Pay a job premium for some important jobs — Some *Special Jobs* take a seller away from selling for a block of hours. Help with the bookkeeping and depositing the sales draft stacks are good examples. Sellers doing *Special Jobs* lose the chance for commissions. Set these jobs up in slow time and pay a premium for doing them. Schedule sellers for some hours selling and some hours on *Special Jobs*.

Allow for meal breaks — Typically meal breaks:

- Are unpaid.

- Last at least 30 minutes.

- Last 45 minutes or less—Talk to your sellers about the length of meal break they need.

- Begin 2 hours or more from the start of a shift.

- Begin 5 hours or less from the start of a shift.

Schedule working meal breaks if you need them. It's easy to schedule meal breaks when you have enough sellers to overlap the breaks. You may have a problem where you have one or two sellers only. In most states sellers can work during a meal break on the employer's time. They take a meal break in the store and interrupt it to sell. Total break time, excluding the selling, adds up to the required meal break. Make a separate payment over and above commission earnings to sellers who take a working meal break. Pay a full hour of base pay. Remember this extra hour when working out overtime.

Check that your local standards allow working meal breaks. Let new sellers know about this plan when you employ them. Make it a condition of employment. Local standards may call for a meal break before sellers go on overtime. A 30 minute meal break is usual before working 3 or more extra hours after a full work day.

Allow for rest breaks — Typically rest breaks:

- Are paid.

- Last at least 10 minutes for each 4 hours worked.

- Begin 3 hours or less from the start of the shift.

- Are as near as possible to the middle of the shift.

Schedule broken rest breaks if you need them. It's easy to schedule rest breaks when you have enough sellers to overlap the breaks. You may have a problem where you have one or two sellers only. Most states allow a broken rest break if the pieces add up to a rest break. Sellers take their breaks in pieces as they fit in. Then you needn't schedule a rest break at a special time. Total break time, excluding the selling, adds up to the required break. Check that your local standards allow broken breaks. Let new sellers know about this plan when you employ them. Make it a condition of employment.

Schedule sellers and set their duties — All selling includes the *Background Jobs* that go along with selling. Set these jobs clearly:

- Seller in Charge of the Start of the Day.

- Seller in Charge of Each Shift.

- Seller in Charge of Each Cash Drawer Used in Each Shift.

- Sellers Using Each Cash Drawer.

- Seller in Charge of the End of the Day.

Include *Special Jobs* sellers do on set days in the schedule too.

Set schedules ahead of time — Post the work schedules in *Daily* two weeks ahead of time. Have sellers who see a problem with their schedule let you know right away.

Make sure sellers know their shifts — Have sellers sign off on their shifts as soon as they're posted. Have sellers check their shifts in *Daily* each time they work. Send *Messages* to sellers if you need to change shifts.

Give two OKs for swapping schedules — Suddenly something comes up that John needs to do. He finds a seller who'll swap with him. That's OK, *if the manager agrees*. Both sellers swapping need an OK from the manager—one OK's not enough. It's too easy for one seller arrange a "swap" and the other seller not know it. You may say no to the swap. The seller John chooses may not have skills needed for his slot. Perhaps the seller he chooses is taking on too much and you want to head off burnout. Control who'll be in the store.

Make a Floor Plan

Make a floor plan and see that your sellers use it until they know it by heart.

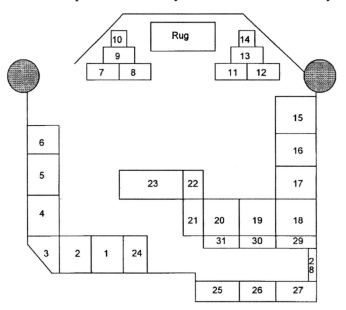

Your floor plan is your own and only you can make it. Having a floor plan gives you a high level of control of your store. Expect to see a payoff in keeping your store looking good to customers. That means extra sales. Expect to see a payoff in managing your displays and storage. That means extra profit.

Make the numbering plan easy to follow. Start from a place that stands out. Run the numbers clockwise. Letter all shelves, drawers, or other sub-units from the bottom up. It's easy to learn this system. Put the numbers on the units but keep them out of sight of customers to avoid a mechanical look to your store. There's no need to put letters on shelves and drawers, since they all go from the bottom upwards. The lowest shelf is always "a," the one above it "b," and so on.

As your store changes, some of the unit numbers get out of order. Live with that until it creates too many problems. Then renumber all the units and start again.

Number and Name the Items

Each item on the *Price List* has a number and a name. Sellers learn a few at a time. They'll pick up numbers and names as they work with items. Follow a standard system like the one set out below.

Item numbers have two parts: 123-1234. The first part's a group number. All scissors sold separately are in group 235. All knives sold separately are in group 236. Group numbers are always three digits long and never end in a zero. Numbers 123 and 256 are group numbers. Numbers 56, 120 and 2345 aren't group numbers.

The second part's the "item in group" number. 6-inch Left Hand Scissors have the number 235-1246. 8-inch Left Hand Scissors have the number 235-1248.

"Item in group" numbers are always four digits long. Numbers -1234 and -1246 are "item in group" numbers. Numbers -12, -123 and -12345 aren't "item in group" numbers. "Item in group" numbers have no meaning without group numbers to go with them. The same "item in group" numbers crop up in different groups. There's item 123-1234 and there's item 124-1234.

Sellers soon pick up the group numbers. Then they pick up the numbers of items they sell most. Then they'll pick up the rest. Most names are easy—they describe the item.

Spell out number and name to stop mix-ups — It's easy to write a number so it looks like a different number. Sellers know you have the wrong number when they see "688-8353 Black Cat" listed when you sell "688-8353 Brown Dog" and "688-8358 Black Cat."

Some names are nearly the same as others. Sellers know they have the wrong name when they see "256-1201 Blue Skirt" listed when you sell "149-1756 Blue Skirt" and "256-1201 Blue Shirt."

Fix bad numbers — Sometimes a *Pricer* puts the wrong number on an item. Re-label the items with the right number and price. First re-label the items on display. Then re-label the items in storage. Put out a *News Sheet* on the correction so sellers can watch out for the problem. That'll also get the attention of the seller who put the bad label on the item.

Use the Price List

The form of your *Price List* is up to you. Write on 3″ x 5″ or 5″ x 8″ index cards. Prepare written, typed or word-processed lists. Set up a computer database system. Each has its advantages and disadvantages. Set up what you're comfortable with and what you can afford. This is a sample *Price List* entry:

> 111-0005   CNDLSNUF   Candle Snuffer
>
> Price: 19.00   Markdown: Sale Price: Spiff:
>
> Display Shelf 2b: 6   Storage Shelf 2b: 24   Reorder at: 18

Spell out item number and name — Always use number and name to be clear about the item. Report "111-0005 Candle Snuffer," not "111-0005" and not "Candle Snuffer."

Use and learn the store's name for each item. The Small Earthenware Bowl may look large to you. The supplier may call it Terracotta Dish. Still call it the Small Earthenware Bowl.

Any short form of a name is OK. The short forms of the names on the *Price List*, like CNDLSNUF, are those used in the electronic cash register. It's hard to remember them. Any short form of a name is OK, as long as it goes with a number. Both "111-0005 C Snuf" and "111-0005 Can Snuf" are OK.

Know the price line — Most items have only a price entry. That's the price you want to sell it at. Prices may change. Begin by trying to sell items at a good profit. Often you'll find you can only sell them at the usual profit, so you change the prices.

Some items you'll mark down because they sell poorly.

> 111-0005   CNDLSNUF   Candle Snuffer
>
> Price: 19.00   Markdown: 9.99   Sale Price: Spiff:
>
> Display Shelf 2b: 6   Storage Shelf 2b: 24   Reorder at: No More

In that case list the markdown price as well as the price. Also change the "Reorder at:" quantity to "No More." There's less profit than you need on this item at the markdown price. For all markdowns, first put on the regular price tag. Cross it through with a pen. Put on the markdown price tag so the customer can also see the usual price. Remember, markdown items carry no commissions.

Some items you'll sell as sale items.

111-0005   CNDLSNUF   Candle Snuffer

Price: 19.00   Markdown: Sale Price: 9.99   Spiff:

Display Shelf 2b: 6   Storage Shelf 2b: 24   Reorder at: No More

Probably you'll make no money on them. For a sale item, the *Price List* has list price and the sale price filled in. Put "Sale" price tags on sale items. Sale price tags include the list price crossed out as well as the sale price. Remember, sale items carry no commissions.

Some items carry spiffs.

111-0005   CNDLSNUF   Candle Snuffer

Price: 19.00   Markdown: Sale Price: Spiff: 5.00

Display Shelf 2b: 6   Storage Shelf 2b: 24   Reorder at: No More

Then the price line has price and the value of the spiff on it. The spiff is the amount that sellers get for selling the item at the normal price. Spiffs are between sellers and the store. Make sure sellers keep quiet about them with customers. Remember, sellers take no commission when they take a spiff. Spiffs pay more than commissions.

Use the display and storage lines — The display entry tells which display counter or shelf the display is on. It also gives the number of items on display. The storage entry tells on which storage shelf to store extra items. It also gives the highest number of items to keep on the shelf.

Reorder items at the "Reorder at:" number — Work out when to reorder. In the sample entry for the *Price List* the number of display items is 6. The storage number is 24. The reorder at number is 18. Start with 6 (display) + 24 (storage) = 30 items in the store. Every time you sell an item, the total in the store drops by 1. It's time to reorder when the number of items in the store drops to 18.

Usually place new orders based on the daily reports of sales. Now and again the numbers get mixed up. Ask a seller to take a *Spot Check* of an item to see if you've reached the reorder number.

Keep Up Displays and Storage

Place great stress on your sellers keeping displays "in shape." A display is in shape when it looks nice and has the full number of items.

Keep displays in shape — A seller sets up a display when a new item comes in stock. The seller notes the display place and number of items on the *Price List*. Customers soon put displays out of shape. Then it's up to sellers to put the displays back in shape.

Fill gaps with fill-in displays — Sometimes a store sells all of an item in storage and most or all of the display. This leaves a gap in the displays. Fill the gap with something else. Perhaps the display next to it should have 10 items. Put out 20 instead. Perhaps the gap is on display counter 5. Put out a copy of a display that's on display counter 12. Make a note of a fill-in display on the *Fill-in Display List* in *Daily*. That way another seller knows to take it down when a new shipment of the original display item comes in.

Keep storage in shape — Storage for an item is in shape when you can get at items in storage easily. Sellers who set up displays set up storage for extra items. They note the storage place and number of items on the *Price List*. Sometimes sellers get in a rush and storage goes out of shape. Put the storage back in shape when things slow down.

Store Highlight Signs when displays end — Put up *Highlight Signs* to make customers notice displays. *Highlight Signs* range from simple price signs to signs showing great imagination. Usually a seller who draws well makes *Highlight Signs*.

Keep the *Highlight Sign* when a display ends. The item may come back in stock and you can use the sign again. Sometimes you know you'll never stock the item again, but keep the *Highlight Sign* for a while. It may give someone an idea for a *Highlight Sign* for another item. Every so often *Daily* directs a seller to flush any unwanted *Highlight Signs*.

Store Highlight Signs in the right place — Look under "Highlight Signs" in the *Supplies and Materials List*. Old *Highlight Signs* left around the store or storeroom on shelves and counters are below the store's standards.

Set Up a Supplies and Materials List

Keep the *Supplies and Materials List* in whatever form you can handle. It's easy to keep as a word-processed or database list, but a typed or hand written list is good enough. Keep the *Supplies and Materials List* on cards if you type it or write it by hand. List one item only on each card.

W	Item	Why?	K	Place	Unit	Low	High	Supplier	Id
	"Back in 5 minutes" sign	Security	m	Shelf 6b					
	Bad Items Area	Repairs	o	Shelf 29c					
	Bags & Purses	Sellers	o	Shelf 25c					
w	Bags, Mini	Sales	u	Shelf 21b	Box of 500	125	625	Bagman	Hydene 5x7
	Bags, T-shirt Med	Sales	u	Shelf 23cF		0	100	Storage	9¾ x 15½
	Bags, T-shirt Med	Sales	u	Shelf 23cR		2x100	5x100	Storage	9¾ x 15½
w	Bags, T-shirt Med	Sales	s	Shelf 25b		2x100	10x100	Bagman	9¾ x 15½
	Bags, Utility Lg	Sales	u	Shelf 23bF		0	100	Storage	17 x 14½
	Bags, Utility Lg	Sales	u	Shelf 23bR		1x100	3x100	Storage	17 x 14½
w	Bags, Utility Lg	Sales	s	Shelf 25b		0	1000	Bagman	17 x 14½
	Binder, Customers	General	u	Shelf 21b					
	Binder, Daily	Control	u	Counter 23					
	Binder, Forms Masters	General	m	Shelf 27c					
	Binder, Forms	General	u	Shelf 27c					
	Binder, Items	Sales	u	Shelf 21b					
	Binder, Old Orders	General	u	Shelf 21b					
	Binder, Seller's Volume	Control	u	Shelf 21b					
	Binder, To Manager	Control	u	Shelf 21b					
	Broom, Witch's	Cleaning	m	Shelf 28b					
	Card 3x5 Stiff (Brown)	Reports	u	Shelf 24a		6	6	Used 3x5 Pads	
	Cash Register	Sales	m	Shelf 21c		1	1	Sharp	ER-2580
	Charge Card Signs	Sales	m	Shelf 21c					
	Charge Slip Container	Charges	m	Shelf 21d					
	City Maps	Tourists	u	Drawer 23d		10	50	Storage	
	City Maps	Tourists	s	Shelf 26a		100	200	Convention Center	
	Clothes Hangers	Sellers	o	Shelf 28c					
	Coats	Sellers	o	Shelf 25d					
	Comb, Pet (Metal)	Cleaning	m	Shelf 28b					
w	Counterfeit Detector Pens	Sales	s	Drawer 21e	Box of 10	10	20		
w	Counterfeit Detector Pens	Sales	u	Register		1	1	Storage	
	Credit Cards, Lost	Sales	s	Drawer 23e					
	Display Wheel	Canadian $	m	Shelf 21f					
	Dry Mounting Press	Displays	m	Shelf 25e					
w	Dry Mounting Tissue	Displays	u	Shelf 25e	Box of 500	40	540	Warshal	K 104 5046
	Duo-Tang Covers	Office	u	Shelf 25e	8½x11	5	30	Trick & Murray	DUO51253
	Dust Pan & Brush	Cleaning	m	Shelf 25a					
	Dusters (Polishing Cloth)	Cleaning	u	Drawer 21e	13 oz Pack	5	10	Crawford Waage	Ace 10433
	Easel	Meetings	m	Shelf 28a					
	Easel Pad	Meetings	u	Shelf 28a	27 x 34	1	1	Storage	
	Easel Pad	Meetings	s	Shelf 28a	27 x 34	1	1	Trick & Murray	AMP-24-028
	Endust	Cleaning	u	Shelf 28b	6 oz	1	1	Storage	
	Endust	Cleaning	s	Shelf 28b	6 oz	1	1	IGA	
	Envelopes, #9	Reports	u	Shelf 21b	3⅞x9⅞	10	50	Storage	
w	Envelopes, #9	Reports	s	Shelf 25c	3⅞x9⅞	10	1x500	Trick & Murray	QUA-10912
w	Envelopes 9x12 New	Reports	u	Shelf 25b		10	50	Trick & Murray	QUA-41472
	Envelopes 9x12 Recycled	Reports	u	Shelf 25b		0	50		
	Envelopes, Clasp	Reports	u	Shelf 24a	9x12		1x100	Storage	
w	Envelopes, Clasp	Reports	s	Shelf 25c	9x12		1x100	Trick & Murray	NAT-00837
	Fake Bill Markers	Security	u	Shelf 21c		2	4	Storage	
	Fake Bill Markers	Security	s	Drawer 30b					

W   Weekly

Check items marked by w weekly.

Item   The name we use for the item.

Why?   Why do we need this item? Be as specific as possible. Look this column over once or twice a year. Get rid of items that outlive their use to the store.

K   Key

     u   =   Supplies in use.
     s   =   Supplies in storage.
     m   =   Materials.
     o   =   Other

Place   Place where we keep the item. All items have a place. That's the only place to keep them.

Unit   For supplies list the size of package we order. Leave blank for materials.

Low   Lowest quantity allowed on hand.

High   Highest quantity allowed on hand.
Watch for suppliers and sellers who try to overstock us.

Supplier   Name of usual supplier. Leave blank for materials.

Id   Anything that helps identify the item clearly. Often it's a size, a catalog number or a supplier's name for the item.

Keep Everything in Its Place

Keep the store neat to make sales. Customers like neat stores—they shy away from messy stores. Have a place for everything. Have sellers find out where things belong and keep them where they belong.

Use the Price List — Look in the *Price List* to find out where we display and store items we sell.

Use the Supplies and Materials List — Look in the *Supplies and Materials List* to find out where we keep everything else.

Keep things where they belong — It's each seller's job to put things where they belong It's not somebody else's job.

Put bits and pieces in the Odds and Ends Box — Kill the mess made by bits and pieces. Now and then something small and unknown turns up. The sellers don't know what it is or where it belongs. Sometimes an item we sell falls apart and a seller finds some pieces but is too busy to pay attention to them. Put these bits and pieces in the *Odds and Ends Box*. From time to time someone sorts out everything in the *Odds and Ends Box*.

Save Sticky Tape for Office Work

Sticky tape includes tapes sold as: Adhesive Tape, Brown Tape, Drafting Tape, Masking Tape, Scotch Tape, Sellotape, Transparent Tape. Sticky tape is fine for office work. It holds papers together nicely and there are lots of other uses for it.

Sticky tape ruins cardboard boxes — Put sticky tape on a cardboard box and somebody will pull it off. That takes part of the cardboard with it. Now you've got a markdown on your hands. Some manufacturers send items in boxes they taped shut. Cut the tape carefully with a razor blade before opening the box. Cut the tape of any box that goes on display. Some customers will try to peek inside the box. They'll pull the tape off and ruin the box.

Sticky tape soils items and woodwork — Taped notices on items or woodwork leave glue behind. The glue stays behind when the tape comes off. After a while, most taped notices fall down and leave a soiled item or soiled woodwork. That's a good way to run a tacky store.

Some manufacturers send items with parts taped together. Take the tape off and clean any item that goes on display.

Taped-up notices show the store doesn't care — Put notices in frames or holders. A store that puts up notices with sticky tape showing has given up being a fine store.

Return Credit Cards Left by Customers

Selling includes seeing that customers take their cards with them. Cards left with in the store cause fuss and expense you can do without. It's the sellers' job to return any credit cards left behind by a customers they serve.

Hope the customer comes back on the shift — Keep the card with the charges and checks.

Tag and store the card at the end of the shift — Keep lost cards in the place listed in the *Supplies and Materials List.*. Put a piece of drafting tape on the card. Write the date, the time and seller's name on the tape. Go through the charge slips to find one with the cardholder's signature. Copy the cardholder's phone number from the charge slip to the tape on the credit card. It's too early to make a phone call. The customer is probably still shopping.

Phone the customer during the next shift — Ask the customer to stop by and pick up the card. Sometimes customers buy again when they pick up their cards.

Ask when the customer will pick up the card. Write a dated and timed note on tape on the card to let other sellers know what's happening—called and got no answer—called and left a message—customer will be in by such and such a date.

Mail cards only to customers who ask you to mail them. It's better for the store to have customers come in to pick up their cards. It gives us another chance to make a sale. Write the name and address of a customer who asks you to mail a card directly on an envelope. Seal the card inside the envelope. Then put the envelope in the *To Manager* binder for mailing.

Keep phoning until you connect — Check each shift to see if the card needs more attention.

Destroy the card after a month — Cut the card into several pieces using the junk scissors in the toolbox. That keeps the scissors we use to cut paper sharp.

Clean the Store

The details of cleaning stores will differ from store to store. Stores may have wooden, tile, terrazzo or carpeted floors or a mixture of types of floors. A store may have its own restrooms or use those in the mall. Stores will arrange their displays differently.

For a store facing a sidewalk, clean the sidewalk. That includes using a *PoopScoop* if necessary. For a store with parking in front, clean the parking spaces too.

Write several short *Guide Sheets* for cleaning the store. It's a mistake to join them into one *Guide Sheet*. Some parts of the store need cleaning more often than others. Some cleaning is once a day. Some is once every few days. Some is once every two or three weeks. Write the *Guide Sheets* and control how often the sellers use them through entries in *Daily*. It's good to break the cleaning into small units so you don't swamp the sellers. Separate *Guide Sheets* for separate cleaning jobs draw the sellers' attention to each job. The rule with *Guide Sheets* is the shorter the better and that's certainly the case with cleaning the store.

Several model *Guide Sheets* for cleaning a store follow.

Clean Every Day

Clean the store every day without fail. A squeaky clean store makes it easier for sellers to sell. Customers like clean stores. They shy away from dirty stores.

Prepare to mop the floor — Fill the mopping bucket before opening the store. Put the mopping bucket aside and mop later. Mopping is an *Early Job*. Keep the mopping water around during the day for touch up mopping. Replace it with fresh water if it gets too dirty.

Start cleaning early in the day — Begin daily cleaning as an *Early Job*. Do the main cleaning when there are few customers in the store. Clean again when it's needed during the rest of the day.

Clean the rug — Sweep it with the dust pan and stiff-bristled brush. Shampoo it at least once a week after the store closes. Spray with rug shampoo and scrub with a scrub brush. Leave the rug to dry overnight.

Sweep the floor — Sweep with the witch's broom. Clean up the sweepings with the dustpan and brush. Roll up the oriental rug while you sweep. Comb fluff out of the broom with the metal pet comb. Hang the broom on its hook when you finish to keep it off its bristles.

Scrape chewing gum off the floor — Use the one-inch putty knife from the toolbox.

Mop the floor — Mop with the sponge mop and the mopping bucket. Mop the whole floor. Make sure you get the mud streaks. Keep the mop water for touch up mopping during the day. Mop once a week with *Mop & Glo*. Regular mopping is an *Early Job*. *Mop & Glo* mopping is a *Closing Job*. Replace dirty sponge mop heads as needed.

Put a new liner in the waste paper basket — Remove old liner with waste in it. Tie a knot at the top and store it by the coat rack. Drop it in the dumpster on the loading dock when you leave the building. Put new liner bag in the waste paper basket.

Empty the mopping bucket — This is a *Closing Job*. Take the mopping bucket to the washroom. Empty the dirty water in the toilet, not in the sink. Rinse the mopping bucket twice and empty the dirty water in the toilet, not in the sink. Clean the sink with a paper towel. Flush the toilet.

Dust and Clean Shelves and Display Counters

Dust and clean a little each day. Follow the plan set out in *Daily*. It's too big a job to dust and clean all shelves and display counters in one day.

Set up a ghost display area — Set up a ghost display area at one end of the sales counter. The ghost display area is the same size as one display counter. Arrange the rest of the sales counter so you can still make sales. Move displays from one display counter to the ghost area. Move the displays to the ghost area one by one. Put each display in the same position in the ghost area as it was on the display counter.

Move displays from the top shelf to the display counter — Move the displays to the back part of the display counter one by one. Put each display in the same position on the display counter as it was on the top shelf.

Dust the wall behind the top shelf — Dust with a clean dry cloth. Dust and clean the top shelf. Begin with a cloth damp with *Endust*. You may need to spray *Fantastik* on the shelf and wipe with a cloth.

Dust and return displays to the top shelf — Return each display to its right place on the top shelf. As you return each display, dust it. Tidy each display.

Follow the same plan for each shelf below the top shelf — Work your way down shelf by shelf for all other shelves.

Dust and clean the display counter — Begin with a cloth damp with *Endust*. You may need to spray on *Fantastik* and wipe with a cloth. Dust and return displays to the display counter. Return displays from the ghost area to their places on the display counter. Dust and tidy each display as you return it.

Clean Upright Surfaces

Clean all upright surfaces. Clean as needed each day. We have these upright surfaces:

- All cupboard doors.
- Base panels set back below the cupboard doors.
- Exposed panel of unit 24.

- Exposed sides of cupboards 6, 7, 8, 11,12, 15, 22.

- Front and rear panels of the counter.

Look at the upright surfaces daily — Most days there's little need to clean the upright surfaces, but it's important to check and do this cleaning as needed. The main problems are:

- Finger marks where we open and close the doors.

- Foot marks and scuff marks on the doors and base panels.

- Ice cream and other smears left by customers.

Clean with *Endust* or *Fantastik*. First, try a cloth damp with *Endust*. Try spraying *Fantastik* and wiping with a cloth if *Endust* fails.

Clean the Windows

Have a window cleaning service clean the outside windows regularly. List the name and number of the cleaning service in use in the *Quick Phone List*. List how often the cleaning service cleans the windows in *Daily*.

Check the outsides of the windows — How do the outside windows look? Are you getting good service from the cleaner? Do you need the windows cleaned more often? Is the window cleaner a no-show? Do you need better service?

Clean the insides of the windows — Have sellers clean the insides of the windows when they set up new window displays. Check the insides of the windows and clean them as needed.

Clean smears and smudges daily — Touch up between the window cleaner's visits. The main problems are:

- Customers lean on the windows with their hands, leaving hand prints.

- Customers make smears and smudges with ice cream and sticky fingers.

- Customers press their faces to the window, leaving nose prints, face prints and breathing patterns.

Spray the dirty areas with *Windex* and wipe them clean with a cloth. Check the insides of the windows for smears and smudges.

Dust Ceiling and Walls

Sloppy stores overlook cleaning the ceiling and walls. So make sure you clean them.

Dust ceiling and ceiling displays — Dust the ceiling with the feather duster on a long stick. Work carefully around the hanging ceiling displays. Stand on the step-stool to dust each hanging display. Get the dust off without breaking the displays. Work out a good balance of dusting, blowing and gentle shaking.

Dust walls and wall displays — Dust with a dry cloth. Take down each wall display. Dust the wall behind it. Then dust the display and put it back on the wall neatly.

Dust Display Stands

Give display stands special attention.

Move a display stand to an open part of the floor — Most display stands are in a nook of their own. Move them one at a time to an open part of the floor so it's easy to work with them. Sweep the floor where the display stand stood. Sweep with the witch's broom. Then use the dust pan and brush to put the sweepings in the waste paper basket.

Set up a ghost display area — Set up a ghost display area at one end of the sales counter. The ghost display area is big enough to store everything from the display stand. Arrange the rest of the sales counter so you can still make sales. Move items from the display stand to the ghost area. Keep the items in order. Then it'll be easy to put them back on the display stand. Dust the empty display stand. Dust with a cloth damp with *Endust*. Put the display stand back where it belongs. Dust items as you return them to the display stand.

Dust Floodlights

Many stores have dirty floodlights because they're hard to reach and are hot when they're on.

Dust floodlights in slow times — Choose a time when there are few customers. The store looks best with the floodlights on. Switch off floodlights and let them cool down. Cooling down takes about 10 minutes. Another way is to clean them before opening the store or after closing.

Dust the floodlights — Stand on the step stool to reach them. Dust with a cloth damp with *Endust*. Dust these parts:

- The track.

- The outside of each reflector.

- The inside of each reflector.

- The surface of each bulb.

Replace burnt out bulbs — Switch the floodlights on and replace any burnt out bulbs.

Use the Phone Properly

Use the phone properly yourself and train your sellers to do the same.

Look in the mirror and smile when you phone — Keep a large mirror by the phone. Look in it and smile when you start talking. Send your smile through the phone. Make mental eye contact with the caller. Write the word "Smile" at the top of the mirror with lipstick or a felt pen.

Put some action in your phoning — The smile starts you off on the right path. Lean forward into the phone. Stand up and move around as you talk. Put your whole body into phoning.

Answer calls quickly — Pick up the phone as the second ring ends and the third ring begins. Picking up the phone on the first ring catches the caller off guard. Get yourself together for the call during the first and second rings. Waiting beyond the third ring's too late. Many callers get bored and hang up.

Answer calls pleasantly — Make it a pleasure to hear you on the phone. Put aside any bad feelings you may have and answer the phone pleasantly. Speak at a middling to slow pace. Avoid sounding like a robot.

Know your answering script — Follow this four part model: "Hello, this is Fred Jones at the Clam Shell Gift Shop. Who's calling, please?"

Greeting: "Hello," "Hi," or something similar. The greeting makes the connection between you and callers.

Full name: "This is Fred Jones." Let callers know they're dealing with a person, rather than a voice without a name. People who identify themselves fully are sure of themselves. They give the store a good image. Give your full name. Be proud of yourself and your actions.

Store ID: "At the Clam Shell Gift Shop." Let callers know they've reached the right place. Set the store name in callers' minds.

Ask for caller's name: "Who's calling, please?" About a third of callers will give you their name when you ask it like this. Knowing and using customers' names helps form relationships with them.

Avoid power answers. Some people use power answers like, "It's a beautiful day, Barbara speaking." They're striking when you only hear them once. After that, they sound unreal. They rarely get you the caller's name.

Use callers' names — Find out who's calling. Many callers don't give their names. Asking who's calling often makes callers clam up. Act as if you think they're someone you know. "Is that Mary Jones?" This leads some callers to give their names. Have some follow up lines ready for those who give their names. "Nice to meet you, Ann." "Mrs. Smith, I'm sorry I didn't recognize your voice."

Some callers don't like to say who they are. Honor their feelings. Otherwise use callers names at least once as you talk to them. "Is that what you have in mind, Mrs. Smith?"

Use callers' names in closing calls. "Thanks for calling, Mr. Jones." "Good-bye, Mrs. Gonzales."

Match calls to callers — Speak long enough to make customers feel important. Speak long enough to find out their needs and get them to come to the store.

Keep business calls short and to the point. Skilled business users finish most simple calls in less than a minute. Three minutes is a long call. Avoid long "business" calls that deal mainly with personal topics. Some business calls take much longer than three minutes. Placing a large order is a good example.

Pace your calls by the pace of callers. Speak slowly to customers who speak slowly. Speak breezily to customers who speak breezily, and so on. It turns customers off when your pace differs from theirs.

Keep your hand away from the mouthpiece — You might put your hand over the mouthpiece innocently. To callers it's as if you're talking about them behind their backs.

Always have pen and paper beside the phone — Putting someone on hold to look for pen or paper makes a bad impression. It annoys some customers to have to wait. It says the store isn't on top of things and customers notice that. More importantly, they notice it when the store's on top of things.

Tell when instead of why — Report when you expect people instead of why they aren't there: "We expect Mrs. Jones at 2:30. May I take a message for her to call you?" This gives the impression that everything's under control and is normal. Be sure to use the word "expect."

You risk giving a bad impression of yourself and the store when you tell why someone isn't there. Normal lunch time is from 12 till 1. Joan is the manager. It's OK when callers hear, "Joan won't be back from lunch till 1 o'clock." Some callers will think Joan takes long lunches when they hear, "Joan won't be back from lunch till 2:30." They won't know she went for a quick late lunch at 2 o'clock. It's even worse if it's 12:05 and callers hear she won't be back from lunch till 2:30. They won't know Joan's having lunch with an important supplier. They won't know she's doing the banking on the way back from lunch. It's even worse if you make it clear Joan takes long lunches. Throw in a tone of voice that makes it clear you frown on the long lunches and it's worse still. "Joan just left for lunch. I doubt she'll be back before 2:30. She usually takes 2 or 3 hours for lunch." This puts down Joan, the store and shows you as a whiner. There may be good or bad reasons for Joan taking long lunches but they're not the business of callers. By talking about it you show yourself as a gossip and you show the store up. Avoid these bad messages. Stick to, "We expect Mrs. Jones at 2:30. May I take a message for her to call you?"

Write clear full messages — These are the facts you need on all messages:

Name of person the message is for.
Time, Day, Date.
Name of caller, Name of caller's business.
Phone number, Times available.
Topic.
Caller's message.
Your name.

Here's a good message:
Mary Knight.
10:30 am Thu, Mar 17th 1994.
Call Joan Smythe (sounds like Smith) of Johnson Suppliers.
123-1234 extension 256 8 am - 5 pm Mon-Fri.
About item 5 on Purchase Order KN1234.
Says it's urgent.
Mark Storey.

Write full names for everyone. Then it's clear to everyone which Mary, Joan and Mark the message is talking about. The manager might keep your note on file after the call. Months later Joan Smythe has left Johnson Suppliers and the manager who asks for Joan reaches Joan Brown.

You make closer contact with customers when you give, get and use full names. You give and you get better service. Sellers who give full names stand by who they are more than sellers who just give first names. In modern society, using just a first name is a way of being without a name. It's a way of avoiding responsibility.

Check the spelling of names. Say to Jackie, "I have J, A, C, K, I, E. Is that right, Jackie?" Then say, "How do you spell your last name, Jackie?"

For names that may be hard to say correctly from the spelling, put what it sounds like in brackets. Smythe (sounds like Smith.)

Customers with hard or unusual names like it when you check the spelling. "Is that M, C or M, A, C, Mr. Mackenzie?" "Is that a capital K or a small k, Mr. McKenzie?"

Ask the name of the company for business callers who don't give it. Check the spelling of the company name.

Add am or pm to times. True, you can't mix up 9:30 if you're open only from 9 am to 6 pm. Later the opening hours may change or you may work elsewhere. Get into good habits from the beginning.

Always add the day of the week to the date. Thurs, June 9th 1994, not June 9th 1994. Add the year to the date. True, most people answer phone messages within hours or days and then throw them away. Some managers keep a few on file after they've used them. It's often useful to know the date of an old note. Get into good habits from the beginning. Date all your notes, including the year.

Be sure to get the phone number. Ask if there's an extension number. Ask for the business hours to call back. Include what the caller wants to talk about. Often the caller will tell you without you asking. Otherwise say, "Please may I tell Joan what you need to talk about. Then she can prepare herself when she calls back." Sometimes callers won't give their reasons for calling. Then write "Wouldn't give reason," on the note. Include any special instructions from the caller.

Read messages back to callers for an OK — Make sure you have the facts right. "I have 'Call Joan Smythe of Johnson Suppliers at 123-1234 extension 256 between 8 am and 5 pm Mon-Fri. It's about Item 5 on Purchase Order KN1234 and it's urgent.' Is that OK, Joan?"

Thank callers for calling — "Thanks for calling, Mrs. Jones. It was nice talking to you."

Get an OK for holds and call-backs — Learn these scripts:

"I'm sorry. I don't know the answer. Would you prefer to hold or have me call back when I find out?"

"Please help me. I'm swamped at the moment and it's difficult to give you the attention you need. May I take your number and call you back in a little while?"

Make two contracts for a customer and phone clash — Sometimes you're the only seller serving customers. Someone else usually answers the phone while you're selling to a customer. Someone else usually sells to a customer while you're on the phone. But now and then a customer in the store and a phone call will both need your attention at the same time.

First deal with the customer in place. Suppose you're on the phone and a customer comes in. The customer on the phone has first call on your attention. Yet end the call as soon as you can. The customer on the floor is more likely to buy than the customer on the phone. Untrained sellers ignore customers on the floor when they're busy on the phone. That makes them feel bad and some leave the store. Treat customers better than that.

Suppose you're selling to a customer and the phone rings. The customer you're selling to has first call on your attention. Untrained sellers cut customers off when the phone rings. They leave customers standing about while they deal with the phone call. You know how bad that feels. Some customers leave the store. Treat customers better than that.

Deal with clashes up front. Make a contract with both customers.

Suppose you're selling and the phone rings. Ask for an OK to answer the phone. Say, "Sir, would you please allow me to let this caller know I'm busy with you? I'll just take a number so I can call back later." Answer the phone if the customer gives you an OK. Otherwise, let it ring. After you've answered with your script, let the caller know you're busy. "Mr. Jones, I'm sorry but I'm busy with a customer in the store at the moment. Please let me take your number and call you back as soon as I can." Thank Mr. Jones and hang up if he gives you his number. Call him back as soon as you can.

Mr. Jones might ask something simple. "I only need to know what time you're open till tonight." In that case it's quickest to tell him what he wants to know. Be firm but polite if Mr. Jones wants to cut in on your customer. "Mr. Jones, I'll enjoy talking to you about this in a little while. At present too much of my mind's on the customer I just left on the floor. I'm too confused to give you the attention you deserve. Please help me by giving me your number so I can call you back in a little while."

Suppose you're on the phone and a customer comes in. Ask for an OK to speak to the customer. Say, "Sir, a customer just came in. Would you please allow me to let him know I'll be with him when I've finished speaking to you?" Usually the caller will give you an OK or will end the call. Otherwise, ignore the customer who came in. After an OK, say to the customer on the floor, "Can you please hang on a minute while I finish this call?" Usually the customer will say "Yes." Then say, "Will that be OK?" Usually the customer will say "Yes." Customers who've said yes twice will usually stay till you've finished the call. Finish the call. Then pay attention to the customer who waited. Thank the customer for waiting.

Make your call-backs — Once you promise a call-back, make it. Have someone else call back if you're too busy to return the call soon. Stay late to call back if there's nobody else to call back. Keep calling till you get a connection. Call the next day if necessary. Leave a *News Sheet* asking someone else to call back if you won't be working next day.

Know how to get to the store — Know how to get to the store by auto and by public transit. Learn the details in the *Guide Sheet* titled *How to Get to the Store*. Many people find it hard to give directions clearly. Follow the *Guide Sheet* to be sure you're being clear.

Take control of windbag callers — Now and then you get a caller who just wants to talk. Be firm but polite when you decide you have to end the call. "Ann, it's always nice to talk to you but it's getting quite busy in the store just now. Is there some way I can help you before we hang up?"

Avoid charges for directory assistance — Most numbers we call often are in the *Quick Phone List* beside the phone. Look up other phone numbers in the phone book. Call directory assistance only when the number isn't in the phone book. Enter the name and number in the *Phone Log* and the *Quick Phone List*. There's a charge for each call to directory assistance. Sellers who don't use the phone book because it's easier to call soon run up a bill. That's not allowed in your store.

Get the manager's OK for long distance calls — It's unusual for sellers to make long distance calls. Check first with the manager. Write all long distance calls in the *Phone Log*.

Check Use of the Phone

Check what goes on when your sellers answer the phone. This is an area many businesses overlook. The seller answering the phone is the first contact many customers have with your store. Make sure it's not the last contact. Be sure to check for phone abuse by your sellers that costs you money.

Call the store often — Call the store to know how customers hear your store. There'll be times you'll call in about the store's business. That's good, but the business will be on your mind. Call at least once a week to ask, "How are things going at the store?" That let's you focus on how the sellers answer the phone.

Add "Call the store" to your *To-do List* for all out-of-store trips. Keep a *Call-in Log* of your store call-ins at the back of your pocket diary. Check your *Call-in Log* once a month.

Keep your checklist in mind when you call in — Do you get a busy line often? Is your store busy or is someone misusing the phone? Let your sellers know politely that it was hard to get through. Ask what's been happening. Count the rings.

Let sellers who answer when the third ring begins know you're pleased. Let sellers who answer before the third ring begins know they're too early. Politely ask other sellers what stopped them answering earlier. Let sellers hear you're serious about answering as the third ring begins. There may be good reasons for delays but drive the lesson home politely.

Let sellers who follow the phone answering script know you're pleased. Let other sellers know they must follow the script.

How do the sellers sound when they answer the phone? Do they project their voices well? Do they speak slowly enough? Many people speak too fast on the phone. It's rare for someone to speak too slowly. Do they answer the phone pleasantly? Do they speak with warmth and a smile, or do they sound like robots? Good or bad, let them know where they stand there and then.

Check the phone bill monthly — Collect cash for any authorized long distance personal calls. Are the calls on the *Phone Log* OK? Deal with bad use right away. Track down any long distance calls not in the *Phone Log*. Collect cash for them if they're personal. Warn the seller involved that this kind of abuse must end. Say good-bye to the seller if it goes on.

Bring sellers who make unneeded directory assistance calls up to standard. Track down any directory assistance calls not in the *Phone Log*. Make sure sellers enter directory assistance calls in the *Phone Log*. Collect cash on all directory assistance calls for personal numbers. Let sellers know they should make directory assistance calls for personal numbers from a pay phone.

Know How to Get to the Store

Your directions for getting to the store are most important. People who call and ask for directions will probably become customers. Make sure it's easy for them to get to you from every direction and by every means of transport. It's well worth making dry runs yourself to make sure you funnel customers right into your store painlessly.

Know the store's hours — Learn the list of opening times in *Daily*. Customers who ask how to get to the store usually also want to know when you're open.

Stress the best — Talk about the best way to the store, the best time of day, the best parking. That's better than talking about traffic jams, crowds and hard parking.

Use directions to boost your list of Personal Customers — Steer customers your way after you've told them how to get to the store:

1. Say, "Can you find your way here with the directions I've given you?" This will get customers to talk to you. You may have to go over the directions again to make them clear to customers.

2.   Say, "Be sure to give me a call if you get lost."

3.   Now say, "Please do me a favor. Please let me know how the directions work out as soon as you get to the store. I'm trying to keep track of how well I'm doing. My name's Mary Smith, please ask for me. What's your name, by the way?"

4.   Then say, " I look forward to talking to you when you arrive, Frank. Have a good journey." Many of these customers will check in with you as soon as they arrive. Begin to schmooze about the journey and lead into the rest of the *Steps for Selling*.

Tell customers how to get to the store — Sellers follow one of the plans you have prepared for the *Guide Sheet*. They follow a plan to stay focused and give clear directions.

Take Charge of Reps

Reps are people who visit the store to sell items or services. They usually ask to see the manager.

Ask reps if they have an appointment — Let the manager know reps who have an appointment are here. Show them where to wait for the manager.

Stop reps blocking sales — Reps have a way of starting to talk to sellers by the cash register. Then they put their bags on the counter and take over. Customers and other sellers have to work around them. Stop this happening. Take charge and lead reps to where they're out of the way of sales and customers. Say, "Let's move over here where we can talk without blocking sales."

Find out why they're here — Say, "What do you have to show us?" Some reps will try to go round you directly to the manager. We won't have that. Your opinions count in this store. You're on the floor and you know what sells. You know what problems the store faces. Say, "Unless you're selling advertising, there's no problem in seeing the manager. It'll help you if I can say something about your business."

Send advertising reps away — Only see reps selling advertising when you are ready to advertise and have sent for the reps you wish to see. Have your sellers smile and say to advertising reps who drop by unasked, "I'm sorry, our current business plan calls for no additional advertising. Thanks for your call. Good-bye." Some reps will try to push over this refusal or get sellers to tell about current advertising. Sellers simply smile and repeat, "I'm sorry, our current business plan calls for no additional advertising. Thanks for your call. Good-bye." Sellers simply repeat this as often as they need. Make sure sellers know it's not part of their job to provide information to reps who drop by unasked to sell advertising.

Talk to other reps — Look at the items or listen to the offer. Take any brochures, fliers and business cards the reps wish to leave.

Set up contacts and appointments — From what reps show and tell you there are four results:

1. *Looks Interesting.* Set up an appointment if you think we need what a rep's pushing.

2. *Keep on File.* We're interested in anything that's the same as or like something we already sell. We want to know about other suppliers. Perhaps we're satisfied with our present bag supplier and aren't thinking of changing. At the same time, we want to keep ourselves out of a trap. We want to know what other bag suppliers offer. We want to know about bag suppliers who're out looking for business. Let the reps know where they stand. Suggest we'll call them when we need something. Suggest reps who want more than that call the manager. Tell them to say they've talked to you. Let reps who insist on an appointment have one.

3. *Not Interested.* The items are outside our store's mission or we've tried items like these and we don't want them. They're on our list of lemons. Let reps know where they stand. Take any brochures, fliers and cards they want to leave. They can call or have an appointment if they insist. Tell them it's not a good use of their time.

4. *Don't Know.* Sometimes you don't know enough to decide. Even when you've worked here a long time there'll be times like this. Take the brochures, fliers and cards. Tell the rep the manager will call if interested.

Daily tells sellers the present time slot for reps' appointments. Keep to that time slot unless it's for something that really excites you. In that case, get the rep in as soon as possible. Enter the appointment on the manager's calendar.

Add comments and pass materials to the manager — Write short comments on what you've seen and heard. Pass all materials in a pocket of the *To Manager* binder.

Get a release on samples — Some reps want to leave samples. That's fine if we asked them to leave samples or if they're free samples. Have reps write a note saying they're free samples, otherwise, we don't want samples. Samples cause a lot of fuss. We get stuck looking after them while the reps take their time picking them up. They get in the way, so we sell them for a song or throw them out. Then the reps bill us.

CHAPTER 10

PROTECT THE STORE

Your store is a rich deposit of valuables which will attract thieves. It is a mother lode veined with cash, the items you sell, the equipment you use, the supplies you use each day and the personal property of those who work there. Take steps to protect the store from thieves who would break in and those who come into your store when it's open posing as customers. Also take steps to prevent those who work for you stealing from you.

Protect the Store from Thieves

The protection from thieves a store needs varies from store to store. Your location, the design of your building and the items you carry are the main facts to consider. A shopping center provides some protection to all its stores. Each store in the center needs to provide less for itself than a free standing store. A free standing store needs to provide all of its own protection.

This is an area where you must consult the experts. Every store has its own structural features and security problems. You must get specific advice on your store. First ask your local police to send someone from the *Crime Prevention Unit* to give advice. Then ask several security specialists to come in and give advice. Look under *Security Control Equipment and Systems* in the *Yellow Pages*.

Lock the store — Put in cylinder locks with pin tumblers. Locks with pin tumblers are more secure than locks with disk tumblers, or lever tumblers. Get rid of old-fashioned warded locks as they give only token security. Locksmiths can change the cylinders of cylinder locks to re-key them without replacing the lock set.

Put in one-inch deadbolt locks on all outside doors. Open the door and turn the key in the lock while the door is open. The bolt thrown by the key that normally fits in a hole in the door frame sticks out. Push on the bolt. You have a spring bolt if the bolt yields with only the resistance of a spring behind it. A deadbolt stays put when you press on it. A spring bolt gives you little safety. You need a deadbolt lock. It's too easy to force a spring bolt back with a thin blade or a credit card. Most locks with deadbolts have a spring loaded latch bolt in addition to the deadbolt. The latch bolt moves when you turn the doorknob. It lets you close the door without locking it and it lets you open an unlocked door. While deadbolts are usually rectangular in cross section, latch bolts taper on the side that hits the strike plate.

Put in double cylinder long-throw deadbolts on doors with glass panels. You have to use a key to lock or unlock a double cylinder lock from the inside and the outside. You can't lock or unlock them by pushing a button or twisting a knob. That means someone who breaks a window and reaches in still needs a key to unlock the door.

Put in locks with cylinder guards and an armored front. A cylinder guard is a protective mounting for the lock's cylinder which stops someone twisting it off. An armored front is a plate covering the bolts or set screws holding a cylinder to its lock. It stops someone getting at the bolts or set screws when the door is ajar.

Put blocker plates over all outside locks. Blocker plates are metal plates that cover the gap between the door and its frame in the region of the lock. They make it harder to jimmy the lock.

Label all keys with an engraving tool and keep track of them. Write code numbers without the name of your store. Check keys out to sellers who need them and get them back when they stop working for you. Change lock cylinders and keys when you lose control of a key.

Lock or otherwise secure roof openings and air ducts. Include skylights and hatches, air conditioners and outside windows. You may need to secure some of these with bars or safety screens.

Replace glass with Plexiglas in service windows. Replace loose or rotted door frames and window frames. Replace locks that work poorly as soon as you notice them. Fill any gaps between doors and door frames that allow easy jimmying.

Upgrade all outside doors — Replace hollow doors with solid doors. Put metal linings on outside service doors to resist drilling and sawing. Put in multiple-point, high security long bolts on double doors. Put in non-removable hinge pins on doors that open outwards. Spot weld any exposed screws on hinges.

Put in alarm systems — Put in an alarm system to guard against break-ins. Connect the alarm system to a 24-hour answering service. Put in holdup alarms if your store is a prime target for holdups. Set off the holdup alarms only for holdups, not for small crimes. Put in the alarm switches at several places in the store. Train sellers to use the alarm systems without setting off false alarms. Check the alarm systems regularly.

Light the store twenty-four hours, seven days — Keep the inside of the store well lit at night. Keep the store window clear. Let passers-by and police patrols see into the store. Clear windows also let your sellers see the getaway car in case of a robbery.

Put a night light over the safe. Put a night light over the cash register. Put lights over all entrances to the store. Light the alley and rear of the store.

Mark valuable equipment — Engrave equipment with ID numbers. Your local police can help with an engraving program through their *Operation Identification*. Engrave your own ID numbers even if the equipment has serial numbers. Write a phone number, including area code. Write a driver's license number, including state abbreviation. Write a Social Security Number. Then police can find you quickly when they recover stolen equipment. Keep a list of all equipment and serial numbers in a safe place.

Protect outside the store — Keep fences behind the store in good repair. Put locks on any gates in the fences. Get rid of hiding places. Keep weeds, shrubs and trash away from doors and windows. Lock up ladders and tools that thieves can use to break in.

Lock the Store

Give the store's keys to sellers in charge of shifts, for use during scheduled work hours only. Sellers may not be in the store outside their scheduled work hours.

Lock the store when stepping out — Sellers lock up when they step out of the store. A lone seller locks the store to pick up coffee from the store across the way. It's not safe to leave it open "for a few minutes" with no sellers in the store. Put up the "Back in 5 minutes" sign to lock the store during opening hours. Take down the sign on return.

Follow the lockup steps to close the store — This is the order of steps:

1. Turn on outside light over back door.
2. Lock the back door from the inside.
3. Check for burglars hiding in the store waiting for you to lock them in. Washrooms and storerooms are places burglars often hide.
4. Check that the inside store lights left on overnight are on.
5. Turn on the outside light over the front door.
6. Set the burglar alarm.
7. Lock the front door from the outside.
8. Check the front door from the outside.
9. Check the back door from the outside.

Remember Your PUN

Have each seller choose a PUN: a Personal Unforgettable Number. Sellers choose a number they'll always remember. They take it from the events in their lives. Perhaps it's the number of the house a seller was born in. Perhaps it's a seller's mother's birthday. Perhaps it's a seller's father's phone number. Perhaps it's the day Elvis Presley died. It's any number a seller will always remember.

Add the PUN to valuable numbers — Make a number only one person can use. Suppose the combination of the store's safe is 1234 and seller's PUN is 765. Add them to get a coded number 1999. It's now safe to write the coded combination in a pocket diary. Only the seller can figure out the real combination.

Get the number back with a hand calculator — "Write" the combination on the screen. Punch the coded number into a calculator and take away the PUN. The real number displays on the screen. Open the safe and then clear the calculator. This way sellers never write the number down, so they never leave it lying around.

Store Cash and Valuables in the Safe

The role a safe plays depends on the kind of store you have. Volume of sales and your store's neighborhood are important factors to think about. Without a safe you'll have a secret place in the store where you keep cash. That's a bad idea. It's nearly the same as having cash lying around. Some stores have a secret place to hide cash because they can't afford a safe. Cash in a box under the counter isn't in a secret place. There should be a safe in your future. Make sure it's a cash safe rather than a records safe. It's easy to go on using a secret place after the time you can afford a safe. Then loss of cash will prompt you to buy a safe.

The safe has two main uses. To store the take from sales before you deposit it in the bank. To store banknotes and coins you use for *Opening Change*.

In theory you can deposit directly from the cash drawer into the bank but that's not likely to work. There will be times when you'll have too much cash in the cash drawer and need to store it in the safe. The cash drawer may even overflow. There will be times when, without a safe, you'll make bank deposits that are too small. There's usually a banking cost with each deposit and there's always a bookkeeping cost.

In theory you can get cash from the bank before you open each day. For most stores that's not going to work. The bank's not open, or it's not open early enough. You don't know how long you'll have to wait in the bank. A Mom & Pop store can keep the *Opening Change* at home. That's not going to work when different sellers open the store.

Position the safe carefully — There are two views on where to keep your safe. One is to put it where people can see it and keep it well lit. That lets passers-by and police patrols see any thieves working on it easily. The other is that out of sight is out of mind. A safe people can see can be a magnet for thieves. On the other hand, hiding a safe gives thieves a hidden place to work.

Skilled thieves who break into your store will get what's in your safe. They'll break it open. They'll carry it away with them unless you anchor it to the floor. So keep only as much as you need on hand in your safe overnight. Your safe doesn't take the place of a bank. It only helps prevent needless loss. It gives you a place to keep valuables safe from impulsive theft. It may save you cash during an armed robbery. Most thieves want their cash quickly. They'll take what's in the cash drawer and run.

Train sellers to use the safe — Your safe plays a role in a pattern of good habits of handling valuables. Let the amount in your safe reflect a plan. Work out the risks you're willing to take or have to take. Work out when and how you make bank deposits. Work out when and how you pick up change from the bank.

Which sellers you let use your safe depends on your store. Only let managers use the safe if you always have a manager on duty. You'll have to trust other sellers too when that's not the case.

Train sellers well in opening and locking the safe. You want them to be able to open and lock the safe in their sleep. Test them and retest them day after day. Test them until they open and lock the safe without thinking about it.

Some safes have a keypad like a touch-tone phone. It's easy to remember the combination and it's easy to open them. They give enough safety for small amounts of cash in everyday use. Typical safes have a dial combination lock. Dial combinations have a series of numbers and an order of turning the dial. You have to line up the number on the dial with a marker line carefully. You can't overshoot the number and go back to it. They're harder to use, but they give you greater safety. Here's a typical combination you'll have to learn:

1. Turn the dial to the left.

2. Stop when the number 50 lines up with the marker for the fourth time.

3. Now turn the dial to the right.

4. Stop when the number 25 lines up with the marker for the third time.

5. Turn the dial to the left.

6. Stop when the number 30 lines up with the marker for the second time.

7. Turn the dial to the right until the bolt opens.

To remember it, shorten it:

L 50 4	Turn the dial to the left. Stop the fourth time the number 50 lines up with the marker.
R 25 3	Now turn the dial to the right. Stop the third time the number 25 lines up with the marker.
L 30 2	Turn the dial to the left. Stop the second time the number 30 lines up with the marker.
R	Turn the dial to the right until the bolt opens.

Disguise the combination with a PUN. Suppose your PUN is 81. L 50 4, R 25 3, L 30 2, R becomes A 131 85, B 106 84, A 111 83, B. You can write that down and it's not likely anyone can use it to open the safe. Keep backup copies of the disguised combination. With combination locks you can forget the number or the order of dialing. Then you can't get into the safe. It's easy to forget the combination when you're tired or ill. Keep a copy hidden somewhere in the store's papers. Keep a copy of the combination at home. Carry a copy with you at all times. Have backup people you can ask or phone. Treat written copies with the same care as the key to the store.

Change the combination — Buy a safe that lets you change the combination quickly and easily. Change it every time a seller who knows it quits.

Learn how to open and lock the safe — Show sellers who need to use the safe how to open and lock it. For safety's sake, write down no details. Have sellers learn the details by rote. Test the sellers until they know them by heart.

Take Care of Personal Valuables

Thieves cruise stores looking for a chance to steal. Sellers are in the store each day and it feels like home but they need to look out for their purses and wallets.

Keep personal belongings at the back of the storeroom — Hang spare clothing at the back of the storeroom. Lock purses, bags, wallets, and so on in the safety cupboard at the back of the storeroom.

Guard the store keys — Keep the keys in a safe place in the store and at home.

Learn police and security phone numbers — Write emergency phone numbers at the top of the *Quick Phone List*. Memorize the numbers for:

• Police, fire and ambulance.

- Mall security.

- Manager's home.

Describe Suspicious Strangers

Sellers may have to describe someone to the police or to other stores. It could be someone they suspect of shoplifting or of working a scam. It could be someone who passes a bad check or uses a stolen credit card. It could be an armed robber or someone who hangs around the store for no clear reason.

Compare the stranger with known people

Go for height, weight, age. "I had to look up to look into his eyes." "The top of his head was about level with my chin." "Well-built body, like Frank Ho." "Fatter than Mike Jones." "Looked younger than my brother, Jim." "Looked about the same age as Earl Smith."

Fill in the details

Go for eyes, skin color and hair. "A blue-eyed bald white man with a fringe of brown hair and a mustache." Any marks or features that stand out? "A small scar under his right eye." "A large mole on the right side of his neck." "A rose tattoo on his left upper arm." "Large ears that stand out from his head, like Ross Perot."

What about ways of speaking and acting? "Talks rapidly in a high pitched voice." "Shifts his weight from one foot to another."

Include clothing and jewelry. "Wearing a brown coat, gray polo neck sweater and gray pants." "Pants cover tops of brown cowboy boots." "Has a belt with a large brass buckle." "Wearing a thin gold wedding ring."

Remember what they say — Write it down before you forget.

See where they're headed — Which way did they leave? See the kind of vehicle and license plate if you can see it without chasing them. Write the details down.

Wage War on Shoplifting and Inside Theft

Shoplifters will steal from your store, so it's up to you to take steps to cut the loss they will cause you. Unless you're unusually lucky with the people who work for you, some of them will steal from you too. Theft by people who work for you can range from petty pilfering of supplies all the way up to large-scale theft of cash and the items you sell that can cripple your store. While you will want to have trusting relationships with your customers and sellers, you cannot afford to turn a blind eye on these unfortunate facts of retail.

Shoplifting and Inside Theft

This section covers background material for managers.

Know shoplifters — Amateur and professional shoplifters will steal from you. Most shoplifters are amateurs and most amateur shoplifters are otherwise respectable people. A few are mentally disturbed people, drug addicts, drunks and drifters. Professionals steal less often but more thoroughly than amateurs.

Almost all shoplifters come into your store with a plan to steal from you. Customers who react to a one-time urge to shoplift are rare indeed. Shoplifters are mainly long-term, regular, orderly thieves. They'll give you every excuse to get you to take pity on them. So-called "first offenders" are usually shoplifters caught for the first time.

Professional thieves prefer to work a large number of small stores. The store detectives soon get to know them in large stores. Professionals may work alone or in groups of as many as 12 or 15. They work at all times but often when there are crowds in the store. They often work at closing time when sellers are tired and are in a hurry.

Know the problems in fighting shoplifters — Private citizens may arrest anyone who commits a crime within their sight or hearing. You can arrest shoplifters but you'll have to prove their taking, their carrying away, and their intent to shoplift in a court. It's easy to find yourself facing charges of false arrest or false imprisonment.

To arrest people you have to touch them. Some may fight back or draw weapons on you. You may find yourself facing charges of assault or being assaulted.

Crooks may set you up. They may steal something and throw it before you make the arrest. They may buy something, put it with unsold items and act as if they're shoplifting it. They may resist arrest and force you to injure them. These are hard cases to fight when the shoplifters have no criminal or arrest records.

You have to know how to search and question shoplifters.

You have to decide whether to prosecute shoplifters. Prosecuting all shoplifters is good but you may not be able to afford it. It pays to find out your local conditions. How long do you and your sellers have to spend in court each time? You may have to strike a balance. You may have to prosecute only enough shoplifters to cut down losses. Prosecution of at least 30% of shoplifters you catch is probably the lowest that will affect the rate of shoplifting. Even stores that prosecute all shoplifters they catch still have losses to shoplifters.

Prosecuting all teenage shoplifters is a good way to go. This makes it clear to teenagers that shoplifting is stealing. The word soon spreads to keep clear of your store. It may steer some from the path of crime. Most shoplifters start as children who learn from older children.

Prosecuting all professional shoplifters is a good way to go. The word spreads that your store is an easy mark when you let professionals off with a warning.

You have to prepare the cases for court. Your knowledge of the laws of evidence will be up against those of a skilled defense attorney. The attorney may even have connections to the court. You'll have to provide proof of value of the stolen items.

It makes sense to have qualified store detectives arrest shoplifters and decide whether to prosecute them. They'll also prepare cases and attend court for the store. A number of small stores can go together to employ a detective. Perhaps you can employ a retired police officer part-time. Work out your loss from shrinkage as a percentage of sales. Is it worth paying to lower it?

Get mechanical and electronic help — Plan the store layout to cut down on shoplifting. Avoid hidden corners where shoplifters can steal in private. Counters stacked too high make it easy for shoplifters to hide their actions. Keep rear service doors locked. Keep valuables and portables away from exits to prevent grab-and-run by drunks and drifters.

Viewing devices can help you cut down shoplifting. You may not want to use them because they spoil the image of your store. Convex mirrors and closed circuit TV show shoplifters you're alert. Less obvious options are two-way mirrors, grilles and peepholes. Viewing devices are largely useful to pinpoint shoplifters for store detectives to arrest when they steal more items. Someone watches and someone arrests. The person making the arrest must see the shoplifting directly.

Mechanical anti-theft devices can help you cut down shoplifting. Tethers and cables with locks hold items in place. Alarm circuits ring when someone breaks the circuit. Alarms ring when someone takes an item off a reverse pressure pad. These devices are generally useful only for special situations. They're awkward and expensive when used on a large scale. Some of them spoil your store's image.

Electronic tags and labels work well and have little effect on your store's image.

Check the number of garments taken in and out of changing rooms. This is a simple way to control shoplifting. Keep this system going if you use it. Using the system at times but not at others signals times when it's OK to shoplift.

Know the problems in fighting inside theft — Stealing by employees probably causes stores more loss than shoplifting. Probably 60% of the population indulge in small scale theft, so it's easy to see why it goes on in your store. Studies with lie detectors have shown stores with nearly 75% of the employees admitting to helping themselves to items or cash. This is an area where it costs too much to look the other way. Let sellers know you discharge and prosecute them if they steal from you. Employees continue to steal from employers who forgive them. Dishonest employees infect other employees. Make sure you note discharge for theft in dishonest employees' files. They often try to get their old jobs back.

Good selection of employees, good control of inventory and good accounting practices cut down inside theft. The best defense is in the initial selection of employees and in making it clear to them that dishonest people don't survive with you. Inside theft is at its worst when managers or supervisors take part in it. Not only are they in a better position to steal, but other employees pick up on the atmosphere and stealing spreads. What managers do molds other employees. It's important for managers and owners to set an example of honesty.

Employees steal cash — The temptation to steal is in the nature of the job. It's rare for the cash to go directly into a purse or pocket. Most dishonest sellers keep track of what they steal and take the total from the cash drawer. Watch for sellers who keep slips of paper with figures by the cash drawer. It's a favorite way of keeping track of their take. Watch for pennies in the wrong coin slot. It can be another way of keeping track of the take. Make sure customers can see the ring on your cash registers. Cash registers that leave customers blind invite sellers to work dodges. These are the main dodges:

No Ring—Customer gives exact change and walks away. Seller keeps the cash.

Low Ring—Seller rings a lower priced item than the one sold to a friend.

Under Ring—Seller rings $1 for $10, and so on. Hopes customers don't notice.

No Sale—Seller rings "No Sale," gives no receipt to the customer and keeps the cash.

Fake Refund—Seller gives a "refund" on a sales slip a customer leaves behind.

Employees steal the items you sell — These are the main dodges:

Sweetheart Deals—Four shirts go in the bag, one shirt goes on the sales slip.

Fake Void—Seller voids an item on a receipt for a friend but bags the item.

Walk-outs—Employees take items for their own use. They may even take enough items to supply a small business. Pay special attention to sellers who've got something going for themselves. Inspect the trash from time to time. Hiding items in the trash is a favorite way of getting them out of the store.

Call in shopping services — Call in shopping services for routine checks or to look into cases where you suspect theft. Shopping services shop under conditions that make it possible for dishonest employees to steal. They swear affidavits and will question suspects for you. They also report on the level of service, both good and bad. Some retailers use a shopping service without letting their sellers know about it. Others let their sellers know that a shopping service will check them. Letting sellers know probably keeps theft in check better than keeping the shopping service secret and then finding out who's stealing.

Watch for Shoplifters

This section covers material that sellers need to be aware of to deal with shoplifting.

Shoplifter: A thief who poses as a customer.

Give service to cut losses from shoplifting — Shoplifters like stores with poor service. Sellers pay little attention to them so it's easy to steal. Giving good service is the surest way to cut down shoplifting.

The *Steps for Selling* keep sellers in contact with customers. Follow the *Steps for Selling* to sell and to cut down shoplifting.

Stay alert for shoplifters in the store — Although most customers are honest, any one of them may be a shoplifter. Watch for signs of possible shoplifting:

See "customers" stealing: The strongest sign that "customers" are shoplifters comes when you see them stealing. You may see an item go into a dress, a pocket, a bag, a parcel, or the like.

Glancing around: Keep on top of all "customers" who glance around the store often. Customers in a store have their attention on the items for sale. "Customers" who have their attention on the store are possible shoplifters. Typically, they're holding or standing by the item they're going to steal and looking to make sure the coast is clear. Someone about to steal rarely looks at the item. Their eyes dart around looking for danger. Then they steal with quick movements of their hands.

Shoplifting props: Shoplifters use many articles to help them steal—loose coats or capes, coats draped over the arm, folded newspapers, bulky dresses, skirts with elastic waistbands,[16] large purses, briefcases, shopping bags, packages and umbrellas.

Dawdlers: Customers who take forever to make up their minds are real enough, but some shoplifters act like this until they see the chance to steal.

[16]These are generally combined with bulky bloomers to store stolen items.

Scenes: Shoplifters working in groups sometimes cause scenes that draw your attention. Other members of the group steal while your attention is on the scene.

Crabby and fussy customers: Some shoplifters pose as crabby and fussy customers. Their aim is to upset you so you'll leave them alone to steal in peace.

Teenagers: Pay attention to teenagers in the store without adults. Most teenagers are honest but teenagers make up more than half of all shoplifters. Many teenagers think it's fun to steal and don't look on it as a crime. Watch groups of teenagers carefully. Tell wild or rowdy teenagers to leave the store. Watch teenagers near items sold as a craze. Crazes prompt shoplifting.

Dropped items: Some shoplifters drop items into bags on the floor. Others drop them on the floor and pick them up. The items go into a bag if the coast is clear, otherwise they go back on display.

Sunglasses: Many drug addicts are shoplifters and some wear sunglasses indoors to hide their dilated or contracted pupils. Any other sign of drug addiction is a warning sign—needle tracks on the arms, long sleeves on hot days to cover needle tracks, the musky body odor of heroin addicts.

Dressed for a Walk-out: Watch customers wearing old shoes into the shoe department. They may put on new shoes and hide the old ones. Watch customers with no coats on in the clothing department. They may have one on when they leave. Watch the umbrellas when it starts to rain. Shoplifters will take one rather than get wet. Watch for women without purses or with old purses by the purse counter.

Badly matched clothes: A shoplifter using a specially designed item of clothing usually has it in only one style and color. Thus a booster skirt used to shoplift may stand out from the other clothes the shoplifter is wearing. Swapping clothes in the changing room is another reason for badly matched clothes.

Signs of strain or tension: Watch customers who seem under strain or tension. They may have money problems they may try to solve by shoplifting. They may be new shoplifters. Nervous customers may have something to be nervous about.

Make no arrests and charge nobody with shoplifting — Arresting shoplifters is a job for a skilled professional. It's easy for others to end up with expensive lawsuits on their hands. Selling is your job, not arresting crooks. Some professional shoplifters are violent and some carry arms. They may hit you, stab you or threaten you with a gun if you try to arrest them.

Never call someone a shoplifter, a crook, a thief, or the like. You may end up in court having to prove it. Knowing you saw shoplifting is different from proving it in court.

Warn the store detective about possible shoplifters — A *News Sheet* in *Daily* lets you know when the detective is in the store. It tells you how to signal your suspicions to the detective.

"Bug" possible shoplifters — Sellers stay with possible shoplifters. They follow them around the store. They act as if they're pushy sellers who want to sell them something they don't want to buy. Sellers go wherever they go and keep asking them if they can help them. Sellers keep showing them things as if they want them to buy. Sellers act stupid but nice. Sellers aim to make them feel so uncomfortable that they leave the store.

Greet all customers — To a customer a greeting is a greeting. To a shoplifter a greeting says, "I'm watching you." Greetings tell shoplifters you know they're in the store.

Take care when showing valuable items — Show valuable items one by one, or at most two at a time. Placing a whole tray of expensive watches on the counter asks for trouble.

Keep your attention on valuable items. Another customer may demand quick service on a small item while you're showing valuable items. It could be a set-up. Say, "I'll be with you, Sir, as soon as I've finished serving this lady." It's better to miss a small sale than to risk losing an expensive item. It's polite to stay with customers you're with rather than dump them for pushy customers.

Shoplifting Footnote

This section covers material for managers working in close collaboration with owners.

Gutsy retailers may like a more active stand against shoplifters — One way is to confront shoplifters and ask them to buy. Then bar them from your store. Know that you run a risk in doing this. It's possible to have shoplifters sue you for defamation for falsely accusing them of a crime. Many would say this risk is quite small—few shoplifters will sue and even fewer of them will be successful. Only you can decide the risk you're willing to take after talking with your lawyer.

Those who follow this plan should deal with the shoplifter out of the hearing of other customers. This plan isn't something you'd want to turn over to any of your sellers. In the beginning only deal with shoplifters yourself. Then train selected sellers when you're comfortable with the plan. It's OK for sellers to alert you about a shoplifter in the store, but it's risky to lock horns with a shoplifter on a seller's say so. Those who confront should see the act of shoplifting themselves.

Say, "Would you like me to ring up the watch you have in your pocket for you now."

Some will deny they have the watch. Say, "I saw you put the watch in your pocket. Please pay for it or return it now."

Some will pay, some will return the watch, some will deny they have it. Say to all of them, "Please leave this store and never return. You're not welcome here. We'll prosecute you for trespassing if you return."

Watch for Scams

A scam is a trick, ruse, swindle, or confidence game. Although they don't happen often, it's good protection for your store when your sellers know about them.

Let Scenes Pass by You

Scenes are acts that get your attention while thieves steal from the store. Thieves working in a group may make an uproar in the store while others in the group steal. Fights may break out between "customers" over who saw a bargain first. Crooks may start a fire. Someone may have a "heart attack" or a "seizure." Someone you find attractive may pay attention to you. The most natural scene is for someone to act like a customer and take your full attention.

Lock up any cash you're working with when a scene starts. Scan the other customers for shoplifters as you phone building security or the police for help. Call to report what's going on while still watching the customers. Unless you have first aid training there's little you can do for a real medical problem but phone for help anyway. It doesn't help for you or other sellers to watch the scene or hover over the victim.

Sellers other than the seller phoning for help spread through the store watching for shoplifters.

Watch for Fake Money

Fake money: Counterfeit money, false money, forged money, funny money, imitation money, pretend money.

Many stationery stores carry the *Fake Bill Marker* (U.S. Patent 5,063,163) under the name Counterfeit Detection Marker or a similar name. The mark it makes on the bill has iodine in it and is yellow. The mark turns black when the paper has starch in it. Real U.S. bills have no starch in them. They're made from 100% rag paper. Most other papers have starch in them to make them stiff and let them print well, but some have no starch. This means a bill which passes the test has no starch in it, rather than it's a real bill. Canadian bills have starch in them, so the *Fake Bill Marker* is useless on them.

The marks made on the bills fade away in time. It's OK to mark U.S. bills unless the marks make the bills unfit for reuse as currency. Writing political slogans or obscene messages on bills are among the marks that make bills unfit for reuse.

Test big bills — Test U.S. bills valued at $20 or more with the *Fake Bill Marker*. The *Fake Bill Marker* is a felt pen that leaves a yellow mark on real bills and on some fake bills. The yellow mark turns black on most fake bills. Bills with black marks are fakes. Bills with yellow marks are probably OK, but could be fakes.

Test by what's right for the store. Some stores get many fake bills and test all bills. Some stores get few fake bills and test only bills they suspect are fake. Some stores test most bills only when they know fake bills are in the area. Newspapers and merchant groups sometimes publish facts about fake bills being passed locally. Some stores test bills following a pattern, like every tenth customer. Some stores test bills by the call they make on whether the customer is likely to be passing fake bills. Some stores test bills presented by foreigners. About 50% of fake money is passed in illegal money exchange in foreign countries.

Know what paper money looks like — Get in the habit of looking at money. Most of us let it pass through our hands without looking at it closely. Begin with new bills fresh from the bank. Then look at used bills.

Know what paper money feels like — Feel new and old bills. Feel how they bend like cloth and feel how ordinary paper is stiffer than bills. Feel the "embossed feel" of new bills. This comes from the engraving process which makes the printing stick out from the bills.

Look at both sides of bills — Hard as it may seem, some crooks can split the front and backs of bills apart. They split a $1 bill and a bill of high value, say $50. They glue the front of the $50 to the back of the $1 and the back of the $50 to the front of the $1. At a cost of $51 they now have "$100" which they pass with the $50 side up.

Watch for raised bills — Raised bills are bills of low value with the numbers from a bill of high value glued on the corners. It's usually a $1 bill that's raised to a higher value, so watch for George Washington's portrait on a higher value bill. They're more a curiosity than a problem. The petty crooks who make these bills have to change the damaged higher value bills for good bills. Banks will do this if more than half the bill is still there, but the bank clerks notice someone who does this.

Know how crooks fake bills — Crooks usually copy a real note. Skilled artists working for the government cut the plates used to print money. Crooks don't cut their own plates often. It's skilled work, it's easy to make a mistake and it takes a long time. They make a printing plate from a photo of a real bill or they use a high quality color copying machine.

Check suspect bills — We've no fake bills to show you. It's illegal to own them. All you can do is make yourself familiar with real bills.

Real bills are crisp. Fake bills are often dull and flat, but they look real unless you look at them closely.

Fake notes may look old and used. Crooks may fold and twist them so they look used before passing them. They do this bill by bill or they tumble the bills in a clothes drier or some other machine. It doesn't matter if ink rubs off bills. Sometimes ink rubs off real bills.

Look for differences. Fake bills look like real bills. They'll fool you if you ask yourself whether they look like real bills. Ask yourself if there are details that are different.

Feel the bills. Fake bills often have a different feel than real bills. Often they have more substance to them than real bills. The way they feel is hard to describe. Get used to the feel of real bills. Look closely at bills that feel different. The difference in feel comes from the paper. The government prints real bills on paper with a high rag content. They're as much cloth as they are paper. They even make it through a washing machine OK.[17] The strict government controls on making this paper force crooks to use different paper.

Look through a lens at the paper. Real bills are made of high linen content paper, 75% cotton and 25% flax. They're more like cloth than paper. There are short red and blue hairs in the paper. Some of the hairs are close to the surface. It's possible to put the point of a needle under the hairs near the surface and lift them out of the paper. There's no watermark.[18]

Fake bills are usually made of normal wood fiber paper. Sometimes crooks use linen paper, but the quality doesn't match the paper of real bills. These are normal papers that usually fall apart in a washing machine. There are no red and blue hairs

---

[17]Normal wood pulp papers and even good linen based commercial papers usually fall apart in a washing machine.

[18]A watermark is a design pressed into the paper when it's made. You can see a watermark by holding the paper up to the light.

in the paper[19] but there may be red and blue hair-like marks printed on the paper. The bill is fake if there's a watermark.

The kind of paper is a good way to find out if bills are fake. The government controls the manufacture of the paper used to print money. Crooks don't make their own paper because it needs machinery costing several million dollars. People with that kind of money have no need to print fake money.

Look for specks scattered on the face of the bill. Real bills have no scattered specks, but many bills made on photocopy machines have specks of toner scattered across them.

Look for three point colors. With real bills the colors are solid when seen with a lens. Fake Bills made on a photocopy machine have each color made of three separate colors. Under a lens each color point shows as yellow, red and blue dots.

Report suspect bills — *Never accuse customers of passing fake money on purpose.* Call the Secret Service if you think a bill may be fake. The number for the Secret Service is on the *Quick Phone List.* Federal law requires you to report suspect bills. Say, "Sir, I think this bill may be fake. Would you mind waiting while I call the Secret Service to check on it?" Some customers will agree. Go ahead and call the Secret Service. The Secret service can often tell you if the bill is a fake by the serial numbers or some other marks on the bill.

Some customers won't want to wait. They may be in a hurry or they may be crooks passing fake money. Say to customers who won't wait, "Yes, I understand. It's a drag to have to wait. I'll put this bill in an envelope for the Secret Service if you'll show me some ID and give me your phone number. Then I'll give you a receipt and you can be on your way." Copy the ID and phone number to the receipt and to the envelope where you store the bill.

Customers may put pressure on you. They may demand the bill back. They may get angry about you delaying them. Be firm—hang on to the bill. Say, "I understand it's a drag, Sir, but the law requires me to report suspect bills. I have to keep the bill and put the Secret Service in touch with you. They'll need your help. You can give me an ID and your phone number and take a receipt or you can wait for the Secret Service to arrive."

Call the police and be able to describe customers who leave the store without the bill and without giving an ID. Customers who leave you with the bill and leave the store may be passing fake bills. On the other hand, they may be angry customers in a hurry, so be sure not to accuse them of anything.

---

[19]In rare cases crooks will bleach $1 bills and print higher value bills over them. These are the only cases where there are red and blue fibers in fake money.

Touch a suspect bill as little as possible. Write your initials, the date and time on the white space of the bill. Write the customer's ID and phone number on the outside of an envelope. Seal the bill in the envelope. Keep the envelope in the safe until the Secret Service or police tell you what to do with it.

Follow through with customers who leave suspect bills — Let customers know what happened when the police arrived. Apologize for the fuss, especially if the bill is OK.

Watch for the Fake Repairs Scam

One way thieves steal valuable equipment is to pick it up for "repairs." Thieves who work like this usually look the part. They may have uniforms, ID cards, and be carrying paperwork. They usually have a "business as usual attitude." They may have a phone number for you to call and check them out. They look and act like people who pick up things for repairs. They work alone or in groups.

Release equipment only with the manager's OK — The manager will let you know when to expect someone to pick up equipment. Call if the manager is out of the store and it looks like the manager goofed. Hang on to the equipment if you can't get through. Say, "I'm sorry, but you'll have to come back when the manager is here."

Stand your ground against pressure — Stand firm if someone pushes you to release equipment. Fake repair people may push by telling you "the manager wants it done as soon as possible." They may push you by letting you know they went out of their way to come to the store. They may let you know they're fitting you into a busy work schedule. They may make you think you'll look foolish when the manager returns and the job is not done. No way. It's the manager who'll look foolish for not letting you know about a real pickup.

Suggest a police ID — Hold your ground if you feel swamped and confused. Say, "Excuse me, but you're confusing me. I'd feel better if I had the police help me with this." Then call the police. Say nothing other than you're confused and need help. Say nothing about theft or scams.

Watch for Use the Phone Scams

In one scam a customer asks to use the phone and gets close to the cash drawer. The next time you open the cash drawer it's empty. In another scam a customer asks to make a local call but calls long distance or overseas. Even stores that refuse to let customers use the phone are at risk for phone scams. The crooks who work them are masters at telling a story that melts even the hardest heart.

Take the phone to customers — Say, "Sure, I'll bring it to you" when customers ask to use the phone.

Stop customers going behind the counter — Say, "I'm sorry but our insurance policy stops us having customers behind the counter." Some customers go behind the counter quietly, as if it's the usual thing to do. Some get worked up by a story they tell of an emergency. In telling the story they move about a lot and somehow push behind the counter. Most customers who start to go behind the counter do it without thinking. Crooks copy what these customers do. Be polite to customers who try to go behind the counter but watch them. Be firm with customers who still try to get behind the counter. Make it clear they can use the phone but they can't come behind the counter. Phone calls work as well from one side of the counter as the other.

Take the phone away from the sales area — Keep the counter clear for sales while a customer uses the phone. Say, "Could you please use the phone here? We like to keep that area of the counter clear."

Dial the number — With a smile, ask the customer, "What number do you need?"

Keep in touch while the phone's in use — Know what's going on. Watch out of the corner of your eye. Listen with the corner of your ear. Keep enough contact to be sure the customer uses the phone properly. Watch for customers who try to slip in long distance calls.

Watch for Wrong Change Scams

Most crooks try a change scam when the store is busy. They want you under pressure and off balance. There are three styles of wrong change scam:

1. *Polite wrong change:* You give change from a ten dollar bill and the customer says politely, "Excuse me, but I gave you a twenty."

2. *Wrong change with a ruckus:* You give change from a ten dollar bill and the customer says sharply, "Excuse me, but I gave you twenty dollars." Whatever you reply, the customer's anger rises. There's a lot of noise and other customers are looking. Suddenly, you're right in the middle of a scene.

3. *Flimflam:* A flimflam is like a cardsharp but using money instead of cards. It makes use of clever handling of cash and skillfully mixing the victim up. The bill the customer used to pay and the change are on the counter. There's a question on the change. Suddenly the customer is handling all the money and you end up giving change for a bill you don't receive.

   In another version of the flimflam a customer asks you to give a large bill for several small bills. You give a $20 bill and the customer expertly palms it and puts a $1 bill in its place. Now the customer says you've given a $1 bill by mistake. Crooks usually ask you to do this when you already have the cash drawer open to give change to a customer. They know they're more likely to mix you up if you try to serve two people at once. Say, "I'll be pleased to make change for you when I've finished serving this customer."

Stop wrong change scams dead by following the rules — Change scams end up with your word against the customer's. The weakest person loses and crooks who work scams are strong. Put a good defense in place ahead of time to beat them at their game.

Some *Steps for the Cash Drawer* help stop problems with change. Have the customer keep the cash until you're ready to take it. Put the customer's cash on the ledge outside the cash drawer. Say, "out of."—"That's 6.95 out of ten dollars." Count change back to the customer and say, "OK?" Count change while the customer's cash is outside the cash drawer. Put the last cash in the drawer folded. Follow these steps each time you deal with the cash customers give you. Then you'll be strong if a problem comes up.

Deal with problems on change calmly and politely — Treat every problem as an innocent mistake It can be an innocent mistake when a customer gives ten dollars and asks for change from twenty. It doesn't make it a scam because the customer gets angry. Some customers anger easily and they find it hard to back down. It won't help for you to join in the anger. It'll likely end the problem if you can show the banknote the customer gave you. Most honest customers will believe you when you can clearly tell them the steps you follow at the cash drawer to head off giving wrong change. Dishonest customers will know you'll be hard to shake.

Offer to make a close-out check — Sometimes no matter what you say, customers still say you're wrong. Sometimes customers come back later. They get down the road and suddenly see themselves short ten dollars. Support a customer's feeling. "I understand you feel that you're ten dollars short." Give your point of view. "I do follow a series of steps at the cash drawer to stop me making this kind of mistake." Explain the steps in detail, if necessary. Make a deal. "There'll be ten dollars extra when I close out the till if I've made a mistake. Please let me have your name and number and I'll call you if that's so."

Call the police to end a scene — Customers may continue to cause a scene. You've offered to check the cash drawer at close-out but they don't want to come back. They want their extra change right now and they're not going till they get it. Say, "I really don't know how to handle this. I'm going to call the police and ask for their advice." Once you've said you'll call the police, call the police. Be sure to call the police if the customer storms out of the store at this point. Report a possible confidence trickster.

Call the police when you get stung — Suppose you broke the rules. You felt foolish when the customer made a scene, so you gave an extra ten dollars change. At close-out you find yourself ten dollars short. Let the police know. Other stores are getting stung too. The police will add this case to their file on this crook.

Keep Cool During an Armed Robbery

Few retailers experience an armed robbery, so it's easy to leave your sellers unprepared. Show your concern for your sellers' welfare by seeing they know how to act in the face of a robbery.

Stay calm enough for you and the robbers — Armed robbers are tense. Many are on drugs when they're robbing and it's easy to upset them. These aren't reasonable people. Your safety depends on keeping calm.

Do what the robbers tell you to do — Move calmly without arguing. Let the robbers know you'll do as you're told. Give only what the robbers ask for. Try to include the marker bills. Sometimes police catch robbers quickly and these bills make a link to the crime. Forget about being a hero. Be careful. We want you out of this without harm.

Look at the weapons — Be able to describe them. Be able to pick them out from pictures of weapons.

Remember what the robbers touch — Anything the robbers touch may give fingerprints. Make sure you and others don't touch these items.

Keep any note the robbers may have used — Handle it as little as possible. It may have fingerprints.

Call the police right away — Call the 911 emergency number. Many robbers will warn you against calling the police. Call the police once they're gone and you feel safe. Stay on the line until the police tell you to hang up.

Close the store until the police arrive — Preserve the crime scene until the police arrive.

Write down what happened — Write down exactly what happened in your own words. Do this before you talk to anyone about what happened.

Help the police — Tell them what happened. Stick to the facts without added drama and without making things up. Answer all questions politely, even if they ask you the same questions more than once. Identify the robbers and appear in court.

Keep the amount stolen secret — Reporters and others may ask about the amount stolen. Say, "We'll need an audit to find out." Telling the amount stolen tells other crooks how much they can expect to get by robbing us. The manager will report the amount stolen to the police.

CHAPTER 11

LIST SALES

Stores that prosper give high priority to keeping track of the flow of cash and of items sold and received each day. The flow of cash is the pulse of the store, while the items feed the store. Pay constant attention to these signs of the store's life. Produce reports on cash and items daily. Take steps right away to maintain favorable events and to correct unfavorable events shown by the reports.

Cash from sales goes into a cash drawer, then into a safe or a bank account. Keep cash in a cash drawer only while sales are taking place, never overnight. Keep only enough there to make sales. Move extra cash into a safe until it's deposited in a bank account. Keep only enough cash in the safe overnight to open selling the next day.

The cash drawer is usually part of a cash register which controls the opening and closing of the drawer and prints receipts. A cash register is larger than a stand-alone cash drawer and this makes it harder for a thief to walk off with it.

A simple cash register may do nothing more than record cash taken and given out as change. An electronic cash register may also keep track of items sold and produce a certain number of reports. A *Point of Sale (POS) System* stores the greatest amount of information about items and sales and produces a large number of reports. Other computer programs can gain access to the data it collects.

Stores using only a cash drawer or a simple cash register will have to record the data about items sold by hand and prepare their own reports. This is hard work, but there's no skipping it if the store is to prosper. Even stores with more advanced equipment cannot overlook the importance of knowing how to record sales and prepare reports by hand. Only the richest of them are able to have standby equipment to get them through times when equipment fails.

Know your sales figures — Keep track of the day's sales. Know your sales day by day and hour by hour. Review each day's sales and know how they fit into your pattern of previous sales.

Know what you sell — Keep track of the items you sell as you sell them. Stores that make a profit keep on top of the items they sell. Then the orders they place clearly relate to real needs and projected needs. Well-run stores know what they sell, how many they sell, when they sell them and who sells them. These are the facts needed to keep track of the pulse of the store. Stores "too busy" to track items as they sell them look back and make estimates. That's another way of saying the managers run the store by the seat of their pants. Most stores sell many items and therefore need many data records. The only way to keep on top of many data records is little by little, as the events happen. Let them pile up, or try to look back at them, and they'll swamp you.

Sum up the items day by day. Keep a running count for sales by day, week, month and year. Update the figures daily.

Choose how to list sales — Your choice of how to list sales may relate to how much you can afford to spend on equipment. Whatever your final choice, explore the section on listing sales by hand to give you a reference point for judging automated systems.

- *List sales by hand*—Write sales slips, track the flow of customers and work out the *Customer Flow Summaries*. Prepare the reports on sales and the *Seller's Sales Summaries*. Prepare the *Manager's Sales Summaries*. Store the cash in a simple cash drawer or a mechanical cash register.

- *List sales on an electronic cash register and by hand*—An electronic cash register will cut down some of your hand paperwork. Analyze the reports it gives you and add to them with hand written reports. Make sure you have some backup for an electronic cash register that breaks down. This won't be a problem if you have four or five registers and can get by in a pinch with three. Where you depend on one electronic cash register, make sure your sellers can also list sales by hand.

- *List sales on a Point of Sale System and by hand*—Think of a *Point of Sale System* as a more flexible electronic cash register. Yet be aware you may still have to produce hand written reports too, even when you have all the modules of the system. *Point of Sale Systems* tend to be inventory related rather than sales related. Take care the system doesn't divert your energies from sales management to inventory management. The problems relating to backup machines are the same as for electronic cash registers, only larger and more critical. This is especially so where a store runs a starter system on one marginal computer. Many *Point of Sale Systems* come in a series of modules with the price of the full system being much higher than the price of a starter system. There's much variation in *Point of Sale Systems* and in the modules in use at any store. Periodic system upgrades are common.

Work with Numbers

Make sure your sellers know simple math and know the use of calculators. Otherwise, see that you teach them.

Round Decimals

Make sure your sellers know how to round decimals.

Round to two decimal places — Figures may run to several decimal places. Suppose you buy four items for a total of $14.19 including the tax. Divide $14.19 by 4 and find you paid $3.5475 each. We say 3.5475 is a number written to four decimal places. With coins we can only use two decimal places. You can pay $3.54 or $3.55—there's no in between.

To change $3.5475 to its value in coins "round to two decimal places."

1. Strike out the last digit, which is a 5.

2. Its value is 5 or above, so raise the digit to its left by one—$3.5475 becomes $3.548.

3. Now do it again and $3.548 becomes $3.55.

Round $3.5423 to two decimal places.

1. Strike out the 3 at the far right.

2. Because its value is below 5, do nothing to the digit to its left.

3. $3.5423 becomes $3.542.

4. Now do it again and $3.542 becomes $3.54.

Round to a whole number — The number 90 is a whole number. The number 90.56 is a decimal fraction. Apply the same rules to round a decimal fraction to a whole number. First 90.56 becomes 90.6, then 90.6 becomes 91.

In stores we often see prices like $99.95. The idea is that $99.95 looks less than $100, but when we round it to a whole number it becomes $100. Round 99.95 to a whole number by the same rules:

1. Drop the five at the far right and add one to the 9 to its left.

2. That makes it 10, so carry the one to the nine at its left.

3. That makes it 10, so carry the one to the nine at its left.

4. That makes it 10, so we end up with 100.

Work Out Percentages

Make sure your sellers can work out percentages.

Know the meaning of percent and percentage — "Percent" means "in every hundred"—the sign "%" means "percent." "Pay me 5% of $1,000" means "pay me

$5 for every $100 in $1,000." There are 10 $100s in $1,000, so pay me 10 x $5, that's $50.

"Percentage" is a rate per hundred—"5%" is a percentage. A dollar has 100 cents. 1% (one percent) of a dollar is one cent. 7% (seven percent) of a dollar is seven cents. Suppose the sales tax is 7%. For every dollar's worth of items customers buy, they must pay seven cents tax. That makes a total of $1.07.

Work out a percentage of a number — Divide the number by 100 and multiply the result by the percentage.

7% of $2.00 (200 cents)

In cents:

1.   Divide 200 cents by 100 to get 2 cents.

2.   Multiply 2 cents by 7 to get 14 cents.

In dollars:

1.   Divide $2 by 100 to get $0.02.

2.   Now multiply $0.02 by 7 to get $0.14.

7% of $12.00

Either:

1.   Divide $12 by 100 to get $0.12.

2.   Multiply $0.12 by 7 to get $0.84.

Or:

1.   Divide the percentage by 100 to get 0.07—Divide by moving the decimal point 2 places to the left. With two decimal places the number 7 is 7.00. Move the decimal point one place to the left to get 0.70. That's divided it by 10. Now divide it by 10 again to get 0.07.

2.   Multiply 0.07 by $12 to get $0.84.

Work out percentages in your head, on paper, or using a calculator. Using a calculator you can work out percentages as you would on paper or in your head. Or you can use the [%] key instead:

7% of $12.00

1.   Enter 12 on the display.

2.   Press [x] press [7] press [%]. The display shows 0.84.

Use a Hand Calculator

Most sellers will probably have used a simple calculator, but make sure they really know how to use one.

Press numbers and signs in talking order — Press keys as you'd say what you're doing: "Two plus four equals," "Two times four equals," and so on.

Pressing [2] then [+] then [4] then [=] gets 6, pressing [2] then [x] then [4] then [=] gets 8, and so on.

Clear machine and clear entries — Clear all numbers from the work area with the Clear [C] key. This sets the display to 0.

Clear bad entries with the Clear Entry [CE] key. This clears only the last number on the display.

1. Press [2] then [+] then [4] then [+] then [5] then [CE]—[CE] clears 5 from the display and replaces it with 0.

2. Press [+] and you see the subtotal so far on the display—That's 6, the result of 2 + 4.

3. Press [7] then [=] and you see the total 13 on the display.

Store figures in the memory — Press [M+] to add to memory. Leave the total 13 on display and press [M+]. That stores 13 in the memory. The letter M shows on the display to let you know there's a number in the memory. Enter more numbers and add them to memory with [M+]. Press [M-] to take away from memory. Enter other numbers and take them from memory with [M-]. Press Memory Recall or Clear [MRC] once to call the figure from memory:

1. Press [5] then [+] then [4] then [=] then [M+] to store 9 in the memory.

2. Press [9] then [x] then [10] then [=] to display 90.

3. Press [x] then [MRC] then [=] to display 810.

Press [MRC] twice to clear the memory. That leaves the contents of memory on display. Use the figures on the display to work something else out or clear the display with [CE].

Work out percentages

7% of 76.

Press [7] then [6] then [x] then [7] then [%] and 5.32 appears on the display—5.32 is 7% of 76.

Use a Simple Business Calculator

Fewer sellers will have used a business calculator than will have used a simple calculator. Make sure they can use the business calculator to its full advantage.

Prepare to use a business calculator — This account is for a simple business calculator. Some have more switches and keys than those covered here.

Know it by its paper tape and control switches — A business calculator has a paper tape as well as a display panel. You can print a list of the figures you enter and cross-check them. There's a Print Switch that lets you choose to use the tape. The Paper Feed Key lets you feed the tape through the machine. An Item Switch lets you count items. If you choose to count items, the item count prints when you print a total.

Set the number of decimals with the Decimal Point Selector — The switch slides to any one of the settings + 4 3 2 1 0 F. + is a good choice for a store. It puts the decimal point in for you. It works well where most of the figures are dollars and cents:

Enter   9995   and   99.95   prints on the tape.
Enter   175   and   1.75   prints on the tape.
Enter   25   and   0.25   prints on the tape.
Enter   2   and   0.02   prints on the tape.
Enter   25.   and   25.00   prints on the tape.
Enter   2.   and   2.00   prints on the tape.

Always enter the decimal point for whole dollar amounts. Your totals will be wrong if you forget it.

Set the number of decimals for display and printing at 4, 3, 2, 1, or 0. Setting 2 works well in a store:

Enter   12.95   and   12.95   prints on the tape.
Enter   12.9   and   12.90   prints on the tape.
Enter   12   and   12.00   prints on the tape.
Enter   1   and   1.00   prints on the tape.

Setting 0 ignores any decimal fractions—it's of little use in a store:

Enter   19   and   19   prints on the tape.
Enter   19.45   and   19   prints on the tape.
Enter   19.95   and   19   prints on the tape.

Setting F is for *Floating Point Numbers*. These numbers always have a decimal point whether you key it in or leave it out. The part of the number after the decimal point stays exactly as you enter it. Floating point echoes what you enter, but the printed tape looks ragged:

Enter	1	and	1.	prints on the tape.
Enter	2.5	and	2.5	prints on the tape.
Enter	4.95	and	4.95	prints on the tape.
Enter	9.3675	and	9.3675	prints on the tape.

Keep the rounding switch set at 5/4 — The *Rounding Switch* has 5/4 and an arrow pointing downwards on it. The 5/4 setting rounds displays upwards:

1. Enter 9.956 and 9.96 prints on the tape.

2. Enter 9.954 and 9.95 prints on the tape.

The arrow setting rounds displays downwards:

1. Enter 9.956 and 9.95 prints on the tape.

2. Enter 9.954 and 9.95 prints on the tape.

Enter a number, then enter what to do — Entering numbers and actions differs from a hand calculator. On a hand calculator press [5] then [+] then [4] then [=] and see 9 on the display. On a business calculator press [5] then [+] then [4] then [=] and the 4 remains on display. Press [5] then [+] then [4] then [+] to see 9 on the display. Press [5] then [+] then [4] then [-] to see 1 on the display.

Enter repeat numbers — Sometimes a number repeats in a list. Press [+] twice after the repeat number instead of entering the repeat number again.

Suppose you're adding 19.95, 29.95, 29.95 and 10.50. Set the *Decimal Point Selector Switch* at +, press [1] then [9] then [9] then [5] then [+] then [2] then [9] then [9] then [5] then [+] then [+] then [1] then [0] then [5] then [0] then [+].

Suppose you hit a run of 8 numbers the same—press [+] 8 times. You could multiply the number by 8 instead of pressing [+] 8 times. That's OK, but it may break your stride to do that. Often it's easier to press the [+] key when you see a repeat number.

Print subtotal or grand total — Print the total as either subtotal or total. The usual sign on a subtotal key is a diamond. Suppose the total on the display is 25. Press the subtotal key and 25 prints on the tape with a diamond beside it. Now press [5] then [+] and the display shows the total 30.

The usual sign on a total key is *. Press this key and the total on display prints with a T beside it. The total remains on the display, but you can't use it. The next number you enter starts the next set of figures.

Recall memory and clear memory with separate keys — Business calculators have more keys than hand calculators. The Memory Recall Key has M and a diamond on it. The Memory Clear Key has M* on it.

Number lists with the Number Key — The key marked # prints the last number you pressed. The number clears so it doesn't take part in what you're working out. On the tape the number prints with the # sign beside it. Number lists of figures with the Number Key:

Press [1] then [#] then [2] then [5] then [+] then [2] then [#] then [30] then [+] then [*] to display 55. The tape reads:

```
1.  #
25.  +
2.#
30.  +
55.  T.
```

Work the Cash Drawer

The basics of working the cash drawer are the same for all stores. They apply equally to a simple cash drawer supported by hand written sales slips, a simple cash register, an electronic cash register and to a computer-based sales system.

Handle Cash Safely

Lean on your sellers to get them to handle cash properly. The most likely losses you can prevent will come from impulse stealing. This will spring from sloppy handling of cash by the sellers. Scams and stickups only occur now and then but make your sellers aware of the main scams. Beyond keeping little cash in the cash drawer there's little you can do about stickups.

Prevent impulse stealing by customers by putting the cash drawer where it's hard to reach. A cash drawer behind the counter is better than one in an open area. It helps if customers can't reach the cash drawer by leaning over the counter.

A store that's running on a shoestring may not have a cash drawer. Avoid a cash box. A cash box almost invites someone to pick it up and walk off with it. A neck purse or a fanny purse is better. The cash is then under the seller's close control. Of course, the seller must wear the purse at the front.

At the other extreme is a store that takes in a lot of cash. Have someone pick up cash from the cash drawers several times a day. Take it to a locked room for counting and locking in the safe. Arrange for a security service to pick up the cash from your safe and take it to the bank.

Keep cash in the bank — The only place the store's cash is really safe is in the bank. The bank guards cash carefully. It's the bank's problem if someone steals from the bank. It's your problem if someone steals from the store.

Aim to make a bank deposit at least once a day. Skip the deposit when sales are dead. Make several deposits when sales are active. Check the amount in the cash drawer against the highest amount of cash allowed in the cash drawer. *Daily* lists this amount. Check the amount you're planning to deposit against the lowest amount of cash allowed for a bank deposit. *Daily* lists this amount.

Lock cash in the safe — Store cash safely between visits to the bank. Keep only the cash you need to make change for customers in the cash drawer. Move the rest to the safe. You need some cash on hand to make change when you open in the morning. *Daily* lists this amount. The safe is the place to keep the cash you need to make change. That's the only amount to keep in the safe overnight. Deposit the rest, unless it's below the lowest amount you allow for a bank deposit. Cash is fairly safe in a safe but thieves break into safes and they also steal them.

Lock cash in the cash drawer — Keep the cash you take from customers in the cash drawer. It's usually the bottom part of a cash register. In stores that write sales slips by hand it's a separate drawer with a lock on it. Lock the cash drawer whenever you move away from it. It only takes a skilled thief seconds to empty an unlocked cash drawer. It's true that a bell rings when a cash drawer opens, but the noise in the store may make it hard to hear. You'll miss hearing it if you're at the other side of the store busy with a customer.

Take care if you're busy at the cash drawer and a customer asks for help. It's natural to turn your attention to the customer and forget the cash drawer. Be safe rather than natural. Say, "I'll be right with you as soon as I lock the cash drawer." Lock the cash drawer and then turn your attention to the customer.

Keep the cash drawer key with you — Wear the cash drawer key on a chain around your neck or wrist. Wear the key all the time. A cash drawer key on the counter or hanging on a nail by the cash drawer is almost the same as an unlocked cash drawer.

Stand beside an unlocked cash drawer — Lock the cash drawer when you go away from it. Lock the cash drawer even if you'll only be away from it "for a few minutes."

Keep the cash drawer closed — Open the cash drawer only as long as it takes to move cash in or out. It asks customers to look the cash drawer over if you keep it open longer than necessary. It sends a signal to crooks that you're careless with cash. Sellers who walk away from an open cash drawer tempt even honest customers to steal. Keep the cash drawer closed while you write credit card drafts.

Count cash in private — Count cash in a locked room. The safest place to count cash is in a separate room behind a locked door. Lock the cash up if you need to open the door to anyone.

Count cash when the store is closed. The store becomes a locked room when it's closed. Wait till the store closes to count cash if you can.

Count cash in a private place where customers can't see you. Some stores without a locked room need to count cash while the store is open. Do this only if there are other sellers in the store. Let them know you're counting. Let them know they can't call on you for anything else while you're counting. Say, "Please don't disturb me while I'm counting cash," to anyone who talks to you while you're counting. Only count where customers can't see you—that's usually at the back of the storeroom.

Count cash on a clear desk. Move everything off the desk before you begin to count. Working around clutter while you count cash asks for trouble.

Hold cash in your hand — This is your fail-safe reaction. Suppose you're handling cash and someone grabs your attention. It's natural to put the cash down, but be safe instead of being natural. Gather the cash up and hold it in your hand. Cling to it until you straighten out and look after it properly. The rule is: Grab the cash and hold on to it if anything spooks you.

Say good-bye to cash you put down — The surest way to lose cash is to put it down while you do something else. Stores attract thieves who react to breaks like that. A pile of cash even tempts normally honest customers to steal. The cash can go almost as fast as you can blink your eyes.

Treat cash in an envelope like cash — Cash in an envelope is still cash. Something happens to many sellers when they put cash in an envelope. Once it's out of sight, it's out of mind. So far they've followed all the rules. Then they seal cash in an envelope and leave the envelope lying on the customer counter.

Cash in an open envelope shouts that it's cash. Customers know it's cash when they can see the edges of the bills.

Cash in a banking envelope shouts that it's cash. Perhaps only customers who saw the cash go into a plain envelope know it's cash. Everyone knows it's cash when it's in a banking envelope.

Treat credit card sales drafts like cash — To the store, credit card sales drafts signed by customers are cash. While someone who steals them probably can't turn them into cash, the store still loses the cash.

Follow safety rules when banking — Write the serial number of a marker bill on the bank deposit form. Leave a copy of the bank deposit form in the store. The number on this copy may help put someone who robs the store in jail.

Make it hard for robbers to work out your pattern. Go to the bank at different times of day if you can. Take different routes to the bank each day. Send different sellers to make the deposits each day. Carry bank deposit envelopes in an ordinary bag instead of in your hand. Carry money bags inside an ordinary bag. Carry money in the trunk of the car when you drive to the bank. Have someone go with you when you bank at night.

Pre-count Cash

To pre-count cash is to count it ahead of the time that you have to count it. The aim is to keep as much cash as possible in counted bundles, working with only a little loose cash.

Pre-count to speed up end of shift counting — At the end of a shift sellers are tired and there's lots to do. One job is counting the cash in the cash drawer. Counting is easier if sellers pre-count cash during the shift.

Pre-count to keep cash safe — As sellers pre-count cash they notice if there's too much cash in the drawer. Move any cash not needed for making change to the safe. As sellers pre-count cash they give it attention and bring it under control. That helps to protect it.

Pre-count between customers — Sellers on shifts by themselves wait till the store's empty to pre-count. Other sellers wait till they're low on *The Wheel*.

Scrap the pre-count when customers show up — Sometimes beginning to pre-count the cash draws customers like bait. Sellers scrap the pre-count even if they've nearly finished it. They put the cash back in the cash drawer and try again later.

Pre-count only one item at a time — Pre-count dollar bills now, dimes later, and so on—pre-count one by one.

Pre-count bills — Take one dollar bills as an example. Sellers take the one dollar bills from the cash drawer and hold them in their hand. Close the cash drawer. Tidy the bills without putting them down—pass them from hand to hand. Smooth creased bills—unfold turned down corners of bills. Arrange the bills "heads up," that's with the picture of George Washington on top and facing the seller. Count the bills by passing them from hand to hand. Count 20 one dollar bills. Separate the 20 bills from the rest of the bills with a finger. Count the 20 bills again to check the count. Keep the bundle of 20 bills in your hand and return the other bills to the cash drawer. Put two bank note rubber bands around the bundle of 20 bills. One rubber band goes near the first T in "THE UNITED STATES OF AMERICA." the second goes near the last A.

Store the bundle of bills in the safe or return it to the cash drawer. Take care to leave enough cash in the cash drawer to make change. Put the bundles under the loose bills in the cash drawer. For $45 that's 2 bundles of 20 bills, with 5 loose bills on top. Take the rubber bands off the top bundle when you run out of loose bills. For bills from $2 to $20 make bundles of 10. For bills $50 and above make bundles of 5.

Pre-count coins — Plan to scoop the coins back into the cash drawer if customers turn up. Open a coin envelope so you have somewhere to put the coins you count. Count on the counter near the cash drawer. It's too hard to count a lot of coins hand to hand without spilling some. Open the cash drawer. Put the coins on the counter close to its edge. Close the cash drawer. Hold one hand cupped below the level of the counter. With the other hand slide 10 coins, 2 at a time, into a cupped hand. Put the 10 coins in a separate pile on the counter. Slide the same 10 coins 2 at a time into a cupped hand to check the count. Put the 10 coins in the coin envelope. Go on like this putting 10 coins at a time into the envelope. Keep a running count in your head or make tally marks on the envelope. There may be less than 10 coins left over at the end. Count them and add them to the coin envelope. Seal the coins in the envelope. Write seller's name, the date and time on it. Write the amount like this: 43 x 0.25 = 10.75. Put the envelope in the *Coin Drawer*. Write the amount in pencil on your *Cash Report* under Extra Coins Out. Write in pencil because you may change this figure later.

Pre-count more to count less — The more sellers pre-count, the less they need to count at closing. The bundles of bills are ready for the bank—leave the rubber bands on. The coins are already in the *Coin Drawer* and on the *Cash Report*.

Set Up a Cash Tray

Know cash tray from cash drawer and cash register. A cash drawer is a drawer to lock up money you take from customers. It can stand alone or can be the bottom part of a cash register. A cash register is an adding machine built onto a cash drawer. Many cash drawers have a tray inside them that you can lift out. The tray has slots to store different values of money separately. Using two trays make sharing a cash drawer easy. While one tray is in use, another seller sets up the second tray. Then at change over time one tray comes out and the other goes in. Some cash drawers have no trays or have only one tray. Cash drawers without trays usually have slots for different values of cash built into them. We still use the idea of separate trays—a "tray" is the cash that goes into the drawer. One "tray" comes out and the new "tray" goes in. It's slower than using real trays but it controls the cash.

Count your tray in a safe place — Get your *Opening Change Envelope* from the safe. Get any extra change from the manager. Get any extra coins from the *Coin Drawer*.

Put bills and coins in their right places — Follow the plan shown in the drawing:

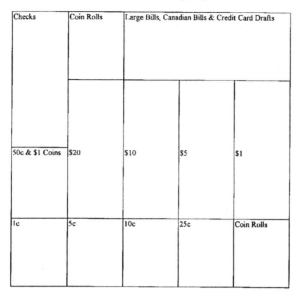

Checks	Coin Rolls	Large Bills, Canadian Bills & Credit Card Drafts		
50c & $1 Coins	$20	$10	$5	$1
1c	5c	10c	25c	Coin Rolls

Only cash, checks and drafts in the cash tray — It's a cash drawer—put odds and ends in the *Odds and Ends Box*. Put credit cards left by customers where they belong. Keep the cash drawer neat so you can use it without fumbling or searching.

Keep large bills out of sight — Hide $50 and $100 bills under the cardboard in the large bills slot.

No extra coin rolls and coin envelopes in the coin slots — Keep the coin slots for loose coins only. Rolls or envelopes of coins on top of loose coins slow you down when you need to make change. Keep the coin roll slot full of rolls and envelopes of coins. Keep some coin rolls and envelopes in the *Coin Drawer* while you sell. It's easier to get at the *Coin Drawer* than it is to open the safe. Store rolls and envelopes of coins overnight in the safe.

Leave Empty Cash Drawers Open

Keep cash drawers locked when there's cash in them. Put all cash kept in the store overnight in the safe. Leave cash drawers unlocked and open when they're empty. Leaving an empty cash drawer open may save the cost of a new cash drawer. Thieves break open closed cash drawers looking for cash. They come in with a big screwdriver and work quickly. They don't spend time checking if a drawer's locked or figuring out how to open a cash drawer.

Follow the Steps for the Cash Drawer

There's some detail in what at first seems to be the simple act of working with customers at the cash drawer. Getting things right here is a big help in keeping your store's reputation high. It also cuts down on expensive mistakes with handling cash.

Focus on customers — Smile as you talk to customers. Keep eye contact. Let customers see your face, instead of the top of your head. Too many sellers act like robots at the cash drawer.

Map out work areas of the counter — In your mind's eye map out *Stack Area*, *Billed Area* and *Bagging Area* of the counter. Stack items in the *Stack Area* before you list them on the receipt. List items one at a time to make sure customers pay for all items. Move each item to the *Billed Area* as you list it. Put a shopping bag in the *Bagging Area* and bag the billed items.

Take control of the items — Customers will put items all over the counter or hang on to them. Group them in the *Stack Area* before you begin listing them.

Follow the steps for listing sales — How sellers list sales depends on whether they use sales slips, a cash register or a *Point of Sale System*. The specific details will vary from store to store. Give the details for your store to your sellers.

Tell the total price including tax — Say something like, "Including the tax that's twelve ninety-five."

Find out how customers will pay as you bag the items — Begin bagging the items. It's too early to take any money yet. Customers usually make it clear how they're going to pay. They get out cash or credit cards. They ask if you take VISA or personal checks, and so on. Otherwise, as you begin to bag the items ask, "Will that be cash, Sir?"

Have plenty of change on hand — Selling goes smoothly when you have enough change in the cash drawer. Asking customers for change slows things down and you look clumsy. Care about customers enough to get ready for them. Customers have a right to expect you to make change for them. Be sure that sellers review their change needs with the manager if they run out of change. Plan so it doesn't happen again.

Bag items while customers search for change — Many customers want to give correct change. They often first give banknotes, then begin searching for coins. Sometimes people with them begin to search too. Let them search for change while you bag the items.

Take all coins customers offer — Take the coins customers offer, even if you already have too many. Some customers ask, "Would you like the correct change?" Others ask, "Would you like some extra pennies?" Answer "Yes, please. That's a big help." These customers want to get rid of their extra coins, or they want to help. Take their coins and make them happy.

Bag while customers sign sales drafts — Have customers sign sales drafts for credit card charges before opening the cash drawer.

Bag while customers write personal checks — Have customers write checks and OK them before opening the cash drawer.

Count items as you bag them — Compare your count with the item count on the receipt. Make sure you charge for all items.

Put a flier in the bag — Give all customers a copy of the latest flier.

Let customers look after their cash until you're ready — Some customers offer cash right away. Say, "Please hold on to the cash until the bill is ready. It'll be safer that way."

Look at customers as you tell price and cash taken — Look and say something like, "That's six thirty-four out of twenty thirty-four." Be sure customers hear you—say it again if they're busy talking.

Work out the change — Use a calculator unless the cash register or sales system works out change.

Keep cash taken in view while you open the cash drawer — Put the cash you take on the ledge of the cash drawer. Leave it on the ledge while you count the change. Then you can show customers the money they gave you if they question the amount.

Count change to yourself while the receipt prints — Count to yourself first—later you'll count to the customer. This gives you a double check as you see in banks. In banks the first count is by the cashier to the cashier. The second count is from the cashier to the customer.

Tell total price, cash taken, and change — Say something like, "That's six-fifty out of twenty. That's thirteen-fifty change."

Put receipts in the bag — Put receipts in the bag unless customers ask for them in their hands. Then we know we gave all customers receipts. Then we can ask for a receipt with every return.

Count change to customers and say, "OK?" Counting change is slightly different for different ways of listing sales:

For registers or systems that print the change on the receipt: Count the change to customers. For a customer who gave a $20 bill for a bill of $6.50: "That's ten, plus one, two, three, equals thirteen. Plus fifty cents, equals thirteen-fifty change. OK?"

For other cash registers and for sales slips: Count the change to customers from the price. For a customer who gave a $20 bill for a bill of $6.50: "Six fifty plus fifty cents equals seven. Plus one, two, three equals ten. Plus ten equals twenty. OK?"

The "OK?" is important. A customer who gives an OK isn't likely to question the change.

Put cash taken in the cash drawer — Put each coin and bill in the right slot. Close the cash drawer. Lock it if you move away from it.

Charge to Credit Cards and Debit Cards

List the kinds of cards you take. Then let your sellers know how to charge to them. The details will vary with the level of automation you have. Where you use an electronic system, make sure your sellers also know how to use a standard imprinter for charges. All electronic systems will fail from time to time.

Make charges electronically — Details will vary with the kind of system in use.

Make charges using an imprinter

- List credit card sales on sales drafts as well as listing them on receipts.

- Write the sales draft before printing the receipt on a cash register.

- Keep the cash drawer closed.

- Have customers sign sales drafts.

- Hand customers their copy before printing the receipt.

Follow these steps with the imprinter.

1. Tell the customer the amount—"That will be 47.08 including the tax."

2. Pull the imprinter handle to the left end of the imprinter.

3. Take the credit card from the customer and check the expiry date. Credit cards are only good to the date on the card.

4. Check the date on the imprinter's date wheel.

5. Put the credit card face up so you can read the writing on the card. The credit card goes in the space above the store's ID plate. Fit it into the guides that keep it in place and make sure it lies flat.

6. Select the right sales draft—MasterCard for MasterCard, and so on. Mark the check box for MasterCard or VISA on shared slips.

7. Mark the check box labeled "Expiration Date Checked."

8. Put the sales draft in the imprinter. Place it over the credit card and the store's ID plate. Fit its bottom corners in the guides that hold it in place. Make sure it lies flat.

9. Run the imprinter handle firmly to the right of the imprinter and run it back to its starting place.

10. Check the bottom copy of the sales draft. Check for a good impression of the customer's credit card. Check for a good impression of the store's ID plate. Run a new sales draft if either impression is not clear.

11. Check the card's expiry date again by reading it from the bottom copy.

12. Write the cash register receipt or sales slip number on the sales draft.

13. Enter the subtotal on the Subtotal line. The subtotal is the total price of the items before adding the sales tax.

14. Enter the sales tax on the Sales Tax line.

15. Enter the total on the Total line.

16. Sign your name on the sales draft in the box labeled "Clerk's Initials" or below the entry for the receipt number.

17. Hand the customer a pen and say, "Please sign and write your phone number" as you point to the Cardholder's Signature area. Hold on to the credit card while the customer signs. That stops a forger copying the signature on the card. Keeping the card also lets you check the signature on the card against the signature on the sales draft.

18. Bag the items while the customer signs.

19. Get the pen back from the customer.

20. Check that signature and phone number are on the sales draft. We can't force customers to give their phone numbers. Act as if it's normal to give them. Smile and say to customers who won't give their phone numbers, "That's fine. Make sure you don't leave your card behind. We won't be able to call and let you know."

21. Compare the signature on the sales draft with the signature on the back of the credit card.

22. Call for an authorization number in these cases:

- Credit card has no signature on it.

- Credit card looks altered.

- Customer asks you about the floor limit.

- Customer buys many items and isn't worried about prices.

- Customer buys, leaves the store and comes back to buy again.

- Customer is nervous or talks too much.

- Customer misspells the name on the card when signing.

- Customer seems like a new credit card user. May not know where to sign the sales draft, and so on.

- Customer takes the credit card out of a pocket rather than a handbag or wallet.

- Customer tries to get the credit card back and cancel the sale when it looks as if you're going to call for an authorization. Say, "This will only take a minute," and continue dialing. Hang on to the credit card. It's the property of the credit card company, not of the customer.

- Customer tries to hurry you along.

- Signature on the card is different from the name on the face of the card. Suppose the name on the card is John Smith and the signature on the card is Mary Jones. It may be that John Smith has given an OK for Mary Jones to use one of his cards. On the other hand, "Mary Jones" may have found the card without a signature on it and have signed it as Mary Jones because she can't pass herself off as John Smith.

- Signature on the sales draft doesn't agree with the signature on the credit card.

- Total amount is over the floor limit for the credit card. Know the floor limits for each card by heart. *Daily* lists the floor limits.

23. Enter authorization number in the Authorization Number box.

24. Give customer the Customer Copy of the sales draft.

25. Return the credit card to the customer.

26. Put store and bank copies of the sales draft in the cash drawer.

27. Close the cash drawer.

Refund charges using an imprinter — Make out a credit card draft to refund on a sale made with a credit card. Never refund cash for a credit card sale. Credit drafts look like sales drafts but are red. They stand out from the blue or black sales drafts. Keep them hidden so sellers don't use them as sales drafts by accident, but see that sellers know where they are. It's important to take care here because credit drafts give money to customers.

Match the right credit draft with the right credit card. It's messy to use an American Express credit draft to refund a VISA sale. It makes extra bookkeeping costs.

Note these differences to filling in a sales draft.:

- List each item refunded as well as the receipt number.

- Customer signs as normal in the Cardholder's Signature area.

- Seller signs in the Merchant's Signature area.

Take Personal Checks

A personal check is a check written on the bank account of the person who signs the check.

You increase sales when you take personal checks. You also increase costs because some checks will bounce. It will cost you sellers' time to track the writers down. You won't find some of the writers and you'll have to write off some bad checks.

Keep score of how much trade you get from checks against the cost of bad checks. That way you can make business decisions about taking checks. Without a score, you'll make emotional decisions.

The personal checks you take will relate to your store's situation. Some stores find they can take almost any personal check. Others find they can take scarcely any. Some stores refuse all personal checks even when the risk of them bouncing is small. They don't want the risk and the bother. That's another way of saying they won't put themselves out to give customer service.

It's better to have all sellers trained to handle checks than to have one seller who OKs checks. You stress a high standard of service. Having only one seller who handles checks puts you on a level with a supermarket. Of course, until you're sure of new sellers, let them know who can back them up when they take checks.

It's easy and cheap to track down hometown customers who write bad checks. That leads some stores to take only hometown checks. That seems safer, but is it? Keep separate scores on hometown and out-of-town checks. It's a pity to turn down extra trade from out-of-towners and cross-border shoppers unless there's good reason. Find out what other local stores do. What about other stores in your shopping center? What about other stores like yours in similar areas of town? Try to find out if they have good reasons for doing what they do. They might have made decisions based on fear rather than facts. Try talking about percentages to see how good their facts are. What was the percentage of bad checks and the percentage of dollars lost on bad checks? Other stores can help you prevent losses you can avoid. They can also give you a sense of fear you don't need.

Some retailers sell expensive items that crooks can resell easily. They have to be extra careful when accepting checks. They need to subscribe to a service that OKs checks. Without this service they can be victims of the after-hours check scam. It's near closing when a well-off-looking customer comes in. This customer runs up a bill that makes mouths water and offers to pay by check. The customer has a story that boils down to it's now or never and it's with the check. It's too late to call your bank manager to get an OK on the check. The retailer loses when greed overcomes sense.

There are several services that guarantee checks. Before you use them, find out how much it will cost you. Then compare that figure to what bad checks cost you now. Consider whether the service will open you up to taking more checks than you do now.

Look into all bad checks right away. Most come from customers who haven't balanced their checkbooks. Let the police know when it looks as if you've taken a bad check from a crook. Let them know, even if it's not worth the effort to you. Watch out for other bad checks. Word may have spread that your store is an easy mark. Find out how the bad check got through your check system. Did the seller go through the steps for taking checks properly? Do the steps need changing? Take it calmly. It's easy to overreact to a few bad checks.

Keep bad checks between you and the writer and possibly the police. Now and again you'll see an angry retailer who displays bad checks in the store window. The image of the store suffers from this open display of anger. There might be a good reason for a bad check. Then the store can find itself with bills for damages and legal fees.

You may need to tell your sellers not to take checks from certain customers. *Daily* is the place for this list. It's a mistake to tape the list on the cash register where customers who peer over can see it. It leaves you open to possible legal action and it makes your store look tacky.

Here's a model for letting your sellers know how you deal with checks in your store.

Take all U.S. and Canadian personal checks — In our store we've had little trouble with bad personal checks. Until we run into trouble, we'll be easy on taking personal checks.

Payroll and government checks aren't personal checks. Payroll and government checks look official. They look as if they're OK. That's why crooks forge them so often. Let the bank take the risk on official looking checks.

Second party checks aren't personal checks. Here's an example of a second party check: John Smith writes a check to Mary Jones. Mary Jones writes on the back "Pay to The Clam Shell Gift Shop" and signs it.

Take charge politely — Take the time you need to handle personal checks. Be polite and stay in charge. You make the rules and you set the pace. Slow down and handle the check properly if anyone tries to rush you. You may only have a pushy customer who's in a hurry. You may have someone who's skilled at passing bad checks.

A customer has no right to pay by check. It's a favor you choose to do for customers. Never say this to customers but know it for times you have to refuse a check.

Take personal checks from strangers only to the amount of the bill — Some customers want to write the check over the amount of the bill. The bill's $50, but they write a check for $70. They want $20 cash in change. Customers write over the amount to save a trip to the bank. It's OK to go up to $20 over for a regular customer. This can be a bad check scam. The point of writing the check is to get the change, rather than the items. Stick to the amount of the bill for a stranger.

Back up the personal check — Say, "That'll be fine" when customers ask if you'll take their checks. Then add, "We need to see your driver's license and a credit card to back the check up." Be sure to use the phrase "a credit card to back the check up." This isn't the same as "two pieces of ID." Steer clear of those words. Most of them will show you the license and the card. Customers may ask what "a credit card to back the check up" means. Tell them, "In case we get a check returned by the bank, we make the charge to the credit card. We also add the bank charges and bookkeeping fees."

Know the current charge for returned personal checks — Some customers will ask what the charge is for returned checks. Know the charge from *Daily*. Make it clear these are costs we have to pay. Say, "The bank charges us $x and the bookkeeper charges us $y. That's a total of $z." The store makes nothing by charging for returned checks.

Take a passport instead of a driver's license — Some customers have no driver's license. A passport or other photo ID identifies them just as well.

Look at the photo ID — Check that you're dealing with the right person.

Watch customers sign personal checks — Have customers sign checks in front of you. Have customers sign checks again if they come with signed checks.

Have customers initial changes — Sometimes customers make a mistake when they write checks. It's OK for them to correct mistakes if they initial all changes. Look all checks over for changes before you take them.

Look for name, address and phone number on the check — Only take checks with a printed name and address on them. Check the printed name and address against the driver's license. Ask about any differences—then decide if you want to take the check. Get a phone number, including the area code. Write it under the address if it's not printed on the check.

Ask if the phone number is OK — Ask, "Are you still at this phone number?" Ask visitors for a local and a home phone number.

Look for date and amount — Check for today's date on the check. Post-dated checks are checks with a date some time in the future. We take no post-dated checks because they cause extra work and bookkeeping.

Fill in a cross on the front of the check — Banks rubber stamp the backs of checks. They'll cover up anything you write there.

Driver's License Number & State or Province or Passport Number & Country.	Customer's Birth Date.
Credit Card Number & Expiry Date.	Day & date. Receipt Number. Your Name √.

Make sure the customer signed the check. An unsigned check has no value. Put a check mark by your name to show you've checked for a signature on the check.

Make sure the customer wrote the amount in longhand and in figures. Check the longhand value against the value in figures.

Check the date on the check.

Take U.S. and Canadian Travelers Checks

U.S. and Canadian travelers checks are about as safe as money. While there are problems with forged and stolen travelers checks, so are there problems with fake money. One advantage travelers checks have over money is that you can ask for an ID from people using them.

Treat travelers checks like money — Travelers buy travelers checks from a bank. Unlike personal checks we know the bank has money to cover them. A travelers check is as good as money when a customer signs it. Suppose a customer's bill is $5. Take a $50 travelers check and give $45 change. Only do that with personal checks when you know the customer well.

You still have to take care with travelers checks. Crooks who forge them and steal them can cost you money.

Watch customers sign travelers checks — Customers sign their names on travelers checks when they buy them. They sign each one in front of the bank officer who sells the checks. Typically, they sign in a space at the top left corner of the checks. Customers sign the checks again when they use them. This time they sign in front of you. Typically, they sign in a space at the bottom left corner labeled: Countersign Here in Presence of Person Cashing.

Ask customers to sign again if they hide the signature — Crooks who pass stolen travelers checks usually sign them ahead of time. It's easier for crooks to forge signatures where they can work at their own speed rather than under pressure in a store. At the store they act as if they're signing, but they hide the tip of the pen. One way is to put a hand between you and the checks. You see the pen moving and think you see someone signing the check. Another way is to sign the top check of a pile of checks. Then lift the top check so it blocks your view of the checks below it. Then fake signing the rest of the checks. The passer gives you the checks but palms the top one.

See the tip of the pen touching the travelers check as it writes. Otherwise, say, "I'm sorry. I missed seeing you sign. Please sign again." Any space on the travelers check is OK for the new signature.

Ask customers who drop travelers checks to sign again — A crook passing stolen travelers checks may buy some in the same name. The passer signs them in front of you, so everything looks good. Then the passer drops them on the floor "by accident" and switches them for the checks with forged signatures. Say, "I'm sorry, but these checks have been out of my sight since you signed them. Please sign them for me again."

Ask customers to sign again after a scene in the store — Scenes are acts that get your attention while thieves steal from the store. A customer gets ready to sign some travelers checks and there's a scene. Perhaps two people start arguing in loud angry voices. The customer has signed the travelers checks when the scene is over. Say, "I'm sorry. I missed seeing you sign. Please sign again."

Ask for an ID — Copy the number and type of a photo ID to the front of a travelers check. A driver's license or a passport is a suitable ID:

"JOHNSHC504PW Washington Driver's License."

Copy the address from the ID:

"149 130th Ave SE, Bellevue, WA 98008."

Write your name and the date below the ID number.

Stand firm when customers get upset — Crooks passing stolen travelers checks may try to make you feel foolish. They may get angry or laugh when you want a new signature or an ID. Stay cool, polite and firm. Smile sweetly and say, "Yes, I know it sounds foolish, but that's what I have to do."

Call the police when customers back off — Everything is OK until you ask for a new signature or an ID. Then the customer backs off, perhaps in anger. Suddenly the sale is off. Let the police know someone may be passing stolen travelers checks.

Compare the two signatures — One person usually signed the travelers checks when buying them. The signature you get must match the original signature. Some travelers checks have names like Travelers' Checks for Two. Two people sign on buying these checks. The signature you get must match one of the original signatures. Refuse the check if it looks as if someone changed the original signature.

Be careful if the original signature is written with a felt pen. Crooks sometimes use felt pens to write over the original signature. Look for signs of a different signature beneath the felt-pen signature.

Take only a reasonable amount in travelers checks — We're running a store, not a bank. Take a $20, $50 or $100 travelers check for a $10 sale. Draw the line at two or three $100 travelers checks for $10 sale. Some customers ask you to cash extra travelers checks to help them out. Crooks try this to pass stolen travelers checks quickly. Let's spread the risk around. Say, "I'm sorry, Sir. The store doesn't allow me to go that much over the bill on travelers checks."

Keep Track of Layaways

Let your sellers know about layaways if you use them.

Try for a credit card before a layaway — Some customers ask for a layaway. Keep the layaway open but try to avoid its paperwork and storage. Say, "Yes, a layaway's fine, or would you prefer to use a credit card?" Suggest a layaway to customers with little cash and no credit card.

Know the terms for layaways

- Down payment is 25% of total including the tax.

- Pay off the layaway within 3 months.

It's OK to allow for payoff within 4 months if it helps make the sale. Only suggest this to customers who say they can't buy because they can't pay in 3 months.

Fill in the Layaway Slip — *Layaway Slips* are like sales slips with a section to enter layaway payments.

O			
LAYAWAY		7	48

Fine Arts Gift Shop
6735 Westlake Avenue
Seattle, Washington
(206) 873-6877

DATE	1 Feb 94	PHONE	688-8353
NAME	Mary Rogers		SOLD BY
ADDRESS	674 Aurora St		BH

	Item	Amount	
1	101/8 Swd Flatware	400	00
2			
3			
4			
5			
6			
7			
8			

I agree to pay the amount due on or before

3 May 94

or the store will return the items to stock.

Mary Rogers
CUSTOMER'S SIGNATURE

SUBTOTAL	400	00
TAX	28	00
TOTAL	428	00
DEPOSIT	107	00
BALANCE	321	00

Payment Record — Keep receipts for all payments.

DATE	SLIP NO	AMOUNT	BALANCE	DATE	SLIP NO	AMOUNT	BALANCE
3/1/94	48-10	107.00	214.00	BH			
4/5/94	68-16	107.00	107.00	BH			

Layaway Slips have three copies. The customer gets the top copy. The second copy is for the seller's paperwork. The third copy is a stiff copy. Tie it to the layaway or staple it to the layaway's shopping bag.

Write the layaway book number in front of the *Layaway Slip* number.

Write your initials in the "SOLD BY" box.

Finish the header with today's date, the customer's phone number, name and address.

List the items put on layaway.

Work out subtotal, tax and total.

Take away the deposit to get the balance.

Enter the date for paying off the layaway in the "I agree ..." box.

Get the customer to sign the agreement.

Stick the date for the final payment in the customer's mind. Say, "The total is $428 of which you've paid $107 deposit. That leaves three more monthly payments of $107. The last payment's due by Tuesday, May 3rd. That's just in time for Jane's wedding."

Prepare a regular receipt for the layaway deposit — Prepare a regular receipt as well as the layaway deposit slip. Write a sales slip or ring a receipt on the cash register or *POS System.*

Parcel out the receipts — See that all copies of receipts go to the right place:

- Give the customer the top copy of the *Layaway Slip* and the receipt.

- Put the seller's copy of the *Layaway Slip* in your *Seller's Report.*

- Tie the third copy of the *Layaway Slip* on the layaway item or staple it to the shopping bag they're in.

- Store the items in the layaway area of the storeroom.

Update the Layaway List — Add items laid away to the *Layaway List* in *Daily.* The store still owns items on layaway, so you can't list them as sold. On the other hand, you can't sell them to someone else. You have to bear in mind items on layaway when you place new orders. The solution is to keep a list of items on layaway.

Add the next payment due to the *Layaway List* in *Daily.* Keep on top of layaway payments. Call customers to remind them when their payments are overdue.

Take payments on layaways — Follow these steps:

1. Write a sales slip or ring a receipt on the cash register or *POS System.*

2. Write the payment on the Payment Record section of the *Layaway Slip.*

3. Write on the store's copy that's with the items.

4. Enter date.

5. Enter the receipt number.

6. Enter amount paid and remaining balance.

7. Squeeze in your initials too.

   Write the same facts on the customer's copy, if the customer brings it. Staple the customer's receipt to the customer's copy of the *Layaway Slip.* Tell customers who forget to bring their *Layaway Slips* to staple the receipt to the *Layaway Slip.*

8. Cross out this payment on the Layaway List in Daily.

9. Add the next payment due to the *Layaway List* in *Daily.*

Handle final payments on layaways — In case of a mix-up we ask customers to show the payment receipts. This guards against customers who fill in "payments" on their copies of *Layaway Slips.* Handle the final payment on a layaway as a sale and give the items to the customer. Write a sales slip or ring a receipt on the cash register or *POS System*. The final payment scores the items as sold items. Cross them off the *Layaway List* in *Daily*. Keep the store's copy of the *Layaway Slip* with your paperwork for the shift.

Deal with layaway problems — Some customers change their minds. Refund all payments made by these customers and remove the items from the *Layaway List*. Avoid saying we'll return all cash on unwanted layaways as a sales pitch. The danger is in planting seeds that grow in the minds of customers. Customers who hear, "We'll refund all you've paid if you change your mind on the layaway" find it easy to back out of the deal. Without hearing this customers feel they're in a firm contract.

Sometimes customers will ask, "What happens if I can't make the payments or if I change my mind?" Then face the question squarely. Say, "We do expect customers to enter the layaway agreement seriously. Should unexpected events make it impossible for customers to live up to the agreement we'll be on their side. Either we'll allow more time for payment or we'll refund all payments, whichever customers choose."

Some customers ask to pick up items before they've made all payments. They often have a sad story—Johnny won't get that bicycle on his birthday unless you let his mother pay later. Say, "I'm sorry, Mrs. Jones. We don't run personal charges in this store. Would you like to put the payment on a charge card?" Leave these problems with customers. It's their job to solve them, not yours. Stay silent after suggesting the charge card.

Handle Non-taxable Items and Sales Tax Exemptions

There's usually no legal requirement that you make tax exempt sales. For cheap items, the fuss and paperwork cost more than your usual profit on the items. Make these sales as a service to customers. It harms your image to send customers elsewhere.

The rules on non-taxable and tax exempt sales differ widely from state to state. Only your state's department of revenue[20] can give you the facts for your state. Search within your state's rules for the exemptions that apply to the items you sell. It's no value to a gift store to know that motor vehicles sold to nonresidents are exempt from sales tax. That's something a car dealer near a state line may use to

---

[20]Different states have different names for the department that deals with sales taxes. Department of Revenue is common. Other names are: Department of Revenue Services, Department of Taxation, Department of Finance, Department of Finance and Administration, State Tax Commission, Franchise Tax Board, Bureau of Revenue, Bureau of Taxation, Budget and Financial Planning Department.

boost sales. Come up with a short list that your sellers can understand and can look up quickly. The rules change from time to time, so keep up with the notices the department of revenue sends you. Keep the list in your *Guide Sheet* up-to-date and post *News Sheets* to let sellers know about changes.

Know non-taxable items — States with a sales tax apply it to most items customers buy. They usually excuse the tax on items like medicine and hearing aids. Foods for humans generally escape the tax, unless they're prepared and sold in places like restaurants.

Look in Daily and the Price List for non-taxable items — *Daily* has a summary list of the non-taxable items we sell. The *Price List* lists every non-taxable item. After programming them, electronic cash registers and *POS Systems* know about non-taxable items.

Know sales tax exemptions — A few customers escape paying sales tax. Some laws free certain customers from having to pay the usual sales tax on certain items. We say such a customer is "exempt from sales tax" or "has a sales tax exemption." Write the details of all sales with sales tax exemptions, including ID seen. Include numbers and dates of expiry for any documents you use for identification. Include the record of all tax exempt sales in your *Seller's Report*.

These are the main sales tax exemptions you're likely to see:

The U.S. Government. The U.S. Constitution forbids the states from taxing direct purchases by the federal government. The U.S. Government buys with a U.S. Government check or a U.S. Government VISA Card.

Customers buying items for resale or for use in making items they'll sell. These customers will give you a Tax Exemption or Resale Certificate to keep on file. Check that any certificate on file is less than four years old.

Handle Refunds

To refund is to give back a payment for the return of an item.

Record the refund — A refund rolls back a sale. Record it on a refund receipt. The store needs a record of:

- The payment it makes to the customer.

- The tax it returned to the customer.

- The items it gets back from the customer.

Mirror the payment for refunds — Aim to pay customers back the same way they paid the store. Aim to give cash only to customers who paid cash. Never give cash to customers who paid with credit cards. Aim to give back checks and travelers checks to customers who paid with them.

Refund cash payments — Refund cash to customers who paid cash. Make out a refund receipt. Give back the cash the customer paid for the items and the tax.

Refund credit card payments on credit drafts — Make credit card refunds to customers who paid with a credit card. Make out a refund receipt. Follow the steps for refunds on credit cards.

Refund for personal checks still in the cash drawer — Return the check when the refund is for the full amount. Suppose a customer gave a $50 check on a bill of $50 and is returning $50 of items, then return the check. Swap the check when the refund is for less than the full amount. The new check is for the amount of the original check minus the amount of the refund. Suppose a customer gave a $50 check on bill of $50 and is returning $10 of items, including the tax. Swap the $50 check for a new $40 check.

Refund for personal checks deposited in the bank — Make out a refund receipt. Decide whether to refund cash or by check:

Refund cash when the amount for refund is $50 or less and you trust the customer. We'll take the risk rather than go through the paperwork of refunding a check.

Refund cash when the amount for refund is $100 or less and you know the customer. Go over the $100 limit as long as you leave yourself enough change to make sales to other customers. Remember, this is only for a customer you know. Otherwise, have the manager mail a check for the refund. Say, "Please write your name and address on this paper. Then I'll have the manager mail you a refund check." Leave a message for the manager in the *To Manager* binder.

Refund payments by travelers checks — Include travelers checks in the refund when you can. Make out a refund receipt.

- Refund cash if the travelers checks have been deposited in the bank.

- Refund cash or cash and travelers checks if the travelers checks are still in the cash drawer.

- Refund cash if the refund is less than the value of a travelers check. Suppose a customer gave a $20 travelers check on a bill of $15 and received $5 in change. Suppose the refund amount is $10, then refund cash.

- Include travelers checks where the refund is more than the value of travelers checks. Suppose a customer gave three $20 travelers checks on a bill of $50 and received $10 in change. Suppose the refund amount is $45. Refund $5 cash and two of the $20 travelers checks the customer gave you. The customer can use the travelers checks elsewhere but may have to sign them again.

Restock returned items — Return all returned items to a display or storage location. Make sure the items are in good shape and have price labels on them.

List Sales by Hand

Smart small stores will begin by listing their sales by hand. It needs no expensive equipment and it needs no technical skills. It is thus the cheapest way to test a store. Does the public want to buy what you have for sale? Are you agile enough to change to meet customers' needs? Do you have what it takes to train sellers and keep a store going?

The downside of listing sales by hand is that tracking inventory takes a lot of work. Yet even this task is manageable with suitable methods.

Small stores that believe they need to automate immediately risk being just another store. Their stress tips from making sales and creating a unique mood in the store to inventory control and advertising. This puts them in up against major chains, and that's a battle they just can't win.

Stores that know how to list sales by hand stay in business when their automatic systems fail. Failure of computer systems is as certain as death and taxes. Only the richest stores can afford the extra equipment and software needed to protect themselves against it.

Get Sales Books Ready

The cheapest way to list sales is by using generic sales books. Buy these in quantities right for your store and neatly stamp them with the store's name. Later you may want to use sales books preprinted with your store's name if you can get them at a good enough price in small enough quantities.

Bring the Ready Pile up to count — The *Ready Pile* is the pile of sales books ready to use to make sales. Get sales books ready for use. Stamp the store's name on every sales slip and put the finished books in the *Ready Pile*. Sales books usually have 50 sets of sales slips, numbered 1-50. Each set has a white top copy and a yellow back copy. Stamp the white top copy with the store's name. Keep the *Ready Pile* within a range listed in *Daily*. It gives a store a poor image if it uses blank sales books.

Test the store's name stamp on scrap paper — Use a self-inking stamp, so don't use a stamp pad. Make sure the stamp prints copies customers can read. Practice stamping until you get the hang of it. Aim to get a good print each time you use the stamp. Get so you can line up the print where you want it on the paper. Get so you print the store's name level on the paper. The store's name on the slant shows us as a sloppy store.

Stamp the sales books — The pairs of sales slips have numbers from 1 to 50 in each book. Stamp the top copy of each sales slip. Watch the numbers as you stamp—then you'll stamp every slip. Stamp the outside cover of each book when you finish stamping its slips. Then it's easy to see the sales book is ready to use. Write your name below the stamp on the outside cover. Take pride in your work.

<table>
<tr><td>

Fine Arts Gift Shop
6735 Westlake Avenue
Seattle, Washington
(206) 873-6877

DATE
NAME
ADDRESS

SOLD BY	C.O.D.	CHARGE	ON ACCT		ACCT	FWD.
1						
2						
3						
4						
5						
6						
7						
8						
9						
10						
11						
12			TAX			
48	SIGNATURE					

</td><td>

OUR BRAND

SALES
BOOK

Fine Arts Gift Shop
6735 Westlake Avenue
Seattle, Washington
(206) 873-6877

Book No. 256
Mahasti Moktashami

4B200

2 Part
50 Sets

</td></tr>
</table>

Number the sales books — Number each book. Begin at number 1 and keep going. Check before you number the books you've stamped. Check the *Ready Pile.* Check the numbers of the books sellers are using. Keep the books in order. Keep the lowest numbered book at the top of the pile. Keep the pile together with two rubber bands.

Get the sales books ready for use — Carefully remove one of the carbon papers from the back of each book. Fold it along the line of holes before tearing it out carefully. Cut along the line of holes with scissors if you find it hard to tear it out neatly. Trim any carbon paper that tears badly with scissors. Check that the carbon is long enough to make a complete copy before using it. Otherwise, throw it out.

Put the carbon between sales slip 1 and its copy. Line it up so it'll make a complete copy. Add the new books to the *Ready Pile*.

Write Sales Slips

Sellers write several kinds of sales slips. Begin with the simple case of a straight payment of U.S. cash with U.S. change and then work through the other kinds. Make sure sellers can write every kind of sales slip used in your store before they sell.

U.S. Payments with U.S. Change

A sale where sellers take U.S. cash and give U.S. change is the simplest sales slip. It's usually the commonest.

Use the lowest numbered sales book that's free — Take the lowest numbered sales book from the *Ready Pile*. This may be a partly used sales book or an unused sales book. Each seller in a shift works from a separate sales book. Return partly used sales books to the *Ready Pile*. Include fully used sales books with your paperwork

Check the carbon paper — Put a carbon paper between sales slip 1 and its copy in new books. Check for carbon paper between the next slip and its copy in used books. Replace the carbon paper if it's worn out. Sometimes sellers get busy and forget to change carbon papers.

Identify yourself for every sales book you use — Sellers identify themselves on the cover of every sales book they use. They write name, initials, and the slip numbers they use. Make sure all sellers' initials are different.

Fine Arts Gift Shop
6735 Westlake Avenue
Seattle, Washington
(206) 873-6877

Book No. 256
Mahasti Mohtashami

Mahasti Mohtashami   MM   1 - 18
Baye Hunter¹   BH   19

4B200

```
            Fine Arts Gift Shop
            6735 Westlake Avenue
            Seattle. Washington
               (206) 873-6877
DATE      1030a Mar 15/94
```

NAME						
ADDRESS						
SOLD BY	C.O.D.	CHARGE	ON ACCT		ACCT.	FWD.
BA						

1	171/1 Bowl Feet	25	00
2	241/2 Chalk Cat as is	29	00
3	101/6 Mag Glass		
4	3 @ 20.00	60	00
5	211/10 Snake Pin	95	00
6			
7			
8			
9	SUBTOTAL	209	00
10	TAX	14	63
11	TOTAL	223	63
12	$ PAYMENT	250	00
48	CHANGE	26	37

Identify each sales slip — The header of the sales slip has a line for the date. Write the time and date on this line. For speed, use "a" and "p" for "am" and "pm" "220p 1/20/94" "10a Mar 15/94." Write initials in the box titled "SOLD BY."

List the items sold — List items on lines numbered 1-8. Enter prices in the two columns at the right. List item number, a short form of the name and the price. Item 171 0001 is a Bowl with Feet at $25. List it as "171/1 Bowl Feet 25.00." Item 241 0002 is a Chalkware Cat at $59. List it as "241/2 Chalk Cat 59.00."

Write numbers and names to avoid mix-ups. Numbers and prices are on the price labels. Short forms of names come out of sellers' head. Any short form of a name is OK.

Note anything special about the item, such as "Sale" or "As Is." "171/1 Bowl Feet Sale 15.00." "241/2 Chalk Cat As Is 29.00." "As Is" means we offer a flawed item for sale at a lower price as it is. It's a case of what you see is what you get. "As Is" on the receipt stops customers from returning flawed items for good items.

Write on a second line for several items of the same kind.

The sign @ means "at a unit cost of."

Use a calculator to work out the cost for all items. To work out "3 @ 9.95" enter [3] then [x] then [9] then [.] then [9] then [5] then [=].

Work out subtotal for items — Use a calculator to add the costs of the items. Clear the calculator: [MRC] then [MRC] then [C]. Add the costs: [25] then [+] then [29] then [+] then [60] then [+] then [95] then [=]. 209 shows on the display—write it on the subtotal line.

Work out sales tax — Sales tax is subtotal amount times the tax rate. The tax rate is in *Daily*. 209 x 7% = 14.63. Use a calculator with 209 showing on the display: press [x] then [7] then [%]. 14.63 shows on the display—write it on the tax line.

Add subtotal and sales tax to get total — Add the sales tax on display to the subtotal in memory. [M+]. Display the total the customer must pay. Press [MRC] and 223.63 shows on the display—write it on the total line.

Say to the customer, "Including the tax that will be two hundred and twenty-three dollars and sixty-three cents."

Note payment and kind of sale — Enter the payment and kind of payment on the payment line. Write these initials:

AE   American Express
D   Discover Card.
MC   MasterCard
PC   Personal Check
TC   Travelers Check
V   VISA
$ Cash

Work out change — Take the payment from the total. Enter on the calculator: Press [C] then [2] then [5] then [0] then [-] then [MRC] then [=]. 26.37 shows on the display—write it on the change line.

Write extra slips for many items — Sometimes you sell too many items to list them all on one sales slip. Work out a subtotal for the one sales slip and carry it over to the next slip. Enter tax, total, payment and change on the last slip.

Fine Arts Gift Shop

Fine Arts Gift Shop
6735 Westlake Avenue
Seattle, Washington
(206) 873-6877

DATE   1030a Mar 15/94

NAME

ADDRESS

SOLD BY	C.O.D.	CHARGE	ON ACCT		ACCT.	FWD.
BA						
1 171/1 Bowl Feet					25	00
2 241/2 Chalk Cat as is					29	00
3 101/6 Mag Glass						
4 3 @ 20.00					60	00
5 211/10 Snake Pin					95	00
6 211/4 Daisy Ering					399	00
7 201/2 Chry Trvt						
8 4 @ 15.00					60	00
9			SUBTOTAL		668	00
10			TAX		Go	
11			TOTAL		to	
12			PAYMENT		Slip	
48			CHANGE		49	

Fine Arts Gift Shop
6735 Westlake Avenue
Seattle, Washington
(206) 873-6877

DATE   1030a Mar 15/94

NAME

ADDRESS

SOLD BY	C.O.D.	CHARGE	ON ACCT		ACCT.	FWD.
BA					668	00
1 111/2 Egypt Cup					38	00
2						
3						
4						
5						
6						
7						
8						
9			SUBTOTAL		706	00
10			TAX		49	42
11			TOTAL		755	42
12		AE	PAYMENT		755	42
49			CHANGE			

Canadian Payments with U.S. Change

The simplest way for most U.S. retailers who take Canadian cash is to take the Canadian cash and pay the change in U.S. cash.

Let sellers know the Canadian money you take — For example: We take Canadian banknotes, travelers checks and personal checks. We take no Canadian coins, not even the $1 and $2 coins Canadians call loonies and toonies. We'd like to take coins but our bank won't take them from us.

Learn the exchange rate at the start of each shift — The seller in charge of the day posts the Canadian exchange rate as *Today's Rate*. Other sellers check the rate as soon as they come on shift. Be able to tell customers the rate without looking at *Today's Rate*.

Work out the exchange value on the payment line — A sales slip for a Canadian payment is like a sales slip for a U.S. payment, except for the payment line. Show the Canadian amount and its U.S. value. Typical payment lines are:

C$300	@	.85	255.00
C$300TC	@	.85	255.00
C$300PC	@	.85	255.00.

Fine Arts Gift Shop
6735 Westlake Avenue
Seattle, Washington
(206) 873-6877

DATE	1030a Mar 15/94				
NAME					
ADDRESS					

SOLD BY	C.O.D.	CHARGE	ON ACCT	ACCT.	FWD.
BA					
1 171/1 Bowl Feet				25	00
2 241/2 Chalk Cat as is				29	00
3 101/6 Mag Glass					
4 3 @ 20.00				60	00
5 211/10 Snake Pin				95	00
6					
7					
8					
9			SUBTOTAL	209	00
10			TAX	14	63
11			TOTAL	223	63
12 C$300 @ .85			PAYMENT	255	00
48			CHANGE	31	37

Canadian Payments with Canadian Change

Retailers near the Canadian border may find it boosts sales if they run a Canadian cash tray in addition to their U.S. cash tray. Make sure it makes business sense if this involves you in traveling to a Canadian bank to exchange coins.

Change the total to a Canadian total — Write the sale in U.S. dollars. Enter the rate of exchange on the Canadian dollar total line. Multiply the U.S. total by the rate of exchange. Enter a line for the Canadian payment. Work out and enter the Canadian change. Make the change from the Canadian cash drawer.

Fine Arts Gift Shop
6735 Westlake Avenue
Seattle, Washington
(206) 873-6877

DATE 1030a Mar 15/94

NAME

ADDRESS

SOLD BY	C.O.D.	CHARGE	ON ACCT		ACCT. FWD.	
BA						
1 171/1 Bowl Feet					25	00
2 241/2 Chalk Cat as is					29	00
3 101/6 Mag Glass						
4 3 @ 20.00					60	00
5 211/10 Snake Pin					95	00
6						
7						
8						
9		SUBTOTAL			209	00
10		TAX			14	63
11		TOTAL			223	63
12 @ .85		C$ TOTAL			263	10
13		C$ PAYMENT			270	00
48		C$ CHANGE			6	90

Charge Card Payments

Charge card payments involve no change given to the customer. Follow the steps set out in *Charge to Credit Cards and Debit Cards* section of *Work the Cash Drawer* in this chapter. Write a sales slip and a charge slip to go with it.

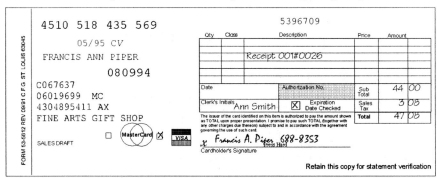

Mixed Payments

Sometimes customers pay their bills part this way and part another way. Suppose the bill is $69.95. A customer might pay $19.95 cash and put $50 on a credit card. Another customer has a bill of $750. $350 goes on MasterCard and $400 goes on VISA. Customers have many reasons for splitting bills like this. Your only interest is that it gets you a sale you might otherwise miss.

Fine Arts Gift Shop
6735 Westlake Avenue
Seattle, Washington
(206) 873-6877

DATE	1030a Mar 15/94					
NAME						
ADDRESS						

SOLD BY	C.O.D.	CHARGE	ON ACCT		ACCT.	FWD.
BA						

1	171/1 Bowl Feet	25	00
2	241/2 Chalk Cat as is	29	00
3	101/6 Mag Glass		
4	3 @ 20.00	60	00
5	211/10 Snake Pin	95	00
6	Subtotal	209	00
7	Tax	14	63
8	Total	223	63
9	Cash SUBTOTAL	100	00
10	Due TAX	123	63
11	Visa TOTAL	123	63
12	PAYMENT	0	00
48	CHANGE		

Take each payment from the last total — Follow this example for a bill that comes to $275.95 including the tax.

Total	275.95
Paid Cash	75.36
	200.59
Paid VISA	100.00
	100.59
Paid MasterCard	100.59
	0.00

Take away each payment from the total. End with nothing owed or an amount of change to pay to the customer.

Go step by step to avoid mix-ups. Write the VISA sales draft, get the signature and write on the sales slip. Then do the same for the MasterCard sales draft.

Squeeze the payments on one sales slip if you can. Otherwise, carry the total from one sales slip to another.

Fine Arts Gift Shop			
6735 Westlake Avenue			
Seattle, Washington			
(206) 873-6877			

DATE   1030a Mar 15/94

NAME

ADDRESS

SOLD BY	C.O.D.	CHARGE	ON ACCT	ACCT.	FWD.
BA					
1 171/1 Bowl Feet				25	00
2 241/2 Chalk Cat as is				29	00
3 101/6 Mag Glass					
4 3 @ 20.00				60	00
5 211/10 Snake Pin				95	00
6					
7					
8					
9		SUBTOTAL		209	00
10		TAX		14	63
11		TOTAL		223	63
12		PAYMENT		Cont	on
48		CHANGE		Slip	49

Fine Arts Gift Shop			
6735 Westlake Avenue			
Seattle, Washington			
(206) 873-6877			

DATE   1030a Mar 15/94

NAME

ADDRESS

SOLD BY	C.O.D.	CHARGE	ON ACCT	ACCT.	FWD.
BA				223	63
1 Cash				13	63
2 Due				210	00
3 American Express				110	00
4 Due				100	00
5 Discover Card				100	00
6 Due				0	00
7					
8					
9		SUBTOTAL			
10		TAX			
11		TOTAL			
12		PAYMENT			
49		CHANGE			

Payments on Layaways

Stores that take layaways have to show their sellers how to write up payments and final sales

Write sales slips for layaway payments — Identify the layaway clearly. Write the customer's name and address. Include the *Layaway Slip* number and the amount paid.

Fine Arts Gift Shop	Fine Arts Gift Shop
6735 Westlake Avenue	6735 Westlake Avenue
Seattle. Washington	Seattle. Washington
(206) 873-6877	(206) 873-6877

Left slip:

DATE: 1130a Mar 3/94
NAME: Mary Rogers
ADDRESS: 674 Aurora St

SOLD BY	C.O.D.	CHARGE	ON ACCT	ACCT	FWD.
BH					

1	Payment on		
2	Layaway 7-48	107	00
3			
4			
5			
6			
7			
8			
9	SUBTOTAL		
10	TAX		
11	TOTAL		
12	$ PAYMENT		
48	CHANGE		

Right slip:

DATE: 1130a Mar 3/94
NAME: Mary Rogers
ADDRESS: 674 Aurora St

SOLD BY	C.O.D.	CHARGE	ON ACCT	ACCT	FWD.
BH					

1	Final Payment on		
2	Layaway 7-48	107	00
3	101/8 Swd Flatware		
4			
5			
6			
7			
8			
9	SUBTOTAL		
10	TAX		
11	TOTAL		
12	$ PAYMENT		
48	CHANGE		

Write sales slips for final payments — Identify the layaway clearly. Write the customer's name and address. Include the *Layaway Slip* number and the amount paid. Include the items sold and count them as items sold.

Percentage Off Item or Subtotal

Sales slips with a percentage off an item or a subtotal are simple for sellers who know how to work out percentages.

Write sales slips with percentage off item — The first sales slip includes a percentage off item. Where there are several items with the same percentage off, add them and work out a single percentage off.

Fine Arts Gift Shop		
6735 Westlake Avenue		
Seattle, Washington		
(206) 873-6877		

DATE   1030a Mar 15/94

NAME

ADDRESS

SOLD BY	C.O.D.	CHARGE	ON ACCT		ACCT. FWD.
BA					
1 171/1 Bowl Feet					
2 1 @ 25.00 - 10%				22	50
3 211/10 Snake Pin				95	00
4					
5					
6					
7					
8					
9		SUBTOTAL		117	50
10		TAX		8	23
11		TOTAL		125	73
12	$	PAYMENT		130	00
48		CHANGE		4	27

Fine Arts Gift Shop		
6735 Westlake Avenue		
Seattle, Washington		
(206) 873-6877		

DATE   1030a Mar 15/94

NAME

ADDRESS

SOLD BY	C.O.D.	CHARGE	ON ACCT		ACCT. FWD.
BA					
1 171/1 Bowl Feet				25	00
2 211/10 Snake Pin				95	00
3 Subtotal				120	00
4 10% off subtotal				12	00
5					
6					
7					
8					
9		SUBTOTAL		108	00
10		TAX		7	56
11		TOTAL		115	56
12	$	PAYMENT		120	00
48		CHANGE		4	44

1. Write all percentage off item lines first.

   a) Clear the calculator: Press [MRC] then [MRC] then [C].

   b) Store the list price of the item: Press [2] then [5] then [M+].

   c) Work out the percentage off: [x] then [1] then [0] then [%]. 2.5 shows on display.

   d) Take the amount on display from the list price: [M-].

   e) Display the list price: [MRC]. 22.50 shows on display—write it on the sales slip.

2. Write the rest of the sales slip as usual.

Write sales slips with percentage off subtotal

1. Write the subtotal on a handwritten Subtotal line.

2. Work out the percentage off subtotal and take it away from the subtotal.

   a) With 120 showing on the display:

   b) Store the subtotal: Press [M+].

   c) Work out the percentage off: [x] then [1] then [0] then [%]. 12 shows on the display—write it on a handwritten % Off Subtotal line.

3. Take the amount off from the subtotal: [M-].

4. Display the new subtotal: [C] then [MRC]. 108 shows on the display—write it on the printed subtotal line.

5. Work out the sales tax. [C] then [MRC] then [x] then [7] then [%]. 7.56 shows on the display—write it on the printed tax line.

6. Add the sales tax to the subtotal in memory to get the total bill. [M+] then [MRC]. 115.56 shows on the display—write it on the printed total line.

7. Work out the change due to the customer.

8. With the customer giving $120: [C] then [1] then [2] then [0] then [-] then [MRC] then [=]. 4.44 shows on the display—enter it on the printed change line.

Discount from Item or Subtotal

Write sales slips with discount from item — Write sales slips as usual but take discounts off items.

<table>
<tr><td colspan="4" align="center">Fine Arts Gift Shop
6735 Westlake Avenue
Seattle, Washington
(206) 873-6877</td></tr>
<tr><td>DATE</td><td colspan="3">1030a Mar 15/94</td></tr>
<tr><td>NAME</td><td colspan="3"></td></tr>
<tr><td>ADDRESS</td><td colspan="3"></td></tr>
</table>

SOLD BY	C.O.D.	CHARGE	ON ACCT	ACCT	FWD.
BA					
1 171/1 Bowl Feet					
2 1 @ 25.00 - 10.00				15	00
3 211/10 Snake Pin				95	00
4					
5					
6					
7					
8					
9		SUBTOTAL		110	00
10		TAX		7	70
11		TOTAL		117	70
12 $		PAYMENT		120	00
48		CHANGE		2	30

<table>
<tr><td colspan="4" align="center">Fine Arts Gift Shop
6735 Westlake Avenue
Seattle, Washington
(206) 873-6877</td></tr>
<tr><td>DATE</td><td colspan="3">1030a Mar 15/94</td></tr>
<tr><td>NAME</td><td colspan="3"></td></tr>
<tr><td>ADDRESS</td><td colspan="3"></td></tr>
</table>

SOLD BY	C.O.D.	CHARGE	ON ACCT	ACCT	FWD.
BA					
1 171/1 Bowl Feet				25	00
2 211/10 Snake Pin				95	00
3 Subtotal				120	00
4 Discount				25	00
5					
6					
7					
8					
9		SUBTOTAL		95	00
10		TAX		6	65
11		TOTAL		101	65
12 $		PAYMENT		105	00
48		CHANGE		3	35

Write sales slips with discount from subtotal

1. List all items as usual.

2. Write the subtotal on a handwritten subtotal line.

3. Write the discount on a handwritten discount line below the subtotal.

4. Take the discount from the subtotal.

5. Write the answer on the printed subtotal line.

6. Finish the sales slip as usual.

Non-taxable Items or Sales Tax Exemptions

In most stores all items are taxable, but some stores sell a mixture of taxable and non-taxable items. All stores may face the need to sell to a person or organization with a sales tax exemption.

Fine Arts Gift Shop 6735 Westlake Avenue Seattle, Washington (206) 873-6877		**Fine Arts Gift Shop** 6735 Westlake Avenue Seattle, Washington (206) 873-6877

Left slip:

DATE   1030a Mar 15/94

NAME

ADDRESS

SOLD BY	C.O.D.	CHARGE	ON ACCT		ACCT.	FWD.
B.A						
1 171/1 Bowl Feet					25	00
2 241/2 Chlk Cat as is					29	00
3 211/10 Snake Pin					95	00
4 201/2 Chry Trvt						
5 4 @ 15.00					60	00
6						
7						
8						
9		SUBTOTAL			114	00
10		TAX			7	98
11		TOTAL			121	98
12		PAYMENT			Go	to
48		CHANGE			Slip	49

Right slip:

DATE   1030a Mar 15/94

NAME

ADDRESS

SOLD BY	C.O.D.	CHARGE	ON ACCT		ACCT.	FWD.
B.A					121	98
1 Non-taxable items						
2 251/1 Slug Butr					5	00
3						
4						
5						
6						
7						
8						
9		SUBTOTAL			126	98
10		TAX			SLIP	48
11		TOTAL			126	98
12	AE	PAYMENT			126	98
49		CHANGE				

Separate all items without tax — Make separate piles of taxable and non-taxable items.

Write a sales slip for the taxable items — Leave out this step for sales where all the items are without tax. Write a usual sales slip except for payment and change lines. Write something like "Go to slip 49" on the payment and change lines.

Write non-taxable items on a separate slip — Write the non-taxable items on a separate slip to avoid mix-ups. Carry the total from the taxable items slip to the top of this slip. Head this slip "Non-taxable items." Finish this slip as usual except for the entry on the tax line.

Refunds

All stores will face the need to write refunds from time to time.

\multicolumn{7}{c}{**Fine Arts Gift Shop**}
\multicolumn{7}{c}{**6735 Westlake Avenue**}
\multicolumn{7}{c}{**Seattle, Washington**}
\multicolumn{7}{c}{**(206) 873-6877**}

DATE   315p Mar 17/94

NAME

ADDRESS

SOLD BY	C.O.D.	CHARGE	ON ACCT		ACCT.	FWD.
BA						
1 Refund						
2 211/10 Snake Pin			-95	00		
3						
4						
5						
6						
7						
8						
9		SUBTOTAL	-95	00		
10		TAX	-6	65		
11		TOTAL	-101	65		
12		PAYMENT	0	00		
33	$	CHANGE	-101	65		

Write refunds on sales slips

On the sales slip write the heading "Refund."

List minus values for refunds

Roll back items on the Item Tally Sheet — Items come back into the store when you write a refund. Roll back the *Item Count* on the *Item Tally Sheet*. The tally mark for a sold item is /. Write -/ to show an item coming into the store. /// -/ adds up to two items sold. Take care to separate -/-/-/-/ from ////. -/-/-/-/ shows four items returned. //// shows five items sold.

Sometimes refunds leave a minus count on an item. For example, someone returns a Snake Pin on a day you sell no Snake Pins.

Keep a Tally of Items Sold

The secret of tracking inventory by hand is to work on it between sales and to complete the tally for the day on the day of the sales.

Item Tally Sheet

Name _Mary Rogerson_ Day _Mon_ Date _16 Mon_ May Year _1994_ Shift _1_ From _1000u_ To _430p_ Page _1_ of _1_

	Item No	Name	Price	TXS	NTS	CMS	NCS	Tally	
	111 0005	CNDLSNUF	19.00	114.00		114.00		*HH* /	6
	181 0003	EAGLE SM	15.00	180.00		180.00		*HH HH* //	12
	111 0005	CNDLSNUF	10.00	10.00			10.00	/	1
	241 0002	CHLK CAT	59.00	118.00		118.00		//	2
	141 0001	TULIPS 2	165.00	165.00		165.00		/	1
	121 0002	EAGL TRV	30.00	60.00		60.00		//	2
S	101 0008	SWD FLAT	400.00	400.00			400.00	/	1
	111 0004	KYLIX	45.00	45.00		45.00		/	1
N	111 0004	KYLIX	45.00		90.00	90.00		//	2
	161 0005	DOLP CS2	85.00	255.00		255.00		/	1
N	251 0001	SLG BUTR	5.00		10.00	10.00		//	2
	Total			1347.00	100.00	1037.00	410.00		

Write slashes as tally marks — Write slashes that slant clearly. Make sure / stands out from the number 1 and // stands out from the number 11.

Keep tally marks in groups of five — Make four tally marks: ////. Then strike a line through them for the fifth item: *HH*. Leave a space between each group of five marks: *HH HH HH* //. Then it's easy to count totals.

Set up a tally sheet — Fill in the header. At the start of a shift the page note says "Page 1 of." Enter the page note of a second sheet as "Page 2 of." At the end of the shift you'll know how many sheets you've used. Then fill in the page notes as "Page 1 of 2" and "Page 2 of 2." These are the column headings on the form:

Item No: This is the item number used on the store's price list.

Name: This is a short form of the item's name. Any short form of the name is OK.

Price: This is the selling price of the item without tax. Fill in two lines on the form when an item has two selling prices. Sometimes an item has two selling prices because we have damaged stock. The normal price is $50 but the damaged items are $25.

TXS: This is a total column for taxable sales.

NTS: This is a total column for non-taxable sales. It's usual for items to be taxable. Write N in the margin beside non-taxable lines. For a sales tax exemption use a different line than for taxable sales.

CMS: This is the total column for sales with commissions.

NCS: This is the total column for non-commission sales. Include items that pay spiffs here. You get paid for spiffs by filling in a Spiffs Slip. Include sale items and markdowns here—these items pay no commissions. Include special orders, seller's discount sales and mall discount sales here—these items pay no commissions. Write S in the margin beside non-commission items that pay spiffs.

Tally: Write the tally marks in this column. Begin a second row for any item where you fill a row with tally marks.

Write item number, short name and price when you sell the first of an item. Then add the first tally mark: 211/2 ELE COIN 19.00 / Leave columns TXS, NTS, CMS and NCS blank. Fill these columns at the end of the shift.

Write the same item at a different price on its own line. You need to do that when you sell a damaged item at a lower price. 211/2 ELE COIN 19.00 / 211/2 ELE COIN 12.00 /

Write taxable and non-taxable sales of the same item on different lines.

Add extra tally marks as you sell more of an item. 211/2 ELE COIN 19.00 ///

Add new items to the list. 211/5 HOOP EAR 79.00 / 231/4 RED PZL 16.99 / As the number of items grows, it gets hard to work with the list. That's because the items are out of order. Make a standard list of items as a form if this becomes a problem. List the items you usually sell and write the others in below.

Keep a running total where you sell large numbers of items — Suppose you sell over a hundred marbles in units of 5 or 10. Then it's better to keep a running total: 5 15 25 30.

Sell first, then tally — Finish selling and tally later when the customer has gone. Sell again if another customer comes along before you've tallied. Tally both sales when the second customer has gone. Keep watch when you put off tallying. The point of a tally is to do it as you go. At the end of a shift you'll be glad your tally sheet is up-to-date.

Check off items as you tally — First make a check mark by the item on the copy of the sales slip. Then make the tally mark on the tally sheet. That way you'll know where you were if someone interrupts you.

Add the tally marks for each line at closing — Write the total at the end of the Tally column. Write in the margin if the Tally column is full.

Work out the sales amounts for each item — Multiply Price by total of the Tally column. Put the sales under TXS (taxable) or under NTS (non-taxable.) Also put the sales under CMS (commission) or NCS (non-commission.)

Add the totals for the sheet — Add sales totals for TXS (taxable,) NTS (non-taxable,) CMS (commission) and NCS (non-commission) columns. Add Total TXS and Total NTS to get Total Sales. Add Total CMS and Total NCS to get Total Sales. Look for errors when the two figures for Total Sales are different.

Fix Bad Labels

Bad labels are labels with the wrong item number or the wrong price on them.

Watch for bad labels as you sell items — Bad labels usually turn up when making a sale.

Labels sometimes have the wrong item number.

• Sell the items.

• Fix the number on the *Item Tally Sheet*.

• Fix the number on all items in the store.

Labels sometimes have the wrong price for the item.

• Sell the items at the label price when the price difference is small. You judge whether the difference is small.

• Sell the items at the true price when the price difference is large. Say, "Oops! Somebody goofed on this one. Let me check the price." Check the price and let the customer know the real price. We go broke if we sell $400 items for $4. Fix the price on all items in the store.

Let others know about bad labels — Sometimes you're too rushed to fix the bad labels. Set up a *News Sheet* warning other sellers. Have them fix the labels. Remove items from display when there's a large price error. Send the *Pricer* a *Message* for all bad labels you fix. The feedback will help the *Pricer* keep on track.

Use Sales Equipment

Equipment to help with sales ranges from simple cash registers, through electronic cash registers to computer sales systems. All but simple cash registers give help in providing a variety of reports and in tracking items sold.

Make Cash Registers Help You Sell

A surprising number of cash registers are of poor design and reflect little knowledge of the psychology of shoppers. Pay attention to some simple basics that apply to all cash registers and computer sales systems.

Let customers see what sellers ring — Make sure customers can see what sellers ring on the cash registers. These are the choices:

- Place cash registers so customers can see the displays.

- Use cash registers with two-sided displays.

- Have separate display units for customers.

Customers get uneasy unless they can see what sellers ring. It's more than customers who think sellers may have something to hide who get uneasy. There's little for customers to do while sellers ring sales. Watching sellers ring sales gives customers something to do and keeps them in contact with their items. Stores that hide the cash register display lose customers. Customers rarely notice they can't see the display. They simply notice they feel better in stores where they can see the display. They rarely figure out why. They shop in other stores because they feel better there.

Make it hard for sellers to tap the till. Let customers see what's going on as sellers ring up and total the items. Then sellers are less likely to work dodges with the store's cash or with customers' cash.

Show details of price extensions — The extension is the cost of several items of the same kind. One bracelet costs $19.95 and a customer buys three bracelets for $59.85. $59.85 is the extension of the $19.95 price to the three items. Go for a cash register that prints receipts that show the details: 1231234 Bracelet 3 @ 19.95 59.85. Avoid cash registers that print only the extension: 1231234 Bracelet 59.85 Many customers find it hard to figure out how much they paid for a bracelet. They feel uneasy with your store. Some shop where they feel at ease instead of at your store.

Keep customers in contact with you — Make sure your receipts identify your store and the sale. Show the facts that keep customers in touch with your store:

- Store name and phone number.

- Date and time of sale.

- Cash register number and *Clerk Number.*

Check Print Darkness Against Sample Receipts

Make sure customers can read the sales slips they receive from you.

Ring No Sale when setting up the cash register each day — The ribbon that prints the cash register receipts wears out. Day by day the receipts get lighter and lighter. The cash register receipt sends a message about the store. A faded receipt lets customers know the store is not on top of things.

Compare the receipt with the sample receipts — Print a receipt at opening time each day. Compare its darkness with a receipt made by a new ribbon. Compare it also with sample receipts rated as "OK" and "Replace." The sample receipts are in a pocket in *Daily*. Keep them between two pieces of cardboard, stapled to a piece of paper. This keeps them in the dark and stops light from fading them. Take them out only to compare them with today's receipt.

Replace the ribbon if the receipt is too light — Write "Replace" on the receipt and staple it to the sheet of samples. Then put a new ribbon in the cash register. Ring No Sale to check that the receipt prints OK. Write "New" on the new receipt and staple it to the sheet of samples. Put the sample sheet between its cardboard covers and return it to *Daily*.

Check Length of Receipt and Journal Tapes

Give your sellers an edge by seeing that receipt and journal tapes rarely run out in front of customers.

Know receipt and journal tapes — Receipt tape is the roll of paper used to print receipts for sales. Use a 2-part cash receipt tape. Tear off receipts and give top white copies to customers. Keep the bottom yellow copies for in-store use. The cash register also prints a copy of all receipts on a second tape. This is the journal tape. Tax officials look at the journal tape to check all sales made on the register.

Check tapes to keep from making customers wait — Most stores change their cash register tapes when the tapes run out. A red stripe appears on the receipts when the tape is coming to an end. Sellers try to choose a gap between customers to change the tape. Often customers have to wait while the seller changes the tape. Even when customers wait politely, the seller is under stress. The level of stress goes up when the cash register or the customer acts up. Serve customers by changing tapes before they run out. Get sellers to check tapes before they start selling. Cut down the times they make customers wait while they change tapes.

Measure the paper on the roll — Measure a full roll of tape before it goes into the register. Lie a roll of paper tape flat on a counter. The paper rests on a central cardboard tube. The longest line from edge to edge of the paper is about 75 mm. The longest line from edge to edge of the cardboard tube is about 22 mm. From the edge of the cardboard tube to the edge of the paper is about 26 mm. We say a full roll is 26 mm thick.

Replace tapes that are too thin — On Sundays replace tapes less than 10 mm thick. On Saturdays replace tapes less than 8 mm thick. On weekdays replace tapes less than 4 mm thick. Keep ends of tapes between 4 and 10 mm thick. Use them as new tapes on weekdays.

Pass used journal tapes to the manager for storage — The manager keeps journal tapes in long-term storage.

Spike Copies of Receipts

Use a spike to keep copies of receipts in order.

Take care with the spike — Spikes are dangerous—treat them with respect and care. Someone gets a bad wound when people are sloppy with spikes. Screw the spike to the back of the shelf and leave little space between the spike and the shelf above it. Leave just enough space to put your hand in and spike a receipt. A screwed down spike stays in one place. Spikes that move from place to place end up wounding someone. With the spike fixed in place you can reach the spike, but not by accident. That's why it's at the back of the shelf. Nobody can reach over it to get something behind it. Make sure the spike is above desk level—that makes it hard to fall on it. There's too little space above the spike to drive your hand down on it. Get a cork to go with the spike. Stick the cork on the spike when the spike is not in use.

Spike copies of receipts till you can work on them — Working from copies of receipts helps keep the displays in shape. Keep copies of receipts to back up paperwork.

Spike copies of receipts near the top — It's natural to spike a piece of paper near the center. That usually puts the hole through something you want to read later. Learn to be unnatural. Spike copies of receipts through the name of the store.

Take copies of receipts to a work area — Leave the spike where it is. Take the copies from the spike and work with them elsewhere.

Electronic Cash Registers

Electronic cash registers come with a user's handbook. It's a mistake to expect your sellers to work from it. In most cases it will have been written by a technically oriented person with little understanding of how to communicate effectively to sellers. In the rare cases where that's not the case, there will probably be too much detail and too many topics of no use to your store. There's always the risk that someone will manage to lose it when it's in general use. Use the handbook and the experience you get by using the cash register to write your own *Guide Sheets* and supporting *Outlines*.

The details of programming an electronic cash register will depend on the model in use. Therefore, this section covers only general features, many of which are often overlooked and end up giving retailers problems. Most of them also apply to electronic cash registers.

Topics for Managers

Like all other topics for managers these topics for using electronic cash registers can be under direct control or be in name only control of a manager. Managers will start by doing them themselves but when they can they will pass them along to trusted sellers as *Special Jobs*.

Set Cash Register and Receipt Numbers

Number all cash registers and all receipts. Then you'll always be able to follow things as they took place.

Set Cash Register Number

Number each cash register when it comes into the store. Keep one number for one cash register only. Give replacement cash registers their own numbers instead of the numbers of the cash registers they replace. Keep a master list of cash register numbers and their model and serial numbers.

Set Receipt Number

The cash register numbers each receipt. Set the receipt number to 0000 when the cash register is first used in the store. Reset the receipt counter when you move the cash register to a new store. Some managers reset the counter on the first of the month.

Set Sellers' ID Numbers

Number all sellers and keep track of the numbers forever. Then you can reconstruct who did what.

Know Clerk Number from Seller's ID — Perhaps the cash register lets you enter numbers for up to 20 sellers. Think of having slots numbered from 1 to 20. Slots 1 to 20 are the *Clerk Numbers*. *Clerk Numbers* always stay the same—slot 1 is always slot 1. You can write any four digit number in each of the slots. In slot 3 you might write "1234." The numbers you write in the slots are the *Sellers' ID* numbers. At different times each slot can have a different *Seller's ID* in it. Perhaps slot 1 now has "1234" in it. Later it might have "9786" in it.

Use smart numbering systems — Use a *Seller's ID* for one seller only. Suppose Joan Smitherson's *Seller's ID* is 1234. Joan leaves and Roy Brown takes her place. Beginners in data handling often reuse the "unused" ID number. They regret it later when they find limits to the use of their data. They come across 1234 and it could be Joan Smitherson or Roy Brown. Let 1234 stand for Joan Smitherson forever. Give Roy Brown his own unique number. Keep a master table of all ID numbers you ever use.

Use four digit numbers, or longer numbers if the cash register allows them. It's easier for crooks to figure out or watch the entry of short ids than long ids. Sellers soon get used to entering their ids quickly.

Avoid natural runs of numbers. It's easier for crooks to crack 1234 than 7927. Avoid numbering sellers one after the other. Suppose Mary has *Seller's ID* 1234 and Joan has *Seller's ID* 1235. It's easy to guess the next *Seller's ID*. It's harder to guess the next *Seller's ID* if their *Seller's Ids* are 9640 and 3581.

Set Training Mode

Training mode lets sellers use the cash register without changing the totals. All receipts sellers ring in training mode have the training flag on them, possibly *TRNG*. Make sure you turn off training mode when training ends. Naturally, only managers know the codes for turning training mode on and off.

Store PLUs

PLUs are *Price Look Up Reference Numbers*, used to keep track of items in an electronic cash register or a computer system. Make them agree with *Item Numbers* used in the *Price List*.

Enter new PLUs or replace existing PLUs — Follow the same steps for entering new PLUs and for replacing PLUs. The cash register prints a list of all entries. Proofread the list carefully. Careful proofreading cuts out wrong PLUs in the cash register. Some cash registers allow grouping of PLUs into departments. Departments are large groupings above the groupings used in numbering items. The department is TOYS and the medium counting frame 100-1234 belongs to group 100 with all other counting frames.

Read all PLUs stored in the cash register — Make sure you have enough time to finish the job before reading the PLUs. The printout takes a long time when there are many PLUs in the register. Run some tests when the store is closed to get an idea of the time it needs. It's rarely a good idea to read the stored PLUs when customers are around.

Make sure there's enough paper on the receipt and journal tapes to print the list. Put fresh rolls in the register and run some tests to get an idea of how much tape the job needs.

Set Tax Rate

Set the tax rate, or tax rates where there is more than one tax. Record any non-taxable PLUs.

Topics for Sellers

The topics sellers need to know to use an electronic cash register mainly match those needed for listing sales by hand. But in addition they need to know which keys press and how to make reports.

Know the Cash Register Layout

Sellers will need to know: the various keyboards and how to use them; how to use the clerk keys; any switches that change between modes of use (for example, Clerk, Manager, Programs, Reports); the position and normal position of the receipt switch. They will need to load and reload the receipt tape, the journal tape and the printer ribbon until they are familiar enough with them to load them under the pressure of waiting customers. This is a good time to review the proper use of the slots for coins and bills in the cash tray.

Try Out the Cash Register

Have sellers try out the cash register. Let them identify themselves to the register and ring some No Sales. Let them display and clear the time display. Make sure sellers can identify the parts of a simple receipt.

```
        FINE ARTS
        GIFT SHOP
        863-6877

    3:23PM03/20/94
        001#0026 B
                1234

    NOSALE
```

001 is the cash register number.
#0026 is the 26th receipt on 03/20/94.
B is the key in the CLERK key slot.
1234 is the Clerk ID.

Recognize and clear warning tones — In most electronic cash registers a warning tone sounds when someone tries to open the cash drawer without a clerk key in the slot. See that sellers can recognize and answer to the warning tone from across a noisy store.

In most electronic cash registers the receipt and journal tapes press down on switch and keep it open. Below a certain weight, the tapes can't keep the switch down, so it turns on an electrical circuit. Then pressing an ending key makes the cash register sound a warning tone. It sounds as if the cash register has broken down when sellers don't know what's causing this tone. The warning tone sounds when either the receipt or the journal tape is near its end. The warning tone also sounds when either the receipt or the journal tape is out of place. This often happens after moving the cash register. Press the Clear key to kill the tone. Then adjust or replace a tape. Put the receipt or journal tape out of place so sellers can correct it.

Know Payment and Change from Pay-in and Pay-out

We take payments from customers and make change for them. Customers rarely pay with the exact amount of cash when they buy. They usually give too much and we give the extra back as change. Payment minus the change equals the cash received.

Pay-in cash belonging to the store — The store's cash that goes into the cash drawer has nothing to do with sales. One *Pay-in* sellers deal with each day is the *Opening Change* they put in the cash drawer. Other *Pay-ins* are possible—a seller might make a *Pay-in* for a personal phone call. Write down the details of all *Pay-ins*.

Pay out the store's expenses and bank deposits — Sometimes the store has to pay expenses from the cash drawer. Payments for deliveries and Spiffs are *Pay-outs*. Write down the details of all *Pay-outs*. Get a receipt from the person who takes the cash. A bank deposit is a special form of *Pay-out*. While it's not an expense, it takes cash out of the cash drawer. Show sellers how to make and sign *Pay-in* and *Pay-out* slips.

```
  FINE ARTS          FINE ARTS          FINE ARTS
  GIFT SHOP          GIFT SHOP          GIFT SHOP
  863-6877           863-6877           863-6877


 Opening Change    Paid to E. J. Bags,   Bank Deposit
                    for Invoice 958
  Joan Smith                            Joan Smith
                      Joan Smith


 3:23PM03/20/94    3:23PM03/20/94     3:23PM03/20/94
 001#0026 B 1234   001#0026 B 1234    001#0026 B 1234

 PAY IN   $99.99   ***P/O   $50.32    BK DEP   $700.00
```

Set Date and Time

Once the date and the time are in the cash register it's rare to have to reset them. Yet date and time are so important for your records and for the image of your store that sellers must know how to reset them. Have sellers check the cash register's date and time every time they come on shift.

Set the Exchange Rate on the Canadian Dollar

The seller who gets the exchange rate also sets it on the cash register.

Enter PLUs with simple cash payments

Begin a receipt with simple PLU entries — Stress how item numbers on price labels relate to PLUs. For example: Item numbers on price labels have this form: 123 1234. 123 is the group number. Then there's a space. 1234 is the "item in group" number after the space. All items have a 3-digit group number and a 4-digit "item in group" number. These are not item numbers: 12 1234, 1234 12, 123 12, 123 12345. All group numbers begin with a digit greater than zero. 110 is a group number but 010 isn't a group number. Often you'll have to leave out the blank in an item number to use it as a PLU. Many cash registers can't handle blanks in numbers. Enter item 123 1234 as PLU 1231234.

Face miskeys right away — The item is 101 0001 but the entry is PLU 1910001. If there's an item 191 0001: The cash register displays the name and price of that item. You expect to see "FIL BIRD 25.00" but you see "TWL RING 8.99." Press [VOID] and begin again. If there isn't an item 191 0001: The cash register displays "ENTER PRICE/DEPT." Press [CL] and begin again.

Enter multiple PLUs — After simple PLUs, enter multiple PLUs. A multiple PLU is the same PLU entered more than once. Example: Three 101 0007 Filigree Birds at $15 each.

End sales — End these sales with payment by cash or travelers checks.

Enter Payment by Canadian Bills or Travelers Checks

In addition to ending the sale with a payment by Canadian Bills or Travelers Checks, make sure sellers can answer customers' questions about exchange rates.

Answer questions about exchange rates — The seller in charge of the *Opening Shift* sets the rate on the Canadian dollar. It's on display for customers as *Today's Rate*. It's in the *Log of Canadian Dollar* in *Daily*. It's loaded into the cash register. Make sure it's the same in all these places.

Customers ask questions like these: "What's the exchange on the Canadian dollar?" "How much U.S. do I get for 9 dollars Canadian?" "How much is this item in Canadian dollars?" Have sellers work out exchanges in their head or on a hand calculator.

Make sure sellers know how you deal with Canadian coins. If your bank won't take them, you don't take them. Say to customers, "I'm sorry, our bank won't take

Canadian coins." Retailers in border towns who cross the border regularly will score points with their Canadian customers by taking Canadian coins.

Handle underpayments — Sometimes the Canadian payment given by a customer isn't enough. Suppose the customer paid a $47.08 bill with a Canadian $50 bill. The cash register shows "DUE 7.08" on the display. Ask the customer for more cash. Suppose the customer gives $10 Canadian. The cash register shows "CHNG 0.92" on the display.

Enter Payment by Credit Card

Electronic cash registers usually have a separate ending key programmed for each credit card you accept. Some electronic cash registers prepare sales drafts for customers to sign. More often, sellers prepare the sales draft separately. Where this is so, write the sales draft before printing the receipt on the cash register. Keep the cash drawer closed. Have customers sign the sales draft. Hand them their copy before printing the receipt.

Enter Payment by U.S. or Canadian Personal Check

See that sellers follow the rules you have set up for taking personal checks. Track sales by checks separately from cash sales as far as possible. Most electronic cash registers have a key programmed for U.S. checks. If there's no key available to program for Canadian checks separately, treat them as Canadian cash but make a daily count of Canadian checks by hand.

Enter Mixed Payments

In mixed payments customers use more than one way to pay a single bill. Customers usually pay a bill by cash or by credit card or by check, but sometimes they pay in two or more ways. They may pay part in cash and part with a credit card. Customers returning to Canada may pay part in U.S. cash and end the bill with a Canadian check or Canadian cash. Some customers use more than one credit card to pay the same bill.

Figure subtotal and enter payments one by one — For example: First payment is $10. Second payment is a personal check for $25.00. Third payment for the remaining 82.70 is by MasterCard.

With some electronic cash registers you may have to enter the credit card last. The cash register charges the outstanding amount to the credit card whose ending key you press.

Handle split credit card billings — Sometimes customers pay with two different credit cards. Make out two different credit card drafts for these customers. Often an electronic cash register won't allow a split credit card billing. Charge the total amount to one of the cards. Correct the "error" later when you fix mix-ups on the *Cash Register Reports*. Always get an Authorization Number for both credit cards. Call in if you don't have electronic card verification. Call in even if both amounts are under the floor limit. Customers who split charges on different cards often have credit problems. Act as if it's normal to call in. Sellers say nothing to customers to suggest they suspect a credit problem.

Enter Payments on Layaways

Finish the paperwork before entering the payment in the cash register, when opening a layaway account or taking a payment on it. Layaway payments are payments Received on Account, and there's usually a key programmed for this.

Sell the items after the final payment. Do the paperwork with the customer, then ring a sale for the items. This sale is for the store's records only. Ring it after the customer leaves. End this sale with the key programmed for Charge accounts.

Enter Percentage Off Item or Subtotal

Electronic cash registers usually have keys for percentage off.

Know percentage off item from percentage off subtotal — Suppose we have a damaged item. Normally, it sells for $10 but we allow 10% off for the damage, so we sell it at $9. That's *percentage off an item*. An electronic cash register usually has a %Off Item key.

Suppose the store's running a "40% off" sale. Four items have original price tags of $23.95, $15.35, $73.15 and $7.58. We could work out 40% of each price and take it from the original price. It's quicker to add the original prices to get $120.03 and take 40% off that, so we sell the four items at $72.02. That's *percentage off a total*. An electronic cash register usually has a %Off Merchandise Subtotal key.

Enter Cash Discount from Item or Subtotal

Electronic cash registers usually have a Cash Discount key.

Know cash discount from percentage off — It may be easier to take a dollar off than work out a percentage. Suppose we sell a damaged $6.95 item for $5.95. That's 14.39% off, while 15% off gives a price of $5.91. Taking a dollar off is quicker and easier to understand. To take a cash discount from an item, enter the discount amount after the item and press the Cash Discount key. To take a cash discount from a merchandise subtotal, enter the discount amount after the merchandise subtotal and press the Cash Discount key.

Clear, Void and Refund

See that sellers can roll back cash register entries. Sometimes sellers sell the wrong item by mistake. Sometimes customers change their minds. Clear, void or refund entries to roll them back.

Clear entries before pressing the PLU key — Sometime sellers notice mistakes as they enter PLUs. Example: a seller enters 1681235 instead of 1861235, notices it and presses the Clear key. PLU 1681235 never makes it onto the receipt and journal tapes.

Direct void — The seller enters the PLU but voids the item before entering the next PLU or pressing an ending key. Example: the seller enters 1010001 and presses the PLU key. The cash register displays and prints PLU, name and price. The customer says, "Forget it." The seller presses the VOID key and then finishes the sale normally.

Indirect void — The seller voids the item after entering other PLUs but before pressing an ending key. The seller enters 1010001—a Filigree Bird—and presses the PLU key. The cash register displays and prints PLU, name and price. Now the seller enters 111005 and presses the PLU key. The cash register displays and prints PLU, name and price. The customer says, "Forget the Filigree Bird." The seller enters 1010001, presses the VOID key and then presses the PLU key. The cash register prints a void line for 1010001. The seller then enters other PLUs, if any, and finishes the sale.

Refund the sale after pressing an ending key — The sale ends and then the customer decides against an item or items. This can happen before the customer pays. Now and then a customer will even walk away from the items. Customers often decide against items after they've paid. Some do it just after they've paid, others later in the day. A few customers return items for refund days or weeks after buying them.

A refund reverses a sale. Here's the sale: 1110005, press PLU key, press Subtotal key, press VISA key. Here's the refund: 1110005, press Refund key, press PLU key, press Subtotal key, press VISA key.

Refund a layaway in the same manner, ending with the Received on Account key. Leave a note for the bookkeeper on a refunded layaway in the *To Manager* binder.

Deal with Bad PLUs

When a seller enters a PLU the cash register can't find a warning prompt appears on the display. Often this will say: "ENTER PRICE/DEPT".

These are the reasons a cash register can't find a PLU:

Sellers miskey PLUs: Entering a wrong PLU may get this prompt from the cash register. All our PLUs have the form 1231234. PLUs like 123123, 121234, and so on, aren't in the register. 9682101 entered for 1682101 gets "ENTER PRICE/DEPT" if there's no PLU 9682101.

Mistakes on labels: The label says 168 2001 but it's a mistake for 168 2101. Entering 1682001 gets "ENTER PRICE/DEPT" if there's no PLU 1682001.

Cash register is wrong: PLU 1682001 should be in the cash register but it isn't, so it gets "ENTER PRICE/DEPT." Sellers who load PLUs into the cash register sometimes overlook items. They sometimes miskey items.

Clear miskeys — Clear miskeys with the CLEAR key and enter the right PLU.

Clear the cash register and clear up mistakes on labels when the mistakes are plain. A plain mistake on a label is one that's easy for the seller to work out. The label says 186 2001 but the seller knows it's item 168 2001. Check the *Price List* to make sure of the price. Clear the display and enter the right number. Clear up the mistake. Fix the labels on all items in the store. Post a *News Sheet* about the mistake. This warns the labelers and the *Pricer* to take care on this item and warns other sellers to look out for this mistake.

Enter other items as problem items — Some mistakes on labels won't be clear to sellers. An item must be in the cash register's memory for a seller to enter it. Enter these items as problem items. Get a price on the item if the price on the label seems out of line. Otherwise, sell it at the price on the label. Enter the price and press [F] on the Letter Keyboard, where F is a "department" set up for problem items. The cash register shows "PROBLM price" on the display. Cash register prints item as PROBLM on the receipt and journal tapes. Finish the sale

Clear up problem items — Find out where the problem lies. Clear up the problem if you can. Otherwise, see that someone clears up the problem.

Clear problem items the same as clearing normal items — To practice clearing, voiding and refunding problem items, reserve a group number with no items in it. For example, have no items in group 888 in the cash register. Then make problem items by using it: 888 1234, 888 1235, etc.

Fix Price Clashes

A price clash occurs when the cash register shows a different price from the label on the item.

Sell at lower price when the difference is small — Sellers judge whether the difference is small. Examples: $12.95 item sold at $12.45, $14.95 item sold at

$12.95. Ring a cash discount to get rid of the difference when the higher amount is in the cash register.

Charge the proper price when the difference is large — Examples: the label says $24.95 but the cash register says $4.95, the label says $4.95 but the cash register says $24.95. Say, "Oops! Somebody's goofed on this one. Let me check the price."

Clear up the price clash. Look into the reason for the price clash. See that someone clears up the clash. Remove items from display while clearing up the clash.

Back Out of Tight Spots

Follow a plan in tight spots. Sometimes things go wrong and panic sets in. It's a busy day and a pushy customer is trying to hurry you along, just when you forget how to do an indirect void. Suddenly another customer slaps down some cash and expects attention right now. Without a plan it's easy to panic.

Ask customers for help — To customers in a hurry, sellers are often part of the furniture. Turn yourself into a person by asking for help. Say, "I'm sorry, Ma'am. I've really messed this up. Please be kind and hang on while I start over." Say, "I'm sorry, Sir. Too much is happening to me at once. Please help me by waiting just a few minutes."

Start over — End the receipt you're working on. Press [#SBTL] Press one of the ending keys, usually [CA/AT/NS]. Close the cash drawer. Tear off the receipt and put it aside. Ring a new receipt.

Refund the receipt and review the problem later Refund the first receipt when things calm down. That puts the cash register's count of items in order. Write a note on the original receipt telling what happened. Include it in your *Seller's Report*. Review the problem that caused the fuss. Sort things out when the pressure is off.

Sell, Void and Refund with Sales Tax Exemptions

Non-taxable items are in the cash register without sales tax on them. Sell them normally. The cash register knows how to handle them.

Sales tax exemptions covers a few odd situations only. In these the law lets a customer off paying tax on taxable items. Sales tax exemptions are rare. Selling items with sales tax exemptions generally involves pressing the No Tax key before pressing the PLU key. Direct void is the same as for voiding sales without sales tax exemptions. Indirect void needs sellers to tell the cash register it's a sales tax exemption. Refunding items with sales tax exemptions generally involves pressing the No Tax key.

Know about Cash Register Reports

Series 1 reports are daily reports. Suppose you take a series 1 report on sales at the end of the day on January 31st 1994. You get a report on sales for January 31st 1994.

Series 2 reports cover a time span. Suppose the last time you took a series 2 report on sales was December 31st 1993. Suppose you now take a series 2 report on sales at the end of the day on January 31st 1994. You get a report on sales for January, 1994.

Most sellers take series 1 reports only. Specially trained sellers or the manager take series 2 reports.

There are two kinds of reports.

X Reports read what's in the cash register and leave it there. Suppose you make sales of $100. An X Report shows you made $100 of sales. Later the same day you make another $100 of sales. An X Report now shows you made $200 of sales.

Z Reports read what's in the cash register and reset the cash register. Suppose you make sales of $100. A Z Report tells shows you made $100 of sales and resets the sales to 0. Later the same day you make another $100 of sales. An X Report or a Z Report now shows you made $100 of sales. Only sellers in charge of cash drawers for *Opening Shifts* and *Closing Shifts* take Z Reports.

X1/Z1 is usually the Mode Key position to take daily Read Reports (X1) and daily Reset Reports (Z1.)

Pick the report by entering a number. Enter a number on the Number Keyboard to pick the type of report. These are examples of useful reports:

Report Number	Report
1	Full sales report.
2	Sales for the key that's in the CLERK key slot.[21]
3	Sales Total for one seller.
4	Sales by the hour.
5	Sales for keys A, B, D and E.
80	Sales by PLUs.
85	Problem Items.

[21] Use the key in this slot to keep track of the day's shifts. A for the First Shift. B for the Second Shift. D for the Third Shift. E for the Fourth Shift.

Fix Problems shown by Clerk Reports

It's important that each seller corrects any errors that show up in the Clerk Report (Report 2 in the above list.) The checks your sellers make will relate to how you use the cash register, but here are some things to look out for:

Check the Q values — Q values are quantities. For example: have sellers make a Q Check on PAY IN, R/A, P/O, DISC, VISA, AMEX, MSTR and USCHEK. The number of each item in the *Cash Drawer Report* must agree with the Q values on Report 2. Suppose Report 2 has VISA 3Q. Expect to find 3 VISA slips in the cash tray.

One Q Value is High and Another is Low: Looks as if the seller pressed the [MSTR] key for a VISA sale.

	Cash Drawer		Report 2	
VISA	29.95	3	24.00	Q2
MasterCard	12.95	1	18.90	Q2
Total	42.90		42.90	

Item Count is Lower than Its Q Value: Suppose Report 2 has VISA 3Q but there are only 2 VISA slips in the cash drawer. The seller has mislaid or overlooked a VISA slip. Find it and redo the adding machine tape.

Item Count is Higher than Its Q Value: Suppose Report 2 has VISA 3Q but the seller reports 4 VISA slips. The seller has probably miscounted the slips—recount them.

Check the amounts — Once the Q values are OK, check the amounts. Check the amounts for PAY IN, R/A, P/O, DISC, VISA, AMEX, MSTR, USCHEK and CDN$. These are possible reasons for wrong amounts when the Q values are OK:

Adding Machine Entry Error: It's easy to enter a wrong value, like 16.00 for 16.60. Check the entries.

Cash Register Entry Error: With PAY IN or PAY OUT it's possible to enter an amount different from the amount paid in or paid out. Perhaps the seller records a *Pay-in* of 159.68 but only pays in 150.68.

Wrong Value on Charge Slip: It's possible to write a charge slip for less than the amount showing on the cash register. The cash register shows $19.95 but the seller writes $16.95 by accident. It's less likely that the seller writes a charge slip for more than the amount on the cash register. Most customers will point that mistake out.

Wrong Value on a Check: The amount the customer wrote and the seller "confirmed" differ from the amount shown on the cash register.

Check Cash in Drawer (CID) — Check CID amount only when all other Q values and amounts are OK. An error elsewhere will likely cause an error in CID. Recount the cash in drawer when there's an error in CID. Shortages come from giving too much change They also come from someone stealing from the cash register. Overages occur when customers walk away from their change. Some customers walk away from small amounts of change.

Check voids and refunds — Managers keep track of all voids and refunds. Know the usual rate of use of these keys. Look into any high use right away. Fake voids and refunds are an easy way for sellers to take cash for themselves.

Fix up the report — After correcting errors on the paper copy of the Clerk Report, sellers correct the report in the cash register and then run a new report.

Fix mix-ups. Suppose the seller pressed [VISA] instead of [MSTR] to end a sale of $12.95. First cancel the VISA sale. Now put the sale on MasterCard.

Fix cash shortage. Make a *Pay-out* receipt for the missing amount. Write, "Missing from Cash in Drawer" on the receipt and sign it.

Fix cash overage. Make a *Pay-in* receipt for the extra amount. Write, "Extra Cash in Drawer" on the receipt and sign it.

Borrow the Cash Register

Sellers need to use the same cash register that printed the report to correct it. This will probably mean borrowing it from its present user. Borrowers will have to do this so there's little break in its use for sales.

Get ready — Sellers need to know what they're going to do and have everything ready to do the job quickly. Clear the use with the seller in charge of the cash register before beginning. Follow any rules the seller in charge of the cash register makes.

Wait for a gap in selling — Block the cash register from selling for as little time as possible. Remove the shift key (A, B, D or E.) Give it to the seller in charge of the cash drawer who puts shift key's key ring on a finger. Put your shift key (A, B, D or E) in the register and make your reports. Switch the Mode Key to REG. Take your shift key out of the register.

Make no sales — Sometimes a customer will ask to buy while you're using the cash register. Say, "Can you please hang on a minute while I finish this report, Ms?" Thank the customer who waits for helping you.

Deal with the Problem Item Report

Correct items you can identify. Many problem items come from wrong item numbers. Some are on labels, while others come from entering the wrong number in the cash register. It's usually easy to work out the right numbers. Correct items in the cash register. Refund the items and "sell" them again under their right PLUs. Include the receipts for the corrections in the *Cash Register Report*. Correct items in the store. Correct all mislabeled items in the store. Write a *News Sheet* when you have no time to do this.

Send a message on missing PLUs. Leave a message for the *Pricer* on all mislabeled items. Some items are problems because they're not in the cash register. It's clearly item 123 1234 but there's no PLU 1231234 in the cash register. Send a message to the *Pricer* about these items.

List the rest of the problems. Make a list of problem items that stump you and send it to the *Pricer*. Include item numbers used, number of items sold and the price. Describe each item on the list

Point of Sale (POS) Systems

There is a large variety of *Point of Sale Systems*, which generally interface with a computer rather than with their own specific hardware. Their advantages over electronic cash registers are:

- Fewer limitations in entering data.

- More extensive reports.

- Easier import of their data into other computer programs.

Take Stock

There will be differences between numbers of items you think you have in stock and the true numbers. It doesn't matter how careful you are in recording your sales. Differences will always creep in. At the minimum shoplifting is always with you. The differences between recorded stock and true stock can be startlingly large. Take steps to correct the differences so you come close to the true stock of your store. You also need to keep track of the supplies you use to make sure you have the right amounts on hand. Also check that the equipment you use is still on hand and is in working order.

Make a Spot Check

A spot check is an inspection carried out at random or limited to a few examples. Make spot checks on specific items when you suspect the count of items might be wrong. Also make spot checks on items of high value, especially if they turn over in high volumes.

Count one item fully — Count to find facts for bookkeeping or ordering. Item 123-1234 is a Round Brass Clock. The *Price List* calls for one on display and four in storage, for a total of five. Count the Round Brass Clocks in the store and find one on display and two in storage, for a total of three. We should have five, but we only have three. So far the spot check shows we're off two items.

Make spot checks only when the store is at full stock — Check for missing items in the *Receiving Area*. The total is OK if the two Round Brass Clocks are sitting in the storeroom waiting for someone to price them. Check any other places where items may be put aside.

Check today's sales — The total is OK if someone just sold two Round Brass Clocks. Check *Item Tally Sheets* and ask other sellers about spot check items. It's usually easy to cross-check on sales. Unless there's a panic on, we only make spot checks when sales are slow.

Make a Spot Check Report — Write on a piece of letter size paper from the *Recycle* binder. Write a header:

Our Store
Spot Check Report
Monday, May 2nd 1994, 11 am
Mary Jones.

For entries begin by copying Item Number, Item Name, Display and Storage Numbers from the *Price List*.

123-1234 2-Drawer Plastic Stacker
D 6
S 12

Take away the numbers you count on display and in storage.

123-1234 2-Drawer Plastic Stacker
D 6 - 6 = 0
S 12 - 8 = 4

Take away any items sold. The numbers left over are *Off Counts*.

123-1234 2-Drawer Plastic Stacker

$D\ 6 - 6 = 0$

$S\ 12 - 8 = 4\ Sold\ 2 = Off\ 2$

Zeros show items that are OK.

123-1235 3-Drawer Plastic Stacker

$D\ 6 - 6 = 0$

$S\ 12 - 12 = 0 = OK$

Pass the Spot Check Report along — Put it in the *To Manager* binder.

Count All Items

A list of items for sale in a store together with the number and value of each item is called an inventory. A physical inventory is a count of all items in the store. It's physical because you touch each item to count it rather than estimate it from written records.

Keep the records straight — Keep track of all the items you buy and sell as you buy and sell them. At the end of the tax year you should know what items you have in the store. Accountants know better than that. They say no matter how well you try to keep track of items, your counts will be off at the end of the tax year. To get your tax records right take a physical inventory at the end of the tax year. That means you have to count every item in the store. So there's not too great a shock at tax time, take a physical inventory at least twice a year.

Share the work — To get the job done everyone comes to work after closing on physical inventory days. Make a separate sheet for each display and storage area. Everyone gets an equal share of sheets. Then tally the items for the sheets. Later put these tallies together as a series of *Odd Jobs*.

Check Supplies Weekly

Keep on top of supplies once a week. Check certain items once a week. Check other items once a month.

Check for items added to the check sheet — Work with a copy of the *Supplies Weekly Check Sheet*. There's a look-up copy of the *Supplies Weekly Check Sheet* in *Daily*. Copy new items written on the look-up copy to your working copy.

Check against the Supplies and Materials List — There may be late changes to the *Supplies and Materials List*. Add them to the *Supplies Weekly Check Sheet* if needed. Add them to the look up copy in *Daily* and to your working copy.

Check fast moving supplies weekly — The *Supplies Weekly Check Sheet* lists the supplies you need most often. They have "w" in the W column of the *Supplies and*

Materials List. Check the places of use for supplies with "u" in the K column. Check the storage places for supplies with "s" in the K column. As you check, top up all supplies in use from supplies in storage.

Check other supplies monthly — Check other supplies after you make the weekly supplies check. Suppose you check the weekly supplies every Wednesday. Choose a Wednesday of the month to deal with other supplies, say the third Wednesday. First finish the weekly supplies check, then check other supplies. *Daily* lists the present choice of day for checking other supplies.

Check other supplies against the Supplies and Materials List — Other supplies have a blank W column in the *Supplies and Materials List*. Write other items you need on the *Supplies Weekly Check Sheet*. Write on the back of the sheet if the front fills up. Write "OVER" at the bottom of the sheet if you use the back. Write "and other supplies" beside "*Supplies Weekly Check Sheet.*"

CHAPTER 12

RUN SHIFTS

This chapter deals with the *Background Jobs* needed to run shifts. From the sellers' point of view they fall into three groups: jobs needed to start shifts, jobs carried out during shifts, and jobs needed to end shifts. It also includes a number of jobs needing the managers attention which spring directly from the sale of items during shifts.

Start Shifts

A number of jobs sellers do to start shifts are best done before opening the store to customers.

Start the Day

Sellers enter the store during scheduled work hours only. They may not be in the store outside their scheduled work hours.

Open the store — Switch off the burglar alarm right away before it rings. Switch the outside lights off over the front and rear doors. Switch the floodlights on inside the store.

Do the outside jobs right away — Lock the door while doing the outside jobs. Check the windows for out of shape displays. Get the mopping water for the day if it comes from outside the store. Clean smears from the windows.

Take Charge of the Store

Let sellers prove themselves at each level before taking charge at higher levels. First get their *Seller's Reports* right. Then they can take charge of cash drawers. Then get their *Cash Drawer Reports* right. After that, they can take charge of shifts and then they can take charge of the day.

Make sure sellers turn in correct reports in fair time. Train them and support them but let them go if they can't or won't learn to make correct reports in fair time. You can't run a store on sloppy reports. You can't afford sellers who take forever to make their reports. You can't spend time making sellers' reports for them. You'll certainly have to correct some errors in reports. Give the sellers feedback and make sure they improve. You need correct reports daily to run a store profitably.

Know who's in charge of selling — All sellers take charge of their own selling. All sellers do their own paperwork for their own selling. The manager gives feedback directly to all sellers.

Know who's in charge of cash drawers — It gives the best control of cash drawers when all sellers have their own cash drawer. Some stores can't afford that and in other stores extra cash drawers take up too much space. When there are several sellers to one cash drawer, one seller takes charge of the cash drawer and does its paperwork. The schedule for the shift lets sellers know who takes charge. All sellers make their sales into the cash drawer.

Know who's in charge of the shift — A seller working alone takes charge of the shift. Where there are several sellers working a shift, one seller takes charge of the shift and does its paperwork. The schedule for the shift lets sellers know who takes charge of the shift. This seller sees that *Daily* runs smoothly and handles problems when the manager is out of the store.

Know who's in charge of the day — Sellers in charge of the day do the paperwork for the day's selling. Sellers in charge of *Opening Shifts* or *Closing Shifts* also take charge of the day. *Opening Shifts* and *Closing Shifts* usually have different sellers in charge of them. The seller in charge of the *Opening Shift* begins the paperwork for the day. The seller in charge of the *Closing Shift* finishes the paperwork for the day. The schedules for *Opening Shifts* and *Closing Shifts* show which sellers are in charge of them and are also in charge of the day.

Log the Kind of Day

Log the kind of day to understand sales patterns. The weather often makes a difference to sales. One Saturday it's like spring but the next Saturday there's a blizzard. Local events may make a difference to sales. The Tall Ships put into port. People come downtown to see them. Afterwards they go shopping and sales go up. The Pope visits and holds a mass at a football stadium in the suburbs. The visit snarls traffic and ties up a lot of people for part of the day. Afterwards they go home to rest and sales go down. At the time you know why the sales are different. Years later you look back at sales figures and wonder why they're different. Keep a written log of the weather and other events. Then you can look back and understand why the sales look the way they do.

The seller in charge of the shift logs the kind of day. Each day has spaces for morning, afternoon, and evening entries. Make an entry for morning and afternoon each day. Make an entry for evening when you're open in the evening. Otherwise write "Closed" in the evening column. Write a simple entry on what you see, feel or hear. For the weather "Bright and sunny" and "Cold and rainy" are good entries. Include anything that everyone is talking about. "First snow storm of the year" is a good entry. So is "Temperature over 100." Also include local events other than the weather.

Play Background Music

For background music use a music machine with no radio tuner. Then you don't tempt sellers to spoil your music program with radio broadcasts.

Some retailers like to go it alone. It needs a good music sense and enough time to listen to and balance a number of disks or cassettes. There are limits to the balance you can give the program because each disk or cassette has a fixed selection of music. Sometimes there are large mood swings between the musical selections. Only some of the selections may be suitable. There may be sound differences from disk to disk or cassette to cassette.

Normal cassette players are a poor choice if you want to choose your own music. The cassettes have too short a playing time for store use. The most you can play is two cassettes on auto reverse. That's better than no music and better than radio, but it's too short a playing time for a store. Get hold of a six-cassette player to offset this limit.[22] You face the need for special equipment if you make your own long playing cassettes. You need lots of time to make them.

Another way is to use a compact disk player that plays five or six disks instead of a cassette player. Get a machine with a disk stacker or carousel. Make sure that it cycles back to the first disk when the last disk ends. That way the music keeps playing when you're too busy to change disks.

Retailers who create their own music programs often overlook copyright problems. In most cases it's a public performance when you play a tape or cassette or compact disk in your store. It's the same with music on the radio played over loudspeakers. It's usually a public performance of music when you play music to your customers. It's usually a public performance when persons outside the normal circle of a family and its friends listen to music. That's so even when the music is recorded or is broadcast on the radio. Someone who runs a greasy spoon restaurant and has the radio on behind the counter is probably legal. The radio happens to be on and perhaps a few customers may hear it. Once you take steps to deliver music to your customers, you face copyright problems.

Expect to pay from \$140 to \$240[23] each year for each music location to both ASCAP[24] and BMI.[25] Their agents visit businesses and collect from them. They'll

---

[22]Pioneer Electronics, Box 1540, Long Beach CA 90801 made 6 + 1 cassette players which may still be available used.
[23]Rough estimates, 1999.

take you to court to collect from you if necessary. Broadcasting music without a license can cost you $5,000 to $20,000 for each copyrighted song you play. You may also have to pay court costs and attorneys' fees.

Professional music services play a useful role.[26] They employ expert listeners to put together balanced music programs. This saves you time, even if you like to choose your own music. You may find it's hard to choose a balanced music program. A professional music service makes skilled choices for you. You can change the style of music you play in your store. You can move from Chinese Instrumental, to Nature Sounds, to Baroque, to Latin Blend. The large choice of styles allows you to try different sound images for your store. It allows you to target age groups and other groups. It allows you to match music to seasons and holidays.

Professional music services take care of all copyright fees. You pay a single fee that covers everything.

Professional services offer a library of four-hour cassettes or compact disks. For cassettes and disks, make sure the player cycles the music. That way the music is still playing when you're too busy to change media. Typically, you borrow six media, then return two and receive two new ones each month. You need special players for these media.

For another way to get professional music service, subscribe to a satellite relayed music service. For good reception you need a small dish on the roof rather than a relay from an earth station.

It's become the fashion for music services to claim they sell foreground music rather than background music. In some cases you really do need foreground music. A punk hairdressing salon is a good example. So is a certain kind of donut shop. Most retail stores need music that's more in the background. Whether the music is foreground or background depends on the music you play and how loud you play it.

Play background music for customers — Background music is an important part of the store. How the store sounds is as important as how the store looks. Without music a store is dead. Most customers prefer stores where music plays. Music relaxes customers and they spend more time in the store. Most customers say music probably plays a part in deciding to buy.

---

[24]American Society of Composers, Authors & Publishers, One Lincoln Plaza, New York NY 10023.
[25]Broadcast Music Inc., 200 Schulze Drive, Red Bank NJ 07701.
[26]AEI Music, 3M Sound Products, Muzak and Yesco provide professional music services.

Play music without voices — Voices grab customers' attention. You want customers' attention on your items. Singers will take their attention away. Announcers will butt in while you're selling.

Keep track of the volume — Play music loud enough to hear but soft enough to sense it. Make sure customers and sellers can talk without the music getting in the way. Noise swamps out the background music when the store is crowded. Raise the volume, but turn it back down as the crowd thins.

Stick to the store's music program — Select your music program to make the store feel right for your customers. The wrong music will drive customers away. Sellers aren't free to change the music to suit their personal taste. They can talk about ideas for a better music program with the manager.

Leave the radio off — Radio programs have an unbalanced selection of music. Radio programs have announcers who talk and distract customers. Radio programs carry ads that distract customers. It costs you a lot to get customers into the store. Sell them something rather than turning them over to someone else's pitch.

Play the music program in order — Play any piece of music only once in twenty-four hours. It shows in the mood of the sellers when music repeats too often. Even regular customers begin to notice the same old music. Play the media in order. Have six four-hour media, each with a number written on it. Play them in order to avoid playing the same media too often. Without numbers on the media it's easy to play one too often. Some sellers do this by accident. Others do it because they like one of the media better than the others.

Refresh the music program — Remove the first two media each month and add two new media. Begin with media 1, 2, 3, 4, 5, and 6. Next month use media 3, 4, 5, 6, 7 and 8. This way each media has a three month life. Wait for a year before using a media again.

Set Up for Credit and Debit Cards

Stores without electronic control of credit cards need to set up for their use.

Set the date on the imprinter — Roll the date wheels to set today's date.

Check blank sales drafts by the cash drawer — Keep sales drafts in a small box by the cash drawer. A card at the back of the box lists the number needed in the box. Bring the sales drafts up to number from the store of sales drafts.

Print a test sales draft — Test the imprinter with the test credit card from the back of the box. Look at the last copy of the printed slip. Check that the copy is good and the date is right.

Set the Exchange Rate on the Canadian Dollar

Stores that take Canadian cash need to check and post the exchange rate daily. Always give a rate of exchange that agrees with or is close to the bank's rate. Trying to make a little extra by giving less than the going rate warns customers that they can't trust the store. Make your money at retail, not on artificial rates of foreign exchange.

Phone the bank for the exchange rate — Call for the rate on the Canadian dollar. Look under "Rate on the Canadian dollar" in the *Quick Phone List*. The *Supplies and Materials List* tells where you keep the *Quick Phone List*.

There are two exchange rates. The buying rate is how much the bank pays you for a Canadian dollar. The selling rate is how much you pay the bank for a Canadian dollar. The bank may buy Canadian dollars for $0.8280 and sell them at $0.8480. That's how the bank makes money on exchanging money. The rate you need is the bank's buying rate. That's how much you'll get for Canadian dollars you take from customers. The bank's buying rate is the lower of the two rates. Get the rate to four decimal places—$0.8280, not $0.83.

Make an entry in the Log of Canadian Dollar — The *Log of Canadian Dollar* is in *Daily*. Fill in all columns.

Log of Canadian Dollar

Day	Date	Rate	Used	Costs	Name
Mon	6/15/92	0.8280	0.83	1.21	Mary Rogerson
Tue	6/16/92	0.8281	0.83	1.21	Mahasti Mohtashami

Write the Rate to four decimal places. You need this figure to work out the exchange for the *Cash Drawer Cash Report*. Round the rate to two decimal places and enter it in the Used column. You need this figure to work out the exchange given to customers. Divide 1 by Used to get the figure for the Costs column. This is the cost of $1 of the items in Canadian dollars.

Display Today's Rate — Use this layout:

Today's Rate

CN $1	US $1
US $0.83	CN $1.21

Know the percentage on the Canadian dollar — A different way of saying the exchange rate is as a percentage. It's common to say the exchange is 21% when a dollar costs CN $1.21. Some stores post a notice saying "Exchange 21%." The 21% is the extra Canadian money to add to the price. One dollar becomes CN $1.21, $10 becomes CN $12.10, an so on.

Work out the Canadian price — Price x Costs = Canadian Price. Where Price is $17.15 and Costs is 1.21, 17.15 x 1.21 = 20.75. The customer pays $20.75 in Canadian dollars.

Read the Daily Readings

Put pointers to all *Daily Readings* in *Daily*.

Read the store's mission daily — Read the store's *Mission Statement* each day and always keep it in mind. Knowing it as second nature helps you steer through problems. Reading it each day is an important part of being part of the store. Although the store's mission only changes now and then, beware of thinking you know the mission so you can skip it. Keep the store's mission fresh in your mind.

Read the charge for returned personal checks daily — Know the *Charge for Returned Checks*. That seems to stay the same, but suddenly it changes. Keep it right by reading it daily.

Read the appointment times for reps daily — Know the *Appointment Times for Reps*. They seem to stay the same, but suddenly they change.

Read the store opening hours daily — Know the *Store Opening Hours*. Know what they are now. Know when they'll next change. Know what they'll be when they change.

Read the work schedules daily Know your present and coming work schedules. The manager sets new work schedules each week, but check them daily. They can change.

Read new News Sheets daily — Scan *News Sheets* as an *Opening Job*. Some news is short enough for you to finish the reading right away. Some news is about something you must do before you open the store. Some news you scan on opening for the day and finish reading as an *Early Job*. *News Sheets* may send you to read new *Guide Sheets*. Finish reading most *Guide Sheets* as *Early Jobs*.

Read any new Messages daily — Scan new *Messages* as an *Opening Job*. Sometimes they're about things to do before opening the store. Sometimes they let you know about something to do later.

Set Up Paperwork

Set up paperwork before starting to sell. There's a lot to do when you finish selling. It's a time when your energy may be low and when you may want to get away as soon as possible. Speed yourself on your way by getting the paperwork set up before you start selling. Fill in the details as you sell and when you finish selling.

Follow the lists of paperwork in Daily — *Daily* lists all papers you set up, so you only have to follow the list. Look over the *Guide Sheets* that ask you to set up paperwork.

Check for a Messy Store

Have sellers check displays when they start their shift. It's their right to find the displays in good shape. Get sellers to thank the last sellers for doing a good job when the displays are in good shape. Tell them, phone them or leave them a note. Be reasonable about this. Sometimes one or two displays need some care. Shape them up as you check the store.

Sometimes a mess is OK. Ignore the mess when the selling is hot. Check the store quickly and join in the selling. Sometimes there was hot selling that's now settled down. Help the last sellers shape up the displays if they're still on shift. Shape up the displays for them if they're going off shift.

Talk about problem messes. Sometimes the store's a mess for no clear reason. Talk about it with the last sellers. Be matter-of-fact. Getting angry won't help you get the mess under control. "John, the store's too messy. Is there some reason for it?" Offer to help if you get a friendly or an embarrassed answer. "Let's pitch in and get this mess cleaned up together." Shape up the displays yourself if you get a hostile answer, then talk about the problem with the manager. Talk about it with the manager when you face a problem mess more than twice from the same sellers.

During Shifts

The problem with *Background Jobs* during shifts is being able to do them properly without them getting in the way of sales. Always put sales ahead of *Background Jobs*.

Sell from the Top of the Wheel

Sellers who get commissions on sales are eager to sell. Eager sellers gain a sense of pride when they sell well. Pride pushes them to make even more sales. That's exactly what you want. The downside is that four problems develop.

1. *Pushy sellers:* Some sellers pounce on customers before other sellers have a chance. Sometimes pushy sellers post themselves near the door. This drives customers away.

2. *Several sellers try to sell to the same customer:* Sellers try to sell to the same customer one after another. This destroys the atmosphere needed for

successful selling. Customers feel your sellers are harassing them. They shop elsewhere next time.

3. *Cherry picking, or skating:* Sellers go through many customers rapidly. They turn aside all but the quick and easy sales. Some retailers call this cherry picking. Others call it skating. Cherry pickers get high sales but the store's sales are low. They waste your customers to make their sales. Stop cherry pickers dead if you want high sales in your store.

4. *Sellers ignore Background Jobs:* Sellers are so busy getting in place for the next pounce they skip the *Background Jobs*. Soon the store has a bunch of eager sellers with little to sell. Its paperwork is behind and there's nothing to support the sellers.

To get the extra sales without the four problems put your sellers *On the Wheel*. *The Wheel* is a list of sellers working this shift that turns like the Ferris wheel at a fair. Selling begins with the seller who is *On Top of the Wheel*. When that seller goes *On the Floor, The Wheel* turns and the next seller is *On Top of the Wheel*.

While waiting for the next customer the seller *On Top of the Wheel* works on a *Background Job* but is wide-awake for sales. The other sellers also work on *Background Jobs* while they wait. The seller *On Top of the Wheel* tells the next seller to *Go to the Top* when leaving to sell. The seller who *Goes to the Top* crosses out the top name and writes it at the bottom of *The Wheel*.

Some people describe the seller *On Top of the Wheel* as being *On the Bubble*. Others refer to *The Wheel* as an *Up List* and the seller *On Top of the Wheel* as the *Up Seller*.

Using *The Wheel* brings sellers under control:

- Sellers are no longer free to decide whether to go up to customers. It's clear whose job it is to sell to the next customer.

- Every customer gets attention.

- Only one seller goes up to each customer. Customers are free of sellers who fight to pounce on them.

- Customers are free of sellers trying to sell to them one after another.

- Sellers share customers equally and fairly. Sellers are eager to sell when they earn commissions on sales. They may be less eager to sell when they only earn a wage.

- Once they get their fair share of customers, many non-pushy sellers make good sales.

- *Background Jobs* have a time and place. Without *The Wheel* some sellers skip their share of *Background Jobs*. They pretend they're selling and leave the *Background Jobs* to others.

- Customers get the attention they need. With *The Wheel*, one seller pays attention to each customer. The seller gives the customer as much or as little time as needed. All customers feel that you pay attention to them.

- *The Wheel* helps sellers to judge the time they spend with customers. Sellers who spend too much time with customers come *On Top of The Wheel* less often than other sellers. They see that's why their sales are low. *Skaters* find they have to slow down and work with customers to make high sales. They're no longer free to make only the quick and easy sales.

- Sellers learn to pace their sales. Some sellers only make quick and easy sales. Some do this because they have doubts about their selling skills. Others know they'll make sales if they ask enough customers to buy. They now know they have time to make their turn with customers pay off. The next turn with a customer may take a while. Their only way to make high sales is to work fully with the customers they get. Their only hope is to use the *Steps for Selling* fully. With *The Wheel*, sellers have time to develop their skills. On the other hand, it's possible to stay too long with customers. Sellers who do this notice when they get fewer turns than others who sell well.

Stick strictly to the rule that names go to the bottom when sellers <u>begin</u> to sell, not when they finish selling.

Stay firm with sellers who try to undercut *The Wheel*:
- *Skaters* try to put their names at the bottom of *The Wheel* after they finish selling instead of when they begin selling. So do some innocent sellers.

- *Skaters* claim their customers were *Askers*. Keep strictly to the rule that *Askers* are only those who ask a non-buying question right away.

- Poor sellers claim it's not fair when they lose a customer to "Just looking." It is fair. Sellers have to turn lookers into buyers.

- Sellers claim it's not fair to lose a turn when they pass a customer along to another seller. Stick to the rule, fair or not. Open the door to a *Pass-along* not being a turn and *Skaters* will skate right through it. Be tough with this one. Do it the same way for everyone.

Jump off The Wheel when sales run wild — Use *The Wheel* for more sellers than customers. Sometimes there are more customers than sellers. Forget *The Wheel*. Stay on the floor going from customer to customer. Just keep selling. Write three pound signs (###) on *The Wheel* when you start using it again.

Run The Wheel right — Draw lots to start *On Top of the Wheel*. Move the seller from the top to the bottom as soon as the seller goes on the floor to sell.

"Just looking" puts sellers on the floor — The *Steps for Selling* turn lookers into buyers. "Just looking" is a challenge to sell.

A Pass-along puts sellers on the floor — A seller sometimes passes a customer to another seller. Sometimes a customer is uneasy with a seller and the seller catches on to it. Sometimes a seller is uneasy with a customer and knows it. A *Pass-along* moves both sellers to the bottom of *The Wheel*.

Askers leave The Wheel unchanged — Some people ask for directions or help. "Can you tell me how to get to the Painted Pony?" "Where are the washrooms, please?" "Can you let me have change for the phone?" They're not customers—they're *Askers*. *Askers* come up to you right away and ask their question. They're customers if they browse before asking, even if they ask for change for the bus. They're customers if sellers go up to them, even if they ask for the washroom.

Callers leave The Wheel unchanged — *Callers* have business in the store unrelated to buying. They include:

- The rent collector.
- Sellers from a nearby store who pick up a key you mind for them.
- Reps who come to visit the manager.
- People making deliveries.

Make a list of *Callers* so everybody is clear who they are. Post the list of *Callers* in *Daily*.

Returns, repairs and layaways cause no movement — The lowest seller handles repairs and layaway payments. The original seller handles returns. When the original seller is out of the store, the lowest seller handles the return.

Personal Customers are extras — Sales are extras when customers ask for sellers by name. Make the sale and keep in position on *The Wheel*. Customers become *Personal Customers* when sellers give good service. Extra sales to *Personal Customers* are a seller's reward for good service.

Answer the phone from the bottom of The Wheel — Sellers answer the phone from the bottom of *The Wheel*. That keeps sellers near the top ready for selling.

Follow the Retail Cycle

Make sure sellers follow the *Retail Cycle*. Begin with *Daily*. Do *Background Jobs* while rising to the *Top of the Wheel*. Click to make sales. Then back to *Daily* for *Background Jobs*.

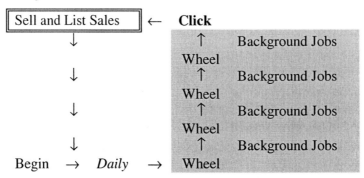

Daily points sellers to Background Jobs — Follow *Daily* step by step to do the right *Background Jobs* at the right time.

Do Background Jobs between sales — Selling needs help and support. Sellers must have items to sell. Nice displays help sales. Sellers must have supplies on hand to help them sell. The list of needs goes on and on. Sales fall off without good help and support. Things only work right when sellers set them up to work right. Sellers minds are only fully on selling when they set things up right for selling. Sellers need things to go smoothly to sell well. Do *Background Jobs* between sales to help and support selling.

Rise to the Top of the Wheel — Sellers go on doing *Background Jobs* when they're *On Top of the Wheel*. Be ready to drop *Background Jobs* to sell.

Rule Background Jobs or they'll rule you — The trouble with *Background Jobs* is that they take over. They take on a life of their own. They demand that you finish them. They push selling into the background.

People have only so much attention. People doing jobs get wrapped up in them. They drift with the tide. It's hard to get their attention. The job becomes a place to hide. It becomes familiar and satisfying. The mind becomes focused. It's easier to finish the job than to leave it for something more important. Here are some examples:

- The manager is training a seller to use the cash register. His back is to the customers. The seller is too scared to look anywhere but at the manager. You cough and shuffle. The manager glances at you and goes on training. You're in the way. You lean over the counter and ask for help loudly. You get a short answer from the manager. It's clear his mind is elsewhere. He's too busy to

serve you. He goes on training. He's in another world where customers are a
nuisance.

- The seller is too busy counting money to serve you.

- The seller is too busy pricing items to serve you.

- The seller is too busy writing up paperwork to serve you.

- The seller goes on arranging items in a cupboard after it's clear you need
  service.

- The owner cares more about putting up a shelf than selling to you.

Click when you sell, then sell when you click — Click every time you start to sell.
Click is a word or action you'll use to turn you on to selling. You might say the
word "Click" to yourself. You might say a nonsense word like "Gozumboo." You
might say a word that has special meaning to you. You might pull your little finger
or tap you knee. A good plan is to wear a rubber band round your wrist. Pull it and
let it go so it gives you a good sting.

After a while, your click will break the spell of the job you're doing. It'll put you
in the mood for selling. Drop what you're doing and start to sell. Pick up the
pieces of the job later. Now you're ruling the job instead of the job ruling you.
Learn to click well. Until you click well, you'll miss sales. You'll be doing
Background Jobs when you could be selling.

Sell and list sales — Make a sale. Then list the sale by hand, by cash register, by
both or with a *Point of Sale System*. Return to *Background Jobs*. Pick up the job
you dropped to begin selling, or take a new one from *Daily*.

Change Prices

Expect prices to change. The *Pricer* tests prices in the market place. The *Pricer*
begins by setting prices that give a good profit. Some items sell well at these
prices. They help pay for items you have to sell at low profit or at a loss.

Some items sell poorly at a price that gives a good profit. Then the *Pricer* sets a
price that gives a normal profit. Some items sell well at this price and they keep
the store going.

Some items sell poorly at a price that gives a normal profit. Then the *Pricer* sets
up a spiff or marks the price down. In bad cases the *Pricer* marks the price down
more than once. *Markdowns* give a slight profit, break even, or sell at a loss.
Markdowns are a drag on the store. Cut the item from your order list after you
mark it down.

Some items the *Pricer* puts on sale at the break-even point or at a loss. Some prices change because suppliers change their prices. Sometimes the rent increases—prices may have to go up too.

Deal with Price Change Sheets — The *Pricer* lists price changes on *Price Change Sheets*. Keep these sheets in *Daily*. *Price Change Sheets* have reminders on them to help you change prices. Follow these reminders or price changes will lead to a mess. The risk is of having the same item with more than one price. It's important to work item by item. It's important to initial each numbered job for each item as you do it. Then the next seller knows where to start.

Leave old price labels only on Markdowns — Strike through the old price on *Markdowns*. Make sure the strike mark stays on the label. Strike marks on items make them hard to sell. Put the new price label beside the old.

Have only two price labels on a *Markdown*. Remove the first *Markdown* label if the *Pricer* marks a *Markdown* down again. Too many labels make items look tacky. Remove old price labels for all other price changes. It looks sloppy when there's one label on top of another. It's important to remove the old label when the price goes up. Otherwise you risk losing a customer who peels off the top label.

Decide price clashes for customers during price changes — Sometimes the *Price List* or cash register and the item show different prices. The label may still say 29.95 when the cash register or *Price List* says 19.95. Sell the item for 19.95. The label may say 8.95 when the cash register or *Price List* says 12.95. Sell the item for 8.95.

Receive Deliveries

Deliveries arrive when the store's open and it's up to sellers to receive them properly.

Count cartons before signing Delivery Sheets — Carriers who make deliveries will ask for a signature on a *Delivery Sheet*. Count the cartons first—then sign like this:

Received 4 cartons.
Joan Brown
10:30 am Thursday
May 12th 1994.

Carriers may try to hurry you along. They may be late on their rounds and they may bring many cartons. Say, "I'm sorry. I can only sign when I've counted the cartons." They may still try to push you. Repeat, "I'm sorry. I can only sign when I've counted the cartons."

Check for damage before signing Delivery Sheets — Handle the cartons to be sure they're not damaged. Carriers may dump cartons in a pile so it's hard to see damaged cartons. They may try to hurry you along so you'll overlook damage. Say, "I'm sorry. I can only sign when I've checked for damaged cartons." They may still try to push you. Repeat, "I'm sorry. I can only sign when I've checked for damaged cartons." Sign for damaged cartons like this:

Received 4 cartons.
2 cartons damaged.
Contents of damaged cartons not inspected.
Joan Brown
10:30 am Thursday
May 12th 1994.

Check Delivery Sheets for supplier's and carrier's IDs — *Delivery Sheets* usually have the supplier's and the carrier's IDs on them. Write missing names, addresses and phone numbers on the sheet. Check for IDs before you sign, while the carrier is still there to tell you.

Get copies of Delivery Sheets — The store needs a copy of the *Delivery Sheet* for its records. Carriers usually give you a copy—otherwise, ask for your copy.

Get a signature if you make a payment — You'll have charge accounts with most suppliers. All you need to do is sign the *Delivery Sheet*. You'll pay a few suppliers on delivery. These are mainly new suppliers and suppliers who only send small orders now and again. In a few cases the carrier charges separately from the supplier. Carriers will ask you to pay if you need to pay. It's not your job to ask to pay. See that carriers sign and mark your copy of the *Delivery Sheet* as paid. Carriers usually do this without asking—otherwise, ask them to sign. Make sure they write "Paid" or "Received" by their signatures.

Pay from the cash drawer in a pinch — For most cash-on-delivery orders you'll find a check for payment in *Daily*. That's the normal way to pay. Sometimes the check is missing. Rather than miss the order, pay from the cash drawer. Only do this if it leaves you with enough change to go on selling. Prepare a *Pay-out Slip* when you pay from the cash drawer. Include the *Pay-out Slip* in the *Cash Drawer Cash Report*.

Note cash payment on Delivery Sheets — Write how you paid on your copy of the *Delivery Sheet*:

Paid with check 1234.
Paid from cash drawer # 2

Staple the *Cash Out Slip* to the *Delivery Sheet*.

Stack cartons in the Receiving Area — Stack cartons neatly in the *Receiving Area* of the storeroom.

Put Delivery Sheets in Daily — Put *Delivery Sheet* in *Daily* unless you go on to check the delivery. Then the another seller can check the delivery. Staple the *Delivery Sheet* to the *Order Sheet* that's already in *Daily*.

Check Deliveries

Once deliveries are in the store the next thing needed is to check them in.

Check items in new cartons — Check items into the store from any new cartons in the *Receiving Area*.

Grandview Supplies Inc.
756 Grandview Avenue   Tel: (206) 778-2356   **INVOICE** 0024386
Seattle WA 98324   FAX: (206) 778-2357   **CUSTOMER ORDER** 940410-1130

Sold to
CLAMSHEL
CLAM SHELL GIFT STORE
765 HARBOR ST
SEATTLE WA 98734

Shipped to
CLAMSHEL
CLAM SHELL GIFT STORE
765 HARBOR ST
SEATTLE WA 98734

INVOICE DATE	SALESMAN	OUR ORDER NO.	VIA	CARTONS	DEPT.
04/12/94	GINA L	A10745	TRANSIT	15	

Item No	Qty	Description	B/O	Ship'd	Price	Amount
1234	10	DRAFTING CHAIR	5	5	*******	*******
1244	6	COAT TREE		6	*******	*******
2321	10	HAWAIIAN LOUNGER		10	*******	*******
8765	2	FUTON FRAME		2	*******	*******

ITEMS NOT SHIPPED HAVE BEEN BACK ORDERED FOR EARLY SHIPMENT.
INTEREST: 2% PER MONTH WILL BE CHARGED ON ALL OVERDUE ACCOUNTS.
ALL GOODS REMAIN OUR PROPERTY UNTIL TOTAL PAYMENT IS MADE.
CLAIMS MUST BE MADE WITHIN FIVE DAYS OF RECEIPT OF GOODS.
NO RETURNS ALLOWED WITHOUT WRITTEN PERMISSION OF SELLER.

QTY	COMP	MORE	TOTAL
23		X	*******

TERMS	INVOICE
NET 60	0024386

CUSTOMER'S COPY

Find the Packing Slips — *Packing Slips* are lists of items suppliers include with shipments. This is supplier's copy of a typical *Invoice* that serves as a *Packing Slip*.

An *Invoice* is a list of items and their prices sent by a supplier to a buyer. *Packing Slips* are usually copies of *Invoices* with the prices blanked out. Some have "Packing Slip" or "Shipping Order" printed on them. Some *Packing Slips* have "Invoice" printed on them. To keep things straight, write "Packing Slip" on *Packing Slips*.

There may be one or more *Packing Slips* for one shipment. *Packing Slips* are usually in an envelope on the outside of a carton. Sometimes the envelope has "Packing Slip" printed on it. Often the envelope is a see-through plastic envelope. Sometimes *Packing Slips* are inside cartons. Staple them together when there are more than one packing slip. Staple them at the top left corner of the sheets

These are typical headings and entries:

Item: Usually an item number: 1234

Qty: Quantity: 10

Description: Drafting Chair

B/O: Number of items back ordered: 5

Ship'd: Number of items shipped: 5

Price: The price of one item or unit, e.g., $10 each, $25 a box. The dollar sign is usually omitted. When the copy of an *Invoice* serves as a *Packing Slip* the price is usually blanked out with stars.

Amount: The extension of the unit price. Ten items at $10 each extends to $100. When the copy of an *Invoice* serves as a packing slip the extension amount is usually blanked out with stars.

Staple Delivery Sheets behind Packing Slips — *Delivery Sheets* are in *Daily* stapled to *Order Sheets*. Staple them behind *Packing Slips* for the delivery.

Open the cartons — Open most cartons with a knife or hard-backed single-edged razor blade. Sometimes you'll need scissors or tin snips to cut strapping.

Write counts on Packing Slips as you unpack Write directly on *Packing Slips*:

Grandview Supplies Inc.		*Packing Slip*	
756 Grandview Avenue	Tel: (206) 778-2356	INVOICE 0024386	
Seattle WA 98324	FAX: (206) 778-2357	CUSTOMER ORDER 940410-1130	

Sold to	Shipped to
CLAMSHEL	CLAMSHEL
CLAM SHELL GIFT STORE	CLAM SHELL GIFT STORE
765 HARBOR ST	765 HARBOR ST
SEATTLE WA 98734	SEATTLE WA 98734

INVOICE DATE	SALESMAN	OUR ORDER NO.	VIA	CARTONS	DEPT.
04/12/94	GINA L	A10745	TRANSIT	15	

Item No	Qty	Description	B/O	Ship'd	Price	Amount
1234	10	DRAFTING CHAIR 3+1+1 ✓	5	5	*******	*******
1214	5			5		
2321	10	HAWAIIAN LOUNGER 4+2+3 *missing 1*		10	*******	*******
2755	2					

- Write 3 near the shipped number if you take out 3 Drafting Chairs: 5 *3*

- Write +1 if you find 1 more Drafting Chair in another carton: 5 *3+1*

- Write another +1 if you find another Drafting Chair: 5 *3+1+1*

- Check the correct total shipped: 5 *3+1+1* √

- Circle damaged or faulty items separately. Write with a bright colored pen to make them stand out: 6 ②+4. This entry shows that of 6 items received, 2 were damaged or faulty.

Store damaged or faulty items in the *Bad Items Area*. Write nothing on the items or their boxes.[27] You'll be able to fix some items and still sell them. It's hard to sell them if there's a negative note on the item or the box.

Search the packing when items are missing — Dump the cartons and packing when every item checks in OK. Set up the largest carton as a trash box. Flatten other cartons and put them in it along with any other packing. Then take the trash box to the dumpster.

Search through the packing when items are missing. Empty one carton and check the packing into it carton by carton. Get another seller to check the packing if you're still short items. Now get rid of the packing and cartons. Note who checked the packing if you're still short items.

Prepare a Packing Slip Alert for problem items — Write on a sheet of 3½″ x 6″ 6-hole lined paper.

Your store
Packing Slip Alert
10:30 am Wednesday
April 20th 1994
Bonnie Rogers
Supplier's Order Number 12345
Grandview Wholesale Gifts
Your Order Number 24567

| 2 | 1244 | Coat Tree | Damaged |
| 1 | 2321 | Hawaiian Lounger | Missing |

Staple the *Packing Slip Alert* to the *Packing Slip*.

Deal with checked Packing Slips — The next step is to turn the *Order Sheets* into *OK Sheets*. Use checked *Packing Slips* to do this now. Or else, staple *Packing Slips* behind their *Order Sheets* in *Daily* so another seller can do this job.

Deal with Damages

More often than you would like deliveries will have damaged items in them. See that your sellers know how to handle them.

---

[27]Typical negative notes are: "X," "NX," "Broken," "Repair," "Fix it," "Needs gluing."

Treat supplies and materials and sales stock differently — Supplies and materials are the things you buy to help you sell. They include things like price labels and staplers. List them in the *Supplies and Materials List*. Sales stock is the items you buy to sell to customers. List items in the *Price List*.

Keep usable cheap supplies and materials — A cheap supply item costs $10 or less. Keep it if it's damaged or faulty and you can still use it. It's too much fuss to return it.

Check for easy replacement of supplies and materials — Some suppliers will replace items on your word. It's too much fuss for them to go through the paperwork. This happens with suppliers who know you're honest and make few returns. This also happens when suppliers know they've got a problem item.

Check for free return of supplies and materials — Suppliers with their own delivery service usually pick up faulty supplies and materials. Some suppliers pay the shipping costs for the return of faulty supplies and materials.

Return other supplies and materials when it pays off — It makes sense to pay $12 to return a broken $300 item. It doesn't make sense to pay $12 to return a $30 item. There's also the cost of a seller's time in making the return. You may have to buy packing materials. It's doubtful you will save anything. The trouble to you and the supplier offsets the little you might gain. It's smarter to buy a new item. Avoid returning items because you're upset that you got burned. That's ego talking. It'll lead you into bad business decisions.

Aim never to return sales stock — Keep long-term relationships with suppliers in mind. This is specially important if the items from suppliers are hard to get. Those are exactly the items you need to keep your store outstanding. Suppose a supplier handles medium-priced items from China. A certain percentage of the items is likely to be faulty. You can return the faulty items but soon you'll have a bad reputation with the supplier. At some time someone will get angry. Then the flow of items will dry up and it'll be hard to run a business.

Allow for reality in pricing items. Suppose you pay $4 per item and 10% are faulty. Those without faults cost $4.44. Base selling price on the true cost of $4.44. Perhaps the 10% are useless—throw them away. Perhaps the 10% are only flawed—sell them "as is" at a lower price. This way you're in business and your supplier is happy. You make sales on an item that rigid retailers won't stock. Customers who buy the "as is" items are happy. You may even make a little extra profit on them. Treat items suppliers will take back for a fee the same way. Returning them takes money from the profit on those you sold. It's better to sell those you're stuck with at a lower price. Aim to break even or make a small profit.

Let suppliers know you stand by them — Talk with suppliers now and then so they know you're eating broken items. They may say they want you to return them, but take that with a grain of salt. Let them know it's too much fuss for you and for them. Suggest instead that they give you a good deal on some other items. They'll know you're easy to work with. Soon they'll come to you with deals that rigid retailers miss.

Return sales stock when there's little choice — Suppose you receive a $2,000 item that's faulty. You have to return it.

Be flexible on sales stock damaged in transit — Sometimes there's a problem when items get damaged in transit. The supplier blames the carrier for bad handling in transit. The carrier blames the supplier's poor packing. You may be the loser on small damages. Fixing the blame may be more hassle than it's worth. Allow a small amount for damaged items when setting prices. Speak to the supplier's manager and the carrier's manager. Make it clear you're not pushing a claim, but you do want them to know they may have a problem.

Claim when there's a lot of damage and it's clear the carrier is to blame. Usually, you've still got a problem. You'll have to keep the items and packing until an adjuster inspects them. That may take weeks. The items are in the way in the storeroom and money is locked up in them. Even if someone ran a bulldozer over the cartons, the adjuster may still blame the supplier.

You can try pressure on the carrier. Tell the carrier you expect an adjustment made within a few days. Otherwise, you'll ask the supplier to use a different carrier. That may work, but it may backfire on you. The other carrier may cost more. Soon the extra shipping costs will equal the cost of the lost shipment. Then you'll be stuck with higher shipping costs in the long run.

Set some deadlines for your own actions when you make a claim. You might decide to throw the items out if the adjuster doesn't examine them by a certain date. Examine the choices you have. Are the items a complete loss? Can you sell them at a reduction and break even? Is it really worth storing the items until the adjuster comes?

Stock Supplies and Materials

Supplies and materials are things you need to run the store. You use them to sell items to customers.

Supplies are things you use up and need again and again. Felt pens, staples and VISA sales drafts are good examples of supplies.

Materials are things you need to get a job done. Equipment is another name for materials. Unlike supplies, you need only one or a few of each of the materials.

Cash registers, staplers and brooms are good examples. Many of the materials use supplies. Cash registers use receipt tape, staplers use staples, and so on.

Stock supplies and materials from Packing Slips — Check them off and initial them on a *Packing Slip* as you stock them.

Work from the Supplies and Materials List — The *Supplies and Materials List* is a list of places for using and storing supplies and materials. It also lists the high and low numbers of items at each place of use and storage. Bring the supplies at each place of use up to the high number if you have enough stock. Put extra supplies in their storage places. Change the high and low numbers for use and storage if they seem wrong. Leave high storage numbers as they are for an overstock that will only last a short time. Sometimes you have to buy a certain number of an item and end up with more than you want. Sometimes the extras store well in the storage place. Avoid crowding the storage place and making it hard to use. Open a new storage area instead. Write the new storage area in the *Supplies and Materials List*.

Stock supplies in order of need — Stock supplies that have fallen lowest first.

Put unfinished Packing Slips back in Daily — Another seller will pick them up and finish them.

Put finished Packing Slips in the Old Orders binder — You can look them up if there are problems about orders.

Turn Order Sheets into OK Sheets

An *OK Sheet* is a list of items it's OK to price.

OK items for pricing — Work with checked *Packing Slips* to turn *Order Sheets* into *OK Sheets*. The *Pricer* works from *OK Sheets*, while the manager uses checked *Packing Slips* to keep on top of orders.

Match Packing Slips to Order Sheets — Look in *Daily* for checked *Packing Slips* and *Order Sheets*. A *Packing Slip* may have your *Order Number* on it. Then it's simple to match *Packing Slips* and *Order Sheets*. Sometimes suppliers forget to use your *Order Number*. Then match *Packing Slips* and *Order Sheets* by the items listed on them.

Update the Packing Slip Alert — Checked *Packing Slips* may have *Packing Slip Alerts* stapled to them. These are notes to the manager from sellers who checked the *Packing* Slip. The notes are mainly about shortages and damaged items.

Your Store
Packing Slip Alert
10:30 am Wednesday
April 20th 1994
Bonnie Rogers
Supplier's Order Number 12345
Grandview Wholesale Gifts
Your Order Number 24567

| 2 | 1244 | Coat Tree | Damaged |
| 1 | 2321 | Hawaiian Lounger | Missing |

Compare the *Order Sheet* to the checked *Packing Slip*. Update the *Packing Slip Alert* if needed. Look for items on the *Packing Slip* that aren't on the *Order Sheet*. Suppliers often include back ordered items and sample items in deliveries.

Write with a different colored pen to update the *Packing Slip Alert*. Add your numbers to the suppliers' numbers. Your numbers are on the *Order Sheets* but not on the *Packing Slips*.

Your Store
Packing Slip Alert
10:30 am Wednesday
April 20th 1994
Bonnie Rogers
Supplier's Order Number 12345
Grandview Wholesale Gifts
Your Order Number 24567

| 2 | 1244 | Coat Tree | Damaged | 435 7723 |
| 1 | 2321 | Hawaiian Lounger | Missing | 421 3379 |

4:30 pm Wednesday
April 20th 1994
John Jones

| 4 | 1244 | *Coat Tree* | *Overlooked* | *435 7723* |
| 2 | 8765 | *Futon Frame* | *Extra* | *456 2375* |

Turn Order Sheets into OK Sheets — Cross out " Order Sheet " and write " OK Sheet." Write in the left margin as an "OK" column. Write the number of items it's OK to price here. Write in details of any extra items. Include extra items sent by the supplier. Include damaged and faulty "as is" items the *Pricer* has ready for release from the *Bad Items Area*. Write the prices of the "as is" items. The *Pricer* gets normal prices from the *Price List*. This makes sure that you use the latest prices.

OK Sheet
~~Order Sheet~~

Order No	940410 1130		Contact	Gerry Reichert
Supplier	Grandview Supplies		Voice	778-2356
	756 Grandview		Fax	778-2357
	Seattle WA 98324		Taken by	Gina Learmonth
Placed by	Fran Smithers		Order No	A10745

Phone ▨   Fax ☐   Mail ☐

OK	Item No	Name	Need	Qty	B/O	Price	Amount
5	567 1107	Drafting Chair	10	10		75.00 ea	750.00
	1234						
4	435 7723	Coat Tree	10	10		75.00 ea	750.00
	1244						
9	421 3379	Canvas Hammock	10	10		25.00 ea	250.00
	2321	Hawaiian Lounger					
							1750.00
2	456 2375	*Futon Frame*					
2	435 7723	*Coat Tree as is @ 90.00*					

Pass the Packing Slip to the manager — Put the checked *Packing Slip* in the *To Manager* binder.[28]

Deal with OK Sheets — Go on to the next step or leave the *OK Sheet* in *Daily* for another seller. For supplies and materials the next step is to stock them. For items you sell the next step is to price them.

Price Items

Price all items before they go on display or into storage in the store.

Finish all Price Change Sheets before pricing items — It wastes time if you price items and then find a price change. Check *Daily* for *Price Change Sheets* before pricing items.

Show the price on all items — Leaving prices off items forces customers to ask prices. That short circuits the *Steps for Selling*. That's beginning to sell by asking customers to buy. Talk prices only when you're sure customers are interested in buying. Get there by using the *Steps for Selling*.

Some customers won't ask the price when there are no prices on items. They know asking will put a seller on their case, so they won't ask.

---

[28]After using them, managers store *Packing Slips* in the *Old Orders* binder.

Customers get used to prices when they see them. The beautiful necklace costs too much. Later a little voice in a customer's head says it's worth the cost. Then the voice tells the customer how to manage paying the cost.

Price items as soon as you OK them for pricing — Sellers receive and check items delivered to the store. Then they OK them for pricing as soon as possible.

Work from OK Sheets — *OK Sheets* are usually copies of your orders. Store them in *Daily*. Orders have your store's item numbers and names on them. They also have the supplier's item numbers and names. This helps keep everything clear. The checkers often write notes on the *OK Sheets* to help the *Pricer*. Sometimes checkers write *OK Sheets* by hand. *OK Sheets* are your guide to the *Price List*. Checkers always include the item numbers and names.

Price from the Price List — After a while you'll know most of the items and most of the prices. Still check the *Price List* for prices. *Price Change Sheets* let you know new prices for old items. *News Sheets* also let you know about price changes. Still check the *Price List* for prices. You'll get the prices right when you check the *Price List*. Take the extra care to get the prices right.

Look at the Price List for prices of new items — Buyers set prices of new items when they order them. Their prices go on the *Price List* before the items arrive at the store.

Match items to the right labels — Label most items with standard labels in the pricing gun. The *Price List* tells you when to use other labels. The other labels you use are mainly string tags. It's impossible to put labels on some small items. Let customers know the price of these by *Highlight Signs*.

Check the darkness of the print on the price labels — Check the first label to be sure the print is dark enough. Change the inking head if necessary. Then run the rest of the labels for the item.

Put price labels on carefully — Some stores slap price labels anywhere on items. It looks as if they've got zombies working for them. Make sure it's easy for customers to see price labels. Make sure customers can still read anything printed on boxes. Take care to keep the labels off pictures printed on boxes. Make sure prices are the right way up on boxes. Let customers see prices as they read printing or look at pictures on boxes. Some miss seeing the price when it's upside down or at an odd angle. Some pick the item up to read the price and put it down with the price showing correctly—that messes up the display. Take extra care when you put the first labels on each new item. Then you'll soon get the hang of where the label goes. After a while you'll come to think of it as the right place for the label.

Change OK Sheets into Stock Sheets — Keep *OK Sheets* in *Daily* as long as there are still items to price. Once all items have prices, cross out "OK Sheet" and write "Stock Sheet."

Deal with Stock Sheets — The next step is to stock the store. Use *Stock Sheets* to do this now or put them in *Daily* so another seller can stock the store.

Stock Items

Keep up the stock of items in the store. Sales go up when the store is fully stocked with items. Think of the store as a bucket with a hole for the sales to run out. Keep the bucket full of water and the high pressure pushes many sales. Let the water fall low and the low pressure pushes few sales. Like a bucket, take care you don't overfill a store. That way you get a mess, not extra sales.

Stock items from Stock Sheets — A *Stock Sheet* in *Daily* shows there are items ready for stocking. Initial items on the *Stock Sheet* as you stock them.

Stock in order of need — Stock displays that have fallen low first.

Work from the Price List to stock items — The *Price List* lists display and storage places for each item. It also lists high and low numbers for items on display and in storage. Bring displays up to their high numbers when you have enough stock. Change high and low numbers for display and storage if they seem wrong. Leave high storage numbers as they are for short-term overstocks. Sometimes you end up with more of an item than you want. Sometimes the extras store well in the storage place. Avoid crowding the storage place—open a new storage place instead. Write the new storage place on the *Price List*.

Put unfinished Stock Sheets back in Daily — Another seller will pick them up and finish them.

Put finished Stock Sheets in the Old Orders binder — That way you've got old *Stock Sheets* on file. You can look up the *Stock Sheets* if problems about orders come up.

Set Up New Items

Set displays and store extras for new items. Some items you stock will be new to the store. Set them up in the *Price List*. Set their display and storage places and their display and storage numbers.

Set displays — Put new items on display as soon as you can. You want to see how well they sell. Call on your creative skills to set up displays. Get help from other sellers until you feel sure of yourself. Learn from them rather than leaning on them. Give new displays a try if you're working by yourself. Then send a *News Sheet* or *Message* asking others to look them over. All displays of new items go through changes. Someone sets them up. Others bring up ideas and make changes to the displays. Gradually, you get it right together.

- Should this item go in the best selling space? Hold the best space for proven sellers. Put it in the best space if you think the new item is going to be a hot seller. Then watch what happens and move it out if need be.

- Should this item be with like items or somewhere it stands out?

- Can you display this item without doing other displays over? Sometimes you need to change other displays to put a new one in. Change the display entry on the *Price List* when you change a display.

- Is this a large item that can sell from a high shelf?

- Does it need a *Highlight Sign*? Make a *Highlight Sign* if the display needs one.

- Is display space tight, or is there lots of it?

- Do you need to buy any props to help the display?

- Do you need baskets or other containers?

Write the display entry for the new item in the *Price List*.

Set storage — Put new items in the storage cupboards neatly. Make sure you can get at them easily. Make sure you can see them when you open the cupboard. Respect another item's space. There may be space in storage only because another item has fallen low. Put the new item in it's place and you'll play musical chairs when the other item comes back in stock. Do that if you have to, but there's less work if you use free space. Try to keep all items of the same kind all on the same shelf. Sometimes you have to store an item in more than one storage place. That makes it easier to overlook items you have in stock. Write the storage entry for the new item on the *Price List*.

Add to window displays — Sometimes the new item will make a good window display. Change window displays only when the *Receiving Area* is empty.

Stocking the store comes first. Leave a *News Sheet* when you run out of time to do the window display. Then someone else can follow up on your idea.

Set Up Window Displays

Fall back on professional window designers only when you have to. Bring them in when feedback says your windows look bad and you're out of ideas. Bring them in them when the mall manager tells you your window is below standard. Some window designers will do a good job. You'll wonder why you paid others. Some put arty ideas ahead of selling items. First try a one-shot deal when you use a professional. Let the design jump-start your own creative ideas.

Some retailers believe items without prices draw customers into the store. Some customers come in to ask prices and sellers sell to them. This risks putting the focus on selling before trust develops. It's also a bounce from the items. Some customers come in hoping that in the store items have prices on them. Some customers don't come in. They think if they ask the price a seller will push them to buy.

Some retailers believe items with prices draw customers into the store. Customers know the price range before they enter the store. They're more likely to buy when they enter. Customers know prices without having to ask about them. There's less pressure, so they're more likely to enter the store. Customers can work on selling themselves high-priced items. They see items they like but can't afford. The prices and items run in their heads. Each time they pass the window the prices seem more reasonable. After a while they enter the store and buy.

Only tests can find out what works for your store. Set up the same window with and without prices in similar selling periods. Then track sales of items in the window and sales in the store. Find out whether showing prices or hiding prices sells more in your store.

Set up your own window displays — Develop your own ideas for window displays. Call on other sellers to bounce their ideas against yours. Find out which items the store needs to push. Find out which items will draw customers into the store. Listen to advisers and critics. Customers, other retailers and friends will tell you how your windows look. They'll give you ideas for making them look better. Seek this help. Few will offer it without you asking.

Clean the insides of the windows — Clean the insides of the windows when you set up window displays. Then clean insides of the windows as needed.

Dust the window displays — It's easy to forget to dust the window displays. It's easy to set up the windows and forget them. That's a mistake. The window is the first part of the store customers see. Many decide whether to enter the store by what they see in the window. Dust window displays as you dust all other displays.

Post price notices — Post price notices to show prices in the window. The normal price labels you use on items are too small for window-shoppers to see them. Price labels on items in windows make the window look tacky. There are too many of them on view. Put price labels on window items so they're out of sight. Then you can sell something from the window easily. Let everyone know the price when you run a special. Otherwise, it's not a special.

Show only items you have for sale — Make sure you have it for sale in the store if it's in the window. Sell it from the window if the last item is in the window. Then fix the window display with a different item.

Review window displays monthly — Keep up the interest in your store. Make new window displays regularly. Review how the window looks monthly. Try to put in a new display. In a pinch, freshen the window by changing some of the items.

End Shifts

The end of a shift can be a time of stress, particularly for sellers who want to be elsewhere quickly. Cut down this stress by having things in order and ready to go.

Follow the list of paperwork in Daily — *Daily* lists all paper work to remind you of the details.

Prepare reports — Sellers prepare *Seller's Reports* and pass them to sellers in charge of cash drawers. Sellers in charge of cash drawers prepare *Cash Drawer Reports* and pass them to sellers in charge of shifts. Sellers in charge of shifts prepare *Shift Reports* and pass them to sellers in charge of days. Sellers in charge of days prepare *Day Reports* and pass them to the manager.

Make bank deposits as needed — Sellers in charge of cash drawers, shifts, or days make bank deposits.

Finish Seller's Sales Summary Sheets

Finish the summaries

Each day:

- Finish the *Seller's Daily Sales Summary*.

- Make an entry in the *All Sellers' Daily Sales Summary*.

At the end of the seller's last shift in each selling week:

- Make an entry in the *Seller's Weekly Sales Summary*.

At the end of the seller's last shift in each calendar month:

- Make an entry in the *Seller's Monthly Sales Summary*.

At the end of the seller's last shift in each calendar year:

- Make an entry in the *Seller's Yearly Sales Summary*.

Store the summaries — Store the *All Sellers' Daily Sales Summary* in *Daily*. Store all other sales summaries in the *Sales Summaries* binder.

Make Bank Deposits

A typical cash drawer has a tray that lifts out. Sellers who use the cash drawer after each other set up their own cash trays. One seller removes a cash tray and the next seller slips another cash tray into the cash drawer. Still use the idea of separate "trays" when sellers use a cash drawer without trays that lift out or when they use a cash drawer with a single tray. In these cases someone's "tray" is just a bunch of money. Protect the cash in the tray. Suppose the amount in a cash tray is $1,000. The *Tray Total* is $1,000. That's too much money to lose to a thief, so put $700 in the safe and keep $300 in the cash drawer. Put the $700 in an envelope labeled with your name, the date and the time. The *Tray Total* is still $1,000. The $300 in the tray is the *Active Amount* and the $700 in the safe is the *Safe Amount*.

Active Amount + Safe Amount = Tray Total.

Keep the Active Amount under control — *Daily* lists the highest *Active Amount* to keep in the cash drawer

Keep the Safe Amount under control — Bank often. A safe with a lot of cash in it tempts thieves. *Daily* lists the highest *Safe Amount* to keep in the safe. Go over the *Safe Amount* when there too few sellers in the store to go to the bank. Make a deposit as soon as you can.

Avoid small bank deposits — It costs too much for the bookkeeper to keep track of small bank deposits. *Daily* lists the lowest amount to bank. Add small amounts of cash to the next *Opening Change* or enclose them in *Cash Reports*.

Follow safety rules when banking — Write the serial number of a marker bill on the bank deposit form. Leave a copy of the bank deposit form in the store. The number on this copy may help put someone who robs the store in jail.

Make it hard for robbers to work out your pattern. Go to the bank at different times of day if you can. Take different routes to the bank each day. Send different sellers to make the deposits each day.

Carry bank deposit envelopes in an ordinary bag instead of in your hand. Carry money bags inside an ordinary bag. Carry money in the trunk of the car when you drive to the bank. Have someone go with you when you bank at night.

Tidy the Store at Closing

Always tidy the store before leaving. A tidy store comforts window-shoppers and sets the tone for sellers who open the next day.

Tidy and clean the customer area — Remove everything from the customer counter. Wipe it with a cloth damp with *Endust*. Leave the customer counter empty overnight. Let it look crisp to customers who peer into the store at night. Clean up around the cash register. Wipe its counter with a cloth damp with *Endust*. Wipe all surfaces of the cash register.

Check the window displays — It's important for window displays to look good overnight. Give window-shoppers a good impression of the store.

Check the in-store displays as seen by window-shoppers — Make sure the in-store displays look good overnight. Window-shoppers see more than what's in the window. They peer into the store. Be a window-shopper yourself. Know which in-store displays window-shoppers can see.

Check the floor — Make sure the floor is clean. Window-shoppers see it through the window.

Do the Change-over Jobs

A *Change-over Job* is a job done when a seller in charge of a shift or cash register passes control to a new seller. Look in *Daily* for the list of *Change-over Jobs*

Do the Incoming Seller's Jobs — The *Outgoing Seller* stays in control while the *Incoming Seller* does the *Incoming Seller's Change-over Jobs*.

Do the Outgoing Seller's Jobs — The *Incoming Seller* takes control as soon as the new cash tray goes into the cash drawer. This frees the *Outgoing Seller* to do the *Outgoing Seller's Change-over Jobs*.

Manager

A number of jobs done by or controlled by the manager arise from the daily sales activity in the store. They are best done every day to prevent them getting out of hand.

Keep on Top of Paperwork Daily

Process papers daily or they'll bury you. Deal with today's papers no later than tomorrow. See that sellers deal with today's papers today. That may leave you time to deal with your part of the paperwork today too. It usually works better to deal with the papers from the sellers the next day. Keep to the rule of clearing your part of the paperwork by the next day.

Do a little paperwork each day. Then look back in surprise at how much you've done with so little effort. That way you reap the reward of up-to-the-minute facts about your store. The other choice is to let paperwork slide for a while. Then look back in alarm at how much piled up. The pile of papers will swamp you. You'll be deep in a mess that's hard to get out of. You won't have any up-to-the-minute facts about your store. That's a good way to undercut your business.

Work down from the top of the pyramid — At the bottom all sellers make a *Seller's Report*. They pass their reports to the seller in charge of the cash drawer they used. Sellers in charge of cash drawers use these reports to make a *Cash Drawer Report*.

Sellers in charge of cash drawers pass their *Cash Drawer Reports* to the seller in charge of the shift. The seller in charge of the shift uses these reports to make a *Shift Report*.

Sellers in charge of shifts pass their *Shift Reports* to the seller in charge of closing the day. The seller in charge of closing the day uses these reports to make a *Day Report*.

The seller in charge of closing the day passes the *Day Report* to the manager.

Some stores need fewer levels of reports. Sometimes there's only one seller to a cash drawer. Then the *Seller's Report* becomes the *Cash Drawer Report*. Sometimes there's only one cash drawer for a shift. Then the *Cash Drawer Report* becomes the *Shift Report*. Sometimes there's only one shift in a day. Then the *Shift Report* becomes the *Day Report*.

Work with the *Day Report*. Dive into the lower reports to sort out any problems that turn up. Your skill in training your sellers decides how much diving you do. Train new sellers to do their reports without mistakes. Aim to do no diving but do some cross-checking. Let sellers lean on you and you're dead. Let sellers know you expect correct reports done in the time you allow for them. Let sellers go who can't or won't do the reports without a fuss. There's not time for you to run a store and do the sellers' routine paperwork for them.

Work through the Day Report item by item — Keep your pulse on the store day by day.

Day Cash Report: Keep a small *Sales Notebook* on you and enter daily sales totals. Total sales for the week, the month and the year-to-date. Look through your *Sales Notebook* more than once each day. Have a clear idea of your sales before you get reports from your bookkeeper. File each day's *Day Cash Report* in your *To Bookkeeper* file.

Full Sales Slip Books or Copies of Cash Register Tapes: File these in case you need them to solve problems. Keep them on file in case an auditor needs to see them.

Cash Register Report Tapes: Study these tapes for what they show about your store.

Full Cash Register Audit Tapes: File these in case an auditor needs to see them.

Customer Flow Summaries: Check where your customers come from. Does it look as if your ads are paying off? Check that your sellers are asking customers, "How did you hear about our store?" Get on top of sellers who aren't asking enough customers. Pass to the seller whose *Special Job* is to prepare the *Storewide Weekly*, *Monthly* and *Yearly Customer Flow Summaries*.

Day Item Sheet: Get the feel of the items that sell rather than just the dollar value of sales. Know your good sellers and your problem items. Check that your *Markdowns* are moving. Pass to the seller whose *Special Job* is helping you to place orders.

Sellers' Sales Summaries: Study the *All Sellers' Daily Sales Summary* each day to keep up with sellers' sales patterns and problems. File in the *All Sellers' Daily Sales Summary* binder. Study the *Sellers' Weekly*, *Monthly* and *Yearly Sales Summaries* on the days they become available. Plan how you'll use them in your next feedback session with each seller. File them in the *Seller's Sales Summary* binders after the feedback sessions.

The Wheel: Check that sellers are using *The Wheel*.

Keep on Top of Bookkeeping

You need to see your store's financial statements for last month by the middle of the next month at the latest. That means you have to be on top of the records the bookkeeper needs right away at the end of the month. It works best if your bookkeeper posts to your books at least every two weeks and you also have informal reports on your store's finances.

Stop doing your own bookkeeping as soon as you can — Get a bookkeeper as soon as you can afford one. The only time to do your own bookkeeping is when you can't afford to pay a bookkeeper. Money spent on a bookkeeper is money well spent. The time you spend bookkeeping is better spent increasing your store's profits.

Steer clear of manual bookkeeping — The days of manual bookkeeping are over. A manual set of books puts your business at risk. People who keep books by hand usually have only one copy of their books. It's possible to make photocopies monthly, but it's an extra expense and fuss and people rarely get around to it. Manual bookkeepers often use large ledgers which are hard to copy. Should you lose the only copy of your books, you'll have a real problem redoing them. You'll be in an awful fix if it happens close to tax filing time.

Manual bookkeepers often meet with you once a month to return last month's vouchers and pick up this month's vouchers. Often you see your books only once a month at this meeting.

Manual bookkeepers rarely prepare financial statements and other summary reports monthly. They usually prepare them only for special occasions like tax filing. It takes too much time and costs too much to do otherwise.

Manual bookkeepers often cut corners to keep down their costs. They may operate the accounts payable on a cash basis instead of as an accrual. This works fine until a business has cash problems. Then you'll wish you had a bookkeeping system that gave you more help.

There must be cases where it's not so, but manual bookkeepers are often behind with the books. Some run months behind.

You need your books to steer your business day by day. With manual bookkeeping there's too much chance of your books becoming history books. Some months after your business fails you'll finally have a record of why it happened.

Replace your manual bookkeeper — Make a change rapidly if you have a manual bookkeeper. Follow a plan for letting the bookkeeper go if you employ a full-time or part-time manual bookkeeper. There's little point in thinking about raising your manual bookkeeper's skills. You definitely don't want a bookkeeper who doesn't keep up with the modern world.

Most small retailers use a bookkeeping consultant who bills for services. That makes it easy to change bookkeepers.

First find a bookkeeper who uses a computer and who can provide the service you need. Work out an agreement spelling out what each of you will do. Also spell out the last services you need from your manual bookkeeper. Agree with the new bookkeeper on a starting date for the new services. This will force you to let your manual bookkeeper go. You'll have created a situation where you'll have to act. Look your manual bookkeeper in the eye and break the news. "I've accepted the advice of a consultant to be more business-like in my bookkeeping. I've decided to have my books done by a bookkeeper who uses a computer, beginning on the first of August. I'd like you to end your services by bringing the general ledger up-to-date as of July 31st." Write a script on paper if you're uncomfortable with speeches like this. Then learn it like a part in a play. Practice it on yourself in the mirror at least eight times.

Choose a bookkeeper who'll guarantee fast turnaround — A good arrangement is a bookkeeper who'll do the work in your place. Either you have a computer or the bookkeeper brings a portable computer. You can always get at your books, vouchers and checkbook ledger when a bookkeeper works at your place. You can solve problems right away. You have your updated books right away. The down side is that you may not have room for a bookkeeper to work in your place. Bookkeepers may also work better in their own work place.

Set times for pick up and return with an off-site bookkeeper. For pick up, the key element is the earliest date you can rely on having a copy of your bank statement. Make sure return of your books is only a few days after pick up.

Stick to your agreed times and expect your bookkeeper to do the same. Act as soon as your bookkeeper misses a deadline. First talk about your concern. Review your understanding of the deadline. Revise it when it's reasonable and still meets your needs. Otherwise, get a commitment for improvement. First find a new bookkeeper and then replace your bookkeeper if the problem goes on.

Choose a bookkeeper who'll meet your needs — Be sure you can get in touch with your bookkeeper. Your bookkeeper is a person you need to contact for advice. Many work alone and aren't there when you call. A bookkeeper with a pager or a cellular phone is a plus. Otherwise, check for an answering machine or service and a commitment to make call-backs two or three times a day. Ask what schedule the bookkeeper keeps for making call-backs.

You may need a bookkeeper whose lifestyle matches yours. You may like to do business evenings and weekends. A bookkeeper you can't phone at those times won't be much use to you. Ask about calling hours.

For an answering machine or answering service, 24-hour, seven day service is a plus. Then you can leave a message at 3 am if it suits you, knowing you'll get an answer the next day. An answering machine that takes long messages is better than one that only takes short messages. Then you can state your problem rather than waiting for a call-back to state your problem.

Be sure the bookkeeping program operates in real-time. In a real-time program any change in any account ripples through the books. The change leads to instant updating of all financial statements and reports. The contrast is a batch mode program. The bookkeeper sends changes in groups. The program only updates financial statements and reports in response to specific requests.

Your bookkeeper will probably do your routine bookkeeping at a regular time each month. The real-time system will serve you well for special inquiries and emergencies. You'll particularly value a real-time program if you have a copy of the program on a computer you use. Then you'll work by having a bookkeeper do the bookkeeping, but look at the data yourself.

Be sure the bookkeeping software keeps perpetual books. Some bookkeeping programs close the books month by month and year by year. That makes it hard to put missing entries in the correct place. The ideal is to complete June's bookkeeping at the end of June. The real world is less perfect. Being able to carry on when things aren't as they should be is useful.

You're stuck if you have missing data when you have to close the books to make reports. You have to delay closing. Delayed reports add up to loss of control of your business. With perpetual books the problem doesn't arise. You can produce preliminary reports. Perpetual books make it easy to use estimated values and correct them later. Perpetual books allow easy analysis of bookkeeping data from prior years. Perpetual books generate traditional bookkeeping reports for specified time ranges.

Here's what you need from your bookkeeper each month:

Reconciliation of Bank Statement: You need the reconciliation stapled to your bank statement. The reconciliation should also list open items.

Financial Statements (Balance Sheet and Income Statement): Steer clear of any bookkeeper who acts as if producing financial statements monthly isn't routine. Without these statements monthly you don't know how well you're doing. A bookkeeper who can't produce them routinely is using the wrong computer software.

Have your bookkeeper include estimates for periodic expenses in your monthly financial statements. You might use your personal vehicle in your business, but only work out true costs once a year. You probably only take a physical inventory once or twice a year. You risk thinking things are rosier than they are if you don't include estimates for each month.

Other Summary Reports: You'll need to see an Accounts Payable report each month. It's useful to know not only how much you owe, but who you owe it to.

You may have set up other specialized reports that give more detail than the normal financial statements. One example would be a report on payments you make to the shopping mall. Only set up special reports when the details in the financial statements aren't enough. You may have particular accounts you need to have printed each month.

Backup Computer Diskettes: You need two backups of your bookkeeping data each month. Find another bookkeeper if yours doesn't want to give you backup diskettes. The bookkeeping data are yours. The bookkeeper merely works with them. You need these backups even if you don't have a computer. Keep one backup in your store and another away from your store. You'll have one copy left if there's a fire, earthquake or theft at either place. You'll still have a copy if one of the diskettes turns out to be bad. Probably each backup will need only one diskette, but it may need more than one. Simply store these backups. You may never need to use them. By some twist of nature, if you don't keep any backups, there will come a time when you need them.

Your bookkeeper will also keep copies of your data. That doesn't end your need to care for your own data. You'll be in a fix if someone steals your bookkeeper's computer and disks and there are no off-site backups. You'll be in a fix if your bookkeeper's hard drive crashes and there are no backups. Computer people know they should keep on-site and off-site backups, but they rarely do so without fail. They say they do, but there are too many stories of people who didn't and lived to regret it.

You may need someone other than your bookkeeper to work on your data with some other computer program. You may have a falling out with your bookkeeper. Know the name of the computer program your bookkeeper uses. Someone who knows bookkeeping programs can find out from the disk, but it's easier if you know the program.

Ask your bookkeeper to test your backup diskettes if you want to be sure of them. Your bookkeeper can restore from your diskettes to a test directory to check that the backups work.

Set up the accounts you need — Your accountant is your main source of advice on the accounts you need. Your accountant is different from your bookkeeper. Accountants have higher skills and cost more. They save their time for accounting.

Your accountant will prepare your tax returns and give you advice on financial management of your store. Be sure to send your accountant copies of your monthly bookkeeping reports. Many retailers make the mistake of being in contact with their accountants only at tax time.

Some accounts you need will relate to your accountant's knowledge of sound business practice. Others will relate to tax needs.

Your bookkeeper can be of some help in setting up accounts. Check your bookkeeper's advice with your accountant. Some accounts will serve your particular business needs. Separate accounts for Checks In-town and Checks Out-of-town will give you better information than a single account named Checks. You'll get a measure of how much business you'd lose by not taking out-of-town checks. Separate accounts for Phone and Copies will warn you of possible abuse. Put them in with other items in a general account Office and things won't be so clear. A Copies account will also alert you to the time when you may be better off buying or renting a copy machine.

Give your bookkeeper the raw bookkeeping papers — Draw up a list of the papers your bookkeeper needs. Here's a beginning:

Copy of checkbook ledger: You need to use your checkbook ledger while your bookkeeper works on the books.

Copy of the Month Item Sheet: You need to use your copy of this sheet while your bookkeeper works on the books.

Day Cash Reports or Monthly Cash Summary: The simplest way is to let your bookkeeper work with the *Day Cash Reports*. That way you'll have a line entry for each day's sales in your books. Another way is to make a monthly spreadsheet from the *Day Cash Reports*. The bookkeeper then makes a single entry for the month's sales, using the spreadsheet as a voucher. Before you go this way, make sure it makes sound business sense. You'll need to train sellers to use spreadsheets and enter data. You may end up paying more than the bookkeeper would cost. This way assumes that you have a computer and the right software. Always keep a sense of how much you're paying for each line entry of bookkeeping. Divide your monthly bookkeeping bill by the number of line entries the bookkeeper makes. The cost per line will astonish you.

Vouchers: Your bookkeeper will need vouchers for everything bought from petty cash. Keep these vouchers in a special file. Bookkeeping will be easier and cheaper if you group the vouchers before passing them to the bookkeeper. Group vouchers by accounts and staple them together with an adding machine tape. Then write store name, account, date and person on the tape:

```
12.95 +
15.89 +
28.84 T
```
Your store
Office Expenses
May 1994
Joan Smith.

Group vouchers several times each month if you have a lot of them. Suppose you printed the above tape on May 16th. Staple more vouchers and another tape on top of it later. A later tape might read:

```
0.
28.84  +
12.95  +
10.36  +
52.15  T
Your store
Office Expenses
May 1994
Roger Jones.
```

The 28.84 value is the total of the first group of vouchers.

Now group the vouchers for all accounts

```
Your store
Petty Cash
May 1994
Roger Jones
Office Expenses       52.15
Copies, Store         12.95
Supplies, Store       27.00
                      92.10
```

Stack Amounts: See the stacks of card charge charges are up-to-date and make copies of the *Stack Slips*.

Keep these materials in the *To Bookkeeper* file. A special file folder in your filing cabinet makes it easy to keep materials for the bookkeeper together. Put these materials in a special briefcase for the bookkeeper to take away. Tell the bookkeeper to keep these materials in this briefcase when not working on them. That'll help stop your records from getting lost.

Find Items to Sell

Always be on the lookout for new items and for new sources of the items you already carry. Much of this work you'll do outside the store, but lay plans during background time when you're in the store.

Search out suppliers — It's your job to find suppliers. Some suppliers will send their reps to your store. You'll have less than the store you could have if that's all you deal with. Even if you're swamped by suppliers' reps, that's only a small part of the possible suppliers. Retailers who go after suppliers soon realize that suppliers do a patchy job of finding retailers. Wait for the suppliers to find you and you put your business in other people's hands. Pretty soon it's not your store and it goes at other people's speed. It might be successful and it might satisfy you but you'll have less profit and personal satisfaction than you could have. Sometimes it can feel as if the source of supplies is a secret known only to a chosen few. Once you make a few contacts you begin to see how easy it is. One thing leads to another and your list grows.

Get your list of suppliers growing — Here are some things you can do:

Go shopping: Most items on retail shelves have labels with the name of the manufacturer, the supplier, or the country of origin. Some even have addresses and phone numbers. Sellers in other stores will usually tell you who makes an item or the country of origin. Visit all the stores you're up against. Visit all stores like yours when you travel.

Ask other retailers: Introduce yourself and your store. Then say, "I really like the line in wool sweaters that you carry. Could you tell me who supplies them?" Some retailers will tell you. You'll have made a business friend. Later, you'll help that friend. Many retailers will brush you off and some will be hostile. At least you tried. Keep your mind fixed on those who help rather than those who refuse.

Go to trade shows: You'll make more contacts with stationery suppliers at a stationery trade show than anywhere else. To find out about trade shows: Ask the suppliers you already have which shows they show at. Write to the Chamber of Commerce in big cities. Read trade journals. Ask your reference librarian to help you locate them. Read these publications:

> *Tradeshows and Exhibits Schedule* and its supplements.[29]
>
> *Shows and Exhibitions* and its *News and Show Updates* issues.[30]
>
> *Trade Shows Worldwide.*[31]
>
> *Exhibitions 'Round the World.*[32]

---

[29]Successful Meeting DataBank, 633 Third Avenue, New York NY 10017 (212) 973-4890.
[30]Shows and Exhibitions Circulation Department, P.O. Box 9100, Station A, Toronto ON M5W 1V7 (416) 496-6035 Fax 593-3310 (Maclean Hunter Canadian Publishing.)
[31]Gale Research Inc., 835 Penobscot Building, Detroit MI 48226-4094.
[32]Trade Winds, Taiwan.

International Trade Fairs.[33]

Ask suppliers about other suppliers: Ask suppliers, "Who are your main competitors and why should I deal with you instead of them?" Ask this question of suppliers you already deal with. Always ask it when you make a new contact with a supplier. Make sure you ask it of all suppliers' reps who visit you. You'll learn about other suppliers and you'll learn which suppliers feel sure of themselves. Suppliers who answer directly and honestly are suppliers you want to deal with.

Look in the Yellow Pages: The *Yellow Pages* often list wholesalers and manufacturers separately from retailers in listings like *Stationery-Whol & Mfrs*. It's easiest to start close to home but you may get better suppliers out of town. Check the out-of-town *Yellow Pages* at your library. Sometimes the *Yellow Pages* have no separate listing for wholesalers and manufacturers. Perhaps the heading just says *Pianos*. These headings often have lists of dealers by manufacturers' names. Call the retailers for the manufacturers' addresses or get them from your library. Sometimes the *Yellow Pages* list only retailers. Call retailers and tell them you're looking for wholesalers. Can they help? You'll get a lot of dead ends but some will give you leads.

Visit or phone your local library: The business and the reference sections of you library will give you a lot of help. Try several different librarians. They differ in their knowledge and in their willingness to help. Tell them your problem and see what leads they give you. "Can you help me find trade journals for a knitting shop?" "Can you help me find suppliers of hard rock candy?"

Many libraries will answer specific questions by phone. "Can you tell me the address of a company named Grahl. It's an office furniture manufacturer?" Once you have a manufacturer's address you can write or phone for the address of the local suppliers.

Write or phone embassies and consulates: Foreign governments will give you leads to follow up. "Can you please let me know the addresses of firms exporting violins from Poland?" The firms who export them will let you know who imports their products. The importers will either supply you or let you know names of suppliers.

Balance your suppliers — Know about many more suppliers than you use. Plan how you'll change if you need to. Suppliers do go out of business. Relationships with suppliers do go sour. You can find better deals and better service.

---

[33]Kuwait Chamber of Commerce and Industry, P.O. Box 775, SAFAT, 13008, Kuwait.

Consider more than price. Price is important, but not without service and reliability. Do you get the items you order on time? Do you get equal service on small orders and large orders? Does your supplier make you feel important or are you just another account? It's rarely a good plan to change a supplier on price alone. Look for a good track record to go with the good price.

There's an advantage in having a few main suppliers. You have less paperwork and bookkeeping. Your account with each supplier is larger and gets more attention. On the down side, you can get stuck in a rut. Gradually, your store gets drab and loses its life. Suppliers begin to take your account for granted. Do the work you need to keep your store alive. Have a good string of small suppliers. Be alert for suppliers who have items you can't get elsewhere. Some of your small suppliers will always be small suppliers. Others may grow as you get to know them and learn you can rely on them. Keep a special eye on those who might grow and replace the suppliers you have. Having credit with the new supplier already in place will help you when you change.

Develop your relationships with your suppliers — Each year give thought to what's new between you and your suppliers. This year should be richer than last. Do you get special deals? Do you get options on end of lines and close-outs? Do you get items that are in short supply when others don't? Do suppliers act on what you tell them? Do suppliers change their ways when they're below standard? Do you have trusting, human relationships with your suppliers?

Set and Test Prices

Test prices all the time and have the courage to change prices. To locate items that sell at good prices in your store all the time you'll have to try many items that don't work out. Cut your losses quickly and move on to profitable items.

Charge good prices — Charge prices that give the profit you need to stay in business. Charge the highest price for each item that sells the number of units needed to give the profit you want. Work out how many units of each item you want to sell. Experience with selling items will give you a feel of what you might expect. There's no shortcut on this. For each item ask yourself if the profit is worth the effort.

Many retailers make the mistake of selling items cheaply. Cheap items have little drawing power. Customers may like a bargain, but they don't like cheap items. Customers often judge quality by price. High price means high quality. Customers will only buy some items at high prices. Low price cosmetics have little appeal. Customers often buy the best or nothing at all. They think it's better to go bare legged than to wear cheap pantyhose. Customers will pay whatever price you ask if they can manage the price and if the item moves them. Meeting the price is an emotional problem in many cases. Customers may shy away from prices they can afford.

Many factors affect the price you can charge. The main one is the value that customers see in the item. Keep this firmly in mind in setting prices. The value that customers see doesn't always relate directly to what you paid for the item. Sometimes customers see more than you'd expect. Other times they see less. You'll come out ahead when you learn to stock items that seem more valuable to customers than they are.

Prices in other stores affect what you can charge. This doesn't mean you have to meet or beat other stores' prices. That can be a good way to put yourself out of business. It's unlikely you can sell many items at $200 when most others sell them for $100, but you might be able to sell them at $110.

Supply and demand affect the price you can charge. You can charge more than usual when you stock unique items customers want. There are still limits. Charge too much for necklaces and customers buy dishwashers instead.

Environment affects the price you can charge. Customers will pay more for items when they shop in a pleasant store.

Ease of shopping affects the price you can charge. It may not matter that your $1.25 item sells for 99 cents somewhere else when customers are already in your mall.

Service affects the price you can charge. You can charge more when you give good service.

These factors act on one another. The value that customers see may relate to the prices they see elsewhere. Poor service can offset a pleasant environment.

Understand markups — The difference between the buying price and the selling price is the markup. It's usual to state the markup as a percentage. Some retailers base the percentage on the price they paid for the item. That's markup on cost. Some retailers base the percentage on the price they sell the item for. That's markup on retail. This table shows how these markups relate to each other:

Cost	Retail	% Markup on cost	% Markup on retail
1.00	1.10	10.00	9.09
1.00	1.20	20.00	16.67
1.00	1.30	30.00	23.08
1.00	1.40	40.00	28.57
1.00	1.50	50.00	33.33
1.00	1.60	60.00	37.50
1.00	1.70	70.00	41.18

| 1.00 | 1.90 | 90.00 | 47.37 |
| 1.00 | 2.00 | 100.00 | 50.00 |

It's easier to use markup on cost to set prices. It's easier to use markup on retail to look at income statements. It's usual to work with income statements by converting all figures to a percentage of sales. That makes the markup come out as a percentage on retail. Understand how percentage markup on cost relates to "times the cost." Some retailers miss that a 200% markup on cost is three times the cost, not two times the cost. Here's how it works:

Cost	Price	% Markup on cost	Times the cost
1.00	2.00	100	2
1.00	3.00	200	3
1.00	4.00	300	4

First work out a base price — Start with this simple formula:

Base Price = Cost + (Cost x Percentage Markup on Cost.)

One part of cost is what the supplier charges for an item. For this formula, cost isn't always what you pay for an item. Suppose a supplier sells an item for $5. Instead of buying 10 at a time you buy a case of 100 at $4.50 each. Cost is $5, not $4.50. Suppose you work out a deal with the supplier. You buy a case of this, a case of that, and two cases of a close-out. You end up paying $4.20 for the $5 item. Cost is still $5.

Resist the urge to "pass the savings on to the customer." You may have no savings to pass on. Or if you do, the savings may be less than you first imagine. You have money tied up in extra inventory. At best it's not earning interest in a bank. At worst you're paying interest to borrow it. You have extra storage costs in space and labor. Stored inventory always loses value as it gets knocked about.

You may make the savings you aimed for if you sell the items quickly. Put that into your profit. You worked extra for it and you took extra risk. It may turn out that you took a bad risk. You may lose money on this deal. You may have been better off paying more for the items ten at a time. You may have been better off placing your orders strictly based on selling rate.

The second part of the cost is what you pay to get the item to your store. Good accounting practice puts shipping costs into your cost of inventory. Shipping costs aren't expenses like the cost of electricity to light your store. Many retailers put them down as expenses for bookkeeping. At tax time their accountants move them to Cost of Goods Sold. Calling shipping costs expenses warps the picture of your store's financial position.

Many retailers ignore the cost of shipping when working out prices. That's a mistake. Suppliers make it hard for you to know shipping costs, since they rarely include them on the *Invoice*. Usually, they show up later on the monthly statement. It's even rarer for suppliers to include the cost of shipping in the cost of items. The same item may have different shipping costs depending on the size of the shipment it comes in. Work out an average shipping cost as a percentage based on cost of the items for a large number of samples. Include that in every item you price.

A third part of cost is the difference between what you paid and the replacement cost. Suppose you paid $10 each for items you have in stock and your supplier now wants $12 each to replace them. Add the extra $2 to your cost. Some retailers think basing price on replacement cost is cheating customers. They think it's fair to set prices on what they paid. Replacement cost is a two-edged sword. Suppose the supplier now charges only $8 for items sold to you at $10. Suppose the store next door buys and prices based on $8. You'll probably have to lower your price. Customers who think it's fair to base price strictly on your cost suddenly stop thinking that way. Customers don't act this way themselves. Find a customer who paid $70,000 for a house that now has a value of $200,000. Try offering $100,000 for it. Houses increase and decrease in value. So does the stock of items you hold. Selling price relates to the value of items.

It's smart to test the selling price based on the replacement cost before you order any items at the replacement cost. Then you can learn if the item has priced itself out of the market without buying new stock.

Percentage markup on cost is simple to use. In some stores all items bear the same percentage markup on cost. In other stores different groups of items bear different markups. Perhaps clothing has 100% markup, while electronic items have a 20% markup. Try to keep to as few markup groups as possible. Keep these groups separate in your bookkeeping or your books will be less useful to you. Using a percentage markup on cost means you have to decide which percentage to use.

There are several ways to choose a markup:

Markup based on historical facts: Suppose you have a selling history for a store. It could be your store or store you're buying. It could be someone else's similar store. It could be a summary from a retail survey of stores similar to yours. Suppose the income statement for last year looks like this:

	Dollars	Percent of sales
Net Sales	600,000	100.00
Cost of Sales	262,680	43.78
Gross Profit	337,320	56.22

| General Expenses | 291,840 | 48.64 |
| Operating Profit | 45,480 | 7.58 |

Interest Expense	4,200	0.70
Depreciation	9,780	1.63
Profit Before Tax	31,500	5.25
Profit After Tax	25,200	4.20

The markup on cost is: (337,320/262,680) x 100 = 128%.

The markup on retail is: (337,320/600,000) x 100 = 56%.

Note that markup on retail is the same as the Gross Profit. That's why retailers use markup on retail in comparing stores. It's already worked out for them.

To set prices use the markup on cost. We see that for $600,000 of sales with 128% markup on cost, there's an after tax profit of $25,200. Does that satisfy you? That's a question only you can answer. It depends on many factors. Do the general expenses include a good manager's salary for you or for a manager? How much do you have invested in the store? Are you getting a good return on the investment? Is this one of ten small stores you own? How close to the limit on price do you really think you are? How much of a risk are you willing to take on raising prices?

You now have a basis for making a plan. Suppose you decide you want to see an extra $20,000 of sales on the same items. The figures now look like this:

	Dollars	**Percent of sales**
Net Sales	620,000	100.00
Cost of Sales	262,680	42.37
Gross Profit	357,320	57.63
General Expenses	291,840	47.07
Operating Profit	65,480	10.56
Interest Expense	4,200	0.68
Depreciation	9,780	1.58
Profit Before Tax	51,500	8.31
Profit After Tax	41,200	6.65

The markup on cost (357,320/262,680 x 100) is now: 136%.

The markup on retail (357,320/620,00 x 100) is now: 58%.

These figures give $41,200 after tax instead of $25,200, an increase of $16,000. The extra $16,000 counts on no increase in expenses. That's unlikely to be true.

Perhaps $12,000 is a more realistic figure. It also counts on selling the same number of units of items. The higher prices may lower the number of units sold, so lower the $12,000 to $10,000.

Bear in mind this markup on cost is an average. To get that average the base markup on cost will have to be higher. Let's go with 145%.

Analysis of Break-even Point: Where you have historical facts, you can crosscheck the break-even cost and markup you need to get it. The break-even cost is where you're spinning wheels. You're neither gaining nor losing money.

Divide the expenses on the income statement by the Cost of Goods Sold. This gives the cost of selling an item that cost $1. $291,840 divided by $262,680 = $1.11. Suppose an item costs $10. It will cost $11.11 to sell it. Add the cost of $10 to the cost of selling to get $21.11. You'll get no profit and no loss if you sell it at $21.11. The percentage markup on cost will be $1.11 divided by $10 times 100, or 110%. Since you're not in business to break even, your markup must be greater than that or you must lower your expenses.

Markup based on tradition: For most items there's a traditional markup on cost. Gift stores usually mark up items 70-100% on cost. For clothing stores it's usually 100% on cost. Florists are higher, 250% or more. Tradition will give you a guide when you have no historical facts to guide you. Tradition will give you something to judge your historical facts against. Here are some ways to find out traditional markups on cost:

Ask suppliers: Suppliers will give you an idea on usual markups. Their figures may be rosy.

Check prices against suppliers' costs: Get prices you'll have to pay from suppliers' catalogs. Ask the suppliers for the names of some stores they supply. Visit the stores and note the prices they charge. Make sure you check the prices of many items. That way you'll get the average markup.

Ask other retailers: Introduce yourself and your store. Ask about the average markup they're able to get. Make sure the other retailer is talking markup on cost. Be crystal clear. Suppose someone says there's a 50% markup on cost. Say, "Let me be sure I've got it straight. Does that mean when you buy for a dollar you sell for a dollar fifty?" Some retailers will brush you off. Others will tell you their markups. As always, help those who help you.

Try all three ways. That way you'll steer round anyone who's confused or is misleading you.

Round prices upwards — Suppose the cost is $4.27 and the markup on cost is 110%. $4.27 + ($4.27 x 110%) gives a base price of $8.97. That's an odd price to sell something. Customers will feel more comfortable with a price that's close to $10. That's the lowest you want to set a test price for this item.

Know the value customers se — Before you settle on the test price, ask some of your sellers how much the item will sell for. Ask them blind. That means they tell you by looking at the item without knowing the cost. The sellers give their ideas on the best price you can sell the item for.

It's important only you and the seller who helps you with orders and pricing know costs in your store. It's not that your costs are something to hide. You want to ask you sellers their ideas on selling prices blind.

Keep track of what sellers say. After a while, you'll find some are better than others at seeing what customers will pay. Keep track of your own ideas too. You might have the feel of it. Your feel might develop as you handle many items. Keep your pride out of this. Go with Mary Jones' ideas if she's closest to what customers will pay.

Suppose your sellers come up with a price that's below the base price you work out. As an example, take the base price that works out to $8.97 and looks like a possible $10 item. Your sellers all come up with a best price of $5. Your test price is still about $10, but watch this item carefully. Let the item decide if your buying it was a mistake. You may have to mark it down, possibly even as low as the $5 they suggest. Do that in stages and hope they're wrong.

Charge more than normal markup — Suppose your normal markup is twice the cost. You buy at $1 and sell for $2. Now and again you may come across an item you can sell well for 4 or 5 times the cost. You buy at $1 and sell for $4 or $5. This is more likely to be a cheap item than an expensive item. Sell it at that markup for as long as you can.

Get out of the habit of thinking it's not fair to charge more than your normal markup. Many items you buy at $1 to sell at $2 sell poorly at $2. You'll get some you may have to sell at 50 cents. Customers will gobble them up without a thought on whether it's fair to you. They'll gladly see you price yourself out of business. Over-markup and under-markup are two ends of a scale. You need over-markup to offset under-markup. It's hard to get over-markup so take it when you can. Customers are free to buy or not buy. They often won't buy and they'll force your prices down.

Start with the high end of price ranges people see — People often answer with a range when you ask how much they'd pay for items. Show one item and they tell you "four or five dollars." Show another item and they tell you "fifty or sixty dollars," and so on. Suppose you were going to charge four dollars and fifty dollars for these items. Charge five dollars and sixty dollars instead.

Compare with stores you're up against — Weigh what others charge for the same items but don't let that panic you into losing your profit. You'll find it hard to make sales if all your items are much higher than the same items in similar stores. Keep your prices high enough to make profits without driving customers away.

Include a premium for the outstanding environment you provide — Keep some prices higher than other similar retailers charge for the same items. Deliberately charge $3.99 for something others sell at $2.99 and see what happens. Take advantage of any items that only you carry. Take advantage of any hot new items you carry. Charge high prices until the novelty wears off.

Set prices at x.99 — By tradition retailers rarely use whole dollar prices. They usually sell $10 items for $9.95 or $9.99. Selling for less than whole dollars dates to the days before sales taxes. There was a danger that some customers would give the seller a $10 bill and walk out without waiting for a receipt. Then the $10 bill could easily find it's way into the seller's pocket rather than the till. Since a nickel or a penny had some value, customers would wait for their change. That forced the seller to use the till.

In modern times retailers say that $9.95 or $9.99 looks less than $10. Possibly such prices do look less to some customers but it could as easily be a myth. Whatever the facts, it's a way of pricing that retailers and customers expect so you'll probably use it.

Be sure to use $0.99, $1.99 and so on instead of $0.95, $1.95 and so on. That's an extra 4 cents each item. That's $2,000 extra on the sale of 50,000 items. On an item you buy for $10 and sell at $19.99 that's an extra 0.4% return on the money you invested. The return is better on low priced items. That's 8% extra on items you bought at 50 cents and sold at 99 cents.

Sell a test order — A test order is small enough to keep losses small if sales are poor. One item is enough if you sell expensive items in small quantities. One necklace in a new style fits in with the rest of your jewelry display.

Where you sell many units of an item each month, the test order must be large enough to have meaning. You don't know if you have an item that sells when you sell one $10 item. The one customer in five thousand who'd buy that item might have walked by.

Buy enough units to set up a nice display of the item. Buy enough units to keep the display in good shape while you're selling the item. Perhaps an item comes in a carton of 100 with 10 inner packs of 10 items. You hope to sell one or two cartons a month. Your test order is one or two packs of 10.

Keep your emotions in check when you place test orders. You may see an item that excites you. You're sure it will sell well but customers may see it differently. Make the test and find out.

Keep your ego in check when you place test orders. This is no time to boost yourself with a big-shot buyer act.

You may face a supplier who only sells in full cartons. Say that you're prepared to buy in cartons once you know the item sells. Speak to the supplier's rep, the manager and the owner about your needs. A supplier who won't meet your needs won't help your store's long-term welfare. Look hard for another supplier who'll meet your needs. Until you find one, you may have to deal with a supplier who undercuts your store. Guess what question you're going to ask all suppliers' reps who come looking for your business.

Begin selling at the test price and watch sales carefully. Set the test price as the selling price when the item sells at the rate you want.

Lower your test price when sales are at less than the rate you want. The rate you want depends on the role the item will play in your store. Some expensive items that help your decor sell at slower rates than day-to-day items.

Wait no longer than a week when you want to sell several or many units of an item each week. The only time to wait longer is when the week is an unusual one.

Lower the test price so there's a difference customers notice between the new price and the old price. There's little point in lowering $12.99 to $12.49. $11.99 and $10.99 may not work unless they're known price points in your store. You may have to lower to $9.99. That's OK, as long as you're not below your base price. Lower the price week by week until you find the selling price or hit the base price.

Each time you lower the test price, remove the old price labels and *Highlight Signs*. Make new ones that say nothing about the old price. You're exploring test prices here, not setting *Markdowns*.

You may hit base price without making the sales you want. At that point look at your markup carefully. Can you make a good profit at a lower markup? Set the lowest price that will satisfy you as a selling price.

Run a new test when new costs raise prices — Treat an item with a raised price as a new item. Suppose you work out a base price of $10 but you have a selling price $12.99 that works nicely. Now there's a change in costs. The supplier raises prices or the rent goes up. It's probably best to keep selling the item at $12.95 if the base price rises to $12. It's time for a new test if the base price rises to $14. Can you sell this item at $14.99 or higher? Try it while you still have some on hand at the old cost.

Mark losers down — Some items won't sell at prices that make them worth selling. You're stuck with them and have to do something about them. First be glad you only bought a test order. Your problem is smaller than it might have been.

One option is to mark the item down and sell it in your store. A certain number of *Markdowns* can draw customers into your store. They can be a form of advertising for you but too many *Markdowns* can mark your store as a discount store. Some customers may expect *Markdowns* and will only buy *Markdowns*. Strike the right balance if you sell items as *Markdowns*.

Work out some figures before you get into *Markdowns*. Aim to break even on *Markdowns*. You lose money if you sell something at what it cost you. You have to add the selling costs. Look at your income statement adjusted and projected for this year. Suppose it shows $200,000 for Cost of Goods Sold and $130,00 in expenses. It costs you 65 cents to sell $1 of items. To break even on an item you paid $10 for you need to sell it for $16.50. Sell it at $10 and you get back $3.50 of the $10 you paid. Sell it below $6.50 and you're better off destroying the item. You may want to give the items to loyal customers as free bonuses.

You might break this pattern with Monday morning specials. Since you sell almost nothing on normal Monday mornings, ignore the selling cost. That's fine if it works. Chances are you'll find customers come to expect "Monday specials" on other days.

Another option is to sell your *Markdowns* in someone else's store. Choose a store far from yours that serves customers less well-off than yours. It might be a regular store or it might be a consignment store. Get an agreement that the other store will never use your store's name. Choose someone you can trust so you can work with little paperwork. Try to get the other store to pick up from you. The other store sells the item that cost you $10 for $10. The other store gets $5 and yours gets $5. Perhaps you have 50 cents expense. You reduce expense if the other store is in an area you visit regularly for some other reason. You clear $4.50 instead of the $3.50 you clear in your store. You keep your store free of *Markdowns* and you keep up your pricey image.

Markdowns may not be your answer for slow sellers. Some items are slow sellers. Suppose you sell an item for $9.99. You sell two each week and want to sell more. You mark it down to $5.99. You still sell two each week. The item is a slow seller at $9.99. Sell the stock you have at $9.99 and decide if you want to order the item again. It may fill a special place in your store that's hard to fill otherwise and it may add to your decor while it does so.

Control the urge to discount. Avoid *Markdowns* to get greater profit from more sales. Mark items down only because you have to. Some retailers get the urge to discount. They see big businesses making money on razor thin markups and they think they can play the same game. Running a discount store is a different ballgame which takes major money and major management skills. Ordinary retailers who try to discount against the major rival up the road usually fail. They understand how discounting works but they fail to see the volume of sales needed for success. The following tables show the extra sales needed to maintain the same gross profit. They show the effects of 10% and 25% cuts in price at selected percentage markups.

No Sold	Cost	Retail	% Markup on retail	Gross Profit	% Cut	New Price	New Gross Profit	New No Sold	Extra Sales %
1	1.00	1.11	10	0.11	10	1.00	0.00		
1	1.00	1.18	15	0.18	10	1.06	0.06	2.90	190
1	1.00	1.34	25	0.34	10	1.21	0.21	1.65	65
1	1.00	1.43	30	0.43	10	1.29	0.29	1.50	50
1	1.00	1.54	35	0.54	10	1.39	0.39	1.40	40
1	1.00	1.67	40	0.67	10	1.50	0.50	1.33	33
1	1.00	1.82	45	0.82	10	1.64	0.64	1.29	29
1	1.00	2.00	50	1.00	10	1.80	0.80	1.25	25

No Sold	Cost	Retail	% Markup on retail	Gross Profit	% Cut	New Price	New Gross Profit	New No Sold	Extra Sales %
1	1.00	1.11	10	0.11	25	0.83	(0.17)		
1	1.00	1.18	15	0.18	25	0.89	(0.12)		
1	1.00	1.34	25	0.34	25	1.01	0.01	68.00	6,700
1	1.00	1.43	30	0.43	25	1.07	0.07	5.93	493
1	1.00	1.54	35	0.54	25	1.16	0.16	3.48	248
1	1.00	1.67	40	0.67	25	1.25	0.25	2.65	165
1	1.00	1.82	45	0.82	25	1.37	0.37	2.25	125
1	1.00	2.00	50	1.00	25	1.50	0.50	2.00	100

Charge sales taxes separately — It's usually a mistake to include sales taxes in prices. Customers dislike paying sales taxes, but they're used to paying them. They complain about them, but they pay them. There's no other legal way to buy in a store. Customers buy less because of high sales taxes when times are bad. Those are the times you have less profit to pay customers' sales taxes for them.

A positive plan for including sales taxes goes like this. An item sells at 85 cents and there's 10% sales tax to collect. Sell it for $1 including the tax. You get more profit and the government gets its tax. Customers feel they've bought without paying tax.

This works well if you only sell one item and its price stays the same. As prices go up, you'll try to keep to the $1 price. Your profit will shrink. You'll try to sell your other items at round figures including taxes. You'll gain on some but lose on others. As prices go up, the number you lose on goes up.

This plan soon cuts your profits. A smarter way to go is to take the 85 cent item and sell it for $1. Then add the tax when customers buy.

Taxes are between customers and governments. Act only as the government agent the law forces you to be.

Track Sales and Orders of Items

Track sales of items and track the orders you've placed. Aim to have the items your customers want to buy in stock without tying up cash in extra inventory. Avoid extra storage costs. There's a fine balance here which needs attention to detail. Avoid placing orders by the seat of your pants.

Track sales and orders of items so you can place orders — Have enough units of each item on hand to last till your next order arrives. Allow for enough units on hand so your displays look good. The trick is to avoid understocks and overstocks. Understock and sales fall because you're short of items to sell. Overstock and you tie up your money and space. That can suck up your profits like a sponge.

Know how long it takes your suppliers to turn orders around. Are some days of the month or week better than others for turnaround? Turnaround time can vary with time of year. Suppliers slow down under high pressure.

Work out a stock plan for each item. Know the highest and lowest number of units you want on hand at any time. Know the number of units you have on hand. Know the number of units you order at a time: each, dozen, case of 100, and so on.

Stock plans rarely work perfectly. Suppliers goof or let you down and they run out of stock. Sometimes they're swamped and your orders arrive late. Work on these problems. Meanwhile, know that you're better off than retailers who place orders by the seat of their pants.

Think of items in three groups. Group A items are the real money makers. Get on top of them first. Group C items are the low priorities. They're items that round out your store. Perhaps you sell only 10 a year and you order them once or twice a year. Group B items are in between. They make money for you but less than Group A items. Get on top of them as soon as your Group A items are in order.

Track sales and orders of items for bookkeeping — Summaries of the sales and orders for items give you a check against figures your bookkeeper uses. Bookkeepers usually have the cost of orders under control from your Accounts Payable Ledger. They can estimate the value of your inventory if they know your sales and average markup. The values you work out from items give you a cross-check. You have some checking to do when your figures and the bookkeeper's figures are different.

Keep a separate Stock Sheet for each item you carry — Here's an example of a *Stock Sheet*:

133-0056 Animal Dominoes, Large. Shang WT085, Jones K234									
Event	**Catalog**	**Cost**	**@**	**Landed**	**O**	**B/O**	**+**	**-**	**=**
Jones 1994 04 27 1245	4.10	4.26	4.10	4.26	12				
Jones 7151 1994 04 29			4.10	4.26		0	12		12
May 1994 Sales								0	12
Jones 1994 05 07 1503	4.10	4.26	4.10	4.26	24				
Jones 7823 1994 05 13			4.10	4.26		0	24		36
Jun 1994 Sales								11	25
Jul 1994 Sales								7	18
Aug 1994 Sales								10	8
Jones 1994 09 02 1125	4.10	4.26	4.00	4.16	48				
Jones 11186 1994 09 07			4.00	4.16		24	24		
				4.19					32
Jones 11593 1994 09 11			4.00	4.16		0	24		
				4.18					56
Sep 1994 Sales								18	38
Oct 1994 Sales								15	23
Jones 1994 11 04 1035	4.2 0	4.37	4.2	4.37	24				
Jones 12765 1994 11 12			4.2	4.37		0	24		
				4.27					47
Nov 1994 Sales								19	28
Jones 1994 12 02 1435	4.2 0	4.37	4.2	4.37	12				
Jones 13052 1994 12 09			4.2	4.37		0	12		
				4.30					40
Dec 1994 Sales								27	13
Inventory 1994 12 31				4.30					13

The header begins with the store's number and name for the item. Next come short forms of suppliers' names and their catalog numbers. Leave a blank line or two so you can add more suppliers. Keep the *Stock Sheets* in order by the store's numbers. These are the column headings and contents:

Event: There are several different events:
Entries like "Jones 1994 04 27 1245" are *Purchase Orders*. Jones is an abbreviation for the supplier. 1994 04 27 is April 27th 1994. 1245 is the time the order placer began writing the *Purchase Order*. Use the 24-hour clock for time and all *Purchase Orders* get their own numbers without looking up a list.

Entries like "Jones 7151 1994 04 29" are *Invoices*. 7151 is the supplier Jones' invoice number.

Entries like "May 1994 Sales" are the number of items sold in a month.

Entries like "Inventory 1994 12 31" are the results of counting the items in the store.

Make an entry for anything else that changes the number or quantity of the item.

Be sure to enter all orders to remind you that you've placed an order. That will prevent double orders by mistake. Also enter any items you return for credit.

Catalog: This is the supplier's catalog price for a single item.

Cost: This is Catalog multiplied by a percentage estimate for shipping. Cost is the figure you use in your formula for base price.

@: This is the price you paid the supplier for the item.

Landed: This is @ multiplied by a percentage estimate for shipping. It's the price you pay for the item landed in your store ready for selling. Landed is the same as Cost when you buy at the catalog price.

O: This is the number of units ordered on the *Purchase Order*.

B/O: This is the number of items back ordered by the supplier. Perhaps you order 48. The supplier may send 24 and put 24 on back order. With a back order the supplier ships the rest of the items when they come in.

Watch back orders carefully or you'll lose control of your store. You may no longer need them when the items come in. You may have passed the peak of the season or sales may have been less than you expected. Cancel back orders you don't need. You can tell suppliers not to place back orders. That way you risk missing items you want. You have to keep placing orders for the same item and you may let them slide. Your suppliers will get fed up with your repeat orders.

+: This is the number of items you receive. Most entries in this column are from suppliers' *Invoices*. Sometimes extra items turn up when you take inventory. Most result from miscounts of sales.

-: This is the number of items that go out of your store. Most entries in this column are sales. Other entries are returns to suppliers, items you break and items stolen from you. Negative numbers often turn up when you take inventory. They result from miscounts, theft and breakage.

=: This is the total number of items on hand at the time of the last recorded event.

The example *Stock Sheet* tracks average value of the items. Suppose you have 8 items at a landed cost of $4.16 each. Now you buy 48 items at a landed cost of $4.26 each.

$$
\begin{array}{rcrcr}
8 & \times & 4.26 & = & 34.08 \\
48 & \times & 4.16 & = & 199.68 \\
56 & \times & 4.17 & = & 233.76 \\
\end{array}
$$

You have 56 items at a landed cost of \$4.17 each (233.76/56 = 4.17.) Tracking the average value of items is one of several ways of managing inventory. It's the easiest to use and understand. Average your inventory unless your accountant has a reason for you to do it differently.

Stock Sheets are valuable in the day-to-day activity of your store. They let you know where you stand on quantities on hand and on order. Read them against the item's status on the *Month Item Sheet* to be really up-to-date.

Stock Sheets are valuable in cross-checking bookkeeping values. Combine the value of all items sold in a month to get the total value of stock sold. Combine the value of all items on hand to get the total value of stock on hand.

Order Items

Fill in your own *Order Sheets* rather than those from suppliers. Keep them simple. Write them by hand if you like. Include store names and numbers where they differ from suppliers' names and numbers. Include the number needed on the store's line. Include quantity ordered and back ordered, price and extension on the supplier's line. Read from *Order Sheets* for phone orders. Make copies of *Order Sheets* and strike out store lines with a felt marker if you fax or mail orders.

Work on Order Sheets daily — Keep *Order Sheets* going for each supplier.

Check yesterday's *Month Item Sheet* against *Stock Sheets* daily. Add needed items to *Order Sheets*. Strike a balance between many small orders and one gigantic order.

You can save on shipping with large orders, but the saving is little compared to extra storage costs, the cost of extra capital and the cost of being stuck with items you need to mark down. Get the items you need at the times you need them in the quantity you need them. Aim to keep items in stock while tying up as little cash as possible.

Cover shipping costs in your pricing formula. Running a medium to high shipping cost is better than running a high storage cost. Running a medium to high shipping cost is better than tying up cash in stock. Keep your extra cash in a bank account that bears interest.

Watch your ego in making orders. You're the small-shot sensible buyer, not the big-shot, no-nonsense buyer. Turn aside pressure by suppliers' reps to place bigger orders than you need. Discounts they offer may lead you to tie up cash in stock and cause a storage problem. Size your orders on good estimates of sales.

Deal in whole cartons of items when the number of items in a carton fits your buying plan. Whole cartons are easier to handle. There's less breakage in shipping than when suppliers pack different items in a carton. These benefits are too small to change your buying plan to get them.

One item usually forces the decision to place the order now. Most items on *Order Sheets* can wait a while. Firm up and place the order when there's an item you must move on now.

Place orders — Watch costs. Many suppliers have toll-free numbers. Watch costs on those who don't so you know how much you're spending to phone orders. Include phone costs for orders in your landed costs as shipping costs. Fax or mail orders instead when phone bills are too large.

Get feedback. Learn about items out of stock and the status of back orders when you phone orders in. Take the chance to go for good prices.

Develop personal relationships with order takers. Look after your relationships with order takers. Through the order takers you relate to the people who put your orders together. From time to time send token gestures to the suppliers' people. Send flowers or a delivery of cake or donuts. Look after the people who look after you.

Follow up to see what's going on. Find out what's going on when orders are slow in coming. Prod gently. These calls buy less goodwill than calls to place orders.

File orders in the "Receive and Handle Deliveries" section of *Daily*.

Aim for a high turnover — Measure inventory turnover. Here's the Cost of Goods Sold in a period:

	Value of items at start of period	20,000
Plus	Value of items bought during period	200,000
		220,000
Minus	Value of items at end of period	26,000
	Cost of Goods Sold in period	194,000

Here's the average cost of inventory on hand for a period:

	Value of items at start of period	20,000
Plus	Value of items at end of period	26,000
		46,000
	Divide 46,000 by 2	23,000

Here's the inventory turnover:

Cost of Goods Sold in Period/Average Cost of Inventory on Hand.

That's 194,000/23,000 = 8.4.

Track the yearly inventory turnover. Values of inventory turnover for a year smooth out the changes from month to month. They're better than values for shorter periods.

Aim to get your figure for inventory turnover to rise from year to year. Be careful of comparisons to average figures for "stores like yours." Many of the stores in the sample may not be like yours. These comparisons make most sense when you know the other stores.

Plan Payments

Pay on time and build your reputation. Your reputation will stand by you in hard times. Paying bills on time is the sign of a business that's under control. Some retailers abuse credit. They pay late and hope suppliers won't charge interest on what they owe. They soon become suppliers' low priority accounts.

Work out a buying, selling and paying plan — To start you may have to pay suppliers when you place or receive orders. Ask and expect to receive items on credit after paying for one or two orders.

Suppliers usually give credit for 30 days. Large buyers may get a longer term of credit. Ask for a longer term when you've been a good customer for a while. Ask for a longer term any time you place a large or special order.

Aim to sell the items before you pay for them. That's hard to do all the time for all items. Suppliers ship during the month and bill you at the month's end. Each shipment comes with an *Invoice*. *Invoices* list the items in the shipment and note any back ordered items. *Invoices* usually have costs of items on them. Don't pay against *Invoices*. Wait for the statement that comes at the end of the month. The statement lists all *Invoices* for the month and their total costs. It's still not time to pay.

On most suppliers' *Invoices* there's a phrase like "2/10 net 30." Suppose it's the statement for March. You have two choices:

1. Pay by the 10th of April and take 2% from the statement amount. That's the "2/10."

2. Pay the full statement amount by the 30th of April. That's the "net 30."

Pay early and earn the 2% savings when you have cash on hand. Make sure it's worth doing when you have to borrow cash to pay early. Delay the payment till the end of the 30 days when you're short of cash. Here's a summary of the options:

		Pay within		
		10 days	30 days	
Buy by	1st	40 days $200	60 days $0	Credit Period Save on $10,000
Buy by	30th	10 days $200	30 days $0	Credit Period Save on $10,000

Pay on time — Schedule one or two definite bill paying days each month. Pay every statement that's due.

Call your suppliers and let them know what's happening should you hit a slow patch and not be able to pay on time. Let them know how soon you expect to be able to pay. Suggest skipping a payment and paying for the next shipment in advance if you have to. That'll give you time to catch up on the missing payment.

CHAPTER 13

REPORT JOBS AND SALES

Daily reports on the jobs sellers have completed and the sales they have made give the facts to keep managers on top of things in the store. All reports begin with each seller. Then join their reports at higher levels to produce a pyramid of reports with the day's reports at the top.

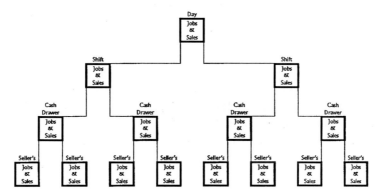

Sellers' Jobs and Sales Reports: Sellers hold up the pyramid. Without sellers there's no store. Everyone sells. Sellers are in charge of their own sales. They also do jobs for the store. They make reports on their sales and their jobs for the manager. The manager uses their reports to keep track of sellers.

Cash Drawer Jobs and Reports: All sellers use a cash drawer. Sometimes more than one seller use the same cash drawer. In that case the manager puts one seller in charge of the cash drawer. Sellers in charge of cash drawers get the cash drawer ready and close it out. They make the reports on sales from the cash drawer. They also group together some of the sellers' reports to make summary cash drawer reports for the manager. Sometimes only one seller uses a cash drawer. In that case the seller's jobs and reports become the cash drawer reports.

Shift Jobs and Reports: Sometimes more than one cash drawer is in use during a shift. In that case the manager puts a seller in charge of the shift. Sellers in charge of shifts make reports on sales for the shift. They also group together some of the cash drawer reports to make summary shift reports for the manager. Sometimes only one cash drawer is in use during a shift. In that case the cash drawer jobs and reports become the shift jobs and reports.

Day Jobs and Reports: Sometimes there's more than one shift in a selling day. In that case the manager puts a seller in each shift in charge of the day. The seller in charge of the day for the first shift starts the day jobs and reports. Then the day jobs and reports pass to the next seller in charge of the day. The seller in charge of the day for the last shift finishes the reports for the manager. Sellers in charge of the day make reports on sales for the day. They also group together some of the shift reports to make summary day reports for the manager. Sometimes there's only one shift in a selling day. In that case the shift jobs and reports become the day jobs and reports.

How the store prepares its reports depends on the equipment it owns to list sales. At one extreme, a store does everything by hand. At the other extreme, a store with an advanced programmable *Point of Sale System* will have a reporting system with a minimum of handwritten reports.

Customer Flow Sheet

Sellers use the facts on the *Customer Flow Sheet* when they do their closing paperwork. At first sellers only use the *Customer Flow Sheet* to make their *Customer Flow Summaries* and their *Sales and Sales Tax Slips*. Later they also use them to work out their *Scores*. Look on the *Scores* as an engine to drive the store. Sellers get rewards for high *Scores*. Low *Scores* force them to work to improve their use of the *Steps for Selling*.

Customer Flow Sheet

Name Mary Brown

Day Mon   **Date** 2   **Month** May   **Year** 1994   **From** 10 am   **To** 4:30 pm

Time	Who?	11	No	TXS	NTS	How?	R	P	I	G	S	A	N
1015	Sam collect rent check	•											
1020	W 25 Ann Jones, Tested Looker	4				Sent by Mary Walker	Y	N	Y	Y	Y	N	N
1025	Mary Brown Alphonso's $5 bills	•											
1030	M in hurry on mission	0	2631	75.95		Walk-by	N	Y	Y	Y	Y	Y	N
1035	M 50 & W 35	11	2635	165.90		Tour bus	Y	Y	Y	Y	Y	Y	N
1050	W 55	3					N	N	N	Y	Y	N	N
1100	M 65 Buy for grandchild	10	2639	36.95		Sent by daughter	N	Y	Y	Y	Y	N	N
1120	W 40 Alicia Jorgensen	7	2641	65.49		Ad in Sun	Y	Y	Y	Y	Y	Y	N
1135	W 28 Edna Jones	7	2644	350.00		Regular customer	R	Y	N	Y	Y	Y	Y
	7		5	693.29			3	5					1

• Visitor, 0 None, 2 Greet, 3 Schmooze, 4 Looking, 5 Move, 6 Find Out, 7 Show-&-tell, 8 Roadblocks, 9 Toe, 10 Ask to Buy, 11 Sidestep, 99 Personal. Register, Praise, Invite, Good-bye, Shape up, After-sale, Note

Managers need to look over the *Customer Flow Sheets*. For sellers not yet using the *Scores*, their *Customer Flow Sheets* give a view of how well they're selling. For all sellers, *Customer Flow Sheets* can warn you about problems in using the *Steps for Selling*.

Have all sellers keep track of all customers they contact and of how they made out with them. Who was in the store? When were they there? Why were they there? Was there a sale? Which of the *Steps for Selling* did the sellers finish?

Look for patterns of activity. Are there times with too many sellers in the store? Are there times with too few sellers in the store? Are there too many unwanted visitors?

Sales Figures

The seller in charge of a cash register prepares the summaries for all sellers using it.

	Mary Jones	John Smith	Jane Johnson	Total
Taxable Sales	2080.50	1807.75	1710.90	5599.15
Non-taxable Sales	109.50	0.00	15.95	125.45
Total Sales	2190.00	1807.75	1726.85	5724.60
Tax	145.64	126.54	119.76	391.94
Total Sales & Tax	2335.63	1934.29	1846.61	6116.54

The seller in charge of a shift prepares the summaries for all cash registers used in the shift.

	Cash Drawer 1	Cash Drawer 2	Total
Taxable Sales	5599.15	1765.90	7365.05
Non-taxable Sales	125.45	0.00	125.45
Total Sales	5724.60	1765.90	7490.50
Tax	391.94	123.61	515.55
Total Sales & Tax	6116.54	1889.51	8006.05

The seller in charge of ending the day prepares the summaries for all shifts for the day.

	Shift 1	Shift 2	Total
Taxable Sales	7365.05	4076.00	11441.05
Non-taxable Sales	125.45	275.00	400.45
Total Sales	7490.50	4351.00	11841.50
Tax	515.55	285.32	800.87
Total Sales & Tax	8006.05	4636.32	12642.37

Items sold

Without true daily records of items sold a store's chances of doing well are low. There's no true record of which sellers are selling which items. There's no true record of which sellers are failing to sell items you want them to sell. There's no true record of which items to reorder to keep profits flowing. Reordering becomes hit-and-miss instead of being under the careful control needed for maximum profits. Electronic equipment speeds this job. But even if it's a job that you have to do partly or completely by hand, it's a priority *Background Job.*

Stores that have their stock partly on display and partly in in-store storage are set to make more money than warehouse-like stores that display everything. But they only make the extra money if their sellers keep on top of stocking the displays. A system using duplicate cash register slips or duplicate sales slips forms a solid base for real time restocking of displays.

Rewards

Keep track of commissions earned, spiffs paid and prizes won by your sellers each day. You'll need these records for working out payroll deductions. You'll need to see them each day to keep on top of your selling programs. How are your reward programs working? Do you need to make changes in them? Are your sellers following the rules?

Time Slips

Time Slips are the record you use to work out base pay. A *Time Slip* is the official record of the hours a seller worked. The law requires you to keep correct permanent records of the time worked. The law looks to the *Time Slip* in any question relating to hours worked, overtime pay due, and so on.

Fill in your own Time Slip daily — Keep your *Time Slip* in the *Time Slips* section of *Daily* till you sign it and hand it in. Get the manager to initial your *Time Slip* if you make a mistake and need to change an entry. The manager checks your *Time Slip* each week. It needs the manager's signature before you get paid. You'll lose your job if you write hours you didn't work on your *Time Slip*. Write hours only on your own *Time Slip*. Filling in or changing someone else's *Time Slip* will lead to discipline. Both sellers may lose their jobs.

Start a Time Slip on the first work day of a work period — Work periods begin on Mondays and last two weeks. Fill in your name, the day and the time you start work.

Fill in hours worked on the day you work them — Keep your hours up-to-date to avoid mistakes. Show each time you arrive and leave. Begin work at your scheduled starting time unless you have the manager's OK to start earlier. Quit work at your scheduled quitting time unless you have the manager's OK to stay later. Show when you leave for lunch and when you return from lunch. Show when you leave and return for other absences during the day. Doctor's and dentist's appointments fit here. Let the manager know when you'll be away during the work day.

Finish your *Time Slip* on your last work day of the work period. Put the finished slip in your *Seller's Report*.

Record time when you come in and there's no work — It's possible that you come to work and there's no work. This can happen during bad weather or because of an "Act of God."[34] There may be a power failure or other utility failure. The computer system may break down. The sewer system may break down. There may be threats to people or property. Government officials may recommend or order closing. There may not be enough work for you to do. Our aim is to call and tell you to stay home, but we may miss. Some things that grind work to a standstill happen suddenly.

We pay you base pay to do *Background Jobs* for two (2) hours when you make the journey and the store is not open. We pay you base pay for two (2) hours when you make the journey and there's nothing to do. Should the store have to close for a period of days or weeks, the time off is without pay. Tune to local stations for news of closings when you think the store may have to close—call in before coming to work.

Record time when the store closes early — In case of bad weather or other situations beyond our control, the store may close early. We pay you base pay for two (2) hours work if we send you home before you've worked two (2) hours. We pay you base pay for the time you worked if you've already worked two (2) hours or more. We may ask you to stay after we've closed because of bad weather. We pay you base pay at time and a half for the hours you work beyond closing time.

Seller's Reports

Have sellers produce a report each time they sell. Electronic equipment may help them, but it's important for sellers to take responsibility for what they do. Sellers gather these reports to make up the *Seller's Report*:

Customer Flow Sheet—Update the totals to finish the sheet.

Seller's Customer Flow Summary—Tally the needed figures from the *Customer Flow Sheet*. Staple to the top left of the *Customer Flow Sheet*.

Item Tally Sheet—Keep the *Item Tally Sheet* up-to-date as you sell. Then bring the last few entries up-to-date and the sheet's finished.

---

[34]"Acts of God" include severe weather, fires, floods, earthquakes, avalanches, and so on.

Write Thank-you Notes—Include *Thank-you Notes* and cards you've written in your *Seller's Report*. The seller in charge of the day will stamp and mail them.

Seller's Sales and Sales Tax Slip—Fill in the totals from the *Customer Flow Sheet*. Fill in the totals from the *Item Tally Sheet*.

Commission Sales Slip—Copy the total of commission sales from the *Item Tally Sheet*. Sign and date the slip. Keep the slip in *Daily* with your *Time Slip*.

Spiffs Slip—Sellers copy items with spiffs from the *Item Tally Sheet*. Enter spiff values from the *Price List*. Work out spiff amounts and spiff total. Sign and date the slip. Swap the slip for a cash payment at the cash drawer now. Sellers in charge of cash drawers check *Spiffs Slips*. Record spiff payments as *Pay-outs*. Keep *Spiffs Slips* for *Cash Drawer Cash Reports*.

Time Slip—Fill in today's work on your *Time Slip*. Finish the *Time Slip* if this shift is your last shift for this work period. To finish a *Time Slip*, fill in the total hours and sign and date it. Then put it in the *Seller's Report*. Otherwise store it in the *Time Slips* section of *Daily*.

Seller's Daily Sales Summary—Include this form if this is your last shift for the week.

Seller's Weekly Sales Summary—Include this form if this is your last shift for the month.

Seller's Monthly Sales Summary—Include this form if this is your last shift for the year.

Seller's Yearly Sales Summary—Include this form if this is your last shift for the year.

Any other notes related to selling—Include comments made by customers. Include problems that came up and how you dealt with them.

Put the *Seller's Report* in its envelope Leave the envelope open. Give the *Seller's Report* to the seller in charge of the cash drawer.

Cash Drawer Cash Report

You want to know the status of cash for each cash drawer for each shift. Then group these shift reports into a cash report for the day. You may have a *Point of Sale System* that produces these reports for you. But the chances are that whatever electronic support you have you'll still need to finish this report by hand.

Cash Drawer Cash Report
Cash Drawer Number __1__ Shift Number __1__

A Monday 2 May 1994 9am-4pm
B Mary Jones 9am-4pm
C *Fran Holly 10am-2pm*
D *John Smith 11:30am-4pm*

#			
1	OCS Total[2]	384.70	(√)
2	Extra in OC[2]	0.05	(√)
3	Extra Cash from		
4	Extra Change[3]	60.00	(√)
5	Coin Drawer[4]	10.00	(√)
6	Cash Drawer #[5] __2__	420.00	(√)
7	Sales		
8	Non-taxable[6]	52.95	(√)
9	Taxable[6]	2735.00	(√)
10	Tax[6]	191.45	(√)
11	Other Income[7]	2.05	(√)
12	Canadian $[8] x __0.20__		
13	Cash __300.00__	60.00	(√)
14	Checks __50.00__	10.00	(√)
15	TChecks __20.00__	4.00	(√)
16	Subtotal 1	3930.20	(√)
17			
18	Missing from OC[2]	0.00	(√)
19	Paid from cash[9]	55.90	(√)
20	Spiffs Paid[14]	131.00	(√)
21	Cash Removed to		
22	Coin Drawer[4]	12.00	(√)
23	Cash Drawer __3__	100.00	(√)
24	New OC	390.30	(√)
25	Deposited[11]		
26	US$	2203.55	(√)
27	US Checks[12]		( )
28	US TChecks[12]		( )
29	CN$		( )
30	CN Checks[12]		( )
31	CN TChecks[12]		( )
32	Amer Express[12]		( )
33	Discover[12]		( )
34	MasterCard[12]		( )
35	Visa[12]		( )
36	Enclosed		
37	US$		( )
38	US Checks[12]		( )
39	US TChecks[12]		( )
40	CN$	300.00	(√)
41	CN Checks[12]	50.00	(√)
42	CN TChecks[12]	20.00	(√)
43	Amer Express[12]	13.55	(√)
44	Discover[12]	27.95	(√)
45	MasterCard[12]	49.95	(√)
46	Visa[12]	576.00	(√)
47	Subtotal 2	3930.20	(√)
48			
49	Subtotal 2-Subtotal 1[13]	0.00	(√)

A Monday 2 May 1994 9am-4pm
B Mary Jones 9am-4pm
C Fran Holly 10am-2pm
D John Smith 11:30am-4pm
A: Day, date & time of shift.
B: Seller in charge of shift.
C & D: Other sellers. Use other side for more sellers.

CN: Canadian
LCCC: List of Credit Cards & Checks
OC: Opening Change
OCS: *Opening Change Slip*
SSTS: Sales & Sales Tax Slip
TChecks: Travelers Checks

[2] Staple OCS

[3] Give Extra Change Receipt(s)
[4] Update Coin List in drawer
[5] Give Cash Moved Receipt(s)
[6] Staple SSTS
Staple SSTS Workslip if more than 1 SSTS

[7] Staple slip(s) to explain it
[8] Enter 1 - exch rate
e.g., 1 - 0.8258 = 0.1472
so enter 0.1472
[9] Staple receipt(s) and workslip
[11] Staple Bank Deposit Slips
[12] Enclose LCCC

[13] Zero or include + or - with amount
[14] Staple Spiffs Workslip & signed *Spiffs Slips*

CHAPTER 14

TUNE UP FOR THE STEPS FOR SELLING

Before presenting the *Steps for Selling* there are some preliminaries to deal with. You will have to:

- Kill the use of "May I help you?"

- Train the sellers to use *Open* and *Closed Questions* properly.

- Make sure the sellers know the items they sell.

Kill the use of "May I help you?"

You have to make sure your sellers forget they ever heard the phrase "May I help you?" Be strict on this. They've heard it in so many stores where they've shopped that they think it's what they should say. Some of them have worked in other stores where they were told to use this retail obscenity and they used it every day. The secret of breaking this habit is to give them the words they need to use. These words will come later, in the *Steps for Selling*. At this point, make a song and dance about this issue as a lead-up to the later treatment. Make sure your sellers know that if you hear them saying, "May I help you?" to a customer your reaction will be the same as if they had waved a red flag at a bull.

"May I help you?" usually leads to "No Sale" — You know the usual answer to this question. You use it yourself when you go shopping: "No, thank you. I'm just looking." Say, "May I help you?" and customers vanish. Might as well chase customers out of the store as say, "May I help you?"

A great relief goes through customers after sellers ask, "May I help you?" They've solved their problems. They've now told themselves why they're in the store. A moment ago they didn't know why they were in the store. Now they do. They're "Just Looking." They put it into words and that makes it true for them. They've written themselves a contract and they'll live by it. Once someone voices a decision there's little hope of changing it.

"May I help you?" forces "No Sale" — Customers who enter the store fully intending to buy often say, "No, thank you. I'm just looking" when sellers ask "May I help you?" They are so used to giving this reply that they do it automatically. They act like robots. Once they've said they're not buying, many customers will feel foolish if they change their mind and buy. So they don't buy.

"May I help you?" invades personal space — It might be your store, but customers have personal space in it. You don't like it when someone invades your personal space. Neither do customers. You brush people off when they invade your personal space. So do customers. They brush you off when you barge in and say, "May I help you?"

"May I help you?" passes over doubts, needs, wants and desires — Customers have doubts. Customers in doubt usually put things off. They say, "No" when you pass over their doubts with "May I help you?" You know nothing about customers' needs, wants and desires. Most customers say, "No" when you pass over needs, wants and desires with "May I help you?"

"May I help you?" is polite for "I expect you to buy" — Many pushy sellers have greeted customers this way before you. So customers defend themselves. You say, "May I help you?" but customers hear, "Buy, buy, buy." "May I help you?" says, "I'm here to sell you something." Customers defend their money. They might need or want something, but they don't like the idea of paying. Almost by second nature, customers defend themselves. Given the chance, many customers will say, "No." "May I help you?" gives them that chance.

"May I help you?" forces a buying decision too early — Some sellers say, "May I help you?" soon after customers step in the store. They hit customers with a buying decision right away. Most customers don't make up their minds to buy that quickly. They say, "No."

"May I help you?" gets customers off the hook — Sellers who ask "May I help you?" strike before they get a nibble. One customer wants an item but hasn't decided whether to buy today. Another customer has a need but hasn't decided which item fills the need. At this point their sellers jump in with, "May I help you?" These customers must now decide, so they answer, "No, thank you. I'm just looking." The sellers have forced these customers to say, "No." The first customer thinks, "Some other day will do. I'm not here to buy. I'm just looking." The second customer thinks, "I don't have to decide what I need. I'm not here to buy. I'm just looking."

"May I help you?" has many disguises — Any questions that sellers ask customers right away without following the *Steps for Selling* will probably have the same effect as asking "May I help you?". These are some of the substitutes that untrained sellers use:

"Anything I can tell you?"

"Anything I can show you?"

"Anything special in mind?"

"Are there any questions, Sir?"

"Are you being helped?"

"Being waited on, Madam?"

"Call me if you need help."

"Can I answer a question for you, Sir?"

"Can I help you?"

"Can I help you find anything, Sir?"

"Can I show you something?"

"Can I tell you about something?"

"Did you find everything on your list?"

"Do you have a question?"

"Do you need some help?"

"Do you want some help?"

"I'm Jan. Let me know if you need help."

"Just let me know if you see something I can help you with."

"Just let me know if you see something I can tell you about."

"Let me know if you need help finding something on your list."

"Like something in travel goods today?"

"Sir, do you want some help?"

"Something I can show you today?"

"Something for you, Madam?"

"Was there anything you were looking for?"

"What can I do for you?"

"What can I help you with?"

Avoid them with the same intensity that you avoid "May I help you?" Almost any question sellers ask customers right away will turn customers off. Even "Nice day, isn't it?" can produce "No, thank you. I'm just looking."

"May I help you?" is the sign of untrained sellers — Most sellers say, "May I help you?" It shows they're not trained or they're wrongly trained. It's their badge of innocence. Sometimes the boss told them to say it. Nobody trained the boss either. Sometimes nobody told them what to say. So they parrot the words they

hear when they go shopping. "May I help you?" sounds like a polite offer to serve. It doesn't sound pushy. It sounds like it's just the trick. Untrained sellers make so few sales anyway that they don't notice "May I help you?" kills sales. Day after day they parrot words that don't work. No wonder their jobs are boring.

"May I help you?" works with customers on a mission — Customers on a mission to buy have decided to buy something before entering the store. Often these customers are in and out of the store quickly, buying only what they came to buy: "May I help you?" "Yes, I need a fine-point black refill for this pen." Your sales are too low if you're only selling to customers on a mission. You're selling less than fully if you ring up the sale at this point.

Ask Open and Closed Questions Well

During the *Steps for Selling* sellers ask customers many questions. It's important that they ask the right questions at the right times. Make sure that all sellers understand the differences between *Open Questions* and *Closed Questions*. Make sure they understand the roles that these questions play in the *Steps for Selling* before moving on to the *Steps for Selling*.

Spot Open Questions by their many right answers — "What do you do on weekends?" Different customers give different answers. The same customers give different answers at different times.

Ask Open Questions to get customers talking — Customers start talking and telling stories when you ask *Open Questions*. They run with the answers. The answers need thought—customers may pause before they answer. Give them time to answer without breaking in. Allow at least four seconds for customers to start to answer. Answers to *Open Questions* often include extra facts. Many of the facts show the speaker's values and interests. Answers to *Open Questions* have hooks on which to hang other questions. It's easy to use the answers to get customers talking.

"What foods do you like?" "Ever since I went to Greece, I just love souvlaki. I had such a wonderful time there." You can be sure this customer wants to talk about Greece. You soon find out facts about travel to Greece, travel agents and costs. You hear about the hotels, the best beaches and the good restaurants. Soon you're talking about things that have nothing to do with Greece. *Open Questions* are keys to developing personal relationships.

Know the question words for Open Questions — Some question words lead *Open Questions*:

"**Who** is going to play the guitar?"

"**What** do you want a computer to do for you?"

"**When** did you first use a washing machine?"

"**Where** are you going to store the guns?"

"**How** do you feel about this refrigerator?"

Add the commands "**Tell me** ..." and "**Tell me about** ..." Put "Tell me ..." in front of *Open Question* words. "Please tell me how you heard about our store?" Say, "Please tell me about ..." to open up answers fully. "Please tell me about your trip to Hawaii" will usually get you a lot of facts. "How did you like your trip to Hawaii?" may only get "Fine, thank you."

Spot Closed Questions by their few right answers — It's easy to call the possible answers to *Closed Questions*. Often "Yes" or "No" answers *Closed Questions*. "Do you want to buy this calculator?" "No, thank you."

Often a single fact answers a *Closed Question*. "How old is your son?" "He'll be five in May."

Know the question words for Closed Questions — Some question words lead *Closed Questions*:

"**Are** these what you had in mind?"

"**Could** I interest you in these shoes?"

"**Did** you look at the new carpets?"

"**Do** you like the fur coat?"

"**Had** a chance to look at the china yet?"

"**Have** you tried our new restaurant yet?"

"**Is** this your style?"

"**Was** the music box in the window the one you liked?"

"**Were** you pleased with the selection of fabrics?"

"**Would** you like these cuff links to go with your shirt?"

Ask Closed Questions to get clear-cut facts — "Do you own a VCR?"

Ask Closed Questions to get customers to decide — Ask a *Closed Question* when you need to know this or that. "Are you interested in a portable or in a desk model?" Ask a *Closed Question* when you want to bring a sale to a head. "Would you like to buy the stereo?"

Recover when you hit a wall — Ask customers to buy when you feel they'll say, "Yes." Sometimes they say, "No" and things grind to a halt. Ask another *Open Question*. "Nancy, for my information, please tell me what you don't like about this stereo?"

Sometimes you ask an *Open Question* and get a closed answer. "How was your trip to Hawaii?" "OK." Follow up with another *Open Question*. "How did you like the weather?"

Steer clear of "Why?" as an Open Question — Questions that put customers on the spot often close them down. Watch out for "Why?" Customers who are really sure of themselves will open up to it. Many customers feel you're attacking them and draw into themselves.

Look for a way to replace "Why?" For, "Why is a 15-digit labeling machine important to you?" Try, "How do you plan to use a 15-digit labeling machine?"

Avoid turning an Open Question into a Closed Question — An *Open Question* becomes a *Closed Question* if you add a choice to it. "How did you hear about our store? In the Sun or in the Star?" Someone who may have said, "From a friend," may name a newspaper instead.

Know What You Sell

Make sure sellers know every item you sell and that they know the prices and the important facts about the items. Then make sure they know how to use the facts properly by building *Show-&-tells* from them and grouping the *Show-&-tells* into *Game Plans*. At the beginning it's important to establish that:

- Every item for sale has a number.

- The *Items* binder lists all facts known about each item.

- Sellers build *Show-&-tells* from facts. *Show-&-tells* are simply plans for showing the item to customers and telling customers about items. Deal with *Show-&-tells* in detail in the *Steps for Selling*.

- Sellers group *Show-&-tells* into *Game Plans*.

Perhaps your items aren't numbered, you have no *Items* binder, no *Show-&-tells* and no *Game Plans*. Simply turn your presentation from "This is what we have and this is how we do it" into "This is what we're going to do." Then get everyone involved in doing it.

Look in the Items binder — The *Items* binder helps sellers to sell items. It's in order by group numbers and item numbers. It has facts, *Show-&-tells* and *Game Plans*.

Facts are the lowest level of help on items and groups of items. Gather the facts about the items you sell from several places. Manufacturers and suppliers will let you have brochures and leaflets. Get facts from labels on the items and from instructions on using them. Write down what reps tell you about items. Write down what customers tell you about items. Look up facts at the library and write them down. *Show-&-tells* are ways of using the facts to sell items.

Write and learn *Show-&-tells* as you learn the *Steps for Selling*. Look at videos of sellers and reps *Showing-&-telling* items. *Show-&-tells* stop sellers swamping customers with facts and killing sales.

Game Plans are ways of linking items together for selling. A *Game Plan* for selling a watch covers a way to interest customers in an expensive watch. It has fallbacks to medium and low price watches. The idea is to sell the best watch you can, but to sell any watch rather than no watch at all. A *Game Plan* for selling a suit covers how to sell other clothing to the same customer. It draws the seller's attention to the other clothing that naturally goes with the suit.

Add to the Items binder — Add any facts you find out about items. Add notes to *Show-&-tells*. Let other sellers know how well the *Show-&-tells* work for you. Write down ideas to make them better. Add new *Show-&-tells*. Items that have *Show-&-tells* always need new ones. New items need new *Show-&-tells*. Aim to have *Show-&-tells* for every item in the store. Play catch up first on your usual items. Begin with the higher priced items and work your way down. Star in the videos *Showing-&-telling* items.

Know many facts about the items you sell — Be able to answer questions about items right away. Customers buy more from you when you sound certain of the facts. Know all the facts about the items you sell.

Use facts to sell as a chef uses salt in the soup — Use only a few facts for each sale. Know many facts about the items you sell but use only a few. It's as if a chef dumped salt in the soup when you dump facts on customers. Customers won't buy from you, as you won't eat the soup.

Example 1: "I need a sleeping bag for camping when it's 10 below zero." The seller knows the temperature ratings of the bags. Reaching a bag from the rack and handing it to the customer the seller says, "This is the one you need." "How much is it?" "$250." "Fine, I'll take it." The seller used only one fact. The customer accepted the seller's know-how. The seller is now ready to schmooze and find out the customer's other needs.

Example 2: "Do you have a cheap sleeping bag?" "This is a nice bag for $150." "Do you have something cheaper?" The seller hands a bag to the customer and says, "Then you need this $99 bag." "Do you have it in blue?" "This one comes in green." "Is it machine washable?" "You take this one to the dry cleaners." "I'll take it." The seller used more facts, but only as many as the customer needed.

Note how the seller turned the negative facts into positives. The customer wanted a blue bag but took the green. The customer accepted that it's normal to take the bag to the cleaners. Compare this to "I'm sorry but we only have green." Compare it to "No, it's not machine washable, you'll have to dry clean it." This customer wanted cheap and was willing to cut corners to get it. The customer would have squeaked if it was really important to have blue and machine washable. The seller would then sell the blue machine washable bag for $120 The seller is now ready to schmooze and find out the customer's other needs.

Example 3: The customer needs a cheap bag to sleep on the couch when he visits his brother, but he doesn't tell the seller his needs. "I'm looking for a sleeping bag." "Yes sir, we have a complete range. These down bags come in either a polyester cover or fire resistant impregnated cotton. The only colors we have at the moment are red, green and blue. There's also a yellow one, but that's out of stock until next week. They no longer make the black one as it wasn't too popular. These over here are our best bags. You can choose polyester or down filling and they're warm enough to sleep in at 40 below zero. I can vouch for that myself as I used one on my last trip to Alaska. You couldn't ask for a warmer bag. They also come with a rainproof fly-canopy... and on, and on, and on" Customer 20 minutes later, confused and exhausted—heading for the door never to return, "I'll check back later in the week."

The seller dumped the whole pack of salt in the soup. Chalk up from one to three lost sales. The seller missed this sale and possible sales to two other customers who came and left because they got no attention.

Know all the facts, but only use the few you need to make the sale. Use different facts about the same item when customers have different needs.

Give customers the facts they expect — Pass the tests customers set for you. Some customers know many facts about items. They'll soon see through you if you're faking it. This is often true with technical items like computers. These customers will only feel at ease dealing with an equal. Keep up with the facts if you want to sell to them. These techie customers are the only ones who like technical jargon. Avoid it with all other customers.

Get help when you don't know the facts — Admit it when you don't know, then find out. Sometimes customers will ask something you don't know. Say, "I don't know, but let's find out." That brings customers along with you and keeps them on the hook. Check in the *Items* binder. Bring another seller in on the deal if you need to. Sometimes you'll go on with the sale. Other times you'll pass the customer along to the other seller.

CHAPTER 15

THE STEPS FOR SELLING

The next diagram summarizes the *Steps for Selling*, using the short forms of the names of the steps. The steps fall into three subgroups. There are steps that take place before the sale (1-11,) steps that take place at the cash register (12-14,) and steps that take place after the sale (15-21.) It's important for sellers to master all three subgroups of steps and to use them smoothly, moving from one subgroup to the next without a break.

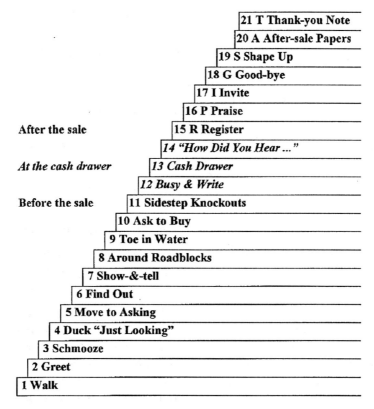

The numbers are in the order that sellers use the *Steps for Selling*. The steps used after the sale have letters in addition to numbers. These letters are useful in checklists and forms.

These are the full names of the *Steps for Selling*, arranged in their order of presentation:

1. Walk the Store.

2. Greet Customers.

3. Schmooze.

4. Duck "Just Looking."

5. Move from Schmoozing to Asking Questions.

6. Find Out Why Customers Want to Buy.

7. Show-&-tell the Chosen Item.

8. Go Around Roadblocks.

9. Put Your Toe in the Water.

10. Ask All Customers to Buy.

11. Sidestep Knockouts.

12. Keep Customers Busy While You Write Up Sales.

13. Follow the Steps for the Cash Drawer.

14. Ask, "How Did You Hear about Our Store?"

15. **R** Register Customers and Register Sales.

16. **P** Praise Customers for Buying.

17. **I** Invite Customers Back.

18. **G** Say, "Good-bye."

19. **S** Shape Up Displays and Storage.

20. **A** Do the After-sale Paperwork.

21. **T** Write Thank-you Notes.

Walk the Store

To *Walk the Store* is to make a mental check of all items currently available for sale in the store. Walk to all displays and look at them. Walk to all storage areas and check them. A stopgap measure which is less complete but still useful is to *Eyeball the Store*. This is to stand in one place and look at all the items you can see. To *Check the Store* is either to *Walk the Store*, or *Eyeball the Store*, whichever is possible at the particular moment. All sellers begin their shifts by walking the store. Make sure that sellers know that a shift is a time period that they work. Common shifts are: all day, mornings, afternoons, evenings. Then during their shifts sellers *Check the Store* from time to time.

Check items — Check which items are on display. Remember what you sell and know the names of the items.

Check places — Check the places where you keep items and you'll remember them. Know where your displays are and where you keep extras.

Check prices — Check prices and remember them. Test yourself while you check. How many prices do you know?

Check displays — Are your displays neat? Tidy any mess. Look at your displays with customers' eyes. Do you like what you see?

Check so you'll feel on top of things — Check the store and you'll feel in charge of things. Without checking you risk feeling foolish. You'll feel foolish when a customer asks about prices and you don't know them. When you can't find an item you want to show to a customer. When you make a customer want to buy an item that's out of stock. When you take a customer to a display that's a mess.

Follow a plan when you check the store — Make a plan and stick to it. Check the display areas in the same order each time. Talk over your checking plan with the manager.

Include the window when you check — Sloppy checkers overlook the window but it's an important check. Customers first see the store's window. Many customers only come in if the window looks nice to them. Always check the window before you enter the store. Check it again when you're inside the store.

Walk the Store when you enter the store — Know how the store looks right now. *Walk the Store* every time you enter the store. That's every time you start your shift and other times too. *Walk the Store* after your coffee break, after your lunch break, after you've done the banking.

Walk the Store after Special Jobs — *Special Jobs* take time. The store may change while you do them. *Walk the Store* after *Special Jobs* to bring your focus back on selling.

Eyeball the Store between sales — Take a moment to eyeball the store as you move from sale to sale.

Eyeball the Store from different places — Some areas will be out of sight when you *Eyeball the Store*. Make up for this by eyeballing from a different place each time.

Greet Customers

Make sure sellers understand that to greet a person is to welcome a person with pleasure.

Greet customers to show you're polite — Show you respect other people by greeting them. A greeting is the natural start of any friendship. Customers feel you've noticed them when you greet them. They feel you ignore them unless you greet them.

Greet all customers who enter the store — Greet all customers, even if you're busy.

Greet customers right away — Greet within one minute of a customer entering the store. That's not when you get around to it. It's before you've finished adding up that list of figures. It's before the customer has had a chance to look around the store. Customers often back off if you first ignore them and greet them later. They think your greeting is part of selling. They're less likely to accept you as an honest person.

Greet customers without trying to sell to them — You've done more than greet if customers back off. Sell only to customers who use your greeting to start talking about buying.

Greet without asking questions — Greetings that ask questions put pressure on customers to talk to you. Avoid greetings like "How are you?" and "Nice day, isn't it?" Welcome customers with simple greetings they can echo: "Good Morning, Sir." "Good Evening, Mrs. Rogers." "Hi there, Joan."

"Hello" and "Hi" are OK, but one or two extra words help open customers up. The extra words show you care.

Greet cheerfully — Look customers in the eye and smile when you greet them.

Greet at a distance — Stay at least three arms' length away as you greet customers. Allow customers some personal space. Enter that space and they'll back off.

Wrap yourself up in a job when you greet — Greet customers while you're busy doing something else. They'll be more open to you than if you focus on them right away. Customers are at ease with busy sellers. They're a relief from the threat of sellers who swim around customers like sharks. There's always a job to do in a store. Check items on a list—hold some papers while you check. Tidy or set up displays—handle the items. Dust the furniture—hold a duster and dust. Clean the glass of the display cases—spray and wipe. Jobs that put you on the floor before customers enter the store are best. Come out and begin a job on the floor if you're behind the counter.

Cross paths with customers when you greet them — Customers may back off if you go straight towards them. They fear you'll force them to buy. You risk scaring customers if you come up behind them. They fear you snuck up on them to force them to buy. Lower customers' fears by crossing their paths. Act busy with a job at the side of the store. Walk nearly at right angles to the customer's path. Pass in front of the customer without coming too close. Without stopping, look the customer in the eye. Smile as you greet—"Good morning, Sir." Keep walking to the other side of the store. Carry on with your job.

Greet to stop shoplifters — Shoplifters love stores where sellers ignore them. They know you know they're in the store when you greet them. Greeting customers helps fight theft.

Schmooze

To schmooze is to gossip, to chat idly, to chatter. The more sellers schmooze with customers, the more they sell. Schmoozing with customers is the main gateway to high sales. Sellers who don't schmooze fall back on common myths about customers that lead them to low sales. See through the common myths about customers:

Customers who need things will ask to buy them.

Some customers will tell you their interests—"I'm thinking about buying a guitar." Some will tell you their needs—"I need a clothes iron." Some will ask you to show them an item—"I'd like to look at that calculator." Some will ask to buy an item—"I'd like to buy that bicycle." But many customers who need or want items will keep silent. They'll leave without giving you a chance to sell to them.

Let customers look around and get used to the store. They'll see things they need and ask to buy them.

After they've looked around some customers will tell you their interests or needs. Others will ask you to show them an item or ask to buy. But most will leave without giving you a chance to sell to them.

Customers are more likely to buy when sellers offer help.

Customers are less likely to buy when sellers offer help. Most of them turn out to be "Just looking." Customers guard themselves from sellers. It's natural to say, "Just looking." Customers say it even when they came to buy.

Schmooze to get close to customers — Some customers have already sold themselves something. They know what they want and they've come to buy. Sellers only have to step and fetch it. They'll buy even when they get poor service or no service. Sellers are missing sales if they only sell these customers what they came to buy. Schmooze to get close to them and sell them more.

Other customers want to buy but find it hard to make choices. They find it hard to act when they've made choices. It's easier for them to do nothing—they fear they'll waste money. Try to help them and you may spook them. Once they've decided they're "Just looking," your chance of a sale drops. Schmooze to get close to these customers and sell to them.

Customers won't let sellers help them, because they don't trust them. After sellers greet customers, the next job isn't to sell to them. The next job is to get them to trust you. Get customers to trust you by schmoozing with them. That's how trust grows in your daily life and it's the same in a store. Greeting customers has opened the way for schmoozing because customers already know you. The chance they'll schmooze with you is now higher than it was before.

Schmooze with all customers who enter the store — That's right—schmooze with all customers. Not just with those who say they want to buy. Not just with those who you think might buy or who look as if they can afford to buy. Schmooze even with those who are "Just looking around" or who came in to get out of the rain.

Begin schmoozing from a distance — Some customers start schmoozing with sellers when they greet them. That's good luck, but usually you're the one who starts schmoozing. Judge when to start schmoozing. Speak too soon and customers feel uneasy. Wait too long and customers leave before you know it. Allow that customers have personal space. Begin schmoozing from a distance. Move close only when trust grows.

Begin schmoozing with Openers — *Openers* are questions you ask to start customers schmoozing. *Openers* are always *Open Questions*. You want customers to talk. *Closed Questions* have no place in schmoozing. Forget you ever heard "May I help you?" It's such a bad *Opener* that you never let it pass your lips. Get customers to start talking. Customers who talk are customers who buy.

Forget about selling — Steer clear of *Openers* that have anything to do with selling. Schmooze, don't sell. Start schmoozing without signaling you're going to sell. It's too early for you to start selling. You don't know what customers need, want, or desire. You don't even know that customers came to buy. It's too early for customers to feel comfortable with you.

Forget about bouncing — *Openers* that bounce from items seem natural, but they're a trap. "That's a beautiful toy, isn't it?" "That silk sure feels wonderful, doesn't it?" "So it's house painting time, is it?" "Well, that time of year has come round again, hasn't it?" "Have you figured it out yet?" "That's a beauty, isn't it?" "That looks good on you, doesn't it?" "How would you like to own that refrigerator?"

A bounce uses an item. Talking about items is talking about selling. A bounce is a pounce. It's a sales pitch. Customers may back off. Only unskilled sellers leap on customers like this. Slow yourself down and sell more. Customers often handle things they find interesting as they pass by. They may want to buy different items. Sellers may waste their time when they bounce. Sellers may put customers off buying altogether.

Bounces rarely lead to personal relationships with customers. Personal relationships open up sales. Develop personal relationships with customers even when they pick up an item and say, "I'll take it."

Start with a natural topic — Start to schmooze with customers as with any stranger. Be honest. Stick to your style of schmoozing. Talk sports only if you're a sports fan. Talk opera only if you like opera. Talk about cute babies only if you really like them.

Take hints from customers to start schmoozing — Customers give hints about their interests and values. Is a customer holding a theater program? A great chance to ask what's playing, who's playing, how the play was, and so on. Is a customer carrying a cook book? Start schmoozing about favorite foods and recipes. See an airline ticket, so start schmoozing about travel. Going? Coming? Where? When? Why? How long? Show you're envious. Someone is carrying a tennis racquet, so ask how the game was. Then there are all those customers wearing T-shirts with messages on them. They're perfect for schmoozing. Chances are she never went to the University of Hawaii, but ask her how she enjoyed the islands anyway.

Look around for hints. See customers wearing uniforms, running shorts, badges, lapel pins, buttons with messages, convention stickers. See customers carrying umbrellas, gloves, magazines, newspapers, shopping bags with the names of stores on them, skateboards, flowers, phones. See customers with shoelaces undone, with wet hair.

Make a list of all the hints you come across. Here are some questions based on hints: "How's the convention going?" "How are you liking 'The Naked Ape'?" "How do you like your Porsche?" "How old is your little girl?" "How was the play?" "How are you liking your visit to San Francisco?" "What language are you speaking?" "Where are you staying?" "Where are you visiting from?" "Who's going to win the big race?"

Pay a compliment now and then — Be careful with compliments—they're personal. Many customers find it hard to take compliments. They can sound fake from a seller. Pay them rarely and only when you're sure of yourself. Saying "That's a beautiful coat" can fall flat. It's a remark, instead of a question. Some customers may find it hard to reply. Some customers feel uncomfortable with praise. Give a reason for the compliment and end with a question: "I like your coat. I've been looking for one like that for my mother. Did you buy it locally?"

Always say something — Sometimes customers give no hints and a compliment feels wrong to you. Try something from the news. Read newspapers and news magazines. What's happening? Michael Jordan? Dodgers? Space shuttle? Take an honest interest in the world around you. Make an everyday comment if all else fails. Be sure it shows an interest in your customer: "Enjoying the sunshine?" "Did you get caught in the traffic jam?" "Get caught in the rain?" "Did you get to see the parade?" "Cold out there, isn't it?"

Avoid hidden sales pitches: "How you doing?" "How's it going?" These are just other words for "Now you've looked around, are you ready to buy?"

Always say something. The biggest mistake sellers can make is to say nothing.

Write your own Openers — Write a list of the *Openers* you can use to start customers schmoozing. Keep adding to your list. Keep score of how well each works. Keep your list in order with those that work best at the top.

Duck "Just Looking"

"I'm just looking" is probably the commonest thing customers say to sellers who speak to them. Sellers have to be able to go through this negative phrase to make sales.

Get ready for "Just looking" — Whatever sellers say, some customers will say, "Just Looking." Some customers won't schmooze. They'll brush you off. Some will schmooze and then brush you off. Whatever you ask, some customers will answer, "Just looking."

Duck "Just looking" — Smile nicely and say warmly, "Fine!"

Then wait a moment and say, "How long have you been looking?" This often starts customers talking.

Keep smiling and ask warmly, "What type of things are you looking for?"

Leave tested lookers alone — Sometimes trying to duck "Just Looking" brings another brush off: "Nothing in particular." "Nothing special." "I'm just browsing around, thank you." "Please don't bother me."

Get the brush off more than once and you usually have a looker. You've tested for a customer and you've found a looker. Leave a tested looker in peace and spend your time elsewhere. Smile and say warmly, "Fine! Enjoy the store." It's a success when you come to this dead end. You've done the job fully. You can't overcome all "Just looking."

Pass customers along — Sometimes you sense a customer doesn't like you. Maybe another seller will be luckier than you. Try passing the customer along. Learn to spot "Jane's kind of customer." See that Jane gets her kind of customer.

Move from Schmoozing to Asking Questions

Never let schmoozing become an end in itself. At the right time, sellers move from schmoozing to asking questions.

Question customers closely and fully — Customers buy things because they need them or want them. They also dream about things they may never own. To sell find out what customers need and want. Find out what they dream about. Find out by asking questions. Ask questions closely and fully.

Move from schmoozing to asking questions — Good schmoozing slides into asking questions. Neither customer nor seller notices the change. Avoid schmoozing sliding into nothing but a gossip session. Know when enough is enough. Watch out for customers who can't stop talking. Watch out for lonely people. They'll waste your time and buy nothing. It's up to you to begin asking questions. Avoid asking questions too soon. Only practice can help you judge the right moment.

Move with "What brings you into our store today?" — Ask this question to move from schmoozing to asking questions. Ask it in any store. Ask it with any items you sell. Other movers are different forms of this basic mover: "So, how come you're visiting us today?" "To what do we owe the pleasure of your company today?" "What brought you here on such a rainy day?" "How come you're in our store on a nice sunny day like this?"

Find Out Why Customers Want to Buy

One of the great mistakes in retail selling is sellers trying to sell things before they fully understand why customers want to buy and what it is they want to buy.

Find out why customers want to buy before showing — Many sellers show items once they've started talking to customers. A customer mentions typewriters and the seller shows several different models. For each model the seller shows this feature, that feature and many other features. Soon there are too many details for the customer to handle. The customer loses interest and doesn't buy.

These sellers make customers feel they're in danger of buying something they're not sure about. They haven't found out why customers want to buy. They only know the general area of interest.

Ask questions to find out why customers want to buy. Question customers closely and fully before you show them anything. Most sellers rush to show items too soon so they waste time and effort. End this waste. Find out the details. Keep asking questions until you get the full story. Know what you'll show to customers before you stop asking questions. Spend more time asking questions than showing items.

Find out needs, wants and dreams — For a customer to buy an item, it must meet a need. Perhaps the typewriter must type in italics. Perhaps the truck has to carry loads weighing 10 tons. Find out needs by asking customers about them. Customers don't always know their needs. You may have to help them explore their needs. Knowing needs helps you choose items to show customers. The needs fence off a few items of the store's many items.

Knowing needs isn't enough to be sure of making sales. Few customers buy things from needs alone. Usually, a feeling makes a customer buy. Feelings even sway customers who pride themselves on their practical buying. Customers buy most items because they want them. Wants get ahead of needs. Often several items meet customers' needs. Among the needs there are items customers want. Sell the items customers want. You win twice when you sell from wants. You satisfy customers. Wants usually cost more than needs.

Dreams are wants that a person isn't likely to get. The child's need is to take the school bus. The want is to fly in an airplane. The dream is to go by rocket to the moon. You need a small truck, but you want an MG and dream about a Lamborghini. Dreams are important in selling. Let customers bask in their dreams. All customers like to feel they can own what they dream about. They'll come to the reality of what they can afford themselves. It's not a seller's job to ruin their dreams. Go along with customers' dreams. Crush customers dreams and they won't buy from you. Let dreams flavor needs. Say to the child, "Hurry for the school bus. It's going to zoom to school like a rocket to the moon."

Find out which items to show — Choose items to show. The goal of asking customers about their needs, wants and dreams is to choose items to show. These *Chosen Items* are the only items to show customers. Any of the hundreds or thousands of items in the store may interest customers. Put aside the wrong items and zero in on one or two items that fill needs and wants. Aim to find a small group of items of interest to each customer. Then find a smaller group within that group. Then find a still smaller group, until you have only one or two items to show the customer.

Match customers to the right items to make sales. One customer needs a portable electric typewriter with a memory. Another wants a manual typewriter with a correcting ribbon. A third customer will buy an electronic office typewriter, but only if the keys make a satisfying click. They all say they need a typewriter. Show only the right typewriter to the right customer.

A customer shows interest in a TV. Before you show a TV, find out who's going to watch the TV. Is it for the family? Is it for the children? Find out where the TV will go. Family room? Den? Bathroom? Bedroom? Find out what other TVs the customer already has. Is this a second TV or the main family TV? Do they have VCRs? Are the TVs the customer has out of date? Do they have good color? As you ask questions, you'll get a good picture of the family and the possible price range.

Plan your asking — Develop a *Question Plan* for each group of items you sell. Follow a plan when you mention items. Ask general questions at first. A sample *Question Plan* follows this section. Keep *Question Plans* for groups of items in the *Items* binder.

Find out the reason for buying — Customers always have reasons that send them shopping. Get the edge in selling by knowing customers' reasons for buying.

Mary must buy a toy for a baby shower at her office. She has to go to the shower, but she'd prefer to go bowling. The shower is on her regular bowling night. She doesn't like the mother-to-be. Jane wants to buy a toy for Ellen's new baby. Jane has known Ellen since they were kids. She's her best friend. It's difficult for Ellen to get pregnant and she's had three miscarriages. She recently gave birth to a fine baby girl. It's unlikely that she'll bear another child. Couldn't you sell a more expensive toy to Jane than to Mary?

Jack is at the jewelry counter. He's a student, but he's scraped together enough to buy a present for Jill. Their first wedding anniversary is in six weeks. Frank is at the jewelry counter. He's a successful banker who likes to spend. He needs to buy a present for Carol. Tomorrow is their silver wedding anniversary. Couldn't you sell a more expensive necklace to Frank than to Jack?

Joan's only reason for buying a dress is to look fabulous for a special date. Talk fabulous. Forget easy to clean. Forget a good bargain. Forget comfort.

Reap the harvest of trust — Customers face many choices. Shopping can be confusing and tiring. Price affects the decision to buy, but not as much as many retailers believe. Customers buy what they want. They buy at a handy store. They buy at prices they can afford. They buy from sellers they trust. Customers trust sellers who are polite and honest. They trust sellers who take a personal interest in them and who respect their point of view. Customers sense when sellers work with them. For this they offer trust. Trust develops when you ask questions to choose items to show. Customers feel you going along with them. Trust develops when you ask questions to find out the reason for buying. Customers feel your personal interest in them. Asking questions builds on your schmoozing. The more you talk without a hint of selling, the more trust develops. You and the customer relate person to person, not as seller to customer.

Ask Open Questions most of the time — Begin with an *Open Question*. Go on with other *Open Questions*. Ask another *Open Question* when one gets you a closed answer "What kind of foods do you like?" "Eggs." "How come you like eggs so much?"

Bounce the second question from the first answer or choose a different topic. Only ask *Closed Questions* after you've asked several *Open Questions*. Ask *Closed Question* to get facts you must have. Ask *Closed Questions* when you're sure they'll make customers buy. Otherwise, ask *Open Questions*. Force a decision with a *Closed Question* when customers are close to buying: "Which do you prefer? The compact washing machine, or the one that washes a full load?"

Listen to customers — Listen to the answer when you've asked a question. Listen until the customer finishes the answer. Listen without breaking in on the customer. Listen as the customer strays from one topic to the next. You learn what customers believe and what they feel when they talk fully. You hear important facts when customers talk fully. Use these facts for today's selling and for future selling. Put aside the urge to break in—it pays off for you in sales.

All human beings need a listener, but they rarely get one. Take the chance to be the only person who lets customers finish their thoughts.

Keep in contact with your body language as you listen. Square your body to customers. Make good eye contact without staring. Keep a good look on your face. Nod your head from time to time to show you're following and you understand.

Make sounds that show you're paying attention. "Ah," "Hmmm" and "Uh-huh" are good. So are one or two words. "Yes," "I see," "I understand," "Good," "Go on," "Tell me more." These act as push-alongs, getting customers to tell you more. They encourage and support customers.

Echo the main points and get customers to agree. "Am I correct in understanding that you must have a small refrigerator with an automatic ice-maker?" "As I understand it ..." "You're saying that ..."

This way you show you've listened. You get stronger commitments from customers. This way customers will know you got their message. They'll be more likely to listen to what you say if you need to suggest something else. Ask for more facts when you don't understand. "Could you please explain to me what you meant by...?" "Please tell me more about ..." "How did you feel about that?"

Steer customers back to the topic when they drift away. Gently guide customers back by asking a question about the topic. Listen well to get customers who'll come to you each time they shop.

Avoid grilling customers — Grilling is when you ask questions and then break in on the answers to ask other questions. Grilling is an "I" activity. It says, "I'm important. You exist to serve me." Listening is a "You" activity. It says, "You're important. I'm here to serve you."

The energy needed to turn thoughts into words goes on flowing when you break in on an answer. Customers have to work against that energy to listen to you. That causes stress. Avoid causing stress in customers.

Grilling customers will cost you facts about customers. Grilling will cost you sales. Listening fully will make the questions you ask a pleasant experience.

Support customers' answers and beliefs — Customers' answers reflect their beliefs. Support them. It's not your job to question customers' beliefs. Remember the saying: "The Customer is Always Right." React to the customer as a professional. Your single aim is to sell. Perhaps a customer says "It's important that a man's umbrella is black." Perhaps you prefer a red one with yellow spots and dislike black. React professionally and lead the customer to the black umbrellas. "Yes, a black umbrella gives a man just the right touch of dignity."

Agreeing and repeating customers' words gives the strongest support. It sends clear signals that you've heard what customers said. Know that when they state facts, customers are voicing their beliefs. Know that customers' beliefs are important to them. You're in the store to sell, not to waste time arguing. You're in the store to sell, not to root for social changes. Arguing with customers will lose you sales. Never argue with customers.

Correct mistaken views with support, tact and questions — Correct customers tactfully when they have mistaken views of items. They'll keep their trust in you if you're tactful. Correcting mistaken views will stop customers returning unwanted items. "With this printer writing 180 characters per second, I'll really get the letters to my clients moving." "It certainly prints at 180 characters per second, but that's in draft mode. For letter quality printing, it slows to 60 characters per second. Do you need letter quality or will the high speed in draft mode be satisfactory, Sir?"

Correct mistaken dangerous views with care. Agree with customers. Then put the blame on a powerful outsider and suggest something else. "It's certainly important to have a warm bathroom. But the electrical inspector forbids the use of these free-standing electric fires in bathrooms. He says they're not safe for that use. Would you consider the baseboard unit instead?"

Always react to Headline Banners — Customers want to talk about the exciting events in their lives. They signal this by waving *Headline Banners*. "We're thinking about a stereo for our daughter's graduation." These parents overflow with joy as they wave that *Headline Banner*:

You can make a sale if you ignore the *Headline Banner* and say, "What type of stereo do you have in mind?" Join the ranks of dull, unimaginative sellers with poor sales. Instead, react like this: "Congratulations. I can see you're full of pride in your daughter. Tell me, what's she going to do now?" Then let the conversation develop. You've stepped on the road to high sales.

Question Plan

Group 247—TVs.

Aim to find out:

Who's going to watch the TV?

Family? Children? Parents?

Where will the TV go?

Family room? Den? Bathroom? Bedroom?

What other TVs are there?

Is this a second TV?

Is this the main family TV?

Are other TVs out of date?

Good color?

Do they have VCRs?

Price range.

Ask one or more *Open Questions*.

Please tell me what you want from this TV.

Who's going to watch the TV?

Where are you going to use the TV?

How will the TV fit in with your other TVs?

Ask a *Closed Question* or two to fill in details if you need to.

Add-ons:

Try using a VCR as an *Add-on* to make the sale.

Show-&-tell the Chosen Item

When sellers have found out what customers want to buy, it's *Show-&-tell* time. The danger is that sellers will go overboard and swamp customers, so there's a way of *Showing-&-telling* to stop this happening.

Make customers desire to own the Chosen Item — Show the item. Tell about one or more of its features and benefits. The desire to own items grows when you point out their good points. Words alone lose to an exciting *Show-&-tell*. A good item is its own best seller. Show it in use. Get customers in contact with items.

The desire to own items grows if customers touch them, hold them, use them, smell them or taste them. Put items into customers' hands at the right moment. You're doing it before trust has developed if customers back off. Items placed in customers' hands outsell the same items openly displayed on the counter. One study showed into-the-hand sales were twenty times better than on-the-counter sales. Give items to customers with both hands. Giving with two hands invites customers to accept. The action says "Please accept this offering." Its grace makes it easy for customers to accept the item. Giving with one hand pushes items on customers. It's aggressive. The action says "Take this." Customers may back off from this command. Customers who accept may become uneasy and lose trust in you. They feel you're pushing.

Talk about Payoffs instead of technical features — Customers buy *Payoffs*. A *Payoff* is what the item does for customers. It's the benefit customers get from owning an item. "This electric stapler staples a half inch pile of paper." Technical features are statements of exact facts. "This electric stapler has a Hyatt K15 200 watt power source." Downplay or skip technical features.

Use everyday words instead of technical jargon — Run from technical jargon. Technical jargon bores ordinary customers and makes them feel foolish. You'll lose contact with customers if you use jargon. They'll be too polite to tell you to shut up. They'll put up with the boredom. Then they'll go away without buying.

Use technical jargon only when customers ask you for it. Any other use is showing off and nobody likes show-offs. Aim to explain items instead of aiming to "impress" customers.

List the Show-&-tells — List *Show-&-tells* for each item in the *Items* binder. Here's a *Show-&-tell* for the Brand X, Model 1234 Typewriter: "One of the nice things about this typewriter is its memory. You can store a one-page letter. Then you just make a few changes each time you send it to a different person. That'll make light work of writing to all your friends and relatives, won't it?"

The parts of the *Show-&-tell* are:

Lead in: "One of the nice things about…" It's a soft entry. It leaves you in a good position for "Another nice thing about…"

Name: "this typewriter…" Give the item a simple name. "The Brand X, Model 1234 Typewriter" is bad. It's too exact. It's too technical.

Feature: "is its memory." The *Feature* must be simple. Avoid the name, manufacturer, catalogue number or size of the memory. Give only one feature in each *Show-&-tell*.

Use: "You can store a one-page letter." Pitch only one *Use* for each *Feature*. Write several *Show-&-tells* if the *Feature* has several uses. A *Use* explains how to use the *Feature*. A use forms a bridge from the feature to the *Payoff*.

Payoff: "Then you just make a few changes each time you send it to a different person." Again, only one *Payoff* for each use. The *Payoff* is what the *Use* of the *Feature* will do for customers. It answers the question, "What's in it for me?"

Hook: "That'll make light work of writing to all your friends and relatives." Again, only one *Hook* for each *Payoff*. The *Hook* is a final statement to make customers agree that the *Payoff* is valuable.

Barb: "Won't it?" The *Barb* of the *Hook* is a *Closed Question* to make customers say, "Yes."

The *Payoff* is the important point, but remember to set the barbed hook. The *Payoff* is what customers buy. The *Payoff* is what the item will do for customers. The *Payoff* is how the item will make life easier, more fun, more exciting. The *Payoff* is how the item will give more power, more status, more beauty. Set the barbed hook right after the *Payoff*.

Try the Show-&-tells in the right order — One *Show-&-tell* may sell best, but it's rare to use only one for a sale. Usually two or three others come before the one that works. Prepare the way for the *Show-&-tell* that makes the sale. Write a small group of *Show-&-tells* for each item.

Build the stock of Show-&-tells — Brainstorming with a group of sellers is a good way to write *Show-&-tells*. To begin, write several for each item and try them. One item can have several *Features*. A *Feature* can have several *Uses*. A *Use* can have several *Payoffs*. Perhaps you can hang more than one *Hook* on each *Payoff*. This means you can write many *Show-&-tells* for each item. Keep track of how well they work. Throw out the losers and write new ones. Aim for about six good ones for each item in the *Items* binder. For most items one *Show-&-tell* does most of the selling. Let it bubble to the top. Different sellers may find different *Show-&-tells* work for them. A seller may need different *Show-&-tells* for different customers.

Show-&-tell item by item — *Show-&-tell* only one item at a time. A mixed *Show-&-tell* that jumps from item to item confuses customers. Begin with the item the customer is most likely to buy.

One result of your *Show-&-tell* is you come closer to the sale. Another result is you learn new facts to choose a new item to *Show-&-tell*. Be sure customers turn down an item before *Showing-&-telling* another.

Show-&-tell Payoffs when asked to compare items — Sometimes customers ask you to compare items. "Which of these is best?" "Which of these would you buy for yourself?" Still sell item by item. Show the good points of each item. Go on asking questions to find out needs, wants and dreams more fully. Customers leaning towards item A buy nothing if you say item B is better. Customers may think you gain personally by selling item B when you say item B is better than item A. This may destroy trust, especially for customers leaning towards item A.

Present the smallest number of facts possible — Use only the facts you need to do the job when you *Show-&-tell*. Few words and few actions are marks of skilled sellers. Aim to move quickly from one sale to the next.

Stop Showing-&-telling as soon as you can — Stop *Showing-&-telling* as soon as customers say, "I'll take it." Stop even if most of your *Show-&-tell* remains. Stop even if you could easily go on with your *Show-&-tell*. Stop even if you're proud of your *Show-&-tell*. Stop even if you're keyed up to go on with your *Show-&-tell*. A customer may say, "I'll take it," before you begin to *Show-&-tell*. Your *Show-&-tell* is over. More selling can only kill the sale after customers say, "I'll take it." Stroke your ego by pride in the sales you make instead of by spinning wheels with *Show-&-tells* customers don't need.

Give self-ending Show-&-tells — Ask questions fully and give good *Show-&-tells*. You've asked questions well and you're giving a good *Show-&-tell*. Suddenly, you hear, "I'll take it." That's a reward for a job well done. The sale came before you asked the customer to buy. You gave a self-ending *Show-&-tell*. Aim to make all your *Show-&-tells* self-ending. Keep a score chart to measure your success and to chart your progress.

Act the part for all Chosen Items and for all customers — Your *Show-&-tell* is a performance, like an actor's on a stage. You expect actors to put their personal feelings aside and express the characters they play truly. Perform for customers in the same way. You expect actors to perform well in all their plays for all audiences. The play fails when actors decide only some plays are worth the work. Sales fail for sellers who decide only some items are worth the work. The play fails when actors decide only some audiences are worth the work. Sales fail for sellers who decide only some customers are worth the work. Give polished *Show-&-tells* for all items and for all customers. Unlike actors, sellers can change the act when they get bored. Sellers get bored when a poor act leads to poor sales. Look at the act and change it. Keep asking as you *Show-&-tell*. Ask questions at every chance. Some customers have only partly told their needs, wants and dreams. Some feel more sure of their choice after you ask extra questions.

Good displays Show-&-tell for you — A good display is a *Show-&-tell* working for you. Pay attention to the window displays and in-store displays and watch your sales go up.

Go Around Roadblocks

Roadblocks are reasons customers give for not buying the *Chosen Item*. Customers will put up *Roadblocks* to selling for a number of reasons, so your sellers need to go around them to make sales.

Listen to Roadblocks fully — Some *Roadblocks* are real and some are a way of asking for more facts. Others are smoke screens that hide the true reasons stopping customers from buying. Listen to *Roadblocks* fully. *Roadblocks* always give clues to what customers will buy.

Put aside the urge to argue against Roadblocks — You'll only go around *Roadblocks* by working with customers. You'll lose the sale if you defend the items, the store or yourself. Customers may insult them all. Jumping in to defend them is the worst thing you can do. You're a professional—put up with the abuse. Help customers instead. You can't help customers if you let their frustrations or rudeness get to you.

Agree with Roadblocks — *Roadblocks* are real to customers even if they're wrong. Always take customers' worries seriously. You put customers down if you don't agree with their worries. Make it clear you're on their side. Enter into customers' feelings and agree with their *Roadblocks*. "I don't like the noise the weed machine makes when you turn it on." "It certainly does make a noise, no doubt about that."

Point out any reason in passing — Point out any reason without laboring it. Keep it simple and avoid arguing. Mention any reason in passing. "Yes, it does make a noise, just like all weed machines."

Go to the next Show-&-tell — The last *Show-&-tell* led to a dead end. The customer said, "No" and you agreed with it. Give a different *Show-&-tell*. Give the customer a new reason to buy. "One of the nice things about this weed machine is that its powerful engine does the job easily in 5 minutes. That compares with 30 minutes hard work by hand. That's a wonderful help, isn't it?"

Prevent Shy-aways with "Feel, felt, found" — Many customers have beliefs that make them shy away from your items. Everyone knows Brand A dishwashers are good, but you stock Brand B because they're better. It's a *Shy-away* when customers say, "Thank you, but I only buy Brand A dishwashers." Customers who've made up their minds won't give Brand B a fair hearing. To make a sale, let customers know why Brand B is better. Let them know without upsetting them. "I know exactly how you **feel**. We **felt** the same way. However, our customers **found** that Brand B does an excellent job too, and causes less streaking on glasses. We also **found** that Brand B needs less than half the repairs needed by Brand A. These are good reasons for thinking about Brand B, aren't they?"

Many customers shy away from items that puzzle them. They prefer not to buy, or to buy something simpler and cheaper. "This VCR looks nice, but it's far too hard for me to use. I'd never be able to use all those knobs and buttons. I'm just no good at mechanical things. I must have something simpler."

Sometimes a simpler item fully meets a customer's needs or wants. Sell the simpler item. Sometimes you know customers will regret buying the simpler item once they get used to it. Let them know why but avoid upsetting them by knowing more than them. "I know how you **feel**. It does look hard to use and it's certainly confusing until you get used to it. Most customers **felt** exactly the same as you do now. However, customers who bought the simpler model **found** they wished they had the features of this model. On the other hand, customers who bought this model **found** they soon got used to it. They were glad of the extra features. I can set this model up so it works simply. Later, when you're used to it, you can try some of the other features. That'll give you the best of both worlds, won't it?"

Are Roadblocks on price based on value or cash? — Customers may want items but think the prices too high for the benefits. Customers see a $20 value and you're asking $35. This *Roadblock* is on value.

Customers may see the value of an item but not be able to afford it. Customers who'd pay $200 for a watch may only have $150. This *Roadblock* is on cash. You can be sure the *Roadblock* is on cash when a customer says, "That's a pity. I've only got $20 to spend."

Some customers speak loosely. Customers without enough cash may let out frustration on the item. "What! $35 for that piece of junk." The *Roadblock* is on cash but it sounds as if it's on value. Customers may have a polite way of saying the price is too high. "I can't afford to spend that much." The *Roadblock* is on value but it sounds as if it's on cash.

With some words it's hard to separate value and cash. "It's too expensive."

Ask this question to find out if the *Roadblock* is on value or cash: "Is the price of this typewriter too high?" Then pause. Then ask this question: "Or is it more than you want to spend today?" Agree with the customer's *Roadblock* before you ask these questions. "It costs as much as that? That's quite a rip off." "I know how you feel, Sir. I feel the same way when I go shopping myself these days. Is the price of this typewriter too high?" Pause. "Or is it more than you want to spend today?"

Show more value for Roadblocks on value — Try a new *Show-&-tell* to give the item more value in the customer's eyes. "This umbrella is nice, but it's just too expensive." "Yes, it is expensive. It has a push button that opens it automatically. That means you can open it with one hand. That's useful when you're carrying a lot of parcels, isn't it?"

Show another item for Roadblocks on cash — Ask this question when the price is more than the customer wants to spend: "How much do you want to spend today?" Then *Show-&-tell* an item in the right price range. Know the prices of items so you can do this well.

Put Your Toe in the Water

Sellers come to a point when they feel customers probably will buy, but they're not quite sure. So they need to ask customers to buy in such a way that they can continue selling without losing face when the answer is "No."

Test the water — Sometimes when you ask customers to buy they say, "Yes" and that makes you feel good. But often they say, "No" and that can feel like plunging into ice-cold water. It takes courage to keep asking customers to buy when the usual answer is like a plunge into icy water. It's easy to back off and pretend it's polite to let customers ask to buy. It's easy to pretend it's normal to let customers ask to buy. Then there's little risk of hearing customers say, "No." That's the way to low sales.

Put your toe in the water first. That way you can tell what's going on. Sometimes you'll find you're in the water without any fuss. It was warm and you slid in without even noticing it. Customers buy with little effort on your part. Sometimes the water is chilly or icy cold and you pull your toe out. Customers aren't warm enough to buy. It's too early to make a sale. That's no problem. You only put your toe in. There's no loss of face. It's not the final word. Go on warming customers for a sale.

Suggest an Add-on to go with the main item — Act as if customers have already bought the main item. Skip asking customers to buy. Suggest extra items that naturally go with the main item.

Think of the extra items as improving customers' lives. Since we add them to the main item, we call them *Add-ons*: "How about a pair of prescription sunglasses to go with your new spectacles?" "How about a pull duck for your granddaughter to balance your grandson's tricycle?" "How about a high-speed hard disk to give your computer real data capability?"

Suggest an *Add-on* in one sentence. Its aim is to sell the main item.

Build each Add-on suggestion carefully — Make sure your suggestions have these parts:

Opening: "How about…" This opening makes sure you'll ask a question and is less pushy than others like, "You need…"

Add-on: the name of the *Add-on*. *Add-ons* in the examples are "sunglasses," "pull duck" and "hard disk."

Improver: a word or words that make the *Add-on* more desirable. Improvers in the examples are: "**prescription** sunglasses," "a pull-duck **for your granddaughter**" and "**high-speed** hard disk."

Reason: Give a reason for needing the *Add-on*. Reasons in the examples are "to go with," "to balance," "to give real data capability."

Ownership: Act as if customers already own the main item. Include "Your," or sometimes "You."

Item: Items in the examples are: "spectacles," "tricycle" and "computer." Describe the item so it stands out when possible. "Your **new** spectacles." "Your **grandson's** tricycle."

Act as if customers own and need the main item — The more you act as if customers own items, the more they'll buy them. Avoid going into a huddle with customers. Avoid asking customers to buy at this time. Act as if there's a natural and clear need for the *Add-on*. Make it seem that when smart customers buy the main item, they also buy the *Add-on*. The need isn't because the main item won't work without the *Add-on*. It's the stereo for the car rather than the wheels. Customers will enjoy the car more with the stereo.

Suggest the Add-on when customers go with you — You've opened and you've asked questions. You're giving your second or third *Show-&-tell*. You've gone around any *Roadblocks* in the way of the sale. The customer is receiving your *Show-&-tell* well. The customer is going with you. Customers may even signal that they'd like to buy. You're ready to suggest the *Add-on*.

Think of the Add-on as an improver rather than a need — Thinking of the *Add-on* as a need will limit your selling. The traditional *Add-ons* in a shoe store are the polish and the laces. Sell odds and ends like these to every customer. The real *Add-ons* are the shoe trees or a second and third pair of shoes. The *Add-on* often improves the main item. It can as easily improve a customer's life. The granddaughter's pull toy isn't a helper or an improver to the grandson's tricycle. It improves the grandmother's life—she'll cause more pleasure. Her sense of self-esteem will be that much greater.

Suggest upward Add-ons when you can — Upward *Add-ons* cost more than the main item. A customer comes in for shoelaces and leaves with shoelaces and shoes.

Grow and weed your stock of Add-ons — List *Add-ons* in the *Items* binder. Every so often write new *Add-ons*. Keep track of those that work and get rid of those that don't work.

Try different Add-ons — Write several *Add-ons* for each item you sell. Add a pair of long-distance glasses for the car to the pair of bifocals. Add a spare pair of reading glasses for the cabin. Add a pair of prescription sunglasses. Add a pair of glasses to use at the computer. Hard protective cases and lens cleaner are *After-sale Add-ons*. Suggest different *Add-ons* for different customers. Different customers respond to different *Add-ons*.

Handle the results of asking for Add-ons — Handle the three main results of asking for an *Add-on* like this:

1. *Customers buy the main item and the Add-on.* Try another *Add-on* or write the sale, whichever seems best. Customers will let you know if you try for too many *Add-ons*.

2. *Customers buy the main item but skip the Add-on.* Try another from your list of *Add-ons* or write the sale, whichever seems best.

3. *Customers object to buying the main item.* Keep asking questions. Begin with "Jim, for my information, please be kind enough and tell me, what is it that

you don't like about this jacket?" You're suggesting *Add-ons* too early if you get too many No Sales. Stop being so pushy.

Suggest After-sale Add-ons too — *After-sale Add-ons* are different from *Add-ons* to make sales. *After-sale Add-ons* are mainly odds and ends like the shoe polish for the shoes. Once you've sold the item, your chance of selling a big *Add-on* falls. Customers are already using the main item in their minds. They're too busy to pay attention even if they see the need for the *Add-on*.

Ask All Customers to Buy

It's nice when customers ask to buy, but that's not their job. It's the job of sellers to ask customers to buy.

Ask all customers to buy — Follow the simple rule of asking all customers to buy and watch your sales go up. Tests show that sellers only ask 40% of customers to buy. Customers who want to buy often leave stores upset with poor service. Plan on asking customers to buy when you start schmoozing with them. Skip asking customers to buy only when they say, "I'll take it" before you get the chance to ask them to buy. Sometimes you'll get the chance to ask customers to buy while finding out why they want to buy or early in your *Show-&-tell*. You'll usually ask customers to buy by putting your toe in the water. Ask customers to buy when you finish your *Show-&-tell*s without making a sale.

Let customers say, "No" for themselves — Let customers choose whether to buy for themselves. Saying, "No" for customers gives you poor sales. Sometimes sellers pass over customers who don't look as if they're going to buy. Buyers don't have any special look. Sellers of expensive items often pass over customers who look as if they can't afford to buy. Some rich customers look just like that. Some customers who look as if they can afford expensive items are broke. Sometimes customers treat themselves. Perhaps a customer can't afford an item, but this time it doesn't matter. Even people living in poverty buy luxuries.

Ask, shut up, and let customers answer — After you ask customers to buy, <u>shut up and let them answer</u>. **Ask them to buy, then shut up.** Say nothing. Avoid starting to talk because the silence makes you feel foolish. Give no extra reasons for buying the item. Push aside any temptation to offer to lower the price. Just keep quiet. Let customers speak next. There are only two results if you speak before customers answer. You'll kill the sale or you'll sell the items at a give-away price. Once you've made your pitch let the customers do the selling for you. Avoid butting into this important process. Customers are working overtime listing the pluses and the minuses. Customers who want items try to find reasons for buying them. Always give customers enough time to talk themselves into buying. It's rude to butt in while customers are still thinking and the only reward of butting in is poor sales.

Teach yourself to wait for an answer. Most customers find it hard to make the choice to buy, especially for expensive items. Wait through long silences if you must. Customers are working for you. You'll destroy what customers are building for you if you try to push the process along.

Keep eye contact with customers while they're deciding to buy. All you need is a quiet, friendly, questioning smile.

Ask customers to buy as soon as they're ready to buy — The *Steps for Selling* are the normal steps for selling. Watch for out-of-step sales. Ask customers to buy when they're ready to buy. This may happen early in a *Show-&-tell*.

Greeting, schmoozing and finding out why customers want to buy may blend into one as customers signal that they want to buy. Ask them to buy right away. Extra *Showing-&-telling* may make customers back off. Top sellers use the least work needed to make a sale. They move quickly to the next sale.

Seeing customers are ready to buy is a skill that grows with practice. Sometimes customers send signals that they want to buy. You become alert to a feeling that grows as you interact with customers. It's hard to describe this feeling. You know customers are coming along with you. You feel customers are ready to buy. Some customers become ready to buy smoothly. Other customers put up many *Roadblocks* along the way. These customers will stay with you if you overcome their *Roadblocks*. As soon as you're sure customers are ready to buy, put all other plans aside and ask them to buy.

Sell early in the Steps for Selling when you can — Here are ways of asking customers to buy during the *Steps for Selling*:

Reflect a question with question: "Is there a smaller one?" "Would you like the smaller one?" Avoid answering "Yes" or "No." Reflect questions back to customers. Customers often answer "Yes." You reflect well when you know the items on hand well.

Meet a comment with "This or that": "This style coat is attractive." "Would you like it in green or red?" A possible answer is, "I'll take the green one."

Tell the price: "How much is this coat?" "Four hundred." Sometimes customers ask the price while you're finding out why they want to buy or *Showing-&-telling*. Tell the price and you've asked them to buy. Allow time for customers to answer. Either it's a sale or keep on selling.

Put your toe in the water: This is so important that it's one of the *Steps for Selling*. You'll rarely need to ask customers to buy directly when you master this step well.

Choose other ways of asking customers to buy — Sometimes it's up to sellers to move ahead with the sale. Try these ways of asking customers to buy when they seem right:

Act as if you've made the sale and ring: A customer went for your *Show-&-tell*. Act as if you've made a sale. Lead the customer to the cash register and begin ringing or begin writing a sales slip. Say nothing.

Act as if you've made the sale and wrap: A customer went for your *Show-&-tell*. Act as if you've made a sale. Say, "Let me wrap it for you," or, "Let me put it in a bag for you."

Cash or charge: A customer went for your *Show-&-tell*. Act as if you've made a sale. Ask, "Will that be cash or charge?"

Sell by reference: A customer wants to buy but raises a doubt. Refer to what happened with other customers. "Yes, they're the strongest we know of. We sell lots to daycare centers and they love them." Often the customer will now ask to buy. Otherwise, ask the customer to buy.

Make a summary: Make a summary of the main points of your *Show-&-tell*. Refresh the customer's memory. Then ask the customer to buy the item.

Ask customers to buy directly: "Would you like to buy the typewriter?" This is the simplest way of asking customers to buy. Sellers don't use it often enough. Ask customers to buy directly when you can think of no other way of asking them to buy.

Be careful with Last Chance — Be honest with *Last Chance*. The seller says this is the last chance to buy the item. Buy it now or never. "We've only three left and they're the last before Christmas." "This price only holds good until Friday." Make sure what you claim is true. Lies will kill future sales.

Last Chance often tries to hurry customers along. Many sellers use *Last Chance* to force a sale but it works poorly. There's little point in telling customers it's their last chance to buy something before they've decided to buy it. Customers will only hurry to buy something they want.

Last Chance kills sales you've already asked for. Sellers who don't wait for customers to answer kill sales with *Last Chance* regularly. They ask customers to buy. Then the silence of waiting for an answer frightens them, so they break the silence to get something to happen. They use *Last Chance* to push the sale along but instead *No Sale* happens regularly. It's no time to put pressure on when customers are deciding for themselves.

Customers usually know about *Last Chance* from advertising. Tell them the facts if they ask you about a *Last Chance*. Try *Last Chance* only when you're sure customers want to buy. Customers may want to buy but want to put off buying. *Last Chance* may help here, but take care. Some customers act as if they want to buy later as a way of saying, "No." With these customers you still need to find out what they want to buy and show them its value.

Sidestep *Knockout*s

Just when sellers think they've made the sale, customers come up with *Knockout*s that stop the sale dead in the water. Only an unprepared seller takes the *Knockout* punch on the chin. Sellers who sidestep the *Knockout* punch either make the sale or get information to help them continue selling.

Wise-up to Knockouts — Customers use certain sentences by habit to say they're not buying. These sentences are *Knockouts*. Customers use them to stop a sale dead. These are the most common *Knockouts*: "I need to think about it." "I need to sleep on it." "I need to shop around before I buy." "I need to talk about it with my partner."[35]

Knockouts often hide *Roadblocks* customers find hard to talk about. Customers also use *Knockouts* to put off making decisions. They may know the items are right for them but they delay anyway. Once customers put off the decision to buy, chances are they won't buy. They get busy with other things and forget their needs and wants. The seller's job is to help customers over this hurdle. The seller's job is to get them home with their needs and wants satisfied.

Agree with Knockouts — "I can understand that you want to think about it. It's certainly an important decision."

Get permission and ask a question — Ask permission to ask a question. "Before you go, may I ask you a question?" Wait for the customer to say, "Yes."

Fish for the true reason for the Knockout — Ask whether customers like the item. Ask a *Closed Question*. "Do you like the typewriter?"

Backtrack when the answer is "No" — Know what customers need and want before you *Show-&-tell* items. You've shown an item a customer doesn't like. This means you were off the mark in knowing the needs and wants, so ask again about needs and wants. Get the true picture and *Show-&-tell* a different item. All sellers have to backtrack like this now and then. Should you find yourself doing this often, it's time to review the earlier *Steps for Selling*.

---

[35] The partner may be a wife or husband, girl friend or boy friend or any other person the customer relates to. Sometimes it's a business partner, an adviser or a boss.

Look for a hidden "No" when the answer is "Yes" — Ask two to four short questions to refresh points used in the *Show-&-tell*. "Will the memory really be useful to you?" "Is it really light enough for you to carry around?" Ask questions to find out needs and wants if you hit a "No." Then *Show-&-tell* a different item.

Ask about price when there's no hidden "No" — Ask, "How do you feel about the price?" Follow the normal steps for handling *Roadblocks* on price. Find out if the *Roadblock* is based on value or cash.

Ask the customer to buy when the price is right — The price is right. All the fishing returned "Yes" answers. So try this approach: "This typewriter seems well suited to your needs. It's a shame to go home without it, isn't it?"

Go around the Partner's Knockout — Customers may stand firm against buying without a partner's OK. "Yes, but I need to talk it over with my partner."[1]

Try, "I can understand that. Tell me—you know your partner. What do you think your partner might not like about the typewriter?" This may bring out hidden *Roadblocks* customers still have. It may give you the chance to build up the customer against fuss the partner may put up. The *Partner's Knockout* may sound foolish when the customer voices it. This may lead the customer to buy.

Offer the Buyer Protection Plan when a Partner's Knockout sticks — The *Buyer Protection Plan* is a money back guarantee. Say, "I can understand your need to talk with your partner. But why spoil the surprise? Since you like the typewriter so well, why not take it with you. We'll certainly return your money if your partner doesn't agree with your choice. You have our word on that."

Save the *Buyer Protection Plan* for the second time the customer raises the Partner's *Knockout*. Treat it like any other *Knockout* the first time it comes up. Customers may still stand firm against buying. "I'd really prefer to bring my partner here." Answer, "That's just fine. I look forward to meeting your partner when you return." There are customers who'll only buy with a partner's OK.

Stop comparison shoppers — These shoppers want the item but they want to check prices in other stores. Some promise to stop back if our price is best. This lets them feel less guilt about the time they spent with you. The chance of a comparison shopper returning is low. You're charging $100. After sweating through three widely separated stores and finding $95, $100 and $105, it's getting late. The customer, who's now tired and cranky, buys at $105 in the last store. Stop this foolish waste of time before it begins.

Try this approach: "I can understand that you want the best value for money. Of course, me knowing our price is good isn't the same as you finding that out for yourself. There are always slight differences in prices from store to store. Perhaps you can save yourself a few dollars if you're willing to put in time and effort on a hot day like this. On the other hand, you can take this typewriter now. You can soon be at home using it in comfort instead of running around town. Then you'll be glad that you didn't waste that time and effort. Doesn't that sound better to you?"

Make a polite good-bye when customers still want to look in other stores. "Well then, I wish you good hunting, and look forward to your return." There are real comparison shoppers. There are people killing time by wandering from store to store.

Keep Customers Busy While You Write Up Sales

Customers who continue to browse while sellers write up sales often buy something extra.

Get customers to look around — Often you do some paperwork to finish a sale. Perhaps it's a credit card sale. Perhaps you use handwritten sales slips. Take the credit card and direct customers to a display. Something related to the sale is best. Say, "I'll leave you looking at these ties while I write up your items." Add it to the sale when customers buy another item.

Add on needed odds and ends close to items — This is the time to add on simple basic needs. Add on the shoe polish and the shoelaces for the shoes.

Add on other odds and ends close to items — Try adding something less basic when customers take basic needs. Try the shoe trees for the shoes.

Add on other odds and ends — Offer items less close to the main item. For customers buying shoes, suggest a tie.

Sell only a few Add-ons — You can pile on the basic *Add-ons*. That shows you think about customers' needs. After that, offer one or two *Add-ons* only. Parading the whole store puts too much pressure on customers.

Make sure customers take their credit cards — Making sure customers take their credit cards is part of the paperwork.

Follow the Steps for the Cash Drawer

Chapter 11 *List Sales* includes the section *Work the Cash Drawer*, which is the basic training for using the cash drawer. Review this material as part of the *Steps for Selling*, and put it together with the training for the particular method of listing sales—by hand, by mechanical or electronic cash register or by a computer sales system.

Ask, "How Did You Hear about Our Store?"

The store must know where its customers come from. It must know how well its ads work.

Keep track of where our customers come from — Find out where all our customers come from. Ask new customers, "How did you hear about our store?" Write the answers on the *Customer Flow Sheet*. Write the answer for every sale. We only want answers from customers who buy. We want to know where our buyers came from, not where our lookers came from.

For known customers ask, "What brought you into our store today, Mrs. Jones?"

Know which ads draw customers — Ads are expensive and many of them don't work. We advertise based on feedback showing that ads work. It's important to ask where our customers come from. Ask regular customers if they saw the ad. Ask, "How did you hear about our store?" even if we're not advertising. We need to know where our customers come from before placing an ad as well as after placing an ad. Then we can see what changes the ad made.

Register Customers and Register Sales

Knowing who your customers are is important for your store. Fill in *Customer Registration Sheets* for new customers. Then keep them up to date.

Customer Registration Sheet

First Name   David   Last Name   Bland   Phone   (206)   123-1234

Apartment #   1705   Street #   7399   Street Name   Sycamore Avenue

Town   Seattle   State/Province   WA   Zip/Postal Code   98117

Birthsign/Birthday   Pisces

Registered by   Catherine Johnson   Date   29 March 1992

dd	mmm	yy	No.	Total		dd	mmm	yy	No.	Total
29	Mar	92	56	89						
13	Apr	92	17	37						
		92		126						
10	Feb	93	27	28						
17	Jun	93	55	43						
23	Aug	93	17	38						
		93		109						
		All		235						
12	Jan	94	12	87						

Say, "Please let me put you on our customer list" — These words up the chance of customers going along with you. You were polite. You asked a favor. Most customers will want to help you. Avoid saying "Are you on our customer list yet?"

Or, "Would you like me to add you to our customer list?" The stress is different. It sounds as if the seller's willing to do a favor for the customer. Busy customers will say, "Don't bother."

Answer customers who ask why you register them — Some customers ask why you're registering them. Choose from these answers: "We try to know our customers." "We let our registered customers know about special events which are only for them." "We have a monthly drawing for our registered customers only. That's in addition to our regular monthly drawing." "We have a special Christmas drawing for our registered customers only. That's in addition to our regular Christmas drawing."

Register customers — Fill in the blanks on the top part of the *Customer Registration Sheet*. Keep the *Customer Registration Sheets* in the *Customers* binder.

Try for birthday by asking for birth sign — You can send birthday cards to your customers when you know birthdays. It's hard to ask for a birthday without asking for date of birth. Asking customers for date of birth is too personal. It's too close to asking age and will drive many customers away. Instead, ask customers for their birth signs. This works well if you're honestly curious about birth signs and can ask naturally. Some customers who don't know their signs will tell you their birthday. Even if all you get is the birth sign, you'll be close to the birthday. You'll build strong bonds with customers interested in birth signs. Sellers interested in birth signs do well at this.

Use phone numbers as reference numbers — Write the phone number at the top right of the *Customer Registration Sheet*. Some customers refuse to give a phone number. Any other number will do. Try a credit card number or the number of an apartment plus the street number. Make sure the number looks different from a phone number. Customer number 223-1234 should be a phone number rather than apartment 223, 1234 Marine Drive.

Enter all customers in the monthly drawing — Respect the wishes of customers who don't want to register. Say, "That's fine. Let me be sure that you get into our monthly drawing. Please let me write your phone number on this slip in case you win." The slip is your copy of the cash register receipt. Afterwards, register the customer as a phone number only. Respect the wishes of customers who won't take part in the drawing. Some customers are just tired of free drawings.

Remember registered customers by name — Sometimes customers will say, "I'm already on the list." Say, "I'm sorry I didn't recognize you. Did I put you on the list?" For "Yes," say, "I'm embarrassed. My name's Catherine. What's your name again? I'll try to do better next time." For "No," say, "My name's Catherine. What's your name? I'll try to remember it for next time."

Register sales to registered customers — Write customers' phone numbers on copies of their receipts. Say, "Let me write your phone number for this month's drawing." Register the sale when the customer's gone. Enter date, receipt number and whole dollar total.

Total the sales to registered customers — Total sales at least once a year. Total sales before special advertising mailings. Send some mailings and special offers only to your big spenders.

Praise Customers for Buying

Keep interest in customers after they've bought. Customers won't respect you if you suddenly lose interest after you've got what you want. Keep that interest by praising them for their purchases. This simple step helps to make sure the items the customer bought stay bought.

Let customers know their choices were right — Let customers know someone else likes the items they buy. "Mrs. Johnson, I think the dress you chose is simply wonderful."

Before customers buy items, you're the seller. Any praise from you sounds like part of selling. You're no longer selling when customers have bought items. Your praise has great effect.

Follow a pattern when you praise — Put yourself where customers are. Praise them warmly. Praise like this:

Name: "Mrs. Johnson…" Get names from the sales slips, credit cards, checks, and so on. Better still, find out names as you schmooze. Even better, know all regular customers by name.

I statement: "I think…" Make it clear it's your feeling. It's nothing to do with the store.

Item: "the dress…" Name the item.

You statement: "you chose…" This makes it clear the choice was hers. You may have been of great help but she made the choice.

Praise: "is simply wonderful." Believe the praise you give. The more you involve yourself in the praise, the better it is. This is the time to gush if you're a gusher. Sometimes it's hard to praise an item honestly. Remember the item pleased the customer. "Mrs. Johnson, I know you're just going to love that dress."

Praise to be polite — Giving praise is polite. It shows you care. Giving praise makes you stand out in a world that's too busy to show care. Praise makes the buyer feel good. Take this chance to make someone feel good.

Praise to reward yourself — You worked with the customer to make the sale. You made the sale happen. As you praise the customer you also send yourself a message: "Hey, I made a sale. That was a job well done." You make yourself feel good when you make someone else feel good.

Praise to build Personal Customers — Praise is important in building *Personal Customers*. Soon customers come to the store asking for you by name. They call ahead to be sure that you'll be there to serve them.

Praise to cut down returns — Some customers take items home and have second thoughts about them. Sometimes customers' partners or friends don't like the items they bought. They knock them, they mock them and they laugh at them. As a result customers sometimes suffer a change of heart. They go through *Buyers Remorse*. They regret what they bought and that results in returns.

It's to your good to cut down returns. That way your commissions stay with you. Customers like the items they buy. Praise the customers for buying the items. Your praise makes customers strong when others don't like the items. They stand up for their values when they have you behind them. Nobody can beat your power to sway customers' feelings. You're first in line to talk to new owners about their items. Your support locks customers onto their items.

Include inside information in the praise — As you sell you find out customers' wants, needs and dreams. You see how they react to the items they buy. You know the most important benefits for customers. Include them in your praise: "Mrs. Johnson, I think the dress you chose is simply wonderful. It really flatters your figure and the color is just right with your tan."

Invite Customers Back

When sellers use the *Steps for Selling* to sell they gain the trust of customers. Trust is the beginning of a friendship. When we meet new people we'd like to have as friends, or when old friends visit, we invite them back. Good sellers develop their friendships with customers and they see it pay of in higher sales.

Invite customers back to build Personal Customers — Many customers drop in to see you when you invite them back. Inviting customers back is a fine way to build *Personal Customers*. They come to the store to see you. They ask for you by name.

Be positive when you invite customers back — Take strong positive stands. "Fred, as soon as you've got your stereo installed, please stop by and let me know how much you're enjoying it." Fred is going to enjoy his stereo. "Mrs. Johnson, will you stop by after the party and let me know how many compliments you received on your new dress?" Mrs. Johnson is going to receive compliments.

Follow a plan when you invite customers — Invites are one sentence with four parts:

Name: "Fred," "Mrs. Johnson." Get names from sales slips, credit cards, checks, and so on. Better still, find out names as you schmooze. Even better, know all regular customers by name.

Your item: "your stereo," "your new dress." Stress that customers own the items.

As soon as possible: "as soon as you've got your stereo installed," and "after the party" ask for action right away. Ask for action while the item and the benefits are still fresh in customers' minds.

Positive command: "let me know how much you're enjoying it," "let me know how many compliments you received." A positive command makes sure customers think positively about items. Close the door on faint praise and on negatives. "Let me know if you're enjoying it," is wrong. "Let me know if you get any compliments," is insulting.

Cut down returns — Sometimes sellers cause returns by what they say. "You can always bring it back if you don't like it." Or, "Be sure to let me know if you have any problems." Such talk makes small doubts grow into large doubts. It moves customers to have a change of heart. You get returns when you invite returns. Positive commands to enjoy items make small doubts smaller and guard against a change of heart. Take returns but don't plant the idea of returns in customers' minds.

Ask for a favor before inviting customers back — Ask customers to do you a favor. "Mrs. Jones, will you do me a favor?" Wait for the reply before going on. Most customers will agree. Then invite customers to return.

Receive Invited Customers warmly — Customers do return and report to you. Customers who pass the store regularly often return. Remember the customers you invite and why you invited them. Remember names and items without customers reminding you. Take an interest in the report you asked for. Praise the item once again.

Invite when customers buy for special events — Events that occur once, or just a few times, in a person's life are special. These include: births, christenings, graduations, special birthdays (21st, 40th, 60th, and so on,) engagements, weddings, divorces, retirements, and deaths.

Big changes are other special events. They include: new schools, new colleges, new apartments or houses, job interviews, new jobs, promotions, new hobbies, and new lovers.

Then there are the special events that occur each year. These include: birthdays, wedding anniversaries, religious festivals, vacations, the seasons, and new fashions.

Customers give and receive invitations to parties and receptions. They receive guests and visit friends. They go to sports and cultural events. Unexpected events are always exciting. So are events which customers see as rewards. The main ones are going to conferences or on special business trips.

For many sales the item itself is a special event. It's exciting when someone stops thinking about a new stereo and buys it. It's easy to pass over the excitement when you sell stereos every day. Keep in contact with how customers feel. Look at sales as customers see them.

Hold back on asking Invited Customers to buy — Pushing *Invited Customers* for more sales will backfire on you. On the other hand be alert for their needs.

One beauty of *Invited Customers* is they often want to buy. *Invited Customers* often have accessories on their minds. They couldn't see the need for an accessory before but they do now. They couldn't afford an accessory before but they can now. Some *Invited Customers* return long after the invitation. They may wait until their next shopping trip. They're likely to be ready to buy.

A second beauty of *Invited Customers* is they seek you out. Congratulations, your list of *Personal Customers* is growing.

Say, "Good-bye"

It's as unthinkable to let a customer leave the store without saying good-bye as it is to let a guest leave your house without saying good-bye.

Say, "Good-bye" to all customers — Say, "Good-bye" to all customers as they leave the store. You greeted customers on entry and made eye contact. You kept up the eye contact during the sale. Keep that eye contact and concern until customers leave the store. Round it off by saying, "Good-bye." Any polite "Good-bye" is OK. "Good-bye, Mr. Smith," or "Good-bye, Sir," is good. Call customers by name if you can.

Perhaps there are also some *Tested Lookers* leaving the store. Try to say, "Good-bye" to them as well.

Go with customers when it's right — Always see customers to the door. — Some customers buy a lot or buy items that are awkward to carry. They like it when sellers help them to their car.

Shape Up Displays and Storage

When customers leave, it's time to shape up the store. How do the displays look? Are the stored items stored neatly? This is the step that makes the difference between a sloppy store and a store where it's a pleasure to shop. Shaping up pays off in extra sales.

Shape up displays you sold from — Shape up any displays you mess up as you *Show-&-tell*. Replace items sold from displays with items from storage. Put the displays in shape as you replace the items.

Unless there's an automated system that tracks inventory in real-time, sellers will have to update an *Item Tally Sheet* from copies of cash register receipts or sales slips.

Sellers will still need to keep track of the display items that need replacing. Usually they work from the *Item Tally Sheet* or copies of the cash register receipts.

Sellers need to check tally marks or receipts as they replace items. Then it's easy to catch up if they serve another customer before they replace all items. Circle any item that runs out.

Sellers go straight to storage places when they know them. Otherwise, they check storage places on the *Price List*. That's quicker than hunting through the storage places.

Make out *Restocking Slips* to help you restock:

124-0368	Gtone Hoops Clasp	1 pr	Drawer 5b	Case
227-1876	Qtz Watch	1	Drawer 17c	Case
124-0266	Rhin Pearl Cab Pierced	1 pr	Drawer 5b	Case
356-1278	Suede Belt Red	1	Hook 7	Rack

Write on recycled paper cut to 4¼″ by 5½″. Throw *Restocking Slips* away after restocking. Used slips lying around make the store look messy.

Shape up displays in order of need:

1. Replace single item displays.

2. Shape up any displays that fall near zero.

3. Shape up displays of hot selling items.

4. Shape up other displays.

Shape up displays messed up by customers — Customers mess up displays as they look through the store. Shape up the displays between sales.

Replace sold out displays with fill-in displays — Sometimes you sell all of an item in storage and most or all of the display. Fill the gap in the display with something else. Perhaps the display next to it should have 10 items. Put out 20 items instead. Perhaps the gap is on display counter 15. Put out a copy of a display that's on counter 12. Make a note of fill-in displays on the *Fill-in Display List* in *Daily*. Replace the original display when a new shipment comes in.

Replace extra items brought from storage — Sometimes sellers bring items from storage to *Show-&-tell* them. Return any left over as soon as customers leave. Put the items where they belong and keep storage in shape. Sales go down when the storage areas become messy. Sellers lose sales when they have to hunt for the items they need to sell.

Put selling ahead of shape-up — Shape up between customers. As long as you're making sales, the displays can be out of shape. Shape up for several sales after a burst of selling.

Do the After-sale Paperwork

Always do the paperwork right away. Paperwork done right away flies away. Paperwork left till later piles up and bogs the store down. Handling the paperwork after each sale is an important step in selling.

Update the Customers binder — Enter new customers or the latest sales in the *Customers* binder.

Update the Items binder — Enter any new *Show-&-tells* used. Enter any new comments on existing *Show-&-tells*.

Put Problems in Selling Notes in the To Manager binder — Sellers note any selling problems they had during the *Steps for Selling*. The manager reviews *Problems in Selling Notes* with sellers at least once each week. This is a typical note:

Thursday, Sep 8th 1994
I need help getting comparison shoppers to stay and buy.
Cynthia Jones

Make the notes on 3-hole punched paper from the *Recycle* binder.

Put Store Problems Notes in the To Manager binder — Sellers let the manager know about any store related problems that come up. Write the notes on 3-hole punched paper from the *Recycle* binder. This is a typical note:

Thursday, Sep 8th 1994

Pricing would be faster if we had another label gun. Then we could have 2 guns for standard labels and one gun for stick-tight labels. Often there are two sellers pricing at the same time who need to use both kinds of labels.

Cynthia Jones.

Write Thank-you Notes

When there are no customers in the store, sellers get down to writing *Thank-you Notes*. These are a great way to keep in touch with customers and to make customer feel good about the store and the seller who wrote the note. Customers who feel good about a store buy more from that store. Customers who feel good about a seller buy from that seller.

Write Thank-you Notes to build Personal Customers — *Thank-you Notes* are great for building your list of *Personal Customers*. The reasons you praise sales and invite customers back are also reasons to write *Thank-you Notes*. Avoid over-kill. Make an invitation or send a *Thank-you Note*. It's too much to use both for the same item.

These are other reasons for writing *Thank-you Notes*:

- A customer helped you.

- A customer left the store upset by your service.

- You're a new seller.

- You dealt with a customer poorly.

- You missed a *Personal Customer* when you were busy.

Learn from examples — Adapt the examples to your store.

Dear Mrs. Kovacs,

Thank you for being so kind to me when you were in the store the other day. I was so nervous. It was my first week in the store. In fact I've never sold anything before. Everything was new to me. You were a real help to me.

Sincerely,

Mahasti Kowal.

Dear Mrs. Nielsen,

I know you'll receive a lot of compliments on your new dress. It looked so good on you. Thanks for stopping by.

Yours,

Catherine Bloor.

Dear George,
I really enjoyed talking with you in the store the other day. I'm glad that in the end you decided the memory typewriter was for you. I know they're a lot of fun. I use my father's one all the time. Stop by and let me know how much you're enjoying it next time you're shopping.
Sincerely,
Peter Davidson.

Dear Mr. Hughes,
I'll bet you were a big hit at Michael's birthday party. The gifts you bought were so wonderful. They'd thrill any child. Thanks for stopping by the store. I enjoyed sharing in your excitement.
Sincerely,
Ken Ouellette.

Dear Mrs. Teglasi,
I hope they've finished remodeling your kitchen and you've been able to use your new kitchen machine. I know it'll save you a lot of time. You'll enjoy the recipes that come with it. The one for Caesar Sauce on page 15 is one of my favorites. Thanks for stopping by the store.
Sincerely,
David Garner.

Write Thank-you Notes by hand on blank stationery — Your *Thank-you Notes* are personal messages. Write them by hand. Write on blank paper and write the store's address by hand. Avoid anything printed, rubber stamped, photocopied, word-processed or the like. Leave the return address off the envelope. It gives your letter an air of mystery when it arrives.

Keep surprises secret — Anniversary cards are wonderful for *Thank-you Notes* when customers buy gifts for their own anniversaries. Otherwise, send *Thank-you Notes* after the event. That way you won't spoil surprises.

Send colored picture postcards — Colored picture postcards are nice for *Thank-you Notes*. Local views remind visitors of their visit. You'll be on their minds when they next visit.

Stick large colorful stamps on colored envelopes — It's fun to get letters and cards with nice stamps. Make the full amount of postage up with several small-value stamps instead of one full-value stamp. Stay away from small plain stamps and go for big flashy stamps. Lay in a store of nice stamps before they go out of print. It's a big mistake to use a postage meter.

Colored envelopes add interest. People like to open mail that looks interesting. Colored paper goes with colored envelopes. Colored paper can match the envelope or differ from it. Try different mixes until you come up with a winner. Change colors from time to time.

Send cards to the items — Instead of *Thank-you Notes* to customers, try sending cards to the items. Send birthday cards—Christmas cards are corny. Birthday cards to items get you back in contact with customers who haven't been in for a while.

Send flowers or gifts — Send flowers or gifts to customers who buy expensive items.

Write Thank-you Notes for items over the Marker Price — *Thank-you Notes* work best when you send them for expensive items. Avoid sending them for common or low cost items. Avoid sending them for many small items that add up to a big bill. Have a *Marker Price* for writing *Thank-you Notes* posted in *Daily*. Send *Thank-you Notes* only for items costing more than the *Marker Price*.

Note Thank-you Notes in the Customers binder — Make notes in the *Customers* binder when you send *Thank-you Notes*. Keep track of how well you're looking after your customers.

CHAPTER 16

SUPPORT THE *STEPS FOR SELLING*

Once the *Steps for Selling* are in place and sellers feel comfortable with them, it's time to move on to supporting them. None of the support items are distinct steps themselves, but instead form a background for using the *Steps for Selling*. Some of the support items we've met before, but it's worth stressing them again. Other support items are completely new.

Know What You Sell

Review the section *Know What You Sell* in Chapter 14 *Tune Up for the Steps for Selling*.

Know Prices

Customers expect sellers to know prices. Customers trust sellers who answer price questions right away without mistakes. Sellers feel like the experts they are when prices are at their finger tips. They feel sure of themselves and they sell more.

Take pleasure in telling prices — Customers ask prices of items. They ask prices even when there are clear price signs and price labels on the items. Sometimes they overlook the signs and labels. Sometimes they need to hear the price to help them buy. Hearing the price can be an important step in getting used to the price.

Avoid making customers feel stupid for asking prices. Sellers do that when they act as if it's a bother to tell prices. Sellers do that when they tell customers that prices are on the signs or on the labels. Sellers do that when they go to items and read price labels. Let customers feel it's natural to ask the price. Let prices come from your head. Tell them pleasantly, with a smile on your face.

Remember that telling prices is asking to buy — You've asked customers to buy when they ask prices and you tell prices. Shut up and let customers answer when you tell prices. You're past "Just looking" when customers ask prices but don't buy. Carry on selling by schmoozing or finding out why customers want to buy.

Salami prices to learn them — It's a big job to learn all the prices, so salami the job. Write a list of prices of 10 or 15 items each day. Fold it so you hide the prices. Carry it with you and test yourself until you know the prices. Learn part of the *Price List* each day. Handle some items and look at their prices each day.

Keep up with prices — Keep up with prices from *Price Change Sheets* in *Daily*. Learn prices of new items from *News Sheets* in *Daily*. It blows everything when a seller tells the wrong price.

Wait for customers to ask prices — Customers will ask prices soon enough. Until then, act as if customers are willing and able to pay the prices. It's the same as asking customers to buy when you talk price. Talk price too early and you risk losing the sale.

Treat prices matter-of-factly — The prices are reasonable and normal for the items we sell. Matter-of-fact statements let customers know this. Sellers lose sales when they say they're sorry about prices. Hints of apology, reservations or regrets in a seller's tone of voice or manner will kill sales.

Know only today's price — Make the sale today at today's price. It's between you and the store if you know about past or future prices. "Pity you missed it on sale yesterday for $300," will kill your sale of a $500 item. "Next week this will be 25% off," is strong enough to turn a sale into a *No Sale*. There's no promise of making the lower price sale next week.

Never invite customers to check out prices — Take pride in our prices without inviting customers to compare them. This boast will cost you sales: "Our price is the lowest in town. You'll see that if you check other stores." This gives customers a good reason for more delay. Many customers meant to shop around. Now there's almost a command to do so.

Contract Customers to Stay

Sellers who have good ways for stacking customers up will sell more than those without them.

Pay attention to customers or they'll leave — Customers often leave while you're busy selling. Suppose you're the only seller on the floor and you're busy selling to a customer when another customer shows up. Most sellers ignore the second customer until they finish with the first one. Chances are the second customer waits a while but soon gets unhappy. Customers get upset when you ignore them. They feel like objects instead of customers. Many leave the store. Others stay, but they're in a bad mood when you start to sell to them.

Get customers to agree to stay — Customers who agree to stay will stay. Most customers will agree to stay if you ask them. You've paid attention to them—now they feel like customers instead of objects. Asking customers to stay turns tigers into pussy cats. Hard-boiled and cranky customers stay. Customers in a hurry stay longer than they should.

Waiting becomes their decision when customers agree to stay. Customers will wait when waiting was their decision. They'll be in a better mood for buying than customers who waited without agreeing to wait.

Get an OK to make a contract — It's rude to break off selling to one customer to talk to another customer. Get an OK to talk to the other customer. "Do you mind if I just let this customer know I'll be with her soon?" Wait for the OK. Then say, "Thanks, I'll be right back." A good break point often comes while the first customer looks at an item. "May I just step aside while you're looking and let this customer know I'll be with her soon?"

Make the contract — Say, "Can you please hang on a minute while I finish with this other customer?"

Make the contract stick — Follow with, "Will that be OK?" when customers agree to the contract. It's a hard contract for customers to break when they agree to it twice.

Return and thank the first customer quickly — Avoid getting sidetracked by the second customer. You have a commitment to the first customer. Say, "Thanks for letting me talk to the other customer." Then go on selling to the first customer.

Go to the second customer as soon as you finish — It's important to keep your part of the contract. Hold off on *Background Jobs* and other customers.

Thank the second customer for waiting — Say, "Thanks for letting me finish with the other customer."

Avoid contracts to stay while you do a job — Only contract customers to stay for emergency jobs. Customers will understand you mopping the floor where a kid threw up. Most other jobs send a message that you have more important things to do than bother with customers.

Reverse contract with reps — You may be talking to a rep when a customer enters the store. Contract to leave the rep to sell to the customer.

Focus on Customers

When sellers have customers everything else in the store takes a back seat to them.

Stick with your customers — Finish with the customers you start with. Stay with customers until they leave the store, or until you're sure they're lookers.

Stay with customers beyond the sale. It leaves a bad impression when you ring a sale and turn off your interest. Sales are pleasant social events. Treat customers like friends. Take an interest in them. Pay attention to them and to their needs. See them from the store pleasantly.

Add interest in customers to the right words. You see robots using the right words at supermarket checkout stands. "How are you doing today?"—rings groceries up without waiting for a reply. "Have a good day"—moves right on to the next customer in line without looking at you.

Keep good eye contact and hold your body well — Show your interest in customers through your eye contact. Let your body language show your interest in customers.

Smile and be pleasant — Keep smiling and customers will be on your side. Smiles are catching. It's hard to be down on someone who smiles. Be pleasant. Leave your personal troubles at the shop door.

Deal with butt-ins — You've been a customer when another seller butts in on your seller. Suddenly, your seller's ignoring you to deal with the other seller's problem. This rudeness is out of place. Bring other sellers back to standard if they forget themselves and butt in on you.

Turn aside the butt-in. "I'm busy with Mr. Jones right now, John. I'll get back to you later." Apologize to the customer. "I'm sorry for the interruption, Mr. Jones." Let the other seller know your store's standard. After the customer has gone, remind John that butt-ins are out of place in this store.

Notice Buying Signals

Buying Signals are words or actions customers use to say "I'm close to buying" in a roundabout way.

Watch for shorthand for "I'll take it" — Some customers buy by asking how they can pay. "Do you take personal checks?" It's safe to act as if these customers have asked to buy. Customers are close to buying when they think of taking the item home. "Do you deliver?" Customers are close to buying when they think of living with the item. "How long is the warranty?"

Watch for the moments when your silence sells the item — Customers have asked to buy when they ask the price. Tell the price, shut up and let customers finish the sale. You're past "Just looking" when a sale doesn't follow a customer asking the price. Go on with schmoozing or finding out why customers want to buy.

Customers want to buy when they ask a partner. "What do you think, John?" The ball is now in the partner's court. Let the partner speak next—you'll kill the sale if you step in. Either you make a sale or the partner puts up *Roadblocks* to the sale. After the partner speaks, sell to the partner. You know the customer who asked the partner the question wants to buy. Go around the *Roadblocks* the partner puts up.

It's time for you to shut up when customers show signs of deep thought. They're working at selling the item to themselves for you. They look as if they're stewing things over. They may pace the floor. They may stroke their chin. They may fold and unfold their arms, and so on.

Watch for signs of great interest in buying — Customers want an item if they pick it up while you're selling to them. Customers want an item if they stop listening to look at the item when you're talking to them. Customers want an item if they knock its price. This is a strong buying signal. They're asking for your help. Sell them on the value of the item.

Trust your feelings — Sense when customers want to buy. Become alert to a feeling that grows in you that this customer is ready to buy now. It's hard to describe this feeling but it comes when customers are going along with you and you feel in tune with them. Everything goes smoothly. Let your mind be free enough to take this gift from the subconscious part of you.

Watch for other signals too — Sometimes customers signal their interest in buying indirectly. These are signals that make it clear you have serious customers:

Angry Customers. Angry customers want to buy. They're angry because they can't get a deal that makes sense to them.

Many Focused Roadblocks. Customers who raise many *Roadblocks* that hang together want to buy. They're focused on what they want and they're working to get it. On the other hand, customers who raise many *Roadblocks* that are all over the place probably just find it hard to say, "No."

Develop Personal Customers

Customers like to buy from sellers who serve them well. Customers begin to ask for you by name when you serve them well. Some call ahead to make sure you'll be in the store when they visit. They become your *Personal Customers*. The idea of *Personal Customers* is informal. There's no agreement between you and the customers. It would surprise many customers to know you think of them as your *Personal Customers*. It's not something to talk about with customers. Simply accept that some customers choose you to serve them.

Regular customers buy more than other customers. Aim to turn regular customers into your *Personal Customers*. You make more commissions when you have *Personal Customers*.

Respect each other's Personal Customers — Accept it politely when customers ask for another seller. It's below our store's standard to try to horn in on other sellers' *Personal Customers*. Let *Personal Customers* know their seller's schedule when customers call in to ask.

Sometimes customers ask for a seller who's off work. Sell to them as you would to any other customer, but that doesn't make them your *Personal Customers*.

Respect customers' wishes — Respect it when your *Personal Customer* leaves you for another seller. *Personal Customers* are like any other friends. You make them and you lose them. Like friends, some *Personal Customers* stay with you. You lose some because you neglect them and you lose others for no reason at all. Some move out of your life. Some customers may be *Personal Customers* of more than one seller.

Outsmart Hagglers

A haggler is a customer who tries to get a special bargain. Hagglers may ask to pay less than the marked price for an item. They may ask you to give them a better deal. They may suggest a lower price or a percentage off. Hagglers may want a sweetener. They'll pay full price for the item, but want you to throw in something else. They may buy the suit but expect a belt and a tie as well. Hagglers may want a special price when they buy a large amount. They may buy 12 umbrellas and want to pay for 10. They may buy $500 of items and want a discount because most customers buy only $50 of items. Hagglers may want to pay less for paying cash instead of by credit card. They may want to pay less because the item is cheaper elsewhere. When you've marked down slow-moving red sweaters, hagglers want fast-moving blue sweaters at red-sweater prices.

Know that we set our prices carefully — Our prices have to cover our costs and give us a profit. We need our profits to survive. Most retail stores go out of business and failure to charge proper prices is one of the main reasons. We won't make that mistake. Our view is simple. We charge the marked prices.

Sometimes we're forced to mark down items that sell poorly. The markdown price is then the price marked on the label that we charge to all customers. We're not going to cut further into markdowns for hagglers.

Know that most hagglers are playing a game — Most hagglers know the marked price is the price. It's a sport for them to see what they can get away with. They haggle in most stores and it makes their day when they find a weak seller and get something for less. It's a game they can only win. They lose nothing when they pay full price—that was the price anyway. They're ahead when the haggling works.

Play a game with hagglers — Suppose a haggler asks for a break. Say politely, "Let me check and see what I can do." Go into the storeroom and stay out of sight for a couple of minutes. Then return and say, "I'm sorry, on that one there's nothing I can do." Then wait silently for the haggler to buy. You're the good guy now. It looks as if you tried to get a break and failed. Hagglers are more likely to buy at the marked price than if you were still the enemy.

Know the false views that hagglers use — We have twelve umbrellas to sell at $20 each. The profit is the same whether twelve customers buy them one at a time or one customer buys them all. We planned on taking in $240 and our expense is the same. Why would we take less? The difference in cash flow isn't worth talking about.

Discounts for paying cash went out with the dinosaurs. Each charge cost a lot when each store ran its own charge accounts. It made sense to give discounts for cash payments. It doesn't make sense when there are few problems collecting charges made to credit cards. It's true we have to pay a fee to credit card companies. To a store that's the same as paying for advertising. Credit card customers spend more than cash customers when they buy. They also spend more often than customers who pay cash. There's less fuss and danger in dealing with sales drafts than with cash. We prefer credit card customers to cash customers.

These are the facts about items that are cheaper elsewhere. In most cases the difference isn't worth the effort of buying elsewhere. Do customers really want to go across town to save a couple of dollars? Suggest customers hurry over to pick up real bargains elsewhere. Sometimes there's a big price difference when a store is going out of business or running a crazy sale. We'll soon be out of business if we try to meet those prices.

Say, "No" — Say, "No" with power and without doubt. Keep the manager out of it—make no offer to ask the manager what to do. Get the "No" over firmly and politely. It's up to you to act for the store. Of course, should a customer ask to talk to the manager when you say, "No," the manager will be pleased to play the game with you.

Act as if hagglers will buy at marked prices. Act as if it's normal to do so. That's easy, because it's true. You may lose a sale because you stick to marked prices. That's fine. You've protected the store's interests. You've made it clear the store's prices are firm.

Sell More to Sold Customers

Sold Customers are customers who know what they want to buy and ask to buy right away. Another way of describing them is as "customers on a mission to buy."

Step around the Pit of Easy Sales — It's easy to fall into the *Pit of Easy Sales*. The last five customers were "Just looking" and you're feeling bad about your selling day. The next customer says, "I'd like to buy the P21 Calculator." Now there's some action—that's a nice sale at $178. You ring up the sale and you feel good. Like most sellers in most stores, you reached for the bait. You fell into the *Pit of Easy Sales*. Like most sellers in the pit, it puzzles you why your sales aren't better.

Sold Customers are nice but they short-circuit the *Steps for Selling*. You still need to find out their needs, wants and dreams. You still need to find out how much they can pay. You still need to schmooze. You still need to find out why they want to buy.

Sold Customers often have a false idea of their needs. Some know exactly what they want and what they're willing to pay. Many only partly understand what they want. Many are willing to pay more for something that serves them better. Take Joan, Fred and Mary who each ask to buy the P21 Calculator. Joan has only enough to buy the P21. It fits her needs for school work. Fred likes the latest electronic toys and has a good income. He'd love the XK15 at $295, if he knew about it. Mary's a busy accountant with two assistants. She needs and can afford three RB34 Calculators at $178 each.

Sold Customers still need *Add-ons*. In the excitement of the easy sale it's easy to overlook selling the *Add-ons*. Even the student with a low budget needs extra rolls of adding tape.

Act out the sale — Go along with the sale to make *Sold Customers* feel at ease. Get a P21 Calculator and take it out of its box to check it over.

Start to sell as you act out the sale — Schmooze and ask questions. Asking about the reason for buying the item is a good *Opener*. "What kind of calculating do you do?

Switch Customers to Items You Carry

Sellers who are able to sell customers items you have in the store sell more than "sellers" who fold in the face of strict beliefs.

Make a positive switch — Say what you do instead of what you don't. Sometimes customers ask for brands you don't carry. "Do you carry Brand X luggage?" "Do you carry Apple computers?"

Take a positive stand instead of answering the question. "We carry Brand Y and Brand Z." "We carry Comtex PCs."

Sellers who answer negatively by saying "I'm sorry, we don't carry that brand" set themselves up for *No Sale*. That's true even if they say "No, but we do carry Brand Y and Brand Z."

Run with the bouncing ball — Ask a question about the item right away. "What kind of items are you looking for?" "How do you plan to use your computer?" Many customers will begin to talk about their needs and wants.

Fight brand loyalty with "Feel, felt, found" — Overcome the brand loyalty *Roadblock* with "Feel, felt, found." Then overcome any other *Roadblocks.*

Know the Promises That Make Customers Act

Make promises to get customers to buy. Be able to prove any promise you make. Customers must care about the promises for them to work. Slim customers don't care about losing weight easily. Know the promises that move customers to act.

Relations with other people — The promise of attracting other people, of satisfying their sexual desires, of finding love, of people respecting them, of people liking them, of someone appreciating them, of belonging to a group.

Image of themselves — The promise of beauty, of losing weight easily, of being in fashion, of protecting their reputation, of showing they have unusual tastes, of owning a unique item, of feeling protected, of feeling free, of having a special identity, of feeling worthy.

Power — The promise of power, of owning the latest, best or fastest model, of being among the first to own something, of being among the few who own the oldest of an item, of owning something unique.

How they feel about themselves — The promise of comfort, of happiness, of showing their own identity, of pampering themselves, of doing their duty, of feeling proud, of meeting their fantasies, of satisfying an appetite, of owning something attractive, of fulfilling themselves, of escaping their troubles.

Money and material items — The promise of financial gain, of riches, of possessions, of a bargain, of owning something valuable, of protecting what they already own, of saving money, of stretching their budget.

Relaxation — The promise of relaxation, of fun, of excitement, of good food, of satisfying their curiosity, of having a good time.

Health and safety — The promise of self-preservation, of safety for self and family, of security, of gaining or preserving health or strength, of getting rid of aches and pains, of living longer, of avoiding hunger.

Work — The promise of work being easier, of saving time.

Nostalgia — The promise of going back to the good old days, of recapturing their childhood.

Survival after death —The promise of eternal life, of people remembering them after they're dead.

Let Customers Think They're Bothering You

Sometimes customers suggest they're bothering you. "I hope I'm not bothering you." "I know you're busy, but I'd like some help."

Get back to work if you're resting on the job and customers are finding fault. Neither deny it nor agree with customers who really care about bothering you. Move along with the *Steps for Selling*. Have the air of a busy person who's professional enough to put customers' needs first.

Customers are in debt to you when you put yourself out for them. Keep this debt alive and let it work for your sales. Avoid saying things like: "It's no trouble at all." "No bother, I'm just killing time." "What I'm doing isn't important." "That's OK. I'm not busy." Saying these things will cancel the debt they owe you.

Burn Your Business Cards

It's rare for sellers who have business cards to make a sale <u>and</u> give out a business card. It's either make a sale <u>or</u> give out a business card. It's better to make a sale.

End your contact with a sale — Sellers who have cards get into the habit of giving them out. Without knowing it, they end up using them to kill sales. Giving a card rounds out the contact with a customer. It's an easy way out. A seller's job is to sell when with a customer and that's harder than giving out a card.

Customers use business cards to knock you out of selling to them. Taking a card is a polite way of saying, "I'm not buying today." It looks as if they've done something. It suggests they'll be back to buy in the future. It gets rid of their guilt. Avoid giving customers this easy way out.

Write the few cards you need — Most customers soon throw away the business cards they take. There are only a few times you need to give out the facts that are on business cards. Write these facts out by hand for customers. Taking the trouble to write makes closer bonds with customers.

Know Birth Signs

Schmooze with birth signs. Birth signs make good *Openers*. Some people laugh at birth signs while others swear they rule our lives. People who laugh at them overlook their value in getting people to talk about themselves. Use them to schmooze if you know birth signs and what they mean. Of course, they only work well when customers are into the signs too.

Find out birthdays with birth signs — Try to get birthdays when you register customers. It's too personal to ask customers their birthdays. That's too close to asking, "How old are you?" Ask for birth signs instead. Sometimes you get birth signs only. Send birthday cards at the beginning of the sign. Sometimes you get birthdays. Someone may say, "Let's see. I was born on the 23rd of June. What does that make me?"

Learn the birth signs and what they mean — Learn the dates of the signs. They run from about the twentieth day of each month to the twentieth day of the next month.

1	Aries	The Ram	Mar 20 - Apr 20
2	Taurus	The Bull	Apr 21 - May 21
3	Gemini	The Twins	May 22 - Jun 22
4	Cancer	The Crab	Jun 23 - Jul 22
5	Leo	The Lion	Jul 23 - Aug 22
6	Virgo	The Virgin	Aug 23 - Sep 22
7	Libra	The Scales	Sep 23 - Oct 22
8	Scorpio	The Scorpion	Oct 23 - Nov 22
9	Sagittarius	The Archer	Nov 23 - Dec 22
10	Capricorn	The Goat	Dec 23 - Jan 21
11	Aquarius	The Water Carrier	Jan 22 - Feb 20
12	Pisces	The Fishes	Feb 21 - Mar 19

Learn the marks of people born under the signs after you know the dates.

| 1 | Aries | The Ram | Mar 20 - Apr 10 |

Like the Ram, people born under this sign are full of energy and life. Lively and full of adventure. Funny and full of ideas. Make friends easily. Friends turn to those born under the Ram to lead them. Impatient, strong-headed, daring. Irritable unless they get their own way. Like to fight. Good at sports and games. Full of drive and spirit.

| 2 | Taurus | The Bull | Apr 21 - May 21 |

Like the Bull, people born under this sign are stable and reliable. Artistic, strong, bullheaded, hard working. Depend on self, rather than others. Practical, patient, easy to get along with. Tough and free from doubt. Take a while to get angry and then get very angry. Plodding and peaceful. Like comfort and food. These people take their time.

| 3 | Gemini | The Twins | May 22 - Jun 22 |

Like Twins, people born under this sign love to share ideas with someone else. Cheerful, lively, change their minds a lot. Often start things and don't finish them. Pass up good chances. Quick, athletic and in touch with others. Curious about lots of things.

| 4 | Cancer | The Crab | Jun 23 - Jul 22 |

Like the Crab, people born under this sign live under a cover. Like the Crab they move sideways instead of directly. Secretive and hard to know. Hang on to things and refuse to give them up. Often shy and sensitive. Need people around them who make them feel safe. Go about things indirectly.

| 5 | Leo | The Lion | Jul 23 - Aug 22 |

Like the Lion, people born under this sign are proud and dignified. Free from doubt, brave, loyal, loving, but bossy. Like to be the center of attention. Pleasant, bright and loving. Roar with anger when people disagree with them. Think big and dislike things with details or dull things. Need plenty of love and attention. Love an audience.

| 6 | Virgo | The Virgin | Aug 23 - Sep 22 |

Like a Maiden, people born under this sign are cool and clear. Readers and thinkers. Have opinions about everything and let people know them. Gentle and quiet. Happy to be alone. Knock others. Youthful and fussy. Enjoy art and beautiful things. Can do more than one thing well. Enjoy traveling. Help others.

| 7 | Libra | The Scales | Sep 23 - Oct 22 |

Like a pair of Scales, people born under this sign balance everything slowly before making up their minds. Want to be fair and are warm and understanding. Slow to take sides in an argument. They are peacemakers. Bad at keeping secrets. Balance everything in their lives. Balance work and play, balance thoughts and emotions. Chase perfection. Need love and companionship.

| 8 | Scorpio | The Scorpion | Oct 23 - Nov 22 |

Like the Scorpion, people born under this sign hide and can be dangerous. Good at making up their minds and getting on with things. Usually thoughtful and quiet but sometimes let emotions take over. Can be excitable and headstrong. Can be dangerous, clever and full of mystery. Quiet, shy and sensitive. Like to keep secrets. Have a strong sense of justice.

| 9 | Sagittarius | The Archer | Nov 23 - Dec 22 |

Like the Archer, people born under this sign like to run free when they want to. Like being with people. Make friends easily. Say what's on their minds and sometimes hurt people's feelings without meaning to. Like sports where they can play against themselves. Need plenty of freedom. Like to start new things, dislike being tied down by a routine.

| 10 | Capricorn | The Goat | Dec 23 - Jan 21 |

Like the Goat, people born under this sign are sure-footed and want to get where they're going. Serious and want to reach their goals. Dislike fooling around and wasting time. Take life seriously. Do things with patience and care. Good at meeting challenges and getting over problems. Make good leaders.

| 11 | Aquarius | The Water Carrier | Jan 22 - Feb 20 |

Like the Water Carrier, people born under this sign share their gifts with other people. Believe in sharing common interests. Believe in equality. Believe that people should do their own thing. Clever, generous, artistic, friendly. You don't know what they'll do next but it'll be interesting. These are giving people.

| 12 | Pisces | The Fishes | Feb 21 - Mar 19 |

Like Fishes, people born under this sign glide through life. Gentle, careful and dreamy, but also moody and changeable. People find them hard to understand. Lively one minute, quiet the next. Fun loving and wise. Love artistic things. Love the water like a fish. Not always brave. Prefer to go along with people rather than swim against the current. Believe almost anything people tell them.

Listen Deeply

For most people "listening" is waiting for a chance to start talking again. A man tells how his wife left him. The listener "listens" by telling how his girlfriend left him. We all want someone to listen to us so badly that we scarcely listen to other people. We jump in and tell about ourselves in the hope the other person will listen to us. The words go round and round but nobody is really listening. Two people tell different stories at the same time. The other person's story is something we put up with. We pounce on gaps in it to go on with our story.

Work at listening — The key to being a good listener is to want to listen. This needs will power and discipline. Active listening needs all your energy but make it look as if you're resting. Value what customers say. Turn customers on by listening to them, really listening.

Make listening pay off — The more deeply you listen, the more customers will talk about themselves. Customers rarely get the pleasure of someone listening to them closely. They feel it when you do it. This excites them and they want to connect with the person who excites them.

Be comfortable with silence — It's natural for customers to pause and think. That's especially so when they deal with hard decisions. Give customers the time to think and decide. Customers answer questions and you can tell they're not finished. Sometimes they may clear their throat, showing there's something that's hard for them to say. Say nothing and customers go on talking. They may start again. They may give you real answers they've been holding back.

Be aware that people hate silence. Someone always speaks to break silence. Let customers do that rather than you. Remain silent and customers begin to feel uncomfortable. So they jump in to kill the silence. You'll often get more from customers by being silent than by asking another question.

Support customers as they talk. Give a slight smile or nod your head to support them. They'll keep on going. What they say will be closer to the truth than if you ask questions.

Say nothing when you're stuck. See what customers say. Relax and look at them. Wait and see what happens. Customers usually go on talking.

Ask a question when you get a blank stare. Try saying you've lost your train of thought and see what customers say.

Let customers speak for themselves — Speaking for customers is rude. Butting in disturbs their rhythm and thoughts. It signals your impatience. It's a form of bullying that shifts attention to you. You miss what customers want to say when you finish their thoughts or sentences.

Be there for customers — Ask simple questions and give the floor to customers. Keep the focus on what's in it for customers. Be careful of turning the focus on yourself. Avoid working out how you're going to answer while customers are talking. Working out answers stops you listening. Thoughts go too fast for there to be time to listen as well. You're there to fill customers' wants and needs, not to impress customers.

Cross check what customers tell you — Customers say one thing, but sometimes there's something else beneath it. Put what customers say in your own words and run it past them. "Let me check what you said. This is what I heard. Is that what you said?

CHAPTER 17

BOOST SALES AND PROFITS

Once sellers are using the *Steps for Selling* well it's time to really start boosting sales and profits in your store. Boosting sales has a firm base in the use of *Scores* that sellers and managers track as sellers sell. Using *Scores* allows managers to give sellers the strongest possible support. Paying sellers commissions on the sales they make boosts sales out of all proportion to the cost of the commissions. Playing games in the store gives the opportunity to boost sales yet again. It's also necessary to master the techniques of making year-to-year comparisons of sales and using them to set goals for sellers.

Understand the Scores

Measure how well sellers sell by their *Scores*. Sellers work out some simple figures to see how well they're selling. They note how many customers enter the store. They count sales slips, the value of sales and the number of items sold. They fill in a form and work out their *Scores*. The basic form is the *Seller's Daily Sales Summary*. Make up figures and fill in forms until you're comfortable with the *Scores*. Study how to use the *Scores* to sell better. See the big picture of your sellers and store by their *Scores*

The *Seller's Daily Sales Summary* is the model for other summaries. The figure shows how the summaries feed each other.

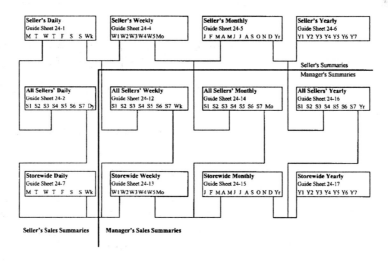

Sellers and managers have their own group of summaries. Managers first fill in the manager's summaries themselves until they feel comfortable with them. Then they train selected sellers to fill them in as a series of *Special Jobs*.

All summary forms are similar to the *Seller's Daily Sales Summary*. Other forms explain any differences. The summaries are linked spreadsheets. You may wish to set them up on your computer if you have the skills. Think about setting up the manager's group of spreadsheets first. Training all sellers to use spreadsheets may be a problem it's wise to avoid. Beware of letting a computer project bog you down. Your priority is to get everyone in your store working with the *Scores*. It drives the *Scores* home when sellers work out their *Scores* on paper.

Follow Scores day by day — Each day sellers fill in one day of the *Seller's Daily Sales Summary* and one seller's column of the *All Sellers' Daily Sales Summary*. Collect the *All Sellers' Daily Sales Summary* in the *Day Report*. Fill in a day of the *Storewide Daily Sales Summary* from the *All Sellers' Daily Sales Summary*.

Follow Scores week by week — Each week sellers fill in the week column of the *Seller's Daily Sales Summary* and one week column of the *Seller's Weekly Sales Summary*. Collect the *Seller's Daily Sales Summaries* in the *Day Report*. Review them and give feedback to the sellers.

Fill in a seller's column of the *All Sellers' Weekly Sales Summary* from the week column of each *Seller's Daily Sales Summary*. Work out the week column of the *All Sellers' Weekly Sales Summary*. Work out the week column for the *Storewide Daily Sales Summary*. It gives you a crosscheck on the week column of the *All Sellers' Weekly Sales Summary*. Fill in a week column of the *Storewide Weekly Sales Summary* after the crosscheck.

Follow Scores month by month — Each month sellers fill in the month column of the *Seller's Weekly Sales Summary* and one month column of the *Seller's Monthly Sales Summary*. Collect the *Seller's Weekly Sales Summary* in the *Day Report*. Look it over and give feedback to the seller.

Fill in a seller's column of the *All Sellers' Monthly Sales Summary* from the month column of each *Seller's Weekly Sales Summary*. Work out the month column of the *All Sellers' Monthly Sales Summary*. Work out the month column for the *Storewide Weekly Sales Summary*. It gives you a crosscheck on the month column of the *All Sellers' Monthly Sales Summary*. Fill in a month column of the *Storewide Monthly Sales Summary* after the crosscheck.

Follow Scores year by year — Each year sellers fill in the year column of the *Seller's Monthly Sales Summary* and one year column of the *Seller's Yearly Sales Summary*. Collect the *Seller's Monthly Sales Summary* in the *Day Report*. Look it over and give feedback to the seller.

Fill in a seller's column of the *All Sellers' Yearly Sales Summary* from the year column of each *Seller's Monthly Sales Summary*. Work out the year column of the *All Sellers' Yearly Sales Summary*. Work out the year column for the *Storewide Monthly Sales Summary*. It gives you a crosscheck on the year column of the *All Sellers' Yearly Sales Summary*. Fill in a year column of the *Storewide Yearly Sales Summary* after the crosscheck. Collect the *Seller's Yearly Sales Summary* in the *Day Report*. Look it over and give feedback to the seller.

Keep the manager's summaries to yourself — Sellers will simplify what the *Scores* mean if you post them for all to see. It looks as if you use *Manager's Sales Summaries* to judge sellers. Sellers will find it hard to believe you use the summaries to help them sell well. Build trust with your sellers by keeping *Scores* between you and them.

Store the Sales Summaries — Three-ring binders with separators for each kind of *Sales Summary* will help you keep on top of the forms.

- Three sellers a day make 1,095 *Seller's Daily Sales Summaries* a year.

- You'll also have 365 *All Sellers' Daily Sales Summaries* and 365 *Storewide Daily Sales Summaries* a year. Move these summaries to bulk out-of-store storage regularly. Keep them in the store long enough to check the *Weekly Sales Summaries*. Keep them in the store long enough to track changes in sellers' *Scores*. You might track a seller's Saturday afternoon *Scores* for several weeks.

- Three sellers a week make 156 *Seller's Weekly Sales Summaries* a year.

- You'll also have 52 *All Sellers' Weekly Sales Summaries* and 52 *Storewide Weekly Sales Summaries* a year. Keep at least a year's copies in the store if you can find the space.

- Three sellers a month make 36 *Seller's Monthly Sales Summaries* a year.

- You'll also have 12 *All Sellers' Monthly Sales Summaries* and 12 *Storewide Monthly Sales Summaries* a year. Try to keep two or three year's copies in the store.

- Three sellers a year for a year make three *Seller's Yearly Sales Summaries*.

- You'll also have one *All Sellers' Yearly Sales Summary* and one *Storewide Yearly Sales Summary* a year. Keep these in the store for several years.

Move summaries to out-of-store storage following a time pattern.

It's tempting to move sellers' summaries out-of-store as soon as they quit. This leads to filing problems in out-of-store storage. It also cuts you off from comparing sellers. It's useful to have summaries of old sellers. Some will be better and some worse than sellers you have now.

Fill in the Seller's Daily Sales Summary

Base all summaries on the *Seller's Daily Sales Summary*. Sellers fill in five *Sales Summaries*. Each Sales Summary depends on totals from the one before it. Begin with the *Seller's Daily Sales Summary*.

Seller's Daily Sales Summary

Store _____ Downtown _____ Year 1994 Mon Jan Seller _____ Mary Jones _____

Sales

		Mon	Tue	Wed	Thu	Fri	Sat	Sun	Total
2	Date						1	2	
3	Hours Scheduled						9-3	9-3	
4	Hours Selling						5	5	10
5	# Entries						28	48	76
6	# Receipts						10	16	26
7	# Items Sold						17	27	44
8	# Items Returned						1	0	1
9	# Items						16	27	43
10	$ Sales						523.88	876.56	1,400.44
11	$ Returns						9.95	0	9.95
12	$ Total						513.93	876.56	1,390.49

Scores

⇧ Average

		Mon	Tue	Wed	Thu	Fri	Sat	Sun	Average
13	# Sales/entry Hit Rate						36%	33%	34%
14	$ Average Sale Hit Value						51.39	54.79	53.48
15	$ Average Item Item Value						32.12	32.47	32.34
16	# Items/sale Item Count						1.60	1.69	1.65
17	# Entries/hour selling						5.60	9.60	7.60
18	# Sales/hour selling						2.00	3.20	2.60
19	$ Sales/hour selling						102.79	175.31	139.05
20	$ Sales/entry						18.35	18.26	18.30

⇧ means work out these averages using totals in the rows above the arrow.

Begin a new form on the first day of the month — Keep the days of each month separate. That makes it easy to sum up facts to monthly summaries.

Fill in the top of the form — The example is for Mary who works on Saturdays and Sundays.

Line 2, Date Work weeks: run from Monday to Sunday. Enter dates for days worked.

Line 3, Hours Scheduled: On Saturday and Sunday Mary works 9 am to 3 pm

Line 4, Hours Selling: Breaks aren't selling time. Time spent on *Special Jobs* isn't selling time. All other time the store is open and you're in the store is selling time. Time spent on *Background Jobs* is selling time. You're in the store to sell. *Background Jobs* fill in the blank time. Mary works 9 am to 3 pm on Saturdays and Sundays. That's 6 hours each day. Both days Mary works one hour before the store opens at 10 am. That leaves 5 hours selling time. Mary's Hours Selling for Saturday and Sunday add up to 10 hours.

Fill in the selling part of the form — **Line 5, # Entries (Number of Entries):** Copy the total number of Customer Entries from the *Customer Flow Sheet*. Other Entries don't count. For Mary that's 28 on Saturday and 48 on Sunday, for a total of 76. These are only the Customer Entries Mary dealt with. Customer Entries for other sellers are on their own *Customer Flow Sheets*. All sellers complete their own *Seller's Daily Sales Summaries.*

Line 6, # Receipts (Number of Receipts): This is the number of sales slips or cash register receipts. It's the number of customers you take cash from. Suppose first you write 5 items on one sales slip for customer 1. Then you write 3 items on another sales slip for customer 2. The Number of Receipts is 2. Count two sales slips you write for one customer as one. This happens when a customer forgets something and comes back to finish buying. Mary made sales to 10 customers on Saturday and 16 on Sunday. Her total for the week is 26.

Line 7, # Items Sold (Number of Items Sold): This is the total number of all items on all of the seller's sales slips for the day. Suppose you write 5 items on one sales slip for customer 1. Then you write 3 items on another sales slip for customer 2. The number of Items Sold is 8.

There are two rules for counting items.

1. Count only items that cost more than the *Marker Price* posted in *Daily*. Items under the *Marker Price* are the odds and ends some stores call sundries. Some odds and ends sell themselves. Other odds and ends are the bait you use as *Add-ons* to sell higher-priced items. Although they don't count as items, odds and ends boost the sales total.

2. Marked down items and sale items don't count as items sold. Marked down items don't count because they're failures. We sell them for salvage value. Their price is low enough for them to sell themselves. Sale items don't count because there's no profit in them.

Mary sold 17 items on Saturday and 27 on Sunday. That's a total of 44 items for the week.

Line 8, # Items Returned (Number of Items Returned): Sometimes customers return items you sold them. Sometimes they have second thoughts about items after you finish the sale. You'll probably handle the returns if they come back later the same day. Sometimes customers take items home and bring them back another day. Another seller will handle the returns if you're out of the store. The return goes on the original seller's next *Seller's Daily Sales Summary*. Sellers who handle returns leave messages for the original seller in *Daily*. Mary had one return on Saturday. That's her total for the week.

Line 9, # Items (Number of Items): Work out the number of items. Take the number of items returned from the number of items sold. That's Line 7 minus Line 8. Mary's Number of Items is 16 for Saturday and 27 for Sunday, for a total of 43.

Line 10, $ Sales (Sales Dollars): This is the total dollars for all of the seller's sales receipts. Suppose a receipt for customer 1 has 5 items at a total cost of $50. Another receipt for customer 2 has 3 items on it at a total cost of $35. The Sales Dollars value is $85 if these are the seller's only sales during the shift. The figures for Sales Dollars don't include any taxes collected. Taxes aren't sales. The store owes the tax money to the government. Mary's Sales Dollars are $523.88 for Saturday and $876.56 for Sunday. That's a total for the week of $1,400.44.

Line 11, $ Returns (Returns Dollars): These are the cash returns that go with item returns. The item that Mary has for a return on Saturday cost $9.95, so Mary gave $9.95 back to the customer. Sometimes a customer who makes a return buys something else in its place. Sellers may even out the return with a sale. They're out of luck if another seller takes a return and makes a sale. The original seller takes the return as an item returned on Line 8. The other seller takes the sale that replaces it. Cut down on returns by selling customers items they need and want. This cuts down lost sales and paperwork.

Line 12, $ Total (Total Dollars): Correct the sales total by taking the value of the returns from sales. That's Line 10 minus Line 11. This changes Mary's sales total for Saturday to $513.93. Add this to her sales total of $876.56 for Sunday. Her sales total for the week is $1,390.49.

Fill in the Scores part of the form — Work out the *Scores* now the Sales part of the summary is done.

Line 13, # Sales/entry (Hit Rate): This is the average number of sales receipts for each entry. Divide the number of receipts (Line 6) by the number of entries (Line 5.) Then multiply by 100.

On Saturday Mary wrote 10 receipts and she dealt with 28 entries. Divide 10 by 28 to get 0.36 as the *Hit Rate*. Then multiply 0.36 by 100 to get 36. This is a percentage figure, so add the percent sign and write 36%. On Sunday Mary wrote 16 receipts and she dealt with 48 entries. Divide 16 by 48 to get 0.33 as the *Hit Rate*. Then multiply 0.33 by 100 to get 33. Add the percent sign and write 33%.

To work out the average *Hit Rate* for the week, use the numbers from the Total column. For the week Mary wrote 26 receipts and she dealt with 76 entries. Divide 26 by 76 to get 0.34 as the *Hit Rate*. Then multiply 0.34 by 100 to get 34. Add the percent sign and write 34%.

Averaging each day's *Hit Rate* also gives the week's average *Hit Rate*. Add 36% and 33% to get 69%. Then divide by 2 to get the average of 35%. Notice there's a small error—the answer is 35% instead of 34%. That's because doing it this way averaged some averages. A math whiz knows that's wrong. Although it's only a small error, we'll work out our figures the right way. Work out all weekly averages from the Total column above instead of from the averages to the left.

Line 14, $ Average Sale (Hit Value): This is the average number of dollars for a receipt. Divide the number of dollars for all receipts by the number of receipts. That's Line 12 Total Dollars divided by Line 6 Number of Receipts.

On Saturday Mary sold $513.93 of items. Divide this by 10 receipts to get $51.39 for each receipt. On Sunday Mary sold $876.56 of items. Divide this by 16 receipts to get $54.79 for each receipt. Mary sold $1,390.49 of items for the whole week. Divide this by 26 receipts to get $53.48 for each receipt.

Line 15, $ Average Item (Item Value): This is all dollars for all sales divided by the number of items on all receipts. That's Line 12 divided by Line 9.

On Saturday Mary sold $513.93 of items. Divide this by 16, the number of items sold. That gets $32.12, the average price of an item. On Sunday Mary sold $876.56 of items. Divide this by 27, the number of items sold. That gets $32.47, the average price of an item.

Mary sold $1,390.49 of items for the whole week. Divide this by 43, the number of items sold. That gets $32.34, the average price of an item.

Line 16, # Items/sale (Item Count): This is the average number of items in each sale. It's all items sold on all receipts divided by the number of receipts. That's Line 9 Number of Items divided by Line 6 Number of Receipts.

On Saturday Mary sold 16 items. Divide this by 10 receipts to get 1.6 items sold on each receipt. On Sunday Mary sold 27 items. Divide this by 16 receipts to get 1.69 items sold on each receipt.

Mary's total of items for the week is 43. Divide this by 26 receipts to get 1.65 items sold each hour.

Line 17, # Entries/hour of Selling (Number of Entries/hour of Selling): This is the number of entries divided by the number of hours selling. That's Line 5 Number of Entries divided by Line 4 Hours Selling.

On Saturday Mary has 28 entries. Divide this by 5 hours selling to get 5.6 entries each hour of selling. On Sunday Mary has 48 entries. Divide this by 5 hours selling to get 9.6 entries each hour of selling. Mary's total number of entries for the week is 76. Divide this by 10, her total hours selling, to get 7.6 entries each hour of selling.

Line 18, # Sales/hour of Selling (Number of Sales/hour of Selling): This is the number of receipts divided by the number of hours selling. That's Line 6 Number of Receipts divided by Line 4 Hours Selling.

On Saturday Mary has 10 receipts. Divide this by 5 hours selling to get 2 receipts each hour of selling. On Sunday Mary has 16 receipts. Divide this by 5 hours selling to get 3.2 receipts each hour of selling. Mary's total number of receipts for the week is 26. Divide this by the total of 10 hours selling to get 2.6 receipts each hour of selling.

Line 19, $ Sales/hour of Selling (Sales Dollars/hour of Selling): This is the average sales dollars each hour. Divide the total sales dollars by the number of hours selling. That's Line 12 Total Dollars divided by Line 4 Hours Selling.

On Saturday Mary has sales of $513.93. Divide this by 5 hours selling to get $102.79 each hour of selling. On Sunday Mary has sales of $876.56. Divide this by 5 hours selling to get $175.31 each hour of selling. Mary's total sales for the week are $1,390.49. Divide this by 10 hours selling to get $139.05 each hour of selling.

Line 20, $ Sales/entry (Sales Dollars/entry): This is the average dollars taken for each entry. Divide the total dollars for all the receipts by the number of entries. That's Line 12 Total Dollars divided by Line 5 Number of Entries.

On Saturday Mary's total dollar amount is 513.93. Divide this by 28 entries to get 18.35 as the average dollars for each entry. On Sunday Mary's total dollar amount is 876.56. Divide this by 48 entries to get 18.26 as the average dollars for each entry. Mary's total dollar amount for the week is 1,390.49. Divide this by 76 entries to get 18.30 as the average dollars for each entry.

Fill in the Total column on the last day of the week — Mary worked only Saturday the 1st and Sunday the 2nd of January. Sunday was her last work day of the week. She filled in the Total column when she finished working on Sunday.

Track Scores to Drive Selling

The *Hit Rate* is the most important score. It's the key to high sales. Aim to get sellers to sell something to everyone. Get the *Hit Rate* high before training on other *Scores*.

Next pay attention the *Hit Value*. That's the total dollar outcome of each *Hit*. Suppose the usual *Hit Value* is $50. Get sellers with $25 to come up to standard and sellers with $75 to beat it for the thrill of topping it.

To raise the *Hit Value* consider the two *Scores* that make it up, *Item Count* and *Item Value*. The *Item Count* is the average number of items on a sales slip. The *Item Value* is the average price of each of those items. Consider these two cases:

	Item Count	x	Item Value	=	Hit Value
Tom	1		60		60
John	5		12		60.

Tom and John have the same *Hit Value* but have different ways of getting there.

Suppose Tom's pattern is to sell a $55 item with a $5 *Add-on*. That shows up as one item at $60. That's because while odds and ends under $10 don't count as items, they do add to the dollar total. Tom can probably sell items with higher prices. He's at ease with high prices. He can use his same way of selling and raise his *Hit Value*. After that he can raise the number and value of his *Add-ons*. Perhaps Tom can sell $120 items with *Add-ons* of $35 and $5 and go to:

	Item Count	x	Item Value	=	Hit Value
Tom	2		80		160

John sells lower priced items to make up his *Hit Value*. John may be skating if his *Hit Rate* is low. Perhaps he's only selling to customers who come in with a list of everyday needs. He may need to improve his *Hit Rate*. Another possibility is that John shies away from higher-priced items. He may need help in learning to sell them. With John moving to higher-priced items, his knack of selling *Add-ons* will help raise his *Hit Value*. Perhaps John can sell $60 items with *Add-ons* of $20 and $5 and go to:

	Item Count	x	Item Value	=	Hit Value
John	2		42.50		85

Then he can follow the track that Tom is on.

Look at the other *Scores*. Number of Entries/hour and Number of Sales/hour give other ways of looking at the *Hit Rate*. Sale dollars/hour give a number that useful in making comparisons. These three *Scores* give a summary picture of hourly activity. Sale dollars/entry is another *Score* to keep track of.

Improve Key Scores — Improve three *Key Scores*: *Hit Rate*, *Item Value* and *Item Count*. As these *Key Scores* improve, so do the other *Scores*

Improve Key Scores one at a time — It's too big a job to improve all *Key Scores* at the same time. Separate them and work on them one by one.

Improve the Hit Rate — The *Hit Rate* is the most important *Score*. Work on the *Hit Rate* before working on other *Scores*. The *Hit Rate* is the key to high sales. As the *Hit Rate* improves, so do *Number of Sales/hour of selling*, *Sales Dollars/hour of selling* and *Sales Dollars/entry*. Aim to sell something to everyone. Keep that aim in mind and watch the *Hit Rate* rise.

Always act as if sellers can get a *Hit Rate* of 100%. That's the right way to improve the *Hit Rate*. Reality will be below that, but there's no special figure. Good *Hit Rates* vary among stores and items and from time to time.

Guide sellers by how they improve. Aim to improve the *Hit Rate* even if it's already high. Guide sellers by how they compare with other sellers. Suppose a seller's *Hit Rate* is 20%—selling to 2 out of 10 entries. Suppose the *Hit Rate* for other sellers in similar time slots is 40%. They're selling to 4 out of 10 entries. The first seller can probably do better than 20%.

Improve Hit Rate step by step — Ask what it is the seller can do better. Give your own input and get input from other sellers. Get them to role play to learn how to get past blocks.

- Does the seller start to schmooze with most entries? If not, work on schmoozing before working on other *Steps for Selling*.

- Does the seller get past "Just looking?" If not, work on "Just looking?" before working on other *Steps for Selling*.

- Does the seller find out why customers want to buy and what they want to buy? If not, work on finding out before working on other *Steps for Selling*.

- Are the seller's *Show-&-tells* self-ending? If not, work on *Show-&-tells* before working on other *Steps for Selling*.

- Does the seller get around *Roadblocks* well? If not, work on *Roadblocks* before working on other *Steps for Selling*.

- Is the seller testing the water with *Add-ons*? If not, work on *Add-ons* before working on other *Steps for Selling*.

- Does the seller ask customers to buy? If not, work on asking customers to buy.

Improve the Item Value — Improve the *Item Value* when the *Hit Rate* is at a high level. As the *Item Value* goes up, so do *Hit Value*, *Sales Dollars/hour of selling* and *Sales Dollars/entry*. As sellers raise their *Hit Rate*, they learned how to deal with customers. They're more sure of themselves with customers than they used to be. Now they can sell higher-priced items, they have less self-doubt to lower their standards. They're past offering the grandfather the $20 toy. Instead they lead him to the $300 train set and say, "Let me show you a toy that will make your grandson remember you for the rest of his life."

Improve the Item Count — It's time for sellers to work on the *Item Count* when they have a high *Item Value*. As the *Item Count* goes up, so do the *Hit Value*, *Sales Dollars/hour of selling* and *Sales Dollars/entry*.

As sellers raised their *Item Value*, they became even more sure of themselves. Now they have the guts to sell higher-priced extra items. Get them to sell the $100 accessories as well when they sell the $300 train set. Then add the $90 doll, "So your granddaughter won't feel left out."

Compare like with like — Different days and different times of day give different chances for selling. Tuesday mornings and Saturday afternoons are rarely equal. National holidays and the days close to them differ from normal days. Compare like with like to use the *Scores* well. How does Tuesday morning selling compare with other Tuesday mornings? How does this Easter Sunday selling compare with last Easter Sunday?

Make sound comparisons — There must be enough customers for the *Scores* to make sense. Suppose a seller works one morning and there's only one customer. Make a sale and that's a *Hit Rate* of 100%. Miss the sale and that's a *Hit Rate* of 0%. *Scores* like that have no meaning.

Group times with few customers. You may need to group ten Monday mornings together to get usable figures for Monday mornings.

Watch out for oddball days and oddball sales — Some days have unusual sales. Outside events change customers' habits. Traffic snarls and customers stay away from shops when the President comes to town. Sales on the first bitterly cold Saturday of the year rarely equal sales for a midsummer Saturday. These are oddball days—they don't let you make normal comparisons. You can compare the first bitterly cold day of winter from year to year. It's unlikely the President will visit you again.

Some sales are unusual. You usually sell an umbrella every two days but XYZ company buys 50 umbrellas from you as presents for its staff. That's an oddball sale—it throws your figures off. Include the sale in your figures, but note it as an oddball sale.

Use Scores to Support Sellers

Use Scores to support sellers — Use *Scores* only to help sellers improve sales. Use them to work with sellers. The *Scores* are useful guides but they have limits. Let sellers know you won't use the *Scores* to judge them or punish them.

It's easy to use the *Scores* badly. Because the *Scores* are numbers it's easy to compare them. It's tempting to make snap decisions from them. Too many factors affect the *Scores* to make direct comparisons of sellers based on them. It would use sellers poorly to let them go just because they have poor *Scores*. The *Scores* only let you know how well sellers were selling at the time they made the *Scores*. At some other time the same sellers may make different *Scores* while using the same skills.

The *All Sellers' Sales Summaries* tempt us to think we can judge sellers on the *Scores*. We can't do that fairly. We can see differences. We can explore why differences exist. We can make plans with sellers to help them improve their *Scores*. It's a mistake to let go of sellers with *Scores* below a supposed standard. The section *Track Scores to Drive Selling* sets out some of the limits to using *Scores*. Be aware of them. Letting sellers go for *Scores* below a standard may lead to lower sales. You'll probably let go as many good sellers as poor sellers. You'll have to find more sellers, with no promise they'll be better than those they replace. You'll destroy the morale of the sellers you keep. A manager who wastes resources like this will find it next to impossible to run a successful store.

Using the *Scores* to judge sellers will place you at a distance from your sellers. Use the *Scores* to bring you close to your sellers. Use the *Scores* to get involved with your sellers. Work with your sellers day-to-day to get better *Scores*.

Now and again you'll find a seller whose selling stays flat in a good time slot even when you lean over backwards to help. It's time to suggest a career change for these sellers who cannot or will not change. Base what you say and do on what you know about the seller, without reference to the *Scores*.

Know the limits of the Scores — Comparing sellers' *Scores* with average *Scores* is a bad way to use *Scores*. It's easy to take all sellers' *Scores* and work out the store's average *Scores*. We can see how far each seller is below or above average, but the average doesn't mean much. The facts aren't solid enough to allow that.

To compare sellers' averages, each seller must work a similar number of hours. During those hours each seller must serve a similar number of customers. On average, each customer must be as likely to buy as the next one. Retail trade doesn't work like that. Put aside any idea of comparing your sellers to an average seller. You'll only fool yourself.

Finding out why sellers have their *Scores* is a good way to use *Scores*. Find the high *Scores* and figure out why they're high. Find the low *Scores* and figure out why they're low. Get some ideas to work with the sellers who have the low *Scores*. Then watch how the *Scores* for sellers change as you support them. See what happens over six or eight weeks. Graph the *Scores*.

Make only sound comparisons. Compare like with like. Leave out oddball days and oddball sales. Work out the similar times in your store. Study sales records from before you began using *Scores* if you have them. Perhaps your sales on weekdays are similar. Perhaps your sales on evenings are similar. Perhaps Saturdays are in a class by themselves. Perhaps Sundays and legal holidays are similar. Compare equal hours. Compare all sellers on 16 hours of weekdays if the low for one seller is 16 hours on weekdays. To get a good sample, stick to the most active times. Switch two sellers in and out of the same hours several times to compare their *Scores*.

Be alert for hidden factors. The gender matches or mismatches of buyers and sellers can affect sales. So can match or mismatch of personalities or lifestyles. It's easier to sell to credit card customers than to cash customers. Payments made to sellers will affect *Scores*.

The *All Sellers' Yearly Sales Summary* is the least useful summary for comparing sellers with one another. It's uneven in an active store. It may compare a seller who worked Mondays in January with one who worked Sundays in December. Some sellers may work most of the year. Others may work only a few weeks

Fill in the Storewide Daily Sales Summary

Follow directions for the *Seller's Daily Sales Summary*.

Storewide Daily Sales Summary

Store _____ Downtown _____   Year 1994 Mon Dec

Sales

		Mon	Tue	Wed	Thu	Fri	Sat	Sun	Total
2	Date	12	13	14	15	16	17	18	12-18
3	Hours Open	11	11	11	11	11	11	11	77
4	Hours Selling	13	13	13	13	12	28	47	139
5	# Entries	87	95	85	80	99	191	324	961
6	# Receipts	42	39	46	49	44	98	174	492
7	# Items Sold	79	84	89	79	90	180	307	908
8	# Items Returned	0	0	0	0	0	0	0	0
9	# Items	79	84	89	79	90	180	307	908
10	$ Sales	4,598	5,798	4,998	4,398	6,200	11,124	18,922	56,038
11	$ Returns	0	0	0	0	0	0	0	0
12	$ Total	4,598	5,798	4,998	4,398	6,200	11,124	18,922	56,038

Scores

									⇑ Average
13	# Sales/entry Hit Rate	48%	41%	54%	61%	44%	51%	54%	51%
14	$ Average Sale Hit Value	109.48	148.67	108.65	89.76	140.91	113.51	108.75	113.90
15	$ Average Item Item Value	58.20	69.02	56.16	55.67	68.89	61.80	61.64	61.72
16	# Items/sale Item Count	1.88	2.15	1.93	1.61	2.05	1.84	1.76	1.85
17	# Entries/hour selling	6.69	7.31	6.54	6.15	8.25	6.82	6.89	6.91
18	# Sales/hour selling	3.23	3.00	3.54	3.77	3.67	3.50	3.70	3.54
19	$ Sales/hour selling	353.69	446.00	384.46	338.31	516.67	397.29	402.60	403.15
20	$ Sales/entry	52.85	61.03	58.80	54.98	62.63	58.24	58.40	58.31
21	# Entries/hour open	7.91	8.64	7.73	7.27	9.00	17.36	29.45	12.48
22	# Sales/hour open	3.82	3.55	4.18	4.45	4.00	8.91	15.82	6.39
23	$ Sales/hour open	418.00	527.09	454.36	399.82	563.64	1,011.27	1,720.18	727.77

Fill in the top of the form — Fill in a new form each week.

Line 3, Hours Open: The number of hours the store is open. For a store open 10 am to 9 pm that's 11 hours.

Line 4, Hours Selling: The total hours all sellers were selling. Suppose one seller sold for 5 hours and 2 others for 4 hours each. That's 13 hours selling.

Copy the total columns from All Sellers' Daily Sales Summaries — Check the figures after you copy them.

Work out the Storewide Scores not given by sellers — **Line 21, # Entries/hour Open (Number of Entries/hour Open):** The number of entries each hour the store is open is the number of entries divided the number of hours open. That's Line 5 # of Entries divided by Line 3 Hours Open. On Monday, December 12th there were 87 entries. Divide this by 11 hours open to get 7.91 entries each hour open.

Line 22, # Sales/hour Open (Number of Sales/hour Open): The number of sales each hour the store is open is the number of sales slips divided by the number of hours open. That's Line 6 # of Receipts divided by Line 3 Hours Open. On Monday, December 12th there were 42 sales slips. Divide this by 11 hours open to get 3.82 sales slips each hour open.

Line 23, $ Sales/hour Open (Sales Dollars/hour Open): This is the average sales dollars each hour the store is open. Divide the total sales dollars by the number of hours open. That's Line 12 $ Total divided by Line 3 Hours Open. On Monday, December 12th there were sales of $4,598. Divide this by 11 hours open to get $418 of sales each hour open. Work out totals and averages for the week. Work out the totals and averages for lines 21-23. Cross check the week column. Cross check against the week column of the *All Sellers' Weekly Sales Summary*.

Keep Track of the Consumer Price Index

The *Historic Dollar Total* is the total sales for a year in dollars of that year. Suppose total sales in 1992 were $441,859. The Historic Dollar Total for 1992 is $441,859. Suppose the total dollar sales in 1994 are also $441,859. Although the Historic Dollar Total is the same as for 1992, the value of a dollar has fallen. Sales for 1994 are less than sales for 1992.

Use the Consumer Price Index (CPI) to compare sales year to year. The CPI is an index worked out by the government to help with year to year comparisons of sales and prices. It's a measure of the average change in prices paid by urban consumers for a fixed basket of items and services. The Consumer Price Index relates to a base number of 100. The base currently in use is an average of the years 1982-1984 (1982-1984 = 100.) Here's a list of Consumer Price Indexes:

1988   118.3
1989   124.0
1990   130.7
1991   136.2
1992   140.3

Suppose total sales were $118,300 in 1988 and $140,300 in 1992. The value of the sales for both years is the same. To show 1992's sales in 1988 dollars, divide $140,300 by 140.3 and multiply by 118.3 to get $118,300. To show 1988's sales in 1992 dollars, divide $118,300 by 118.3 and multiply by 140.3 to get $140,300.

Use the right Consumer Price Index — Use CPI-U, not CPI-W. The government works out two Consumer Price Indexes. CPI-U covers all urban consumers. It covers 80% of the U.S. population that doesn't live in institutions. CPI-W covers only wage earners and clerical workers. It covers only 30% of the U.S. population that doesn't live in institutions. Its main use is in wage negotiations.

Put the CPI background in place — Get the background data for your store from your local library. Look in the latest copy of CPI Detailed Report (ISSN 0161-7311,) U.S. Department of Labor, Bureau of Labor Statistics. The government publishes these reports monthly with subtitles like Data for January 1993. Expect to find January's data at the library by mid-March. Table 24 is the most useful.[36]

---

[36] See also: Consumer Price Index Home Page at the Bureau of Labor Statistics http://stats.bls.gov/cpihome.htm and All Urban Consumers - (CPI-U) ftp://ftp.bls.gov/pub/special.requests/cpi/cpiai.txt

Historical Consumer Price Index for All Urban Consumers (CPI-U)
U.S. City Average All Items (1982-1984 = 100)

	CPI-U	% Change			% Change
1980	82.4	13.5	1990	130.7	5.4
1981	90.9	10.3	1991	136.2	4.2
1982	96.5	6.2	1992	140.3	3.0
1983	99.6	3.2	1993	144.5	3.0
1984	103.9	4.3	1994	148.2	2.6
1985	107.6	3.6	1995	152.4	2.8
1986	109.6	1.9	1996	156.9	3.0
1987	113.6	3.6	1997	160.5	2.3
1988	118.3	4.1	1998	163.0	1.6
1989	124.0	4.8			

CPI-U, U.S. City Average
All Items (1982-1984 = 100)
1992

Jan	138.1
Feb	138.6
Mar	139.3
Apr	139.5
May	139.7
Jun	140.2
Jul	140.5
Aug	140.9
Sep	141.3
Oct	141.8
Nov	142.0
Dec	141.9
1st ½	139.2
2nd ½	141.4
Annual	140.3

Keep up-to-date on the CPI — Get the latest CPI from the CPI hotline. Look in the U.S. Government listings in your phone book for the local Consumer Price Index hotline. Look under the heading U.S. Department of Labor, Bureau of Labor Statistics. Expect the indexes for January at the end of the second week of February. For help with the Consumer Price Index beyond what you can get at your local library call 415-744-6600 or 213-752-7521.

Set up listing the CPI as a *Special Job* and add it to *Daily*. Keep on top of the Consumer Price Index by phone each month and avoid extra trips to the library.

Use the CPI — Estimate the month's CPI when you set sales goals for the coming month. Post the CPI in *Daily* so sellers can use it to fill in the *Seller's Yearly Sales Summary*. Use the CPI to fill in the *Storewide Yearly Sales Summary*.

Fill in the Storewide Yearly Sales Summary

Follow directions for the *Seller's Daily Sales Summary*. Fill in this summary as you fill in the *Seller's Daily Sales Summary*.

Storewide Yearly Sales Summary

Store _____ Downtown _____

Sales

	Year	1992	1993	1994			
3	Hours Open	3,644	3,644	3,644			
4	Hours Selling	3,800	3,765	4,259			
5	# Entries	22,276	20,389	25,685			
6	# Receipts	7,573	6,524	9,893			
7	# Items Sold	13,880	12,625	18,026			
8	# Items Returned	85	63	54			
9	# Items	13,795	12,562	17,972			
10	$ Total Historic	441,859	385,466	759,824			
11	CPI	140.3	144.2	148.8[1]			
12	$ Total Current	468,629	397,762	759,824			

Scores

		⇑ Average	⇑ Average	⇑ Average	⇑ Average	⇑ Average	⇑ Average
13	# Sales/entry Hit Rate	34%	32%	39%			
14	$ Average Sale Hit Value	61.88	60.97	76.80			
15	$ Average Item Item Value	33.97	31.66	42.28			
16	# Items/sale Item Count	1.82	1.93	1.82			
17	# Entries/hour selling	5.86	5.42	6.03			
18	# Sales/hour selling	1.99	1.73	2.32			
19	$ Sales/hour selling	123.32	105.65	178.40			
20	$ Sales/entry	21.04	19.51	29.58			
21	# Entries/hour open	6.11	5.60	7.05			
22	# Sales/hour open	2.08	1.79	2.71			
23	$ Sales/hour open	128.60	109.16	208.51			

⇑ means work out these averages using totals in the rows above the arrow.
[1]This number is a guess made in early 1993.

Fill in the top of the form — Fill in a new form each year. Write column headings for each year since the store opened. Suppose it's 1994 and the store opened in 1992. Write headings for 1992, 1993 and 1994.

Copy this year's column from the Storewide Monthly Sales Summary — Copy lines 4-9 of the Total column to lines 4-9 of this year's column.

Copy line 12 $ Total to line 10 $ Total Historic and to line 12 $ Total Current. The Historic Dollar Total is the total sales for a year in dollars of that year. Suppose the total sales in 1992 and 1993 are both $250,000. Sales are the same in terms of Historic Dollar values. Since the value of a dollar generally falls in value from year to year, 1993 sales are of less value than 1992 sales.

Copy lines 13-20 of the Total column to lines 13-20 of this year's column

Enter the Consumer Price Index (CPI) — The Consumer Price Index is an index calculated by the government. It allows us to compare year to year sales and prices. Here's a list of Consumer Price Indexes:

1988	118.3
1989	124.0
1990	130.7
1991	136.2
1992	140.3

Suppose total sales were $118,300 in 1988 and $140,300 in 1992. Expressed either in 1992 dollars or 1988 dollars these sales are exactly the same. Enter the CPI on line 11.

Copy earlier years' figures from last year's Storewide Yearly Sales Summary — Copy all figures on shaded lines directly to this year's summary.

Enter earlier years' CPIs — Copy the CPIs from last year's *Storewide Yearly Sales Summary*. Check them against the figures posted in *Daily*. There may be updates to the figures you used last year. The latest CPIs on the list are sometimes estimates. Enter earlier years' CPIs on line 11.

Work out earlier years' sales in current dollars — Suppose this year's Consumer Price Index is 148.8 and last year's is 144.2. For last year's sales of $385,466 divide by 144.2 to get $2,673.13. Now multiply by 148.8 to get $397,762. That's last year's sales in current dollars. Enter earlier years' sales in current dollars on line 12.

Work out earlier years' Scores — Work out earlier years' *Scores*.

Take Line 12 $ Total Current as the sales total. Fill in all unshaded lines in the *Scores* section of the summary. Now you can compare the *Scores* from year to year.

Pay a Commission on Sales

Let your sellers profit so you can profit. Pay your sellers more for selling more and end up with more profit. That's the simple idea behind paying a commission on sales. Sellers will sell more when they know they'll get more cash.

The idea of paying commissions scares many retailers. They fear they'll lose cash by paying commissions. They feel they have better control of their store if they pay wages instead of commissions. In fact, every retailer pays a commission on sales. Suppose you pay $25,000 in wages and have sales of $200,000. That's a 12.5% commission on sales paid as wages. The commission paid as wages goes up when sales fall. You pay more to get less. The commission paid as wages goes down when sales go up. Since there's nothing to drive sales up, expect sales to stay the same or go down rather than go up.

Pay commissions to make a good profit in retail sales. Here's a simple model of how commissions work:

	Last Year		Last Year Adjusted		This Year Goal		Gain
Sales	214,078	100%	235,486	100%	270,809	100%	15%
Cost of Goods	109,115	51%	120,027	51%	138,112	51%	15%
Gross Profit	104,963	49%	115,459	49%	132,696	49%	15%
Fixed Expenses	44,069	21%	48,476	21%	48,476	18%	0%
Variable Expenses	7,860	4%	8,646	4%	9,943	4%	15%
Wages	25,674	12%	28,241	12%	27,081	10%	-4%
Profit	27,360	13%	30,096	13%	47,197	17%	57%

Goal	15%
Commission	10%
Inflation	10%

The columns with dollar amounts have columns beside them showing the amounts as a percentage of sales.

First adjust last year's figures to allow for inflation. The example uses a 10% rate of inflation to raise all figures. You may have better figures on fixed expenses from your landlord. Use them instead of the straight 10%. Only raise the base wage figure when you're paying minimum wage and that's gone up. Push your wage increase into commissions.

The model shows a sales increase of 15% as this year's goal. As percentages of sales, Sales, Cost of Goods Sold, Gross Profit and Variable Expenses stay the same. Fixed Expenses stay fixed, so as percentage of sales they fall from 21% to 18% of sales.

Wages are now a commission of 10% of Sales. As percentage of sales, that's shaved 2% off wages. Wages paid have risen from $25,674 paid last year to $27,081 to be paid this year. That's an increase of $1,407, about 6% of $25,674. So, it costs less, as a percentage of sales, to give a 6% increase in pay. Note that this wage payment is less than last year's wage payment adjusted by 10% ($28,241.)

Look what's happened to Profit. That's risen from 13% of Sales to 17% of Sales. The amount has risen from $30,096 to $47,197. That's $17,101 extra—about a 57% increase in profit, for an extra payment in wages of $1,407.

In practice you'll pay more than $1,407 because of extra bonus payments along the way to spur sellers to the goal. Perhaps you'll take another $2,000 or $3,000 from the $17,101 to pay the sellers. Your commission payments are still rewarding you well.

Here's the same table with a goal of 20% increase in sales:

	Last Year		Last Year Adjusted		This Year Goal		Gain
Sales	214,078	100%	235,486	100%	282,583	100%	20%
Cost of Goods	109,115	51%	120,027	51%	144,117	51%	20%
Gross Profit	104,963	49%	115,459	49%	138,466	49%	20%
Fixed Expenses	44,069	21%	48,476	21%	48,476	17%	0%
Variable Expenses	7,860	4%	8,646	4%	10,375	4%	20%
Wages	25,674	12%	28,241	12%	28,258	10%	0%
Profit	27,360	13%	30,096	13%	51,356	18%	71%

Goal	20%
Commission	10%
Inflation	10%

Fixed expenses fall to 17% of sales. Profit rises to 18% of sales. Wage payments are $2,584 greater than last year for an extra profit of $21,260, excluding any bonus payments.

These are models. Reality will differ from them, but the ratios are in your favor. Through commissions you can pay sellers a little more and get a lot more profit. With figures like the above models, there's nothing to lose by paying commissions. Simply promise to pay the same wages as last year or 10% of sales, whichever is greater.

Put no limits on earnings — Work out your commission payments properly and stick to them. Avoid the greed that sets in with some managers. They see sellers earning "too much" and it upsets them. They work dodges to cut down on payments to sellers. That upsets sellers and leads to trouble. Morale falls, sellers leave and sales fall. Aim to pay a lot to have sellers sell a lot so you earn a lot. As long as paying commissions earns extra profits, it's not possible to pay sellers too much. To win in retail share the success and the profits.

Get the Scores in place before paying commissions — You need facts on your store's sales before you can set up commissions. You probably have general sales figures that will help you already. It's easier to set up commissions when you know how they'll affect each seller. *Scores* will show you this. You'll need to bring some sellers up to standard. You'll need their *Scores* to do this. Have the *Scores* in place with sellers selling from the *Top of the Wheel*. You must have *The Wheel* in place before you pay commissions. Otherwise your sellers will turn customers off.

Choose your plan for commissions — There are several plans for paying commissions. One that's well suited to retail stores is to pay a wage against commission.

Wage against Commission. Suppose you pay a commission of 10% of sales. You guarantee a wage, say $7 an hour. Each pay period you pay $7 an hour. At the end of the month you work out the commission at 10% of sales. Suppose the seller's sales for the month were $14,890. The commission is $1,489. You take away what you've already paid at $7 an hour. Suppose the seller worked 8 hours a day for 22 days of the month. You've already paid $1,232. You write a check for $257 to make up the difference between $1,232 and $1,489. You write no check if the seller's sales were $12,320 or less. This way the sellers know they'll get their base pay when they work. They feel safe. They'll feel they did well when you give them their check for commissions.

Always give a separate check for commissions. That way the sellers see their commissions. Sellers don't see their commissions as clearly if you add them to a regular pay check. They see a regular pay check that happens to be bigger. They don't have the same sense of doing well.

Wage Plus Commission. Pay a wage, say $7 an hour. For 8 hours a day for 22 days of the month you pay $1,232. In addition you pay a commission on sales. Suppose you pay 1.73% of sales and the seller sold $14,890 for the month. At the end of the month you write a check for $257.60. You'd pay the same for sales as you would in the wage against commission example. State a minimum sale for the commission. Otherwise you'd still pay a commission if the seller sold less than $1,232. This system lacks glamour. It makes you sound like a cheapskate when you pay 1.73% commission instead of 10%.

Commission Only. Pay no wage, only a commission. You pay $1,000 on $10,000 sales if the commission is 10% of sales. Commission only isn't realistic for most retail stores. It needs sellers who are sure of themselves. It needs an inventory of big ticket items. Commission sellers look for big rewards. To get big rewards they're willing to risk having no income.

Variable Bonus. Pay a commission related to the markup. Items with different markups pay different commissions. In practice the items fall into groups, so you have several rates of commission. Control what you pay by a sticker system or by numbers or letters in the item number. Most people find this clumsy and prefer to pay a commission that averages out.

Share in a Group Commission. To get your sellers working together divide the total commission among the sellers according to the hours they worked. At its simplest, someone who worked 20% of the hours worked this month gets 20% of the commission for the month. Jane works Monday mornings. She makes few sales, but she does valuable *Background Jobs* that make it possible for sellers to sell at other times. Mary sells on Saturday afternoons and does few *Background Jobs*. Under this plan, Jane and Mary support one another. In practice, it's better to relate the percentage of the commission paid to the time slots. An hour worked on Monday morning could score as one commission-hour, while an hour worked on Saturday morning scores as 2.5 commission-hours. Time slots with lower commission-hours can serve as proving grounds from which sellers work their way into the higher paying time slots.[37] Where there's a share in a group commission the good sellers start helping the weak sellers, especially when a goal is in sight but the store might miss it.

Some stores pay sellers commissions strictly related to the sales they make themselves. These stores can offer a share in an extra group commission. Suppose you have a goal for the store to sell $40,000 this month. Offer to pay 1% store commission if the store meets the goal. Take this $400 and divide it among the sellers according to the hours they worked. Another way to pay it is on each seller's sales as a percentage of total sales. It's a good plan to hold this extra commission in reserve. Bring on the extra commission when you see the store running behind the goal. That helps the push for the goal.

Work out your pay structure — Try these ratios for base pay. For a part-time seller, pay about 1.5 times legal minimum wage. For a full-time seller, pay about 1.8 times legal minimum wage. For a manager, pay about 2.1 times legal minimum wage. See how these rates compare with what you get by asking around. Then adjust them so they're similar.

It's easy to employ sellers when the wage you pay against commission matches the wage paid by other retailers. It works for you if most retailers pay $7 an hour

---

[37] Of course, there may be some "Monday morning sellers" who stay there because that's the only time slot that fits their personal schedule.

and you pay $7 an hour against commission. You can pay less base pay when you have a track record of paying well based on your commissions. You can pay your commission against minimum wage. Sellers will push harder for their commissions if they know it's hard to live on base pay.

It's easiest to work out commissions when you have last year's income statement. 12% increase in sales is a good goal. It's not too low and it's not too high. Goals below 10% have too little challenge in them. On the other hand, it must be possible to reach the goal. Otherwise it's a fantasy, not a goal. Sellers soon see there's no way of reaching it and they stop trying. Goals higher than a 12% increase are possible, but only if you've done something to make them possible. Special training for sellers and carefully put together advertising plans are good examples.

Set the wages goal at 10% increase over base pay. From 8% to 11% is the lowest amount over base pay that will really get sellers moving. As the percentage drops lower, it has less effect. It has no effect when it drops to 1% or 2%. Strike a balance between your goal, the extra you pay to reach it and the extra profit you want.

Set weekly goals — Set a commission rate that sellers can work out in their heads. That way they'll work out earnings as they sell. That feedback will push them to make more sales.

Set a goal for every seller for every week. It's not good enough to set a goal for a month. That way it's easy to fall behind. It's easy for sellers to think they'll catch up later in the month after a slow start. That's no way to reach a goal. Let sellers know how much you expect them to sell each week.

Use sales figures from last year to set goals. Always collect and keep daily sales figures. Keep the figures for sales by time of day too if you have an automated cash register or *Point of Sale System.*

Base goals on equal weeks. Adjust for special calendar days like Easter that move from year to year.

Pay commissions in steps — Pay commission in steps rather than a flat rate. Try a plan like this:

- Pay 6% for reaching Last Year's Adjusted Total.
- Pay 8% for reaching the goal.
- Pay 9% for reaching the goal plus 10%.
- Pay 10% for reaching the goal plus 20%.

Keep aside a percentage of sales to use in some imaginative way. You may wish to use different figures. Find out what figures work for your sellers and use them. It's important to pay for reaching Last Year's Adjusted Total. It's important to have the largest step between it and reaching the goal.

Look back to see if you can pay more — Look back over each seller's sales each month. Pay more if the sales have stacked up over time. Work out the total goal and the total commission paid so far. Pay more if there's a case for paying more. Make it clear to sellers that the more they sell the more they make.

Point out items without commissions — Pay commissions to push sellers to sell items at full price.

Pay no commissions on markdowns. A markdown is already a loss to the store. It's already at a giveaway price. You can't pay extra for sellers to get rid of losers. Get sellers to use markdowns as hooks for real sales.

Pay no commissions on sale items. A sale item is one brought into the store as a bargain to attract customers. It has little profit on it or even a loss. Get sellers to use sale items as hooks for real sales. That's the only reason they're in the store.

Pay no commissions on top of spiffs. A spiff is a special payment, or bonus, for selling a certain item. You pay it right then and there at the time of the sale. It's like hitting a jackpot. The reason for a spiff is to focus sellers on an item you want sold. You may want it sold because it's an expensive item with a good profit. You're willing to pay extra to sell it. You may want it sold because it's a lemon. You try paying the sellers extra to sell it before you mark it down for customers and lose even more on it. You're making the best of a bad situation. You hoped to sell it for $100, but it looks as if you'll have to mark it down to $50. Before you try that, you offer a spiff of $25 for each one sold.

Pay no commissions on discounts. Items sold at a discount lack the profit needed to pay commissions. Seller's discount sales and mall discount sales are sales the sellers make as a professional courtesy. Other planned or unplanned discounts given to customers cut into profit. They're bait on the hook which get customers to buy other items that carry a commission.

Let sellers know how you pay — Keep the *Guide Sheet* on commissions up-to-date. Let sellers know how you pay when you interview them.

Say good-bye to sellers who don't learn — A few sellers can't or won't learn to sell. They don't meet their goals when others do. Give them strong support. Give them extra training. Make sure they have customers to sell to. It's time to say good-bye when you're sure the problem lies with them and not with you. Make your decision on sellers by the end of the 6th week of employment.

Pay managers a commission — Pay managers by how well the managers get the sellers to sell. It's usually easiest to pay the manager by the same plan as the sellers. Wage against commission is common

Play Games to Push Sales Up

Bring back the excitement of selling with games. Sales rise when you use *Scores* and pay commissions in your store. They reach a peak and begin to fall. Watch out. They may even fall lower than when you began to use *Scores*.

At first the *Scores* are new and they're fun. After a while, sellers get used to them. At first the commissions push sellers, but after a while sellers expect commissions. Commissions become a regular part of wages. Sellers still want commissions, but they push less hard for them. It's time to push sales up again.

Play games for prizes. Games bring back the competition and excitement of selling. There's always something happening when you play games. They drive sales up.

Watch the pattern of sales. Play a game when sales begin to drop. Look for a burst of sales to a higher level. The game ends and after a while sales begin to drop. Bring on another game.

Start small while you feel your way — Begin with a few dry runs and work your way up. Sellers will play for fun when you first start games. Then offer small prizes while you test the waters. Get the measure of what the games do to your sales. Work out the sizes of game boards. Is the game going to last a day or a week? Is the game for single sellers or for teams? Can you set up games between different branch stores?

Work out the game values of sales. Does the sale of one item move a seller one space on the board? Does the sale of $10 move a seller one space, or does it need $20? These factors will vary with what you sell, how much you sell and the number of spaces on the board.

Move on to better prizes for some games when you get control over games. Look for large spurts in sales when the prizes are valuable.

Search out ideas for prizes — Store owners often have good things they can give away. They can make good prizes at no cost. One owner had a collection of hats that he lost interest in. Sellers of both sexes scrambled to win them. Another owner grew out of his hippie phase. His earrings and necklaces made fantastic prizes. Come up with your own list. Here's a start:

- Coffee for two.

- Day off with pay.

- Dinner for two.

- Dinner for two with limousine service.

- Gift certificate.

- Good parking spot for a month.

- Higher commission for a week.

- Leave work early.

- Lunch for two.

- Magazine subscription.

- Rare coins from the coin dealer.

- Taxi home.

- Tickets to a concert.

- Tickets to a show.

- Tickets to a show and limousine service.

- Tickets to sports event.

- Transit pass for a month.

- Trip to a trade show.

- Trip to Hawaii for two.

- Week off with pay.

Look for discounts from other stores. In a mall other stores may swap discounts with you. Restaurants will often give a discount if you ask. Some want new customers to sample their meals.

Brainstorm with your sellers. Do this after you've given some prizes and the range of values is clear to the sellers.

Allow choices. Different things turn on different sellers. Suppose you're going to give a prize valued at $200. Raise the interest in the game by getting sellers to say what they want. Have sellers bring in pictures of their items. Set up a catalog of prizes.

Play games to raise a Score — Aim to raise a single *Score* when you play a game. These are the main *Scores* to raise:

- Hit Rate (Sales/entry.)

- Hit Value (Average Sale.)

- Item Count (Items/sale.)

- Item Value (Average Item.)

Score these directly in games or score the parts that make them up. For example, sellers can score on:

- Average sale on a sales slip.

- Gross sales over a period.

- Highest sale on a sales slip.

- Number of items on a sales slip.

- Total sale on a sales slip.

Give sellers who are behind in their selling the chance to catch up. Plan some games based on the greatest improvement. Put poorer sellers in the action. Play games based on anything else you can measure. Here are some ideas:

- Highest number of two pairs sold to a customer.

- Lowest number of credit cards left behind.

- Lowest returns over a period.

- Quiz on Item Sheets.

- Quiz on prices.

Set time spans for games — Run most games for a day only. Run them only on days they'll boost sales. There's little point in playing games on days you usually have only two customers. Run games with big prizes longer. A week is long time for a game. Two weeks is very long. Games longer than a day or two call for special steps to keep up interest

Set Up Games

Choose a safe place for the race boards. Decide where you can keep race boards so nobody upsets the game while it's in play. Keep race boards on a counter or shelf in the storeroom if you have space. Otherwise, use a bulletin board on the wall and pin the race board to it. That way sellers can see it easily and will less likely knock it over. It's usually easier to find wall space than flat space in a crowded storeroom.

Set up race boards — Draw a large version of the race board. Bright colors and decorations make the games more fun. Another way of making large versions is to make copies of the race board on an industrial copy machine. To make many large copies of a race board, have a blueprint company enlarge the race board onto a vellum transparency. Then run blackline blueprints from the transparency.

Where the design allows it, make different length race boards. Give the Coiled Snake more coils to make the game longer. Give it fewer coils to make the game shorter. Different length race boards are a good help in controlling the games. Make games long enough to be interesting but short enough to keep in touch with them. Unless the stakes are high, sellers will get bored with games that go on too long.

Set up pieces — On flat surfaces you'll need to move pieces. Checkers or coins are OK. So are pieces of heavy card or small figures. It helps to make them personal with names or photos. On a bulletin board you'll need to move flags on large pins. Color them and make them personal with names or photos.

Fill in a Game Details Sheet — Let the players know the rules.

Game Details Sheet

Game	Coiled Snake, Guide Sheet 25-4
Race board	Based on Form 25-4 with 44 diamond spaces
Number of pieces	One for each player
Score	Total of Sales Slip
Value of score	$10 difference moves 1 space
Players	All sellers on their own-no teams
Time of play	All day Sunday June 19th, 1994
Winner	First on snake's head, or nearest to head
Prize	Small ruby ear stud
Other	

Juggle parts of games to get the right mix for your store.

Try different length race boards: One game of Coiled Snake may have 20 diamond spaces, another 44.

Try different scores: Play Coiled Snake on total of the sales slip. Play it on highest item or average item on the sales slip. Play it on number of items on the sales slip.

Try different values for scores: It may cost a $10 sale to move a piece a space. It may cost $20 or $50. Selling one item may move a piece a space or two spaces. It depends on what you decide. Up to $100 it may cost $20 a space but for the value over $100 may cost $10 a space. Selling $120 then moves 7 spaces instead of 6. Perhaps only sales over a certain value count, as when sellers move a piece one space for every sale over $200.

Try different groups of players: Sometimes sellers play alone, sometimes in teams. Run teams through time as well as teams where members play at the same time. Sellers A and B work the first shift. Sellers C and D work the second shift. Team A + C plays against team B + D.

Try different times of play: Some games are over in a shift. Others are over in a day. Others go on for days or weeks.

Try different prizes: Work out prizes by the extra sales the games bring. The extra sales pay for the prizes and help give the store extra profit. Prizes range from tokens that cost a few dollars to trips to Hawaii for two.

Give prizes by points in long games — Spread the chance at a prize by using a points table. This gives different sellers working different hours a chance at a prize in games that spread over weeks. Plan these games so most sellers receive a prize. Then set up a point table and a catalog of prizes listed by point values.

The table sets out points for *Item Count* for the week. Each week the game goes on each seller looks up the table to get points for the week. They add these over the weeks of the game and then look in a catalog to choose prizes.

In this table points begin at an *Item Count* of 1.11 - 1.15. For each step in the column, points go up by half the previous value. There are four columns for hours worked. To get the points in each column, multiply the column number by the points in column 1. Point values in column 4 (31-40 hours worked) are 4 times as large as in column 1. Round the

Item Count for Week	Points for Hours Worked			
	5-10	11-20	21-30	31-40
1.00 - 1.10	0	0	0	0
1.11 - 1.15	5	10	15	20
1.16 - 1.20	8	15	23	30
1.21 - 1.25	11	23	34	45
1.26 - 1.30	17	34	51	68
1.31 - 1.35	25	51	76	101
1.36 - 1.40	38	76	114	152
1.41 - 1.45	57	114	171	228
1.46 - 1.50	85	171	256	342
1.51 - 1.55	128	256	384	513
1.56 - 1.60	192	384	577	769
1.61 - 1.65	288	577	865	1153
1.66 - 1.70	432	865	1297	1730
1.71 - 1.75	649	1297	1946	2595
1.76 - 1.80	973	1946	2919	3892
1.81 - 1.85	1460	2919	4379	5839
1.86 - 1.90	2189	4379	6568	8758
1.91 - 1.95	3284	6568	9853	13137
1.96 - 2.00	4926	9853	14779	19705

figures to whole numbers. Work out a table that suits your store for the game at hand.

Put up a bonus to makes a game like this interesting. Perhaps an extra 300 points to sellers with a day's sales over $500.

CHAPTER 18

ADVERTISE AND PROMOTE THE STORE

Beyond a general interest in knowing what lies ahead there are only two reasons for reading this chapter:

1. Your store is off the beaten track and advertising is the only way customers will know it exists.

2. The *Scores* for your store tell you it may be sensible to explore advertising.

Separate Advertising from Other Promotions

Promotion is any way you make customers notice your store or its items. Aim to make those who notice your store buy from it and become regular customers.

Promote your store in a number of ways — These are the main ways to promote your store:

Advertise: Pay the media to let people know about your store and its items. Ads make customers aware of what you sell and ask them to buy from you. They usually ask customers to buy directly but sometimes they ask indirectly. Indirect ads rely on customers being so attracted that they'll want to buy.

Seek publicity: Make your store and its items newsworthy. The main vehicles are press releases and publicity stunts.

Engage in public relations: Provide and support community service. Give to charities. Sponsor sports and cultural activities. Join professional groups. Make speeches to community groups. Run open houses. Write newsletters.

Carry on in-store promotions: Put up displays, posters and signs. Run in-store sales and offer premiums.

The different types of promotion aren't always clear-cut.

Seek a direct payoff from advertising — See worthwhile results from ads. Take steps to see that you make advertising clear-cut. Expect ads to pay for their cost and to make a profit. Be firm with what you expect from ads. They're only ads if they pay off.

Seek an indirect payoff from other promotions — Publicity and public relations bring your store to public attention without asking people to buy from you.

Sometimes publicity leads to a spurt in sales but you can't rely on that. Look for a background effect with most publicity. Your store may lend its name and give its support to a good cause. Hope that people will remember you when they want to buy. Don't expect a direct payoff from public relations.

Publicity and public relations can be expensive. You may never know how much you get back from the expense. Pay for expensive publicity and public relations only when you're making enough to afford them. Pay for public relations only when you believe in the causes you support. That way it doesn't matter what they bring back to you. During Heart Week you may wish to pay for a billboard that says, "Please Give to the Heart Fund." It will have the name of your store on it too. You'll feel good about it. People will respect you. Some of them may shop with you. You'll know you spent your money well. You'll be content even if there's no payoff to your store.

Publicity and public relations can cost you little more than your time. Writing a news release is a good example of seeking publicity. News releases can lead to good publicity if you can spare the time and they work out well. Many don't work. Those that do work may have little effect on your trade. A few really put a store on the map.

Write press releases right away when your store and its items are eye-popping new ideas. Write them right away when you have the knack of seeing human interest angles that others overlook. Otherwise, write them when you've made your store rather than to make your store. Beware of putting them ahead of getting your store in shape.

Be aware of different uses of the word promotion — To some retailers a promotion is an advertised markdown. A store may offer a $50 item for $25 for a limited time and call it a promotion. Radio stations call ads that plug the radio station promotions. That way they skip counting them in their total of advertising time.

Put Advertising at the Bottom of Your List

Few stores need advertising at the top of the list. Let customers know where you are if your store is off the beaten track. To get customers through the door you've no choice but to advertise or go out of business. Advertising goes right to the top of your list of needs. In this case, look on the cost of advertising as extra rent. Hope that your location gives you payoffs that offset the cost of advertising. The payoffs are usually lower rent and easy parking. Put advertising on hold if you have a steady flow of customers.

Your store may be losing money or barely making it and you want to change that. Your store may be profitable but you want to increase the profits. Advertising seems to meet these needs and seems natural to us. Daily, we swim through a sea of ads. Large and successful companies advertise. We hear that advertising pays and we feel it must be true. It's a simple chain of thought. Expect more customers if more people know about your store and what you sell. Expect more sales if you have more customers. Expect the extra sales to pay for the advertising and leave you with extra profit. It doesn't always work that way.

It costs a lot to advertise. Advertising can be yet another expense that eats up profits. It's easy to spend money and time on advertising and see loss rather than profit. Change "Advertising pays" to "Sometimes advertising pays, but mostly it doesn't." That's a better slogan for retailers who want to advertise wisely.

Advertising expense has one feature not shared by other expenses. You don't have to advertise. You can get rid of that expense and that's exactly what many retailers should do.

Put advertising completely out of mind until measurements show your store is ready to think about advertising. Then learn how to advertise and learn how to measure how well ads work before you try advertising.

Shape up your store — Make sure all sellers have good backend skills in place.

Make sure all sellers are selling fully to customers who enter the store now. Put your effort into training sellers until they're doing an excellent job. Until then, you need better sellers, not more customers. Until then, your sellers are wasting the customers you do have.

Make sure your sellers turn customers into regular customers. Successful stores depend on regular customers.

Take major credit cards and debit cards before you advertise — Major credit cards and debit cards will increase your sales. Customers who wouldn't otherwise buy will buy with credit cards and many will buy more often than cash customers. Many will buy more items than cash customers and they'll often buy higher-priced items. You only pay for credit card service when you make sales. It's a better deal than advertising. You pay for advertising whether it works or not. A store that pays to advertise before taking all major credit cards has it backwards.

Firm up your store's identity before you advertise — Develop a strong identity for your store before you think about advertising. What exactly does your store offer customers? How have you positioned your store? Why would customers want to shop with you? It's unlikely you can write good ads unless you have a clear view of your store's identity. Think about these parts of a store's identity:

Mission: Review your store's *Mission Statement*. Is your mission down-to-earth? Are there enough customers interested in it? Does your mission make your store one of a kind? Are you just like the other stores that sell similar items? Is your store unusual? Are you trying to be everything to everyone? Do you live up to your mission or have you drifted away from it? Has your mission changed? Do you need to push your store in a new direction? No advertising can offset a poor mission.

Payoffs: Are you in touch with your customers' needs? Do you sell items that customers want to buy? Customers won't buy if they see no payoffs in buying the items you sell. Have you made the mistake of selling items you like and want to sell to customers who want something else? No advertising can offset a store with few payoffs to customers.

Value: Do customers see value in the items you sell? They won't buy if they don't. Value isn't lowest price. You're not offering much value if all you're offering is low price. Customers are willing to pay good prices when they see value. Unless you offer value for money, your store will fail no matter what you do. No advertising can offset lack of value.

Service: You're killing sales if your store is a mess. Filthy restrooms will make customers uneasy. Unless your sellers are friendly and helpful, they're driving customers away. No advertising can offset poor service.

Name: Betty's Jewelry Nook tells more than Betty's Nook. A well-chosen name for a store is its own ad.

Know your present customer line before you advertise — Find out who your customers are. Where do your customers come from? Why are they in your store? Survey your customers to find out. Knowing your present customer line gives you a base to compare with when you place ads. Does each ad you place change your customer line? How many extra dollars did each ad bring in? Are you getting value for money on your ads? It's easy to spend money on ads that don't pay.

Keep surveying. It's not good enough to run a survey now and then. That way you only know your customer line now and then. It won't relate to each ad you place. Chances are you can't depend on your surveys when your sellers only survey now and then. They need practice to develop the survey skills. They'll push the surveys aside if you let them. Survey of the customer line is part of the *Steps for Selling*. Train sellers to survey as they sell.

Sellers ask, "How did you hear about our store?" Most customers will tell them when sellers ask this question pleasantly. The time to ask is while sellers chat with customers after each sale.

Keep records of the answers. There's a space on the *Customer Flow Sheet* for sellers to write answers down. Then they sum up the answers on the *Seller's Customer Flow Summary* in their *Day Reports*. Then you know the sales dollars you receive from each source of customers.

Teach sellers to ask "How did you hear about our store?" early in their training. Have them asking it before they hear anything about the *Steps for Selling*. It's the same with the *Customer Flow Sheet*. That's part of the system for working out the *Scores*. Start sellers using it before they learn about the *Scores*.

Know Scores before you advertise — Know your store's *Scores* before, during and after placing an ad. Did your Sales Dollars/hour of selling go up while the ad ran? That's the most obvious figure. You may have a paying ad if Sales Dollars/hour of selling rise sharply. You do have a paying ad if *Customer Flow Summaries* also show customers are in the store because of the ad.

Suppose sales increase but *Customer Flow Summaries* don't favor the ad. Perhaps customers aren't giving honest answers. So look at Number of Entries/hour of selling. Did that rise? Was there anything other than advertising that caused it to rise? It's unlikely the ad is having an effect on sales if Number of Entries/hour of selling didn't rise. What happened to Hit Rate, Hit Value and Item Value? Did the ad change them?

Improve your Scores before you advertise — Hold off advertising if *Hit Rate, Hit Value* and *Item Value* are low. Your sellers aren't doing a good job with the customers they already have. It's a mistake to give them more customers. They need your help to sell better to the customers they already have. Work with your sellers on their *Scores*. First see them go up. Then see them flatten at a high level. Then keep them at a high level. Then you're ready to think about advertising.

Control climate before you advertise — Customers leave quickly if they shiver in winter and sweat in summer. There's little point in advertising for more customers only to drive them away. Control your store's climate and work with the customers you already have.

Snag passers-by before you advertise — Pull people passing by into your store. Some people pass by only once. Make the most of the chance you have to draw them in. Other people pass by regularly. Aim to turn them into regular customers. Fresh attractive window displays and clean windows draw passers-by into your store. A visible attractive store sign draws passers-by into your store.

Fight the Pressure to Advertise

Swear you'll only advertise on your terms. Swear you'll advertise only when your store has high and stable *Scores*. Stick by that decision. Stay firm on this when advertising reps try to sell you space. Swear you'll advertise only when you're already making good sales. That's when you can afford the luxury of testing what advertising can do for your store. As a luxury you can afford, advertising is a challenge you'll enjoy. You can make it pay off if you work at it, but it's never a sure bet. Swear that you'll seek the places where you advertise. Depending only on reps who come to your store may cripple your store.

Beware of advertising reps — Advertising reps want to sell you advertising space, period. They want to sell it whether you need it or not. Their view is that you need it and most of them can't imagine that you can do without it. They support their view with half-truths, like "Advertising pays." They play on retailers' lack of experience and readiness to believe in the power of advertising.

Advertising reps make no guarantees. They sell you space and suggest the ad you place in it will improve profits in your store. Deep down they must know this usually isn't true. They certainly back off when you ask for a guarantee.

Contrast advertising reps with how you sell in your store. You sell items that give customers payoffs at fair prices. Customers who buy and find the payoffs aren't real return the items. Customers who buy and decide the price wasn't fair return the items. You give them back their money cheerfully. You only want satisfied customers.

Advertising reps don't sell by these standards. Reps would stand by their product if they offered a deal that worked in most cases. They fall back on the truth when pushed on the issue. They sell you space to advertise in and nothing more. The advertising is your problem. Writing an ad that works calls for special skills which you may not have yet.

Advertising reps usually suggest that advertising pays. They stress your need to get the name of your store before the public. They stress the need for long-term campaigns to build traffic in your store. They stress that successful stores advertise. There's truth in these lures, but they're not the full story. Sometimes advertising pays but often it doesn't. Advertising reps encourage you to believe that all advertising pays. It doesn't. This myth is easy to believe because of the successful advertising that surrounds us. But look closely at all advertising and you'll find that much of it doesn't pay. Sometimes advertising even makes sales fall. Stores do succeed without advertising. They have features that customers want.

It's nice to get your name before the public. It may bring you extra customers. How much do you want to pay for them? It's not often you can be sure you get value for money. Advertising to build traffic can be useful but too often you can't be sure it works. Suppose you spend $1,000 each month to develop one new customer. Suppose this customer spends $500 a year for the next 10 years. With

100% markup on cost and excluding expenses, the new customer will pay off the $1,000 after four years. For the remaining 6 years you'll make profit on the ad. Even if you have spare cash to tie up like this, how do you know this rosy picture will hold up? The customer may spend $100 this year, $20 next year and nothing after that. Advertising reps paint rosy pictures. You have to deal with reality. Deal only with ads that turn a profit or break even in the month you place them. Look on extra long-term customers as an added bonus.

Certainly successful stores advertise. They can afford it. For some of them, it pays. For many it's an extra tax they bear because they lack the courage not to advertise. Many factors affect the success of stores. Sometimes stores succeed by themselves and advertising takes the credit.

Send advertising reps away promptly and firmly — Choose the advertising reps you'll talk to when you're ready to advertise. Until then, send advertising reps away. You have better things to do than spend time with them. Be firm, clear and as polite as you can. The sooner the advertising rep is out of your store, the better. Say, "I'm sorry, but we've already mapped out our business plan and we have no need for extra advertising. Thank you for stopping by. Good-bye." Then move away quickly and get busy with something. Take any cards and pamphlets reps want to leave. Meet any attempt at further talk with, "I'm sorry, I'm quite busy now. I'll be sure to call you if we need your services in the future."

Support community activities — Sometimes the "advertising rep" is from a community group. Typically firemen, policemen, guides or scouts have a newsletter. They ask for cash and will print your business card in their newsletter. Always give to these causes. The cost is small and it will come back to you in some way. Always give a small donation to community groups who ask. As you prosper, increase your donations. These groups speak for the community that supports your store. It's fair to support them.

Sidestep the urge to advertise — You may feel tempted to advertise before you're ready. Try writing news releases instead. News releases will give you practice in writing and will only cost the time you put into them.

Measure the Results of All Ads

Force all ads to pay their way. The only purpose of advertising is to make sales. Make every ad you place pay for itself and leave you with a profit. Kill all ads that make no profit. You're chasing dreams if you hope they'll pick up.

Never advertise to keep your name before the public. Advertise and make a profit. That will keep your name before the public.

Never advertise to develop your image. Advertise to make a profit. Develop your image at the same time.

Never advertise to draw future customers. Advertise to make a profit. That will draw future customers. Ads that break even may draw future customers. You haven't lost but you want to do better than that. Do something to make break-even ads pay off. Ads can lose money but pay for themselves with future customers. It's difficult to prove that in a retail store. It's largely an advertising rep's fantasy.

Avoid artistic ads. It's unlikely you can make a profit with an artistic ad. Beware of turning your advertising over to artists who operate computer drawing programs. There's no end to the fancy gimmicks they'll push on you as they enjoy themselves at your expense. Someone who knows about advertising needs to control and channel their creative efforts.

Place only ads you can measure — Work out a way to measure sales that result from each ad. Otherwise, forget the ad. Avoid spending money blindly. Always know if your ads bring results. A business can grow for many reasons. Advertise while your business grows without measuring ads and you risk giving ads false credit.

There's no such thing as general advertising. It's a way of fooling yourself. General advertising is like scattering money in the wind and hoping for a return.

Judge by results instead of the look of ads — Ads that look nice and pay off are fine. They can lead you to think nice looking ads pay off. It's easy to put your attention on making ads look nice. It's easy to fall into the trap of thinking nice looking ads pay off. Only sales that result from ads count. Write ads that pay off at the lowest possible cost. It doesn't matter if ads that pay off are ugly. Avoid anyone who talks of creativity in putting ads together.

Measure how well ads work — *Scores* are your best guides to the value of ads. Take the *Scores* on similar days before, during and after placing ads. Use the Consumer Price Index to adjust last year's *Scores* when you compare from year to year.

Survey your customer line to find out if the ad brought new customers. Make sure sellers ask regular customers if they saw the ad and ask new customers what brought them into the store. A bonus keyed to the ad can measure the ad's pull. Offer a bonus you can afford and customers want. A rental furniture store that offers a month's free rent will have most customers who saw the ad ask for it.

Advertise an item at a good price and see if its sales go up. It'll score low for customers who read the ad but don't want the item. It'll score high for customers who haven't seen the ad but see the item in the store. Get a measure of this by selling it at the good price before you advertise it.

Advertise a special but post the normal price in the store. Customers who saw the ad have to ask for the special price. This scores low because it makes some customers feel ill at ease to ask. Offset this by including "when you mention this ad" with the price in the ad.

Services for tourists are cheap, easy to measure and can be popular. "Pick up a copy the Sales Tax Rebate Form. It's free and there's no obligation." "Visitors, pick up a list of our favorite restaurants. It's free and there's no obligation."

Schemes involving coupons for drawings give some information but they score low. Ads for free drawings rarely pull many customers into a store. They've seen too many of them and they've grown tired of them.

Nurse the Customers You Already Have

Customers who already shop with you are your easiest source of new sales. It's easier to keep a customer than to get a new one. They know your store and the items you sell. They value your good service. They'll shop again. They'll tell their friends about your store.

First advertise to your customers — Always have a flier about coming sales and events in your store. Make sure one goes into every customer's bag. Mail a newsletter to customers from time to time. Let them know what's new in your store. Announce new products and include newsy chit-chat.

Go to bat for your customers—support what they believe in. Support conservation if yours is an outdoor store. Write letters urging conservation and give your customers copies. Let customers know they can sign up for petitions at your store. Lobby for safer toys and against violent toys if yours is a toy store. Let your customers know you act for them.

Support your sellers in developing Personal Customers — Are you satisfied they write enough *Thank-you Notes*? Have you let your sellers forget about sending them? Check the figures. Look at the *Customer Flow Sheets*. Opinions aren't enough. How many *Personal Customer* sales are they writing? Check the figures. Look at the *Customer Flow Sheets*. Opinions aren't enough. You have no figures? You don't need to advertise yet. Pay attention to the customers you have before you get more of them. You have figures but they show few *Personal Customers*? Change that before you waste money advertising.

Work on your Registered Customers List — Are sellers registering enough customers? How do the registration rates compare from seller to seller? You need figures instead of guesses. Look at the *Customer Flow Sheets*.

Do you have someone to plan and make mailings? Set mailings up as a *Special Job*. There's little point to a list if you only use it now and then. Offer really fine specials for your regular customers. Money spent here beats money spent advertising elsewhere. Let your regular customers know these specials are only for them. Have sellers include handwritten messages to some of their *Personal Customers*. Weed your customer list. There's little point mailing to someone who last shopped years ago.

Follow These Rules for All Ads

To place ads that work you'll have to do a lot of background work.

Advertise store or items — Advertise your store or the items you sell. Try both kinds of ads and see which works better for you. Your store tags along when you advertise items. It comes at the end, as the place to get the items. This way you build your store indirectly. It may lack glamour, but if it builds your store, it builds your store. Sometimes suppliers will help pay for this kind of ad.

Develop your store's image as you advertise — What's special about your store? What do you offer that no other similar store offers? What's your unique selling position? What's your image? That is, what first comes to customers' minds when they think about your store.

Manage your image in your ads. Your aims are in your *Mission Statement*. Now is the time to update it. Be clear about the image you have and the image you want. Keep them in mind as you develop your ads. See that your ads develop and support your image. Stick to your image. Like a fad, your store will be here today and gone tomorrow if you jump on fads. Never advertise for image alone. Keep your image in mind as you advertise for profit.

Find out why customers come to your store — Listen to what customers say about your store. Ask regular customers why they shop with you. Listen to their reasons. Listen to the words they use to tell you their reasons. What's the promise that will most likely make customers buy from you? A customer may say your styles are "up-to-the-minute and beyond." Grab it. It beats "latest styles." Your customers can give your ads real turns of phrase. Listening to your customers works wonders for your ads. It gives you an advantage. Most retailers are too busy to listen to their customers and use their input.

Find out how stores you're up against attract customers — Study ads from stores you're up against to get ideas for your ads. They give you a check list of points you may overlook. Present only ideas that blend with your image. Look for better ways to present their good ideas. Be careful of picking up their bad ideas. Most retail stores don't check that their ads work. You'll find a lot of bad ideas in other stores' ads.

Run with ideas stores you're up against miss. Stress the special features of your store. Set yourself apart from the pack. Take over the truth when you can. You're close to the Sky Train station. So are others. They don't say it, but you do.

Send *Your Shopper* to the stores you're up against. *Your Shopper* talks to their sellers and customers while shopping. *Your Shopper* finds out why customers are in the other stores. *Your Shopper* gives you a check list of points you may overlook. Bring your store up to standard where you can. Meet the stores you're up against and beat them in all possible areas. You're ahead when you take the trouble to know the stores you're up against. It's too much trouble for most retailers. They find it easier to go on hunches.

Aim for a target — Be single-minded in your ads. Ads that try to reach everyone reach only a few customers. They cover too many topics lightly. Few customers take them seriously. Ads that work reach into a target group. Begin advertising your single most mouth-watering point. Stress one key payoff of this point for your target group.

Focus on desires and payoffs — Advertise only what works for your customers. Put aside all payoffs to you when you write an ad. Work for your customers. Customers must see payoffs for themselves in shopping with you. They must see the promise of satisfying their desires when they shop with you. Customers are people and people are interested in themselves. To work, your ad must promise a payoff. Showcase payoffs your customers care about. Advertise payoffs your customers believe. Support your claims with facts, photos and testimonials.

Boasts and appeals to your self-interest limit your store. Any argument you make for payoffs to you makes customers fight you. Customers don't care about your interest or your profit. They'll gladly buy at prices that will put you out of business.

It's your self-interest speaking when you make the same claims as other stores and try to shout louder than them. Instead, tell the reasons you make the claims. Most other stores fail to do this.

It's your self-interest speaking when you claim you're the best in town. You may be the best, but what do you offer that makes you the best? An empty claim to be best is another way of saying, "Shop with me, not with the other guy."

You don't have to be best. To gain customers you have to show you're a good store with good items. Without a strong reason to go elsewhere, customers will come to your store. Your job is to write ads that are more honest and tell more facts than ads from stores you're up against. Then customers will feel sure about you and less sure about them. Then they'll shop with you.

It's your self-interest speaking when you claim you're the original. You may be the original. It would be nice for you if others hadn't copied you. What is it you offer now that others don't offer?

It's your self-interest speaking when you claim you're a family business. You appear to take your right to customers as given. What is it you offer your customers because of your special background? Did you learn the business on your daddy's knee? Are your items cheaper than in stores you're up against because you own the building and are free of the lease payments they make?

Most claims to give service are idle boasts. A good example is the robot-like clerk at the checkout stand who wears a button saying, "I'm a Service Specialist." Head down with no eye contact. There's no hello, no good-bye and no thank-you. Slap the groceries in the bag. The receipt is too faint to read. Service is something you give. It's not something you claim. Serve customers well and they'll speak for your service. Talk about something you did if you want to advertise your service. Give customer service, not lip service.

Write simply — Stick to simple everyday words.

```
An ad isn't the place to show you went to a good
school. Your schooling may work against you. Without
knowing it, you may use words many people don't use. Be
clear. Go over all you write to make sure you use only
simple everyday words.
```

Compare the paragraph above with this one:

```
An advertisement isn't a forum to manifest your
meritorious erudition. Your profound achievements in
education may impede your capability to compose
comprehensible prose. Unconsciously, you may employ a
vocabulary beyond the comprehension of the multitudes.
Eschew obfuscation. Amend your writing to ensure it
employs only an appropriate vocabulary.
```

Text with simple everyday words is easier to read even if readers understand all the showy words. Stick to short words that people know. Replace long words with short everyday words. One short word is better than one long word. Several short words are better than one long word. Write short simple sentences. Aim for sentences shorter than twelve words. Avoid commas if you can. Otherwise, use only one comma in each sentence. Write short paragraphs. Aim for paragraphs with three sentences or less.

Write headlines that attract customers you want — Telegraph what you're going to say. Headlines are a short way of saying what's in the ad. That's their purpose. That's what people expect them to do. Trick headlines turn people off. A headline that says, "Want to earn $250 an hour?" attracts people who want to earn $250 an hour. The ad loses people when it begins, "Until you can, stretch your present earnings at Joe's Grocery…" Readers will put Joe's Grocery on the list of stores they avoid.

The headline is the most important part of your ad. It's the only part of your ad most people read. Always have a headline. Without a good headline you have no ad. Your headline goes up against other headlines for people's attention. Make it stand out well. People it interests will want to know more about your offer and they'll read your ad. But people are in a hurry and they already have too much to read. They skip most of the reading they pay to get. Spend more time writing the headline than the rest of the ad. Your ad is a waste if the headline doesn't work.

Headlines that make people curious work. Curiosity is one of the strongest forces that cause people to do things. Headlines that promise a payoff work. Headlines that promise to make a dream come true work. Headlines with news work. A new store is news. A remodeled store is news. A new line of items is news. A new management is news.

Include your target group in the headline. Attract only people who'll become customers. Get it into your headline if you sell only outsize men's clothing. Outsize men know from experience that ads for clothing aren't for them. They ignore them. The word "outsize" attracts them.

Write long headlines if you need them. Short headlines are OK if they tell everything you need to tell in the headline. Otherwise, use long headlines. Less than ten words is a short headline. Avoid long headlines that come from sloppy writing. Start by writing everything you want to say in the headline. Then try to chop it down to six words or less. First prove that a short headline won't work before you use any extra words.

Include the name of the city in the headline if you can. People take an interest in what happens where they live.

Tell a true and interesting story — Tell only the truth. Tell only the truth that will stand up in a court of law. It may have to do that. Make sure customers know you as an honest person.

Tell a story. Write as you'd write a letter to a friend, one person to another. Let customers follow a thread. Tell a story, even if it's an ordinary story. You'll be ahead of the pack. Most advertisers think it's enough to flash their name.

Tell an interesting story. Pitch appeals to emotion rather than to reason. A detergent that makes dishes unbelievably beautiful outsells one that cleans them. Promise overweight people a fast, painless way to become attractive. You'll outsell a diet that avoids health hazards.

Make your first paragraph a grabber. Get the readers by the throat or they'll soon go away. Make sure your first sentence is less than twelve words.

Tell the full story — Put aside the common idea of an ad. Most ads give few facts. Most ads have a pretty picture. Most ads look pretty.

Put aside the myth that people won't read long ads. Interested people will read them. Once you've captured their interest with the headline they want to know more. People will read your story if it's interesting. It shows you have something to say when you write a lot. Write it well and people will read it.

Begin by writing everything you need to make your point. Include every fact and argument that helps make your point. Most people will read your ad once, so let them get the facts at one reading. Some will buy for one reason, others for different reasons.

Tell the full story. Put no limit on space or cost at this stage. Map out everything you need to say. Begin with the promised payoff. Explain how it works. Prove that it's true. State the action you want customers to take. Include your name, address and phone number. Include the price if you're advertising an item. Avoid flowery writing. It will only turn people off. You need an interesting story, plainly told.

Now firm up your copy. Make it read well. Get others to read it and note their reactions. Edit your copy to the point where it has no spare words but tells the full story.

Now see if it fits your space and budget. Sometimes your ad doesn't fit your space and budget. Can you shorten it and still tell your story? You may have to tell a different story that takes less space and money. It's better not to run the ad than shrink it to fit the space you can afford. Shrunk down ads have no pulling power.

You'll add to your problem by including pretty pictures. Pictures have three jobs:

1. To get attention.

2. To replace text because they explain something in less space.

3. To show something you can't describe.

These jobs add to the selling value of the ad. Only use pictures that do one or more of these jobs. Some ads use pictures to decorate or be artistic. These pictures add no selling value to the ads.

You'll add to your problems by including a lot of white space. Include some spacing to assist reading but be careful of the argument that you need lots of white space. It may make your ad look better but does it make the ad sell more?

Take only positive stands — Stress payoffs customers will get by shopping with you. Steer away from negatives. People have more interest in rewards they'll gain than problems they'll avoid. Expect a diet that melts fat off while you sleep to outsell one that prevents heart trouble.

Avoid knocking stores you're up against. You may be better than a store you're up against. Brag about it and it looks as if you're bragging. Customers are uneasy with sellers who brag. You risk fixing the name of the other store in customers' minds. You've seen those ads on TV where Brand A battery brags it's better than Brand B. How many people do you know who can't remember whether it was Brand A or Brand B that was better? Someone is doing some advertising for someone else.

Include testimonials — People accept what other people say about you more easily than what you say about yourself. A magazine or newspaper may have written nice things about your store. Customers may make nice comments about your store. Get permission and use their comments in your advertising. People eagerly accept nice things experts say about you.

Replace puffs with figures — Puffs are general statements made to impress customers. Puffs take the form of "We offer the widest selection of merchandise." Customers have heard this kind of talk too often and it makes little impression on them. They expect such claims. They're used to advertisers putting their best foot forward. The looseness of the puff makes people ignore it. Tell the real figures instead. "We stock 1,356 items for you to choose from."

Show things in use — Show items in use when you use pictures of items. This adds a story to your picture. It adds action and it makes your pictures interesting. It saves you words in telling the story of your item. Show the product instead of the parts. Show the salad instead of the vegetables to make the salad.

Get action now — Get people who read your ad into your store. A simple way to get that is by including an offer with a time limit.

Test ads to make them work — List and test different ways of telling your story. As you write an ad, different ways of telling your story come to mind. List them and test them. In your ad you're going to make one appeal out of several that occur to you. In making that appeal several different phrases will occur to you for each point you make. List them and test them.

You write an ad based on how you see things. Your ad might be good or bad. Ask your sellers and friends for their help. Their input will be valuable, but it's unlikely you'll ask enough of them. They may agree with you too easily. The things that you and I desire may not appeal to most people. Nothing takes the place of the results you get from placing the ad.

Consider each ad you place as a test. Make a change to it and see how the change affects the results. Make only one change at a time so you'll know what changed the results. Feel your way. Learn from the ads that don't work. Without tests and mistakes you're flying blind. Get the appeal right for your ad to work. Changes in the headline or text can lead to surprising gains in sales.

The most important thing to test is the headline. People select all their reading by headlines. Get the right headline and get attention. It's like someone shouting your name in a crowded room. Changes in headlines have great effects on how well ads work. One headline may have ten times the pulling power of another.

Give some thought to how the ad looks. Make it attractive but not at the cost of sales. Beware of anyone who talks about balance or movement in an ad. Only the sales an ad brings in count.

Change or kill losing ads — Change or kill ads that don't pay for themselves. Sometimes changes to ads make them pay. Try changes you think might make them pay and keep track of the results. Each time an ad fails to pay off, change it or kill it. It doesn't work to hope that next time you run an ad some magic will make it work. Hoping an ad is building profits in future sales doesn't work either. Go for sales now. It's foolish to place ads and fail to check how well they pay off. Keep track of all ads. Change or kill dud ads quickly and cleanly.

Cling to winning ads — Keep running ads that work. It's hard work to get a winning ad. It costs a lot of money to get a winning ad. Make winning ads work for you. Keep running them. After a while, you'll get bored with ads that work. Ignore that feeling. Because you're bored with an ad is no reason to change it or stop running it. It's still brings new customers and it's not scaring regular customers away. It's a brand new ad to each new person who sees it. Think of the ad as a billboard beside a river of people. Run every winning ad until it stops winning.

Pay ad by ad until you get a winner — Be careful of bulk rates on ads. Perhaps an ad that costs you $450 placed in one issue costs only $400 per issue if placed in 10 issues. Pass up an offer like this until you have a winning ad. You're out $1,350 if you run an ad three times and it still fails. At the bulk rate it runs 10 times and you're out $4,000. Change the ad each time when you take out three ads at $450 each. You get three shots at making the ad work.

Follow These Rules for Printed Ads

Printed ads are the commonest, so it pays to know what works with them and the things to avoid.

Set text in ordinary size type — Set type in sizes normal for the publication where the ad appears. Text described as 11 point or 12 point is about the right size for body text.[38] The smaller the number of the point, the smaller the text. Small type always loses readers with poor eyes. On the other hand, there's no proof that using large type for body text brings more sales.

Avoid using small type to squeeze your ad into a small space. Pay for more space or write a smaller ad. Ads that people have to squint to see have no pulling power.

Set ads in public places in large type. Be sure readers can read ads from where they normally stand or sit. Use type large enough for readers with weak eyes who don't wear glasses.

Set text in ordinary type styles — Set type in styles normal for the publication where the ad appears. Set body text in a type with serifs. Serifs are small lines used to finish off the main lines of a letter. You can see them easily at the top and bottom of an m. Sans serif type has no serifs and it's harder to read in body text. It's fine for headlines.

Text with serifs: mw.

Text without serifs: mw.

Set text in **bold** or *italics* to make it stand out. Bold or italics make a word **or a phrase stand out.** In long ads it's OK to set a key sentence or a short paragraph in bold or italic. But setting the whole ad in bold or italic type doesn't increase sales. It's like shouting to get people to notice you. Shouting everything turns people off.

Put blank lines between paragraphs to make them stand out.

Set headlines people can read — Headlines are larger than text and are often bold. Set them in normal type styles to make sure people can read them easily. Crazy arty headlines people have to puzzle out are no use. *Type that looks like handwriting is hard to read.* Let people read your headlines easily or you waste your ads. Headlines have no periods at the end. It's OK to put headlines in quotation marks.

---

[38]The text of body type in this book is 11 point. The type in this footnote is 10 point.

Add subheads in long ads to keep readers interested. Subheads are larger than body text but smaller than headlines. Try them every two or three inches of text. Instead of subheads try bullets (•) or asterisks (*) or notes in the margin to set points off. Try numbering the items in a list of related facts.

Set ads in black type on a white background — Black on white lacks glamour but tells your story with no problems. Reverse type is white type on a black background. Because it's hard to read, it cuts down sales. Steer clear of colored type on a colored background. It sometimes looks good but mostly it's hard to read and cuts down sales.

Use upper case normally — Setting an ad or headline in capital letters makes it hard to read. Everyday text is mainly lower case letters with a few capitals. Parts of some lower case letters rise above the line and parts of others drop below the line. These letters help readers see words as words. People read lower case text word by word or in groups of words. CAPITAL LETTERS ARE ALL THE SAME SIZE. NONE HAVE PARTS ABOVE OR BELOW THE LINE. IT'S HARDER TO READ TEXT IN CAPITALS WORD BY WORD. PEOPLE READ WORDS IN CAPITALS LETTER BY LETTER. THEY GET BORED AS THEY SLOW DOWN AND THEY STOP READING YOUR AD.

In typed text people sometimes use capitals to make a phrase or a word stand out. That's not necessary in printed text. Make **a phrase** or a **word** stand out by using a different style or size of type.

Set type for reading, not for design — Steer clear of arty effects based on type. These are hard to read so they can't help sales:

- Headlines set in a single column down the page.

- Odd shapes filled with text.

- Type set at an angle or set on a curve.

- Type set so you read it from bottom to top of the page.

Leave these games to stores with money to waste.

Set type in columns — Columns are easier to read than text spread right across the page. Set columns of text about 40 characters wide. Make the narrowest column at least 35 characters wide. Make the widest column no more than 45 characters wide.

Stick to ragged right margins — Ragged text is easy to read. Text with words at the ends of lines split by hyphens is harder to read. So is text spread out by using more than one space between some words. Sometimes you can balance lines by changing words for words of different lengths. Be careful to use only words that sell for you.

Begin paragraphs with drop initials — Drop initials are initial letters that take more than one line of text.

Text lines after the first line of text wrap back against the drop initial. Begin paragraphs in ads with drop initials. They draw the reader's eye to the beginning of each paragraph. They help the reader by marking paragraphs clearly. The rest of the paragraph forms a solid block.

Pay for more space only for more sales — Resist making an ad larger to make it look better. A larger ad is fine if it brings extra profit. The general claim in print advertising is the more you tell, the more you sell. Larger ads may sell more for you, but only if you tell more and you tell it well. Balance larger size against extra cost. You may already be telling enough. Making an ad larger by setting the body text in a large point size is unlikely to bring extra profit, unless the text is too small to read easily. The same text set in 24 point type instead of 12 point type isn't likely to bring extra profit.

Test size both ways. Make an ad larger to find out if it brings extra profit. Make it larger again if there's extra profit to see if it brings still more profit. Make it smaller if there's no extra profit and see if it brings as much profit as before. Make it smaller again if it does. Test until you find the smallest ad that pays off.

Include pictures when they add selling value — Include pictures to stand out from the ads you're up against. Include pictures to replace text—a good picture can save 1,000 words. Include pictures to show things you can't describe.

Pictures that simply show items can be useful in an ad. A good picture shows what the tea set looks like while it's hard to describe it.

Include photos rather than drawings. Only use drawings when photos print poorly. Then use scratch board drawings. Make sure photos tell a story. Arouse curiosity. Make customers ask themselves, "What's going on here?"

Steer clear of photos of yourself. Photos of you may please you but probably won't sell anything for you. Think about using your photo only if you're sure you could get work as a professional model. Would someone else with a store like yours pay to use your face to make a selling difference in their ads? Then you may be able to use your face to sell your product. Most ads with the advertiser's photo answer to the advertiser's vanity rather than to a selling need.

Include color photos when you can afford them. Color photos are better than black and white, but cost more. Four color photos are best but they cost the most.

Test photos as you test headlines. Find out which photo draws most attention. Photos that interest you may not interest most people. Photos of babies and animals draw the most attention. Women look at pictures of women doing things. Men look at pictures of men doing things.

Follow the formula Picture, Headline, Text — Follow what people do. Most people first look at the picture, then read the headline and then read the text. So, set up ads with picture at the top, then headline, then text. Placing the headline above the picture or below the text are common mistakes in ads. Always have a headline—it's a big mistake to leave it out. Always have text.

Keep text off pictures. Text printed over a picture is usually hard to read. Sometimes people can't read it at all. Text on a picture takes away from the picture. Why are you using the picture? Have you fallen into the trap of using it to decorate? Set text in a small stick-on if you do put text on a picture. A stick-on looks like a small Post-it note on the picture. People can read stick-ons because they have text on a clear background.

Follow These Rules for Magazines and Newspapers

Ads in magazines and newspapers are the commonest ads for many retailers.

Test your ad in different magazines and newspapers — Start with one ad in one newspaper or magazine. Does it pay off? Keep running it if it does. Otherwise change it, kill it or try it elsewhere. Try a second ad elsewhere when you get a winning ad running. Does it pay off? Does it cut into the first ad?

Low quality publications may pay off. Many specialty stores think ads in smart magazines work better than ads in newspapers but ads in newspapers often work better. Make your own tests. Likewise, ads in ordinary newspapers may work better than ads in quality newspapers. Make your own tests.

Know your targets before you place an ad — Know who reads the publications. Number of copies sold is important but it's important to know the number of copies sold to people who buy what you sell. The smaller number of copies sold of a boating magazine may sell you more boats than a daily newspaper. Only a test will tell.

Judge target newspapers and magazines only by number of copies sold. Be careful if there's no outside check of this number. Ask to see the results of an independent audit of circulation.

There are usually more readers than copies sold. Several people may read the same newspaper in a home or restaurant. How often copies appear affects the number of readers. Few people read yesterday's newspapers. Weekly or monthly magazines are around for at least that time. They may stick around after that. Publishers give rosy estimates of the number of readers. One may claim five readers for every copy sold. Another may claim six readers. Ignore these estimates to compare one magazine or one newspaper with another. Compare the number of copies sold. The rate of readers to number of copies sold is probably similar in similar magazines.

An outside check on the number of copies given away is a must for free magazines and newspapers. Those delivered house to house probably have less readers than the number of copies given away. Those picked up from boxes on the street may have more readers than the number of copies picked up. Look into the reputation of free magazines and newspapers. Some are excellent but many are weak.

Some people take a magazine or newspaper they rarely read. They used to read it. Now they don't have the time to read it but they still like to feel in contact. They think that next week, or next month, they'll get time to read it. Their lives and values have changed but they cling to the familiar. They meant to cancel, but they haven't got around to it yet. People pay for a lot of material they don't read. Publishers ignore this when they estimate the number of readers.

Look into rival ads before you place an ad — Rival ads for what you sell can help you. The magazine or newspaper works for others, so it can work for you. Rival ads for what you sell can kill you. You may be unable to meet the prices and services others offer. Rival ads for what you sell can drown you. There may be so many ads that few readers read them.

Gain experience before you use supplements — A supplement is a lift-out section of a newspaper or magazine. It has several pages of your ads. It's your own news section within a magazine or newspaper. A supplement is expensive. Make sure your single ads work before you try supplements.

Follow These Rules for Direct Mail

Once you have a target audience direct mail can be a useful form of advertising.

Target the customers you want — With direct mail you choose the readers. Choose the readers well and your mailing will interest most people who receive it. There are many places to get mailing lists: Look under *Mailing Lists* in the *Yellow Pages*. Contact clubs and other groups. Keep your own list of customers.

Be honest with lists — Usually, you buy lists for one mailing. You'll pay a penalty if you use them for extra mailings. The list owners salt the lists with marker addresses. Mail to these addresses ends up with the list owners and they'll come after you if you cheat. Think about buying lists for multiple mailings. Hit customers with three different mailings in a row. Keep track of how well multiple mailings work for your store.

Send several small mailings and measure the replies — With direct mail you can key the replies. Include a numbered coupon or a special offer in each mailing. This means you can change your letter from mailing to mailing. That way you'll know which letter gives the greatest payoff.

It's a mistake to start with a big mailing. Mail a few thousand only. Get your letter right and get some profit before you mail many thousands at a time. For commercial mailing lists, look for a 1% or 2% reply rate.

Tell the full story — Take as much space as you need to tell your full story. You can write a lot before it costs you more to mail it. With direct mail the more you tell the more you sell. Aim for three to five pages or more. One or two pages isn't enough. Write well and tell an interesting story. Make the first sentence short and interesting or your mailing will fail.

Tailor your message to your readers — Send different messages to different groups. Send messages in different languages.

Add a PS and a PPS — Most people read the PS and the PPS, so make them pay for you.

Go first-class — People will treat your mailing as junk mail if it looks like junk mail. First-class in a plain envelope gets people to open the envelope. Test a first-class mailing against third class mailing before you try to save cash by mailing third class. Handwritten addresses get your mail opened. Attractive stamps make your mail appealing. Colored envelopes make your mail appealing. Leave off the return address and people open your mystery mail. Some people throw out mail unopened based on the return address.

The downside is you need to be sure of your addresses. The post office opens letters it can't deliver to find out who sent them. Then it mails them to you at your cost. Expect to pay two or three times the cost of first-class mail for each item returned to you.

Sell by mail or bring customers to the store — Use direct mail to sell by mail order. Use direct mail to bring customers into the store.

Look into Brochures

Turn to brochures to add to profit rather than to bring profit you lack. Get into brochures when your store is making money and you're looking for ways to make more money. Keep away from brochures while your store is struggling.

Send out brochures to bring in tourists and Askers — Get tourist bureaus and hotels to give out brochures. They're also useful to send to people who write or phone to ask for facts about your store. Measure their payoff just as you measure the payoff of other ads.

Hide brochures in your store — Keep brochures out of sight in your store. The role of brochures is to bring customers into your store. Once customers are in your store you want them to buy. Many customers will pick up brochures instead if you give them the chance. Some will pick up brochures as an excuse "to buy later." Brochures get them off the hook. Others will find their attention taken by the brochures and use up their buying energy without buying. They'll busy themselves reading and dreaming instead of buying. Keep only a few brochures in the store in a drawer that's hard to reach. Keep them for the rare cases when customers in the store demand them.

Go first-class with brochures — The only worthwhile brochure is a first-class brochure. Pass over brochures until you can afford a first-class brochure. Write interesting text. Design brochures with nice colors. Include photos with a story and professional artwork. Drawings alone aren't good enough for first-class brochures. Always include photos or use photos only. One large photo on the cover is better than several small photos.

Set up brochures vertically — Check that your brochures will fit the slots in the racks you'll be using. Typical brochures measure 3½″ to 4″ wide by 8½″ to 9″ tall. They fit upright in racks. See that your text and pictures fit the width of the folded brochure. Some designers make the mistake of fitting text and pictures to the length of the folded brochure. People have to turn their heads sideways to read these brochures when they're in the racks so they skip them.

Put the selling message on the brochure cover — The selling message is your headline. It belongs on the cover where people will see it. They'll skip your brochure unless it has a good headline.

Put store name and location on the brochure cover — Make sure people can find you. Let your location sink in even to people who pass over your brochure.

Make your brochure worth keeping — Include useful information about your store and your community. Include a map. Draw a map to show where your store is in your community. Then people will keep your brochure with them when they visit your community. They'll use your map to find their way around your community and your store will always be in mind.

Look into the Yellow Pages

Ads in the *Yellow Pages* of the phone book pay off for some stores. They work well for services that customers need quickly in times of crisis. They work well for plumbers and funeral homes. They can work well for stores that take orders by phone. Florists are a good example. They can work for stores where customers call in and you talk them into coming to your store. You may get customers who don't phone. They look you up in the *Yellow Pages* and then drop in.

Ads in the *Yellow Pages* may not pay off for you. The *Yellow Pages* reps will help you spin fantasies. They'll stress their satisfied customers. They do have satisfied customers. There are people who depend on the *Yellow Pages* to stay in business. Keep your feet on the ground. Do the *Yellow Pages* ads pay off for your kind of store? There are many who can show no payoff from their *Yellow Pages* ads.

Measure the results of Yellow Pages ads — Customers from *Yellow Pages* ads show up in *Customer Flow Sheets*.

Track the payoff of high cost *Yellow Pages* ads for phone orders. Install a separate phone with it's own number for the ad. Buy a phone with a color that stands out, say yellow. Then score orders from the yellow phone. Try the yellow phone for a test period of one to three months. Then disconnect it and forward its calls to your regular phone. Keep a record of all customers who call on the yellow phone. You'll have their names, phone numbers and credit card numbers. Track what they buy in the future. From this test you'll know exactly how much cash your ad brought you in both the short term and the long term. You'll know whether this ad in the *Yellow Pages* works for you. Give up the idea of the expensive ad in the *Yellow Pages* if the yellow phone test seems too expensive. You've already decided it's not going to pay off. You doubt the profit will equal the monthly phone fee and a share of the installation cost.

Profit from one Yellow Pages before you use the next — Test the *Yellow Pages* one by one. Profit from the *Yellow Pages* in Minneapolis before you use St. Paul's. Profit from the Bronx before you use Queens. Fantasy has a way of taking over when planning ads in the *Yellow Pages*. Say, "No" to the *Yellow Pages* reps who push the surrounding areas.

Choose your heading well — Think about the heading you want to appear under.[39] For many stores the heading to use is clear. You're a dispensing optician, so you want Opticians-Dispensing. For other stores it's less clear. Perhaps John's Sporting Goods started as a general-purpose sports store. Now most of its trade comes from skis. Skiing Equipment is a better heading than Sporting Goods. This may be a hard decision. There's little ski trade in the summer. Know the heading you want before the *Yellow Pages* rep asks you. Otherwise, you'll decide in a hurry and you may regret your choice.

Profit from one heading before you use the next one — It's possible to list some stores under more than one heading. Choose the heading for the main line of

---

[39]*Yellow Pages* reps call the headings "classifications."

business, or one of two equals. Only consider listing under a second heading when the first heading pays off.

Stay out of the district "Yellow Pages" — Reps sell space in local directories modeled on the *Yellow Pages*. Typically, they cover a district of a city like Forest Hills. District *"Yellow Pages"* suffer from poor distribution and low use by people who receive them. There must be exceptions to this. Make sure yours is one before you advertise in it.

Know the options in the Yellow Pages — Most business phones get a "free" listing in the *Yellow Pages*. This is the routine listing that comes when you put in a business phone. The listing is of company name, address and phone number. These listings are in columns and there are four columns on a page. Each listing has one line for the name of the business and one line for street address and phone number. These listings are in small plain type.

The *Yellow Pages* groups similar businesses into classes under headings. The headings are alphabetical. They appear in the columns and as indexes at the top of the page. Businesses under each heading are in alphabetical order.

You can pay for options to make you stand out from the crowd. Many businesses set their names in larger boldface capitals. A few set their phone numbers in larger boldface type.

You can change the column listing into a column ad marked off by a box. The boxes are slightly narrower than the columns, but you can stretch the box down the column. You can use a whole column or more than one column. The boxes allow you to use a variety of types and to use colored type as well as black.

You can also place display ads in the *Yellow Pages*. The display ads are from one to four columns wide and come in several heights. Display ads can occupy a whole page. In display ads you can use fancy typefaces and artwork. Size and seniority decide their position within the *Yellow Pages* heading. Whole page display ads come before half pages, and so on. Within the same size display ads the ad that's been running longest comes first. Buy a large ad to move closer to the front of the heading. Renew your ad from year to year to move closer to the front as other advertisers drop out.

Know how customers use the Yellow Pages — Customers turn to the heading that interests them. Within the heading they often need a special product or service. They often need a place that's easy to get to and hours that fit their needs. Most customers start looking near the beginning of the heading. As soon as they find what meets their needs, they stop looking. Most customers make life easy for themselves. First they look at the larger display ads near the front. Then they look at the rest of the larger display ads. Then they look at the smaller displays and larger boxes near the front. Then they look at the rest of the displays and boxes. Then they look at the line listings. Being near the front of the heading pays off.

Choose your store name well — Name your store so you're near the top of the listing. Suppose Ann's Flowers and Wanda's Flowers are next door to each other and have similar column ads. Bet that Ann's gets more calls than Wanda's. That's not to say position in the *Yellow Pages* should be the only thing you weigh in naming a store. Flower Patch Florists gives a good position in the White Pages. Wonder Flowers is a more imaginative name and might bring you more customers. Forest Hill Flowers will show your location better. You may still have to choose a name for your store. Try choosing a good one that's early in the alphabet. You may have two or three possible names in mind. Position in the *Yellow Pages* might tip the balance for you.

Be careful of being too near the top. Sometimes a listing in the *Yellow Pages* begins with a few names at the bottom right of a page. Many customers skip them.

Some names that bring you to the top bring problems. Names made simply to bring you to the top of the list may make you look hopeless. Some people will wonder if they can trust A-AA-ABA Plumbing. Is this all they have going for them? Some of these names turn some customers off. They feel tricked and that makes them uneasy. Some customers will stay away from your store if they feel uneasy about it. Aardvark Printers is a gamble. Aardvark Pizza might get you some free publicity, but will upset some customers who imagine you're cooking aardvarks. Customers will expect to find plush aardvarks at Aardvark Gifts and Toys.

Use the name in your business if you use an odd name to get near the top of the listing. Some phone companies call to check how businesses answer the phone. Aaace Aaappliances will get listed as Ace Appliances if that's how they answer the phone.

ABC, as in ABC Plumbers, is OK for stores without style. It's common, so someone else may already have it.

Be careful of A, as in A Flower's Touch. You may end up listed as Flower's Touch. It's hard to pin down reps for the *Yellow Pages* on how they'll handle short words so it's better to steer clear of them.

Perhaps your store already has a name and you're near the end of the list. You'll need a display ad to move to the front.

Locate your store well — You'll get more calls if your store is on a street that most customers know. Let customers know how to get to your store when it's off the main drags. Let them know the nearest well-known streets. Maps can be helpful but only in large ads where you really have space for them.

Estimate your needs — You need little to stand out in a list of a few stores. Some *Yellow Pages* headings have only a column or two of stores listed. In these your name is your ad when it tells your story. Herbs from Around the World is fine. Take a small column ad if you want to tell more. You need more to stand out if your store's heading has many pages of stores. Customers mainly look at the display ads and the larger column ads. The regular column listings stand little chance of getting attention.

Boldface the phone number in column listings — Most stores in column listings boldface the name. That's OK if the name tells a different story than the story in the heading. Under the heading Florists–Retail, **Takamatsu Bonsai** tells a story. **Grace Florists** adds nothing to the heading.

It would be better to boldface the address and phone number line instead of the store name. Then customers looking for a handy store would find you easier. That would make it easy for customers who run a finger down the column and for customers who glance at the column. Unfortunately, most *Yellow Pages* only allow a boldface name or a boldface name and phone number. The boldface phone number is useful. Many people know districts of a city from the first three digits of the phone number.

Highlight services and items rather than store name — The *Yellow Pages* is basically a list of names. This leads most advertisers in the *Yellow Pages* into a trap. They try to catch your eye with the store name. The heading tells us we're in Florists–Retail. Taking a third of the ad with the name

Flowers by Connie in large bold type tells us nothing new. Connie gives

a fantastic service: Free Delivery Three Times Daily to Mercy Hospital. That's something to shout about but there she has it tucked away in small type. Put

Mercy Hospital in big red letters to stand out from the crowd. Then give

the pitch on the delivery in smaller letters.

Highlight store name when you've made a name for yourself — Customers know Crazy Benny's as the place to buy sporting goods. Highlight the name. Customers who need to jog their memory will scan the *Yellow Pages* for it.

Let your place of business catch the eye — Include street address and the nearest well-known cross street. 2084 W. Grand at Main. Include local district: Rosedale. Include shopping center: Metrotown Mall. Include well-known places or buildings: Opposite City Hall. Set your place of business in colored type. Make it stand out to customers scanning the pages.

Put the phone number in very large type — Make it easy for people with poor eyesight who dial from the phone book. Numbers ¼″ to ½″ high are good.

Say something about credit cards and standard services — Major Credit Cards Accepted by Phone. Flowers by Wire. Include credit card and service logos. Normally it pays to keep logos out of an ad. They make an ad look as if it's an ad and that cuts down the number of readers. It's different in the *Yellow Pages*. Customers turn to the *Yellow Pages* because they want to read ads.

Include unusual hours — Open 24 hours, 7 days. Open 7 am to 7 pm.

Leave off borders — Most ads in the *Yellow Pages* look like funeral announcements. Those heavy black borders cost you extra and bring you no extra trade.

Commit to the Yellow Pages issue by issue — It's easy to trap yourself into an endless ad. It's better to contract for one issue only. Mark your calendar with a date to review whether the ad paid off. Review well in advance of the last date you can cut off the ad. Do this even when you have a winning ad. Feel sure this year's winning ad will also be next year's winning ad before you place it.

Look into City Transport

Get your message to people as they travel through the city. Most people in buses and subways just sit there and look at the ads. Only a few bring something to read. Even fewer bring their knitting. Even those listening to music on cassette players look at the ads.

Most ads on public transport tell too little. That's a mistake. People have time to read all you want to tell them. The type has to be big enough to read from the seat opposite the ad.

Treat the outsides of buses like mobile billboards.

Apartment elevators are small versions of buses and subways. Fewer people see elevator ads than see ads in buses and subways, so pay less for them. Many who see elevator ads see them every day, so tell a long story. People stand close to elevator ads, so you can use small type to tell your story. People only need to read it from across the elevator.

Look into Billboards

The classic billboard is a large sign on a city street or beside a highway. Other forms include:

- Signs on the outside of vehicles.
- Signs on subway walls.

- Electronic message signs.

- Banners trailed by airplanes.

Keep billboards simple — Deliver the selling message by a headline. Use very large type and strong pure colors. Strengthen the selling message with a picture when you can. Tell your place of business.

Look into Other Printed Items

Look around for other prospects in the print world.

Theater programs — In most cases, advertising in a theater program is like giving to charity. You're unlikely to see a payoff. Give to charity when you can afford it. Look on these ads as public relations.

Shopping bags — Most stores like to have their own shopping bags. They add to the image of a stable store and they cost little more than plain bags. Your own bags can wait a while. Look on them as a nice extra when your store is firmly on its feet rather than something to put your store on its feet. It's unlikely that any store made big sales because of a message on a shopping bag.

Calendars — Your own calendars put your store's name and phone number on the wall all year round. They're most useful for business offering services, especially services needed in a hurry or needed often. Otherwise, they're mainly for public relations. Unless you're offering services, a store calendar may be for you when you're looking for luxuries to polish your image.

T-shirts — You may want T-shirts if your customers will buy them and cover your costs or make money for you. They're not urgent, but they can be fun and for trendy stores they do make money. Think about them only when you can put the cash into them without it troubling you.

Follow These Rules for Radio

Radio ads have different rules from print ads.

Promise the benefit early — Get attention before you get tuned out. Many listeners switch stations or go to the bathroom during ads. Hook them before they leave you.

Identify products early and often — Bring brand names in early if your ads rely on them. Use brand names often during ads but use them without making listeners angry.

Point to your store clearly — Give your name and place of business at least twice. Include the nearest well-known streets. Include phone number if you want phone-ins.

Ask for action — What do you want customers to do? Visit, phone, or send you money? Ask them to do it. Tell them the hours of business for visits and phone calls.

Repeat ads often — You have little time with a radio spot. Even people who want to answer the ad need time to write the facts down. Then they need prompting to get around to answering it.

Hire a professional announcer and recording studio — Perfect recording of a perfect delivery is everything in a radio ad.

Follow These Rules for TV

TV ads are a special area of advertising with high expenses. Work with an agency to produce ads for TV. Be sure you work with people interested in seeing your bottom line improve. Steer clear of directors who want to make an artistic statement. Most of the things that work in TV advertising are corny. Look for someone who's not bored by them and who can bring a new twist to them.

Know some of the options Review these options:

Radio options: The options used on radio also work on TV. Make them richer on TV with moving pictures.

Talking heads: An announcer praises and tells about your store or items. This works well for new stores or new items. Someone talking on camera is better than a voice talking over a picture.

Testimonials: Customers tell why they like shopping in your store. Ordinary people can work as well as well-known people. Viewers remember your store or item rather than the person. Well-known people piggy-back your store on their standing in the community or on their glamour. Testimonials by experts are good.

Items in use: Let people see items in use. Action gets attention. People see what items do. Showing items in use works well for items that make problems go away.

News: A new store or a new direction for your store is news. So is a new item or new line of items. So is a new way to use an item.

Emotion: Appeals to the desires for family and friendship work well for some stores. So do appeals to the good old days, or to charm or sentimentality.

Sound: Sound effects are good in an ad. Background music is OK, but you don't need it.

Try News Releases

A news release, also called a press release, is a news item about your store which you send to editors in the hope they will publish it.

Scratch an editor's back — Help editors out. Editors who find your news release interesting may use it exactly as you prepared it. They may edit it to their needs. They may use it as the starting point for preparing their own news item. Most retailers write news releases but news releases can be videos or films. There's no guarantee that anyone will use your news release.

Put news in your news release — A news release is news, not an ad. Nobody will publish a free ad for your store. What's news will depend on the publication and the event. The local newspaper may publish what a major daily will ignore. Try:

- Store openings and major remodeling.

- New ownership and new directions.

- Major new items and services. Tell what they are and what they mean to customers and the community.

- Unusual hours. In some places a bookstore that's open twenty-four hours is news.

- Anything that's unusual.

- Anything with a human interest.

Make your news release interesting — Tell a good and interesting story. Interesting means interesting to the public. Dull news releases go straight in the waste basket. Grab attention with an interesting headline. Get attention with the first sentence.

Write your news release well — Keep the editors' needs in mind. Know the publications and what they stand for. Write your news release so editors can publish them with few changes.

Match the lengths of your news releases to the usual lengths of stories in the target publications. You may get lucky. An editor may have a space to fill to make up a page. An editor may take your news release as is, or strike out a sentence or two and you're in the publication.

Include pictures when you can — Interesting pictures raise your chance of getting published. Photos are better than drawings. Color photos are better than black and whites for magazines that publish them.

Follow the layout of a news release — At the top write "FOR IMMEDIATE RELEASE," or "FOR RELEASE ON date." At the top write "FOR MORE INFORMATION CONTACT John Smith (123) 123-1234." At the end write "END."

Keep your fingers crossed — You always put a lot of work into news releases. You can end up with nothing published. You can get published but see little new business resulting from it. You can get published all over the place and really put your store on the map.

Look into Newsletters

A newsletter is your own publication which customers turn to for facts. For customers to rely on your newsletter, you have to rise above yourself. It's not your advertising supplement. Suppose you sell computers. Your newsletter may have an article on how to back up data. It may have an article on the latest hard disk technology. You don't make a direct pitch for items you sell. Instead, customers see you know what you're talking about. They'll feel comfortable in buying from you. A good newsletter can be your best public relations tool.

Have the resources to support your newsletter. Newsletters cost time and money on a regular schedule. Be sure you can live up to the schedule. Perhaps you can write the newsletter yourself. Do you have the time? You may have to pay for the articles as well as the publication costs.

Look into Community Service

Community service is as American as apple pie, so do what you can.

Use the small openings — Give at least a token amount to good causes that ask for support. Many groups you support will mention you or publish your business card in their newsletter.

Go for the big openings only when you've made it — Give back to the community that supports you. There's no limit to what you can spend. There's no limit to the time it will take. There's no direct measure of the good it does you. Spoil yourself through major community support when you're a success.

GLOSSARY

Back End Skills: The skills that support selling, like operating a cash register.

Easter Sunday: the first Sunday on or after the Vernal Equinox. Look it up in a calendar each year.

Front End Skills: The skills needed for selling.

Full-time: Scheduled for 40 hours a week.

Half-time: Scheduled for 20 hours a week. A special case of part-time.

Immediate family: Your parents, your spouse or domestic partner, your spouse's or your domestic partner's parents, your children, your spouse's or your domestic partner's children by a former marriage or relationship, your brothers and your sisters.

Part-time: Scheduled for less than 40 hours a week.

Rep: Short for representative, as in Advertising Rep, Supplier's Rep, and so on.

Travelers Check: See "Travelers Cheque."

Travelers Cheque: Most travelers checks have "Travelers Cheque" printed on them. This use of the British spelling adds interest to the product in the U.S. and is the normal spelling in Canada.

INDEX